Power and Legitimacy

Power and Legitimacy

Reconciling Europe and the Nation-State

PETER L. LINDSETH

OXFORD
UNIVERSITY PRESS

OXFORD
UNIVERSITY PRESS

Oxford University Press, Inc., publishes works that further Oxford University's objective of excellence in research, scholarship, and education.

Oxford   New York
Auckland   Cape Town   Dar es Salaam   Hong Kong   Karachi   Kuala Lumpur   Madrid   Melbourne
Mexico City   Nairobi   New Delhi   Shanghai   Taipei   Toronto

With offices in
Argentina   Austria   Brazil   Chile   Czech Republic   France   Greece   Guatemala   Hungary   Italy
Japan   Poland   Portugal   Singapore   South Korea   Switzerland   Thailand   Turkey   Ukraine
Vietnam

Copyright © 2010 by Oxford University Press, Inc.

Published by Oxford University Press, Inc.
198 Madison Avenue, New York, New York 10016

Oxford is a registered trademark of Oxford University Press
Oxford University Press is a registered trademark of Oxford University Press, Inc.

Library of Congress Cataloging-in-Publication Data
Lindseth, Peter L.
   Power and legitimacy : reconciling Europe and the nation-state / Peter L. Lindseth.
      p. cm.
   Includes bibliographical references and index.
   ISBN 978-0-19-539014-8 (hardback : alk. paper)
1. Administrative law—European Union countries. 2. International and municipal law—European Union countries. 3. Legitimacy of governments—European Union countries. I. Title.
   KJE5602.L56 2010
   342.24'06—dc22   2010011750

Note to Readers
This publication is designed to provide accurate and authoritative information in regard to the subject matter covered. It is based upon sources believed to be accurate and reliable and is intended to be current as of the time it was written. It is sold with the understanding that the publisher is not engaged in rendering legal, accounting, or other professional services. If legal advice or other expert assistance is required, the services of a competent professional person should be sought. Also, to confirm that the information has not been affected or changed by recent developments, traditional legal research techniques should be used, including checking primary sources where appropriate.

*(Based on the Declaration of Principles jointly adopted by a Committee of the
American Bar Association and a Committee of Publishers and Associations.)*

You may order this or any other Oxford University Press publication by
visiting the Oxford University Press website at www.oup.com

"The best way of being right in the future is, in certain periods, to know how to resign oneself to being out of fashion."

—Ernest Renan (1882)

Contents

Preliminary Note on the Euro Crisis

THIS BOOK WAS IN PRODUCTION when the Greek debt crisis intensified in the spring of 2010, precipitating a broader crisis that threatened the future of the euro as a viable common currency. Given the timing, it was impossible to assess the many implications of the developing euro crisis here. Nevertheless, even at an early stage, one could still note several institutional aspects of the unfolding drama that were entirely comprehensible from the perspective of this study. These included the relatively marginal role of European Union (EU) bodies in addressing the crisis in the first instance; the correspondingly critical role of national and intergovernmental politics; and the functional pressures—political and economic realities—that were pushing nonetheless toward greater supranational coordination to ward off a possible spread of the crisis elsewhere in Europe.

As of this writing (mid May 2010), it could not yet be determined whether the euro crisis would lead to a new institutional settlement for integration. The "special purpose vehicle" established to manage the new mammoth bailout fund, along with proposals for increased supranational surveillance of national budgets, certainly suggested the possibility. But events are moving fast, and the crisis could still lead to an institutional transformation well short of, or even orthogonal to, some form of European "economic government." Indeed, if Greece and other vulnerable Member States prove unable to satisfy market concerns regarding their public finances, the crisis could still lead to a default (in the form of a debt restructuring) or perhaps an unraveling of the EMU or worse, including a broader European banking crisis with untold consequences for the global economy. It could not yet be determined, moreover, whether the crisis would precipitate a new ruling from a national high court on the legal limits of integration relative to national constitutional orders, although that too was a possibility.

Regardless of the outcome, the euro crisis will again force the EU to reconcile, just as it always had, two key but contradictory features of integration. The first is the cultural persistence of national democratic and constitutional *legitimacy* in the European system of governance. The second is the functional and political requirements for greater denationalized regulatory *power* in pursuit of integration. As this study seeks to show, the tension between these elements has characterized the integration project since its inception, profoundly shaping the contours of European public law over time. Short of a complete breakup of the EU (something I do not foresee, although some kind of transformation looks increasingly unavoidable), I fully expect this tension will continue shaping European public law as integration proceeds into an uncertain future.

Preface

I WROTE THIS BOOK for the most part over the course of 2007 to 2009, as a decade of institutional agonizing in the European Union (EU) appeared to be drawing to a close. Following the rejection of the Constitutional Treaty at mid-decade and the troubled ratification of the Treaty of Lisbon toward its end, many in Europe's political class had hoped that the seemingly endless debate over supranational governance would now largely be behind them. The final approval of the Lisbon Treaty had yielded an institutional settlement that, although falling short of old federalist aspirations, still might allow the EU to move more confidently and efficiently into the future. Unfortunately, the economic crisis that began in 2008 would, over time, begin to test even that more modest hope at fairly regular intervals. As the great recession developed beyond its initial stages, the core focus of this study—the gap between the EU's governing legitimacy and its regulatory power—would reveal itself once again as a feature of European governance as unavoidable and complex as ever.

Among scholars of European integration, the upheavals of the last decade have caused not merely exhaustion but also confusion and disorientation. Older frameworks for interpretation have been challenged, while the outlines of new ones are only now beginning to emerge. The purpose of this book is to help that latter process along. It seeks to draw on history to develop a better interpretation of the nature and legitimacy of European governance going forward. My aim is to suggest an alternative legal-historical synthesis that presents European integration as a further stage in the development of *administrative governance* over the course of the twentieth century. By administrative governance, I am referring to the diffuse and fragmented expressions of regulatory authority reaching well beyond the political summit of the state (that is, the "legislature" or the "executive" in their highest institutional forms). The administrative realm is not merely technical or limited, as some may take the term to suggest. Rather, it is deeply political and discretionary, often beyond hierarchical control, if not de jure then at least de facto, given the diffusion and fragmentation of modern governance more generally. And yet, despite this effective degree of autonomy, administrative governance also remains deeply dependent on the centrally *constituted* bodies of representative government on the national level (legislative, executive, and judicial) for both legal authority and ultimate democratic and constitutional legitimacy.

This book analyzes integration in terms of this paradoxical combination of autonomy and dependence. The synthesis presented here seeks to supplement and also challenge several alternative interpretations that have gained prominence in the scholarly literature over the last two decades. European governance is of course *multilevel* and perhaps even *polyarchical*, as two commonly deployed rubrics describe it. But it is neither as *sui generis* nor as autonomously *constitutional* as conventionally supposed. Although the implications of European integration for national democracy and constitutionalism are reasonably well known, it is also well known that the EU has been unable to attain democratic or constitutional legitimacy in its own right. Rather, as this study shows, European governance has, over the last fifty years, evolved in a quite different institutional direction. The public law of European integration has instead converged around the legitimating structures and normative principles of what this study calls the *postwar constitutional settlement of administrative governance*, adjusted to the demands of integration.

This convergence toward the postwar settlement is reflected in integration's reliance on mechanisms of oversight exercised by nationally constituted bodies—most importantly, by national chief executives, but also by national high courts and national parliaments. Together, these provide the broad legitimating framework within which the now complex forms of Europeanized administrative governance may otherwise operate. These legitimating structures in turn reflect integration's grounding in the core normative-legal principle of the postwar constitutional settlement, *delegation* (or "conferral" as it is now called in the European treaties). By conforming to the normative demands of delegation (what this study calls *mediated legitimacy*), European public law has sought to reconcile, however imperfectly, the functional realities of integration with the continuing role of the nation-state as the primary locus of democratic and constitutional legitimacy in the European system.

* * *

Aside from the inherent complexity of European governance itself, a number of factors complicate any attempted historical synthesis along these lines.

The first is linguistic. This study draws primarily from the scholarly literature in English and secondarily from material in French and German, with additional sources in Italian providing some further perspective. This hardly exhausts the varied and multilingual literature covering all 27 Member States of the European Union, soon perhaps to be 29 or more. Thus, there are almost certainly particularities and cross-national variations that have escaped my analysis—although none, I hope, that undermine the basic validity of my proposed synthesis. I stand to be corrected on that point, of course, as future researchers test my claims more broadly.

The second challenge is not linguistic but disciplinary. As a work of historical synthesis, this book tries to integrate the lessons of a diverse body of secondary literature on European integration and governance, including works by political scientists, sociologists, as well as legal scholars and historians, among others. In trying to be cross-disciplinary in my synthetic ambitions, I run the risk of satisfying the demands of none of these disciplines fully (which is no doubt true). But my aim is nevertheless to foster a greater degree of interdisciplinary dialogue among the various fields. This sort of dialogue is admittedly already common among lawyers and political scientists. But with the obvious exception of Alan Milward and his magisterial work, the voices of integration historians have been relatively isolated in these discussions. Thus, I have made special attempts to incorporate their findings into my analysis where appropriate.

The final synthetic challenge stems from the fact that history does not stop. Numerous developments of obvious importance have taken place just in the past decade, indeed, even in the months and days leading up to the final submission of this manuscript at the beginning of December 2009. I finished the empirical chapters over the summer of 2009, not long after the German Federal Constitutional Court (*Bundesverfassungsgericht*) announced its wide-ranging decision on the constitutionality of the Treaty of Lisbon. In early October 2009, when I was finalizing the manuscript and the cite-checking, the people of Ireland returned to the polls in a second referendum on the treaty, won decisively by the "Yes" side, after an initial defeat in 2008. And just a few weeks before my final submission, Czech President Vaclav Klaus finally signed the Treaty of Lisbon after a long holdout, compelled to do so by a second decision of the Czech Constitutional Court reiterating the treaty's constitutionality under national law. Thus, when I submitted the manuscript to the publisher, the entry into force of Treaty of Lisbon was finally assured, after an extraordinarily long and difficult political and legal struggle.

* * *

Fortunately, in the long process of trying to complete the manuscript, I was able to rely on material that I previously published elsewhere. Chapter 2 is a condensed (and partially revised) version of an article I published in *The Yale Law Journal* in 2004, entitled "The Paradox of Parliamentary Supremacy: Delegation, Democracy, and Dictatorship in Germany and France, 1920s–1950s." Reprinted by permission of The Yale Law Journal Company, Inc. and William S. Hein & Company, from *The Yale Law Journal,* Vol. 113, pp. 1341–1415. I also took advantage of smaller portions previously published in Peter L. Lindseth, Alfred C. Aman, Jr., and Alan C. Raul, *The Administrative Law of the European Union: Oversight,* George A. Bermann, Charles H. Koch, and James T. O'Reilly, eds. (Chicago: ABA Publishing, 2008). These are reprinted by permission as well.

Numerous institutions have also provided support, both tangible and intangible, in the several years it took to bring this book to fruition. First and foremost, I must extend special thanks to the University of Connecticut School of Law, which has been my intellectual home for the last decade. This book simply would not have been possible without the tremendous support of my dean, Jeremy Paul; my associate dean, Anne Dailey; as well as the many members of the UConn faculty who commented on earlier drafts. I am also especially grateful to the efforts of then-acting dean Kurt Strasser and then-associate dean Paul Chill, who secured approval of my request to combine a sabbatical with a leave so that I could undertake extended research and writing over the last two years. To Kurt and Paul especially, but also to all my friends and colleagues in Hartford, I thank you.

As a consequence of this time away, I have benefited from extended visits to a number of other schools and institutes, each of which contributed directly to this book's realization. I was a fellow and visiting professor at Princeton University in 2008–2009, in the Law and Public Affairs (LAPA) Program at the Woodrow Wilson School of International and Public Affairs. Directing LAPA is the incomparable Kim Lane Scheppele, whose encouragement and wise counsel I have always cherished. At Princeton, I must also extend heartfelt thanks to Leslie Gerwin, associate director of LAPA (and adjunct professor of law at Cardozo Law School); Judi Rivkin, events manager; and Jennifer Bolton, office coordinator, each of whom made my life easier and productive in so many ways. Because of their great generosity and good humor, I doubt that I will ever again have as much fun in an academic setting as I did at LAPA.

In the summer of 2008, I had the pleasure of being a visiting fellow (*Stipendiat*) at *Max-Planck-Institut für europäische Rechtsgeschichte* in

Frankfurt am Main, Germany, where I was surrounded by a wonderful group of legal historians from all over Europe. Perhaps most importantly, my stay at Max Planck gave me the chance to exchange ideas on sustained basis with one of the greatest legal historians of this or any generation, Michael Stolleis. For that, I am deeply grateful and feel the manuscript benefited immeasurably as a consequence.

Finally, I spent the 2008–2009 academic year as a visiting professor at the Yale Law School, an extraordinary intellectual community full of ideas and energy permeating both the student body and the faculty. The many exchanges I had at Yale about this project improved the final product in ways too numerous to list here. Because of the understanding of the then-dean, Harold Koh, as well as the current dean, Robert Post, I was able to extend my stay at Yale Law School into the summer of 2009. This allowed me to bring the manuscript to near completion before packing up my boxes once again for the return trip to Hartford. There is simply no way I could have finalized this work without the benefit of my extended time in New Haven, for which I am deeply grateful.

I have also been fortunate throughout these last several years to have had the opportunity of presenting earlier drafts and excerpts in a variety of locations, beyond stimulating workshops at UConn, Princeton, Frankfurt, and Yale. These included the research seminar of the American Bar Foundation in Chicago; the "Seminar on the Law and Politics of the European Union's 'Constitution'" at Trinity College, Dublin; the annual meeting of the American Society for Legal History in Ottawa, Ontario; and the "Transcending Boundaries Conference" at the University of Connecticut School of Law. Thanks to all the participants in these gatherings for their numerous helpful questions and comments.

There is a long list of individuals who have been extremely generous with their thoughts at various stages, sometimes unaware of their impact on my broader project. It is difficult to name them all, but allow me to try. The list includes Bruce Ackerman, Alex Aizenstatd, Michael Thad Allen, Karen Alter, Paul Schiff Berman, George Bermann, Antonella Bettoni, Francesca Bignami, George Bustin, Gráinne de Búrca, Pepper Culpepper, Laura Dickinson, Catherine Donnelly, Jeff Dunoff, David Dyzenhaus, Geoff Eley, Dan Ernst, Michael Graetz, Dieter Grimm, Carol Harlow, Carol Heimer, Larry Helfer, Paul Kahn, Dan Kelemen, Maciej Kisilowski, Nico Krisch, John Langbein, Kathrin Linderer, Miguel Poiares Maduro, Isabella Mariani, Daniel Markovits, Jerry Mashaw, Jean Massot, Walter Mattli, Franz Mayer, Gabriele Mazzotta, Patricia McCoy, Tom Merrill, Andy Moravcsik, Andreas Th. Müller, Jan-Werner

Müller, Sophie Meunier, Fernanda Nicola, Bill Novak, Aidan O'Neill, Nick Parrillo, Bob Paxton, Ingolf Pernice, Will Phelan, Judith Resnik, Susan Rose-Ackerman, Stefan Ruppert, Joanne Scott, Alec Stone Sweet, Francesca Strumia, Nadia Urbinati, Miloš Vec, Neil Walker, Patrick Weil, and Peer Zumbansen. I also thank the anonymous peer reviewers who provided detailed comments on an earlier draft.

I also could not have finished this work without the help of several excellent research assistants. The team of Caroline Edsall and James Montana of Yale Law School, and Daniella Azevedo of UConn Law School, tracked down numerous sources and verified citations, often in difficult foreign language materials. Caroline, in particular, is worthy of special mention: She very generously proofread the entire manuscript in its near final form, pointing out typographical errors and missing words, while also making several subtle suggestions that added to the overall sense and style of the book. In addition, Jonathan Justl of Yale Law School provided very helpful assistance at a key juncture. To each of these students, I extend my deep thanks and best wishes for the future.

* * *

My ultimate and most profound thanks, however, must be reserved for my wife, Lise Martina, and our two boys, Paul and Nicholas Martina Lindseth. They have tolerated my many absences but have never missed the opportunity to rib me about my slow progress ("So Dad, have you reconciled Europe and the nation-state yet?"). This line always brought a smile to my face even as it captured the sometimes quixotic nature of the overall task. My family gave me a refuge from the isolation of the big project, while reminding me again and again that books are meant to be finished. Lise, Paul, and Nicholas will no doubt be happy to see me move on to other things, even if they will have to come up with other ways of bringing me down to earth. For their great love and support, this book is dedicated to them.

New York/Hartford
Peter L. Lindseth
December 2009

Citation Forms

THROUGHOUT THIS WORK, I use an author-date style for citing secondary sources (books, journal articles, etc.), modified from *The Chicago Manual of Style,* 15th ed. (2003). For sources published in multiple editions or as a translation, I have tried to specify both the date of the edition and/or the translation used, followed by the date of the original publication in brackets. To streamline the text, however, I have moved the author-date citations to the footnotes but have otherwise kept the complete citations in the list of references at the end of the book.

Primary legal materials, by contrast, are generally cited only in the footnotes and do not appear in the reference list. There are a few prominent exceptions, such as the ruling of the German Federal Constitutional Court on the Lisbon Treaty in 2009 (which I cite throughout as the "German Lisbon Decision (2009)" and provide a complete citation in the reference list). Also for primary legal materials, I have tried to follow the citation style that prevails in the particular legal system from which the material is drawn (i.e., European, French, German, etc.). My aim is to make the citations intelligible for lawyers and scholars from that system. For the rare bits of American primary legal materials cited below (Supreme Court decisions primarily), I follow the standard format of *The Bluebook: A Uniform System of Citation.* All translations from foreign language material are my own unless otherwise indicated in the footnotes or the reference list.

[Note: In May 2010, while the book was in production, I added a very small amount of new material to certain footnotes in light of the developing euro crisis. That new material, which is largely confined to Chapter 4 and the Conclusion, is set off by brackets to signal to the reader its later addition.]

Abbreviations

A.C.	Appeal Cases (3d Series) (UK)
BGBl.	*Bundesgesetzblatt* (Germany)
BVerfG	*Bundesverfassungsgericht* (Germany)
BVerfGE	*Entscheidungen des Bundesverfassungsgerichts* (Germany)
CAP	Common Agricultural Policy
C.C.	*Conseil constitutionnel* (France)
C. cost.	*Corte costituzionale* (Italy)
CE ... *Rec.*	*Conseil d'Etat* (France), decision reported in the *Recueil des décisions du Conseil d'Etat* (*Recueil Lebon*)
CE Ass.	*Conseil d'Etat, Assemblée du contentieux* (as reported in *Lebon*)
C.M.L.R.	*Common Market Law Reports*
COREPER	Committee of Permanent Representatives of the Member States
COSAC	Conference of Community and European Affairs Committees of Parliaments of the European Union
EAC	European Affairs Committee (Denmark) (also generic)
EC	European Community (or Communities)
ECJ	European Court of Justice
E.C.R.	*European Court Reports*
ECSC	European Coal and Steel Community
EEC	European Economic Community
EMU	European Monetary Union
EP	European Parliament
EU	European Union
EuR	*Europarecht* (Germany)
Giur. Cost.	*Giurisprudenza Costituzionale* (Italy)
IGC	intergovernmental conference
I.L.M.	*International Legal Materials*
I.R.	*Irish Reports*

J.O.	*Journal Officiel de la République Française*
MEP	Member of the European Parliament
MNP	Member of a national parliament
O.J.	*Official Journal of the European Union* (or *Communities,* depending on the date of publication)
Parl. Deb., H.C.	Parliamentary Debates, House of Commons (Hansard, UK)
QMV	qualified-majority voting
RGBl.	*Reichsgesetzblatt* (Germany)
SEA	Single European Act
SI	Statutory Instrument (UK)
TEC	Treaty establishing the European Community
TEU	Treaty on European Union
TFEU	Treaty on the Functioning of the European Union (replaces TEC)
U.S.	*United States Reports* (as used in citations to Supreme Court cases; otherwise refers to the United States)

Introduction
Reconciling Europe and the Nation-State
in Law and History

IN NUMEROUS WAYS, the European Union (EU) has been among the most exceptional yet paradoxical political achievements of the last half century. It has been exceptional because it now encompasses a vast market-polity transcending national boundaries, one that includes (as of this writing) 27 Member States, nearly 500 million people, and somewhere between a quarter and a third of world economic output, depending on the measure. But in attaining this extraordinary scale, the process of European integration has also been deeply paradoxical, even contradictory. This is particularly so with regard to the principal concern of this book: the EU's simultaneous dependence on, but also deep disruption of, the forms of constitutional, representative democracy on the national level.

This combination of dependence and disruption, I will argue, flows directly from the often misunderstood nature of European governance. To put it bluntly, European governance is *administrative, not constitutional.* The process of European integration has had, without doubt, profound constitutional implications for its constituent states. It has both disciplined certain negative externalities of national democracy and offered market actors a range of transnational rights and duties, all to construct a new market-polity transcending national borders. Nevertheless, this polity has had great difficulty being understood as constitutional in its own right. That is, it has struggled to be seen as the embodiment or expression of a new political community ("Europe") capable of self-rule through institutions historically constituted for that purpose. Rather, in this critical regard, the EU is fundamentally administrative, with a ruling legitimacy still ultimately derived from the historically constituted bodies of representative government on the national level.

The resulting system of Europeanized administrative governance, like its counterpart in the administrative state, has been built in response to demands for increased regulatory capacity and efficiency in the face of an array of

1

political, social, and economic challenges. The institutional strategy for satisfying these demands, both nationally and supranationally, has been to diffuse and fragment normative power *away* from the historically constituted bodies of representative self-government on the national level.

As I use the term, *historically constituted bodies* refers not merely to elected national legislative assemblies, although these are undoubtedly the most important in historical terms. Rather, it also refers to national chief executives and cabinet ministers, as well as to national courts and venerable court-like institutions (such as the French *Conseil d'Etat*). Over the course of the nineteenth and twentieth centuries, these bodies, together with the legislature, became the primary vehicles of democratic and constitutional legitimation of the many instances of administrative governance in modern industrial and post-industrial society. These historically constituted bodies on the national level, this study will show, have provided the essential means of democratic and constitutional legitimation in the EU as well. This legitimation occurs even as the process of integration has entailed the shift in significant regulatory power beyond the direct control of these same nationally constituted institutions.

Integration is thus best understood as a supranational manifestation of the broader historical process of diffusion and fragmentation of regulatory power that characterizes modern governance. European public law has operationalized the key normative-legal principle of administrative governance—*delegation*—through a range of national oversight mechanisms that I will discuss in greater detail in Chapters 3 through 5. These mechanisms challenge the idea, widespread among legal scholars of integration, that European governance is built on a set of "institutions constitutionally separated from national legitimation processes."[1] To the contrary, the mechanisms studied here have developed specifically to overcome the seeming disconnect at the heart of integration, between otherwise autonomous exercises of supranational regulatory power, on the one hand, and the national sources of democratic and constitutional legitimacy of that power, on the other.

Much less than reflecting the purportedly sui generis character of multi-level or polyarchical governance in Europe, these mechanisms have an identifiable historical provenance: They are grounded in models of administrative legitimation that emerged in postwar Western Europe in response to the disastrous constitutional failings of the interwar years. For that reason, to

---

1. Menon and Weatherill (2002), 118.

understand the legitimation of European governance over time, historical attention to the antecedent stabilization of administrative governance on the national level is essential. It is there that one begins to see how Europe's "administrative supranationalism could be re-anchored in the Member States' constitutional orders," as one commentator on my work has queried.[2] Historical analysis reveals the basic features of what this study calls *the postwar constitutional settlement of administrative governance* on which the legitimacy of European governance would also ultimately come to depend. It has been through recourse to the legitimating structures and normative principles of this postwar constitutional settlement that European public law has tried, albeit often *sub silencio,* to reconcile Europe and the nation-state for more than fifty years.

As will be explained in greater detail in the chapters that follow, this reconciliation has tolerated a good deal of autonomous regulatory power in what has become an increasingly dense and complex sphere of Europeanized administrative governance, one that now encompasses both national and supranational actors.[3] Nevertheless, this process of reconciliation has also included a significant amount of normative resistance to the autonomously constitutional pretenses of European supranationalism (as if the EU embodies or expresses the legitimacy of a new polity over and above the Member States). The history of European public law—at least outside the confines of the European Court of Justice (ECJ)—in fact reflects a consistent refusal to recognize supranational institutions or processes as autonomously constitutional in that way.

This resistance, most recently reflected in the collapse of the Constitutional Treaty and the struggles to ratify the Treaty of Lisbon, flows directly from the administrative, not constitutional character of the integration process. To introduce ourselves to the intricacies of the argument, we must begin with some basic considerations about the nature of representative democracy both in relation to European integration as well as to administrative governance more generally. This Introduction explores those considerations in greater detail, while Chapter 1 situates my argument within the broader

---

2. Joerges (2002), 27.

3. My analysis of European governance is primarily external, focusing on its legitimating framework rather than its internal operations. For more detail on the internal intricacies of administrative governance in its now Europeanized form, see, e.g., the contributions in Weatherill (2007); Egeberg (2006); Hofmann and Türk (2006); Kassim et al. (2001) and Kassim et al. (2000).

theoretical literature on integration over the last several decades. Chapter 1 also specifically addresses a common misconception of my administrative characterization of integration—that it is somehow meant to suggest that European governance is "non-political," "technical," or "limited."[4] For those readers less interested in the theoretical and methodological debates among integration scholars, they could skip Chapter 1 and proceed directly to the empirical chapters that follow.

Those subsequent chapters (Chapters 2 through 5) show quite explicitly how the institutional evolution of supranational governance in Europe has been a deeply *political* but nevertheless still fundamentally *administrative* phenomenon—at least in relation to integration's sources of democratic and constitutional legitimacy on the national level. These chapters outline the development of the broad normative framework within which a now-Europeanized administrative governance operates. The Conclusion then reflects on some of the legal and institutional implications of this ultimately administrative character of European governance going forward.

※ Representative Government, Democratic Legitimacy, and "Europe"

From a historical perspective, it is fair to say that European integration would have been unthinkable without the reconsolidation of some form of representative democracy on the national level in Western Europe after the disaster of 1933–1945. The same would of course also be true of the extension of integration to Greece, Portugal, and Spain after their transition to democracy in the 1970s, as well as to Central and Eastern Europe after the collapse of communism in 1989.[5] The European treaties confirm this

---

4. See Chapter 1, nn. 12–13 and accompanying text.

5. Sheehan (2009), 185–87, 192–95, and 224–25. In the case of Central and Eastern Europe, the extension of representative institutions after 1989 was arguably aided by a critical but extremely delicate consequence of the postwar period: the consolidation of the state system around realigned national communities, greatly diminishing the "minorities problem" that had plagued the region from the nineteenth century into the interwar period. Whether a consequence of the horrific violence of World War II itself, or of the forced population transfers after the war, this process, as one historian has explained, "turned Versailles's dreams of national homogeneity into realities," vastly increasing the political identity of government and governed throughout Europe after 1945. Mazower (2000 [1998]), 218, citing Schechtman (1963), 363; see also Mazower (2008), 549–50 (describing "the triumph of nationality politics across eastern Europe" as a consequence of

historical dependence: "The functioning of the Union shall be founded on representative democracy" reads the new Article 10 of the Treaty on European Union (TEU), which came into force with the Treaty of Lisbon in December 2009.[6] This provision builds on Article 6 TEU in its pre-Lisbon form, which identified "democracy," along with "liberty," "human rights," and the "rule of law," as one of the several foundational principles of European integration. The TEU then specifies (in Article 49, in both the pre- and post-Lisbon versions) that membership in the EU is open to any European state that respects these principles.

This acknowledged foundation in representative democracy, both historical and textual, has done little, however, to dissipate a nagging concern regarding the nature of European governance, even among its most enthusiastic supporters. As Joschka Fischer put it in his famous Berlin speech in May 2000 on Europe's constitutional future, European governance has long been understood, not without cause, as a largely "bureaucratic affair run by a faceless, soulless Eurocracy in Brussels."[7] More recent statements by other European leaders, both pro-European and Eurosceptic alike, echo the same theme.[8] For example, in an article otherwise intended to encourage participation in the elections to the European Parliament in June 2009, German Chancellor Angela Merkel and French President Nicholas Sarkozy jointly criticized what they called "a bureaucratic Europe that mechanically applies nit-picking rules (*règles tatillonnes*). . . . We want a European Union

---

postwar expulsions); and Sheehan (2009), 141–42. The importance of these developments would become clearer post-1989, with the collapse of communism and the extension of representative democracy to Central and Eastern Europe. The problem of minority populations would persist in the Balkans, however, leading to a tragic renewal of nationalist bloodshed and ethnic cleansing in the 1990s. More recently, the controversy over the Treaty of Lisbon indirectly reminded Europe of the historical and political significance of the postwar expulsions: in October 2009, Czech President Vaclav Klaus indicated that one of his primary concerns with the treaty was whether its Charter of Fundamental Rights could cast doubt on the validity of the Beneš Decrees, the series of measures of the Czechoslovak government-in-exile dispossessing and expelling ethnic Germans and Hungarians from the new postwar state. Klaus (2009). For a detailed legal analysis suggesting the weakness of Klaus's concern, see Peers (2009). There is, in addition, continuing tension between Slovakia and Hungary over the Beneš Decrees and the treatment of ethnic Hungarians within Slovakia.

6. Hereinafter, the TEU post-Lisbon.

7. Fischer (2000).

8. This work uses the British spelling of "Eurosceptic" and its variants (e.g., "Eurosceptical") throughout this work.

that listens to the citizens."[9] Conversely, British conservative leader David Cameron, as part of the general hardening of his anti-EU rhetoric in the 2009 European parliamentary election campaign, suggested EU governance operates outside "the realm of democratic politics" and is "completely unaccountable to the people of Britain."[10]

These statements, of course, merely remind us that invocations of integration's infamous "democratic deficit" have been a consistent feature of European political discourse for more than two decades.[11] But the paradox of European governance is more profound than what might be implied by familiar bureaucratic epithets, or by expressed desires for greater participation, transparency, or accountability in the EU's policy processes. This paradox is not merely a consequence of Europe's famous "no *demos*" problem—the lack of a single European "people," so to speak—although it is related to it. To understand the paradox more fully, we must reflect in greater depth on a number of historical tensions at the heart of European integration.

Over the last fifty years, and more particularly over the last two decades, the geographical scope, organizational complexity, and regulatory reach of Europe's supranational institutions have grown significantly. And yet, over the same period, the specifically democratic and constitutional legitimacy of European governance—its sense of embodying or expressing the capacity of a historically cohesive political community to rule itself through institutions constituted for that purpose—has remained stubbornly weak, at least relative to the nation-states that comprise it. Sympathetic European scholars have struggled mightily to reconceive the nature of democracy and constitutionalism in order to bring supranational governance within their ambit.[12] And yet the idea of the EU as democratic and constitutional in its own right—that is, as an expression of representative government directly

---

9. Merkel and Sarkozy (2009). In a contemporaneous interview, an advisor to President Sarkozy echoed these talking points, speaking of integration as "an incomprehensible, bureaucratic project, indifferent to the sentiments and aspirations of people." Guaino (2009). He had earlier said much worse, of course, calling integration "a bureaucratic monster which only serves its own interests." Babelparis (2008), citing Cohn-Bendit and Guaino (1999).

10. As quoted in Charlemagne (2009a).

11. For a graphic depiction of the rise of this discourse, both in the popular media and the scholarly literature, see Rittberger (2005), 28–29, Figs. 1.1 and 1.2.

12. See, most famously, Habermas (1992) and (2001a). For a succinct summaries, see Cederman (2001), 155, and Rittberger (2005), 29–33.

"*of* the people," the capstone element of Lincoln's classic formulation[13]—has remained suspect, at least when measured against the perceived legitimacy of institutions on the national level, with all their many flaws.[14] As we shall see below, this weakness hardly makes the integration project illegitimate in some ultimate sense (as many hardened Eurosceptics might have it). But it does mean that integration's democratic and constitutional character is broadly understood, even among the most fervent advocates of integration, as attenuated and indirect.[15]

European institutions today enjoy other kinds of legitimacy, to be sure, perhaps most importantly as *instruments of peace* among historically warring nation-states. In the now famous words of the Schuman Declaration of 1950, the purpose of integration was originally to make another European war "not merely unthinkable, but materially impossible."[16] And in that effort, the integration process has been a clear success. This achievement is no doubt partly due to the fact that European institutions also enjoy a broadly recognized *legal legitimacy*, grounded in the commitments of the Member States (both express and implied) that are found in the various European treaties and secondary law. From the perspective of the ECJ (that is, the institutional mechanism created by the Member States to enforce those commitments), the treaties can be understood as a "constitutional charter of a Community based on the rule of law," in which the ECJ itself serves as the ultimate oversight mechanism.[17]

---

13. Emphasis added. Several authors have used Lincoln's formulation in the Gettysburg Address as a point of entry into the discussion of European democracy. See, e.g., Schmidt (2006), 21–22; Rittberger (2005), 29–30; see also Auel (2007b), 496. These analyses generally focus, however, on procedural legitimacy ("by the people") and consequential legitimacy ("for the people"), rather than the question of what might called *demos*-legitimacy ("of the people").

14. See, e.g., Joerges and Neyer (1997), 292–93 (describing the failure of "inevitably one-sided and parochial or selfish" nation-states to take into account of "the interests and concerns of non-nationals," particularly where national policies have negative international externalities, which Joerges and Neyer analogize to "taxation with representation"). For a critique, see Lindseth (1999), 735–36, n. 528. For a more nuanced recent account, see Joerges (2006); see also Menon and Weatherill (2008), 404. For a different take on national democratic flaws, see the discussion of the "deparliamentarization" thesis in Chapter 5, nn. 56–60 and accompanying text.

15. Cf. Habermas (2000 [1998]), 155–56, as cited in McCormick (2007), 208.

16. Schuman Declaration (1950).

17. Case 294/83, *Parti écologiste "Les Verts" v. Parliament*, 1986 E.C.R. 1339, 1365, para. 23. For a useful recent overview of this dictum, with an examination of some of its potential "constitutional" import in the hands of the ECJ, see Pech (2009).

And perhaps most importantly, European institutions enjoy a considerable degree of what could be called *technocratic legitimacy*, rooted in their ability to produce sound regulatory policy for an increasingly integrated social and economic space transcending national borders. From this perspective, the aim of integration is not simply to construct competitive markets—the old ordo-liberal aspiration.[18] It is also to increase regulatory capacity of Europeans to address complex challenges (for example, in the environment, food safety, or the financial markets) whose effects are no longer confined within national boundaries, and which have the potential of imposing negative externalities on the residents of adjacent Member States. This sort of denationalized "output legitimacy," as Fritz Scharpf famously termed it,[19] can certainly be placed under serious strain in moments of economic crisis, when older inward-looking habits risk coming again to the fore. But the record of achievement is still significant, through periods of both prosperity and downturn. Whether measured in terms of the production or enforcement of regulatory norms for the internal market (goods, labor, and capital); the redistribution of income (especially but not exclusively in agriculture); the regulation of a range of social risks (environmental, financial, etc.); or the making of monetary or even foreign policy, supranational institutions play a significant role in modern governance in Europe.[20]

And yet none of these alternative bases of legitimacy amount to anything close to the sort of classic democratic and constitutional legitimacy that executive, legislative, and judicial institutions of the nation-state still are generally believed to enjoy.[21] The relative strength of national institutions in this regard holds even as a secondary, specifically European political identity

---

18. See Joerges (2009), 340 ("[I]n the ordo-liberal account, the Community acquired a legitimacy of its own by interpreting its pertinent provisions as prescribing a law-based order committed to guaranteeing economic freedoms and protecting competition at the supranational level. This legitimacy was independent of the State's democratic constitutional institutions.").

19. See, e.g., Scharpf (1999), 10–23.

20. For a detailed defense of EU's "output legitimacy" as necessary to the continued legitimacy of national governance, see Menon and Weatherill (2008).

21. This holds true even as several European nation-states—e.g., Belgium—are finding it difficult to claim to represent a coherent national *demos*, which in turn makes the claim of democratic and constitutional legitimacy vastly more difficult to sustain within those polities. The fact that, in certain Member States, pressures exist to drive the institutional locus of legitimate governance *downward* from the state to the regional level (not just in Belgium, but also in Spain or the United Kingdom, for example) hardly supports the claim of democratic and constitutional legitimacy at the *European* level. If anything, such pressures reinforce the conclusion that democratic and constitutional legitimacy resides at

may slowly be emerging, one that could eventually be invested in European institutions for this purpose (although this does not seem to have happened yet).[22] Indeed, the strength of national institutions holds even as the foundations of a genuinely European public sphere may also be appearing, albeit one underdeveloped compared to its national counterparts.[23] And the comparative strength of the nation-state holds even as legal and political theorists seek to reconceptualize democracy and constitutionalism away from centralized institutions of representative government on the national level, often around more abstract values such as "autonomy, dignity, participation, fairness, equal respect and concern, collective belonging, interest aggregation, and so on."[24]

This effort to invest Europe with a new, denationalized sense of democratic and constitutional legitimacy, one commensurate with its functional regulatory reach, is obviously appealing on many levels. It is particularly so given the dark history of extreme nationalism in Europe in the first half of the twentieth century, something now deeply ingrained in Europe's collective memory.[25] But it is also appealing for many others who welcome "the growth of a transnational economy" because it "rubs away the rough, unrepresentative and (in market terms) illegitimate pretensions of the Member States."[26] From this perspective, "national polities have a twofold deficit: [O]n the one hand, they do not control many decision-making processes which affect those polities but take place outside their borders; on the other hand, national

---

the level of sub-European political communities, not at the level of the European transnational community.

22. The literature on the development of a European identity is vast. For a succinct overview, see Strumia (2009), 154–60.

23. The German *Bundesverfassungsgericht* recently stressed this point in its ruling on the constitutionality of the Treaty of Lisbon, which acknowledged that, "due to the great successes of European integration, a joint European public . . . is evidently growing." Nevertheless, the Court also found "that the public perception of factual issues and of political leaders remains connected to a considerable extent to patterns of identification which are related to the nation-state, language, history and culture." German Lisbon Decision (2009), para. 251 (citing, inter alia, Trenz (2005)).

24. Walker (2006d), 331. For some examples of efforts to reconceptualize democracy or constitutionalism beyond the state, see, e.g., Pernice (2009), 365–66; de Búrca (2008a); Kohler-Koch and Rittberger (2007); Kumm (2006a); Halberstam (2005); Baquero Cruz (2002); Gerstenberg and Sabel (2002); and Cohen and Sabel (1997). For a critique of Gerstenberg and Sabel (2002) in the same volume, see Lindseth (2002), 140–43. For a more general critique of various strands in this literature, see Bellamy (2006).

25. See generally Mazower (2000 [1998]).

26. Menon and Weatherill (2002), 119–20.

polities exclude from participation and representation many interests which are affected by its decisions."[27] Such negative international externalities become, from this more modern perspective, a kind of "taxation without representation," or a public burden that citizens of adjacent states must endure while remaining powerless to alter it through electoral means. And because European supranationalism seeks to correct this flaw, from this perspective at least integration is "to be understood as a fundamentally democratic concept."[28]

But there is a basic problem with this concept, as the events of the present decade have shown (again, the collapse of the Constitutional Treaty as well as the struggle over the Treaty of Lisbon). Despite these scholarly reconceptualizations of democratic legitimacy, Europeans are not yet prepared, as a matter of political culture, to experience European governance in precisely these novel, purportedly democratic terms.[29] And therein perhaps is the real rub. Much less than serving as a "constitutional moment" for Europe,[30] the events of the present decade revealed once again that a crucial disconnect exists at the heart of integration—between the perception of European governance as bureaucratic and distant, on the one hand, and attachments to national institutions as the true loci of democratic and constitutional legitimacy, on the other. The tension between these two sentiments manifests itself most importantly not in momentary public opinion polling (although this can sometimes be telling) than in the outcomes of institutional politics over time (the focus of this study). European institutional politics can be understood as a persistent effort to manage the tension between the need for supranational regulatory power, on the one hand, and national democratic and constitutional legitimacy, on the other—a challenging undertaking over the last two decades particularly, when both supranational regulatory power vastly increased and the discourse over Europe's "democratic deficit" gained greater momentum.

"Legitimacy, unfortunately, is not solely a question of what is conceptually possible," I wrote in 2001, before the EU embarked on its ultimately unsuccessful experiment with drafting a written constitution: "If that were so, then scholarly solutions to the myriad of constitutional challenges in the EU could

---

27. Poiares Maduro (2003), 86, quoted in Menon and Weatherill (2008), 404.

28. Joerges and Neyer (1997), 293.

29. On the importance of how legitimacy is "experienced," see this chapter, n. 73 and accompanying text.

30. See Walker (2004).

be unproblematically translated into institutional and legal reality, without being filtered through a complex process of political, social, and cultural contestation on the national level."[31] Despite the already extensive transfers of regulatory power to the supranational level, the institutional politics of the past decade suggest that the historically constituted bodies of the nation-state still seem to enjoy (in certain key constituencies at any rate) considerable advantages in what might be called *legitimacy resources*. These go beyond integration's undoubted capacity to act as an instrument of peace, legality, or prosperity. They are rooted, rather, in a widely shared sense of identity or connection to national institutions as embodiments or expressions of self-rule (an attitude perhaps most palpable in Central and Eastern Europe after years of foreign subjugation).

This species of legitimacy builds on more than merely legal and technocratic foundations—indeed, on more than what Max Weber called "the directly economic disposition of goods and services." Rather, it is grounded in what Weber described as a "particular pathos" and "enduring emotional foundations" derived from a history of "common political struggle." Such a history of common struggle, even as it has been placed under considerable strain by the processes of Europeanization and globalization, nevertheless creates a "'community of memories' which ... [still] constitutes the ultimately decisive element of 'national consciousness.'"[32]

In the immediate postwar decades, many thought (as many still believe) that the devastating experience of the first half of the twentieth century, as well as the ongoing, internal logic and basic attractiveness of the integration process itself, would eventually push European governance into a decisively "post-national" phase.[33] But subsequent institutional and political history has shown this transition to be partial at best. Even as many aspects of governance have been denationalized, indeed "Europeanized,"[34] the same has not occurred in the realm of political culture, at least not to the same extent. In the realm of political culture, the institutions of representative

---

31. Lindseth (2001), 163.

32. Weber (1978 [1922]), 2:902–03. See also Renan (1996 [1882]), 51 ("A community of interest is assuredly a powerful bond among men. Do interests, however, suffice to make a nation? I do not think so. Community of interest brings about trade agreements, but nationality has a sentimental side to it; it is both soul and body at once; a *Zollverein* is not a *patrie*.").

33. See, e.g., Habermas (1992) and (2001a).

34. See, e.g., Olsen (2002).

government within the nation-state have retained their central role in terms of democratic and constitutional identity.

But this then leads us to perhaps the greatest paradox of European governance. Despite the widely acknowledged handicaps of European institutions in terms of *legitimacy*, the functional migration of normative *power* to an increasingly dense and complex supranational regulatory sphere has continued, or at least not been reversed (although the new Treaty of Lisbon does make intriguing allusions in that regard).[35] Indeed, even as the nation-state retains its political-cultural role in terms of legitimacy, it largely accepts the penetration of supranationally produced regulatory norms into the national legal order. How do we account for this seeming disconnect between supranational regulatory power on the one hand, and national democratic and constitutional legitimacy on the other?

From one perspective—not the one advanced in this study—this reality is not puzzling at all. It simply proves once again that older notions of legitimacy tied to the historically constituted bodies of representative self-government on the national level (executive, legislative, and judicial) are no longer that important, at least in a functional sense, in the face of the demands of output legitimacy.[36] But the institutional and political history of European governance over the last half century does not, in fact, support that assessment. Rather, what the record suggests, rather strongly in fact, is that European governance has continued to depend on forms of legitimation that are still mediated through democratic and constitutional bodies on the national level in critically important respects—in effect, borrowing the legitimacy of the nation-state in aid of the supranational process of integration. These national mechanisms include, most importantly, collective oversight of the supranational policy process by national executives (see Chapter 3), judicial review by national high courts with respect to certain core democratic and constitutional commitments (see Chapter 4), and increased recourse to national parliamentary scrutiny of supranational action, whether of particular national executives individually or of supranational bodies more broadly (see Chapter 5).

---

35. See Article 48 TEU post-Lisbon (the "ordinary revision procedure," which speaks of "proposals . . . either to increase or reduce the competences conferred on the Union by the Treaties.").

36. See, e.g., the work of Charles Sabel, discussed in detail in the Conclusion, nn. 28–60 and accompanying text.

These practices should be understood, this study maintains, as reflecting a convergence of European governance around the legitimating structures of the postwar constitutional settlement of administrative governance (see Chapter 2). They also reflect an ongoing process of contestation and (potential) settlement in the institutional evolution of European governance over time. To capture the full import of this process, one must undertake an examination that is sensitive to change along three interrelated historical dimensions: first, the "functional," in which existing institutional structures and legal categories come under pressure and are even transformed as a consequence of objective social and economic demands (e.g., international competition, the extension of markets beyond national borders, transnational environmental challenges, etc.); second, the "political," in which divergent interests struggle over the allocation of scarce institutional and legal advantages in responding to these structural-functional pressures; and third and finally, the "cultural," or the ways in which competing conceptions of legitimate governance (often legally expressed) are mobilized to justify or resist these changes in institutional and legal categories or structures.

The interaction of these dimensions results in a complex interplay of reciprocal influences that can only be explored historically, through an analytical narrative of institutional evolution that tries its best not to privilege change along any single dimension at the expense of the others.[37] A durable institutional settlement can only emerge, I theorize, if the processes of change along these various dimensions are somehow *reconciled* in some roughly stable way—that is, if structural-functional and political demands are satisfied but

---

37. For an outline of a similar approach, see Mashaw (2008), 1574; see also Müller (2009). Of course, the various dimensions of institutional change overlap and the causal relationship among them is varied and multidirectional. Functional change is often seen as the prime mover (see, e.g., Sabel and Simon (2006), 403, suggesting that "social development" is "jurisgenerative," even if "seldom synchronized" with law). But functional change should not be understood as the independent variable in a social-scientific sense—if that were the case, then we would observe much greater evolutionary change in legal and political institutions instead of their notorious *stickiness*. Such stickiness can be explained by the fact that structural shifts in the functional dimension (e.g., the extension of markets beyond national borders) are promoted and resisted in the political dimension (e.g., the creation of, or opposition to, transnational forms of governance to regulate those markets), and then are aided by justifications and interpretations mobilized in the cultural dimension (e.g., theories of constitutionalism or democracy "beyond the state," or invocations of "sovereignty" to define the true locus of legitimate governance as "national").

the outcome is still recognizable from the perspective of persistent, although evolving, cultural conceptions of legitimacy.[38]

In important part, the attempted historical synthesis set forth below is a sustained effort to show that, in the context of integration, national legitimating mechanisms have developed to do the work of reconciliation in precisely the sense I just described. These mechanisms strive to balance the evident functional and political demands for supranational regulatory solutions, on the one hand, with the continued cultural attachment to the nation-state as the primary locus of democratic and constitutional legitimacy in Europe, on the other. Put another way, these mechanisms establish a legitimating framework within which the otherwise undoubted complexity of Europe's policymaking processes—characterized by significant amounts of functionally autonomous regulatory power, distributed across multiple levels of governance—can operate *without evident democratic and constitutional legitimacy of their own,* at least as classically understood. To borrow an apt phrase from Robert Dahl, nationally grounded legitimating mechanisms can be seen as efforts to reduce the "costs to democracy"[39] (as well as to "constitutionalism," in some sense the same thing),[40] which inevitably flow from the transfer of regulatory power outside the traditional confines of representative government on the national level.

❦ Administrative Governance and the Distinction between Control and Legitimation of Regulatory Power

Other scholars have certainly acknowledged the legitimating functions of national institutions in European governance, at least in a limited sense.[41]

---

38. As one commentator has put it nicely, my work tries to get at is "the cultural legibility of our political arrangements." Walker (2006b), 355 (commenting on Lindseth (2006)). For my earlier efforts to develop and deploy this historiographical theory, see Lindseth (2002), (2004), (2005a), and (2005b). For its underlying theoretical inspiration, see Hauriou (1925). For its linkages to constructivist approaches to institutionalism, see Chapter 1, nn. 105–106 and accompanying text.

39. Dahl (1999), 34.

40. In this regard, I specifically adopt the historical concept of constitutional democracy set out in Rubenfeld (2001).

41. See, e.g., Bartolini (2005), 175 ("[I]t is difficult to identify any other sources of legitimacy [for the EU] than the direct borrowing of national legitimacy through the governments' representatives."); see also Pernice (2009), 390–91; Claes (2007), 35–36; Wouters (2000); de Búrca

Indeed, this is something that the TEU post-Lisbon now explicitly recognizes (in Article 12, for example, on the role of national parliaments in European integration). And thus, from that perspective at least, my argument may not appear to be particularly original.

My aim, however, is to offer a more helpful analytical and historical framework for understanding the role of national legitimation in European public law. In so doing, I also hope to offer a deeper challenge to the persistent impulse in the scholarship to characterize EU governance in autonomously constitutional terms. By virtue of delegations from the historically constituted bodies of the nation-state, I claim that European governance *as a whole* (including the European Parliament as well as the European Court of Justice) is best understood as an extension of administrative governance on the national level over the course of the twentieth century. This is not simply a repackaging of Giandomenico Majone's well known characterization of supranational bodies as an "independent fourth branch of government" in Europe, analogizing to the American administrative experience.[42] Majone's characterization certainly captured an underlying reality in European governance, although the claim in fact entails a good deal more historical and legal complexity, which this book tries to illuminate.

When I refer to the constituted bodies of representative government on the national level, I mean those institutions—notably national legislatures, but also chief executives and cabinets, as well as courts or court-like jurisdictions like the French *Conseil d'Etat*—which, over the course of the second half of the nineteenth century, evolved into the preeminent expressions of ruling legitimacy within nation-states (see Chapter 1). Tocqueville foresaw this development in *Democracy in America* (1835), when he spoke of the process of "centralization of government," particularly in elected assemblies, with the English Parliament being his paradigmatic example.[43] Latter-day political sociologists often refer to this process as national "consolidation" in

(1995), 352–53, citing Seidel (1995), 230. Cf. as well Habermas (2000 [1998]), 155–56, as cited in McCormick (2007), 208.

42. Majone (1994a). On the distinction between my argument and Majone's and related views, see Chapter 1, nn. 19–23 and accompanying text.

43. Cf. Tocqueville (1889 [1835]), 64–67 (associating "centralization of government" with the elected legislature, distinguishing it from decentralized "local administration" in the United States).

nineteenth-century Europe, a development with territorial, political-cultural, and institutional dimensions.[44]

And yet, almost from the moment of the seeming triumph of national assemblies and other Tocquevillean expressions of the "centralization of government," these bodies were confronted by extraordinary, countervailing functional pressures for diffusion and fragmentation of normative power.[45] The need to address a range of new regulatory challenges posed by urbanization, industrialization, and the globalization of markets in goods, capital, and labor forced centralized bodies to begin transferring regulatory authority outward and downward over the course of the second half of the nineteenth century.[46] Despite our images of national "consolidation" during this period, one could just as easily conclude, based on these countervailing pressures, that the late nineteenth century European nation-state—indeed, the nation-state throughout the North Atlantic world—was very much a "leaky and porous . . . vessel."[47] This administrative "leakiness," if you will, would be one of the identifying attributes of the modern governance well into the twentieth century, as the nation-state in the North Atlantic world confronted even more intense functional and political pressures to regulate a whole range of social and economic phenomena, both in war and peace.

My aim here, then, is to understand European integration as a new stage in this historical process of diffusion and fragmentation of normative power, which has operated in tension with the "centralization of government" in the Tocquevillean sense on the national level (see Chapter 1). It is in linking European governance to this deeper history of the rise of administrative governance that one can begin to see the basic truth in Alan Milward's famous, although controversial, assertion that integration is "one more stage in the long evolution of the European state."[48] To gain a more complete picture of

---

44. See, e.g., Tilly (2002), 178; Rokkan (1999), 163; Holton (1998), 45–46.

45. Mashaw (2008) beautifully traces this process in the American case from 1829–1861.

46. For a suggestive overview of those pressures over the late-nineteenth and early-twentieth centuries, as well as the emergence of "social politics" in the trans-Atlantic world, see Rodgers (1998). For a discussion of the corresponding shift from "classical legal thought" to "social law," see Kennedy (2006).

47. Bright and Geyer (2002), 65. For more elaboration on this point, see Chapter 1, nn. 40–42 and accompanying text.

48. Milward (2000 [1992]), x. For more detail on the relationship of my argument to Milward's work, see Chapter 1, nn. 44–50 and accompanying text. See also Bartolini (2005) for a similar effort, albeit more theoretically oriented, to view integration in terms of the longer-term evolution of state structures.

how this is true, however, one must go beyond a focus on the functional and political dimensions to a perspective more sensitive to institutional change along the cultural dimension as well. As an extension of the functional diffusion and fragmentation of regulatory power, supranational governance in Europe has necessarily relied on elements of the same legal-cultural settlement that provided the foundation for the postwar welfare state (*Sozialstaat, l'Etat providence*) (see Chapter 2). When social scientists emphasize certain features of "multilevel" governance in Europe—for example, "deparliamentarization" or "executive dominance"—they are in fact referring to elements of this same settlement. Moreover, when they suggest that integration somehow caused the development of these features,[49] they are in fact ignoring this deeper history on the national level and below.

The postwar constitutional settlement of administrative governance ultimately entailed a new balance among the executive, legislative, and judicial branches, while also reflecting a reworking of the meaning of representative democracy (see Chapter 2). The postwar settlement was born of the desire to master a number of legal-historical crosscurrents, which went beyond human rights and the need to recalibrate the relationship between state sovereignty and international law, two factors usually invoked to explain the legal-historical foundations of European integration in the postwar decades. These crosscurrents included strains on the boundaries between public and private; between differing levels of governance (local, regional, national, and eventually supranational and international as well); between formal and informal exercises of public authority (now often called "hard" and "soft" law); and, perhaps most importantly for our purposes, between constituted legislative, executive, and judicial powers, each of which saw increasing migrations to the administrative sphere.[50] The postwar settlement reflected a rethinking of the nature and scope of executive power (both internally and externally), the role of an emergent class of political actor (the technocrat), and the proper function of the legislature and the judiciary in vindicating the values of representative (i.e., parliamentary) democracy in an era of increasing diffusion and fragmentation of regulatory authority. To the

---

49. See, e.g., Börzel and Sprungk (2007); see also, Chapter 5, nn. 56–60 and accompanying text.

50. See McCormick (2007), chap. 3, and more specifically p. 83 (discussing Weber's analysis of the transition from the *Rechtsstaat* to *Sozialstaat*); but see also McCormick (2007), chap. 4, and more specifically p. 156 (discussing Habermas's adoption of Weber's basic diagnosis in his own analysis of the same transition). Cf. also Grimm (2005).

extent that European governance is properly called "sui generis,"[51] this is primarily because of challenges that unavoidably arose in the effort to translate the postwar constitutional settlement into workable supranational form. Nevertheless, the origins of these mechanisms remained fundamentally national, emerging out of a similar effort to reconcile representative government and "leaky" forms of administrative governance on the state level.

By spelling out the relationship of European governance to the postwar constitutional settlement, I seek to challenge the claim, so prevalent in the work of leading European legal theorists on integration over the last several decades, that autonomous regulatory power demands an equally autonomous form of "non-statal constitutionalism," or "constitutionalism beyond the state," as it is sometimes less awkwardly called.[52] This claim is an extension of what a new voice in European legal theory has called the dominant "constitutional narrative" of integration[53]—which, although ultimately inconsistent with integration's actual legal-historical character, has nevertheless guided legal analysis for much of the last thirty years.[54]

Among the narrative's core assumptions today, I would maintain, is the idea that the EU "has passed a threshold of authoritative capacity and normative penetration beyond which its structures require a direct rather than indirect and state-mediated mandate from those who fall within its jurisdiction."[55] The historical record, unfortunately, does not support that claim. To the contrary, the record suggests that supranational regulatory power need not be—indeed, for the most part, has not been—exercised by

---

51. See Chapter 1, n. 4, and accompanying text.

52. Weiler and Wind (2003), 4.

53. See generally Avbelj (2008b).

54. Beginning, one might say, with Stein (1981).

55. Walker (2006a), 148; see also Walker (2006c), 80–81 (noting how the "double movement, accelerating over the 20 years since the signing of the Single European Act, towards expanding the scope of the EU from internal market regulation to large areas of social and security policy combined with the reduction or sacrifice of national veto positions in legislative and other decisional procedures, suggests such a profound transformation of both the scope and autonomous capability of the EU as to undermine the claims for indirect legitimation and underline the demand for direct legitimation"). The analogue to this position in the security domain is that it is a "'historical incongruity'" for Europe to be "'an economic, commercial, technological power [and yet] remain a minor power on the strategic plane,'" a position critiqued in Sheehan (2009), 222–23 (quoting Pascal Boniface).

the same institutions that supply its democratic and constitutional legitimacy, just as in the administrative state.

The legitimation of supranational regulatory power (its "mandate," so to speak) has never been successfully located supranationally, whether in the elections to the European Parliament, in the deliberations of the European Commission, or even, dare I say it, in the judgments of the ECJ, the ultimate bastion of a seeming supranational constitutionalism. Rather it has been located, however tenuously, in the enabling treaties themselves, akin to enabling legislation on the national level, empowering the supranational exercise of regulatory discretion within the capacious limits defined by those treaties.[56] Moreover, that mandate finds its ultimate foundation in national constitutional provisions and processes, authorizing the enforcement of European norms in national orders, the sine qua non of European integration.

This empowerment and authorization is best understood as another expression of the *administrative, not constitutional* character of integration. In this sense, EU institutions exercise power that is understood to be derived from national constitutional orders, rather than being autonomously constitutional in itself. It is on the basis of that derivative mandate that supranational regulatory power has been lawfully exercised, subject to ongoing forms of legitimating oversight from national bodies, as well as whatever additional supranational mechanisms that the Member States have chosen to create to increase accountability in the EU. As we shall see below (notably in Chapter 2), this sort of separation of regulatory power from the ultimate sources of legitimacy has been among the most important elements of the constitutional settlement of administrative governance in the twentieth century, whether national or supranational.

Of course, one might argue in a more constitutionalist vein that this separation is not unlike what occurs, conceptually, when a political community— a "people"—legally constitutes bodies of public authority in the first place.[57] But the separation of power and legitimacy is in fact quite different in the constitutional and administrative contexts. In the constitutional context, the constituent power—again, the "people"—has the plenary authority to structure governance as it sees fit, subject to certain limitations imposed, inter alia, by human rights. In the administrative context, however, the already constituted bodies of representative government do not have the

---

56. Contrast de Witte (2002) (speaking of the "semi-permanent treaty revision process" as a "constitutional conversation"). See also Smith (2002); Cohen and Sabel (2004), 161.

57. See, e.g., Grimm (2005), 451.

same nearly plenary discretion. Rather, when these bodies transfer power to an administrative agent, this raises the classic Lockean concern regarding the constitutionally permissible scope of delegation, a concern still very much with us since Locke first articulated it in the *Second Treatise of Government*:

> The power of the *legislative*, being derived from the people by a positive voluntary grant and institution, can be no other than what that positive grant conveyed, which being only to make *laws*, and not to make *legislators*, the *legislative* can have no power to transfer their authority of making laws, and place it in other hands.[58]

In a system of representative government, in other words, those bodies that have been historically constituted by the people itself (Tocqueville's "centralization of government") have an obligation to remain the locus of governing power, at least in some historically and culturally recognizable sense. These bodies should not be able to abdicate that power to others.

And yet modern governance seems to be grounded in precisely this sort of diffusion and fragmentation of normative power both within and beyond the state, in the face of often intense functional demands. So the real question is this: How has the Lockean objection been overcome? *Delegation* is the short answer, albeit not in the sense of an immutable rational-choice regime in which constitutional principals *control* administrative agents, as some readers might suppose. To understand modern administrative governance, we must dispense with an idealized understanding of a "Westphalian" principal with unbridled power to direct regulatory outcomes within a particular territory, an ahistoric reading of state sovereignty if there ever was one.[59] This caricature of the principle-agent relationship in delegation is far from the actual historical reality, not just supranationally but also nationally. As Chapter 1 will outline in greater detail, delegation has evolved as a much more flexible normative-legal principle, in which the power of control,

---

58. Locke (1980 [1690]), § 141 (emphasis in original). See also Lindseth (2004), 1356.

59. See generally Sheehan (2006). The capacity for hierarchical administrative control is generally overstated even within states, often on the basis of stylized principal-agent models. See, e.g., Curtin (2007), 524–25. As a corrective, one might usefully recall the infamous "Crichel Down Affair" in Britain in 1954. For an overview, see Griffith (1955). For reflections on the continuing limited capacities of principals to exercise "control" over agents in modern administrative states, see Thatcher (2005); see also Thatcher and Stone Sweet (2002), 6 (discussing how, in situations of administrative complexity, "the analyst cannot assume that principals can control agents").

whether de facto and de jure, is often greatly diminished, if sometimes nearly relinquished entirely, except in all but the most extreme circumstances.[60] Over the course of the twentieth century in particular, constitutional principals have needed to settle for something less than actual control—perhaps merely supervision, coordination, or what an American administrative lawyer would call "oversight."[61]

This brings us, then, squarely to the distinction between control and legitimation, which is at the heart of the historical synthesis below. The shift away from actual control necessarily has given rise to the need to reconcile, in cultural terms, the socioinstitutional reality of diffuse and fragmented governance with conceptions of Tocquevillian "centralization of government" inherited from the past. In this process of reconciliation, both the reallocations of regulatory power (delegations) and the conceptions of legitimacy tied to representative institutions on the national level (and below) have necessarily adjusted in the face of the reciprocal demands of the other, in an intensely political-cultural process of contestation over values but also in deference to functional realities. The result has been an uneasy balance, not merely in European integration but in administrative governance more generally. While the diffuse and fragmented administrative sphere came to exercise significant and often seemingly autonomous regulatory power of varying types (rulemaking, enforcement, adjudication), that sphere has never been understood *culturally* to enjoy an autonomous democratic and constitutional legitimacy of its own, at least in a historically recognizable sense. Rather, the possessors of regulatory power have remained answerable, in terms of the rationality and limits of their actions, to the oversight of historically constituted bodies in the nation-state (legislative, executive, and judicial) in order to satisfy these cultural demands for legitimacy.

In this process of contestation and reconciliation, one could also say that the very nature of public law has itself deeply evolved. It has become less a system of rules marking seemingly clear lines between "valid" and "invalid" exercises of authority, as classical understandings of the *Rechtsstaat, l'Etat de droit,* or the rule of law might have demanded.[62] Instead, public

---

60. See Chapter 1, nn. 101–111 and accompanying text.

61. Lindseth et al. (2008); see also Strauss (2007).

62. Young (2000), 1594 (describing "a regime of invalidation norms" as opposed to one of "resistance norms"—the former being a system in which "governmental action is perfectly unproblematic even though it pushes right up to the constitutional limit; that limit, however, amounts to an inflexible line beyond which any government action is barred").

law has evolved toward something more focused on "the allocation of burdens of reason-giving,"[63] or, as European scholars are increasingly calling it, "accountability."[64] Such accountability mechanisms are best understood as a system of "resistance norms," operating "as a 'soft limit' which may be more or less yielding depending on the circumstances"—to borrow a powerful distinction first advanced by Ernest Young, an American public law scholar.[65]

The idea of public law as primarily a system of "resistance norms" is intimately linked to the legitimation-control distinction, which as we shall see is essential to understanding the administrative character of European governance. The distinction between legitimation and control is admittedly spectral rather than dichotomous (perhaps no more so, as we shall see below, than in the integration context). But the key difference is this: Control entails a power of specific policy direction, whereas legitimation does not, or at least not necessarily.[66] There are clearly elements of control within some forms legitimation, but legitimation also permits a larger measure of functional autonomy in the agent exercising delegated authority. Legitimation, rather, serves the purpose—to borrow from another American administrative law scholar, Peter Strauss—of "maintaining the connection between each of the [constitutional] institutions and the paradigmatic function which it alone is empowered to serve, while also retaining a grasp on [administrative governance] as a whole that respects our commitments to the control of law."[67]

Although the diffusion and fragmentation of regulatory authority clearly has marked a breakdown in older conceptions of separation of powers (not to mention a deep blurring of the line between the domestic and

---

63. Somek (2004), 58 ("Der Rechtsstaat verwandelt sich in ein System der Allokation von Begruendungslasten"), quoted in Kumm (2006b), 532.

64. Benz et al. (2007), 445, drawing from Bovens (2007) (depicting accountability as "a process of communication in which information is transferred and reasons for policies discussed," and as "a significant institutional element of effective and legitimate organisations, not the least of a democratic political system or a polity governed in accordance with the rule of law. There is, in other words, as strong a link between accountability and legitimacy as that between transparency and accountability, accepted by every discipline as an essential aspect of principal–agent theory").

65. See again Young (2000), 1594. For further elaboration on the role of "resistance norms" in European integration, see, e.g., Chapter 4, nn. 155–156, and Chapter 5, n. 31, and accompanying text.

66. In this regard, I would place many if not most of the "steering mechanisms" that governance theorists now place under the rubric of "control" within the category of "legitimation." See, e.g., Scott (2002).

67. Strauss (1987), 488.

the external), the traditional constitutional principals have nevertheless retained a key role as separate *mechanisms of legitimation* in the emergent system of administrative governance (what Chapter 2 terms "mediated legitimacy"). The diffusion and fragmentation of normative power over the last half century has resulted in a complex regulatory system that no single institution could claim realistically to "control" even within administrative states. Nevertheless, that system has been experienced as adequately "under control," even if only indirectly and systemically rather than intentionally and hierarchically, thanks to the various mechanisms of legitimation that have developed in modern administrative governance.[68]

National Legitimation and the Administrative Character of European Governance

As in the administrative state, so too in the process of European integration: The persistence and growth of national oversight mechanisms in European public law have worked to "maintain the connection" between supranational regulatory power and the historically constituted bodies of the nation-state, providing an essential means of legitimation of administrative governance in its now supranational form. In the integration context just as in the administrative state, the separation of regulatory power from democratic and constitutional legitimacy has been accomplished through transfers of authority that are best understood culturally (if not always functionally) as *delegations* in an administrative sense—that is, as transfers from constitutional principal to administrative agent—*not* as the establishment of a constitutionally original or autonomous level of governance at the supranational level.[69] Although

---

68. Moe (1987), 291. Cf. also Scott (2002), 60 (attempting to broaden the notion of "control" to encompass "the whole variety of mechanisms by which steering of behaviour occurs and to all levels of activity: citizens, civil society, and undertakings; local, regional, and national state bodies; EU and other supranational institutions."); and Harlow and Rawlings (2007), 545 (questioning whether "sanction is an essential element in accountability, though we accept that lawyers may be predisposed to think that it is.").

69. This latter claim, rejected here, has provided the premise for much supranational case law and legal theorizing about integration over the last several decades. See, most recently, joined cases C-402/05P & C-415/05P, *Kadi & Al Barakaat International Foundation v. Council and Commission*, judgment of the Court of Justice of the European Communities (Grand Chamber), 3 Sept. 2008, http://eur-lex.europa.eu/LexUriServ/LexUriServ.do?uri=CELEX:62 005J0402:EN:HTML (last visited July 5, 2009); and more particularly the Opinion of Advocate General Miguel Poiares Maduro, delivered 23 Jan. 2008, para. 21, http://eur-lex.europa.eu/LexUriServ/LexUriServ.do?uri=CELEX:62005C0415:EN:HTML (last visited July 5, 2009).

now obscured behind the language of "conferral" in the treaties (Article 5 of the Treaty Establishing the European Community [TEC]/Article 5 TEU post-Lisbon), the role of delegation is increasingly hard to ignore as a foundational normative principle in European law. In particular, this concept has arguably animated the national high court jurisprudence over the last two decades (see Chapter 4). As the German Federal Constitutional Court (*Bundesverfassungsgericht*) recently reminded us in its decision on the Treaty of Lisbon in June 2009:

> The principle of conferral is a mechanism of protection to preserve the Member States' responsibility. The European Union is competent for an issue only to the extent that the Member States have conferred such competence on it. Accordingly, the Member States are the constituted primary political area of their respective polities, the European Union has secondary, *i.e. delegated,* responsibility for the tasks conferred on it. The Treaty of Lisbon explicitly confirms the current principle of conferral.[70]

Of course, it is quite possible to acknowledge a "thick pattern of 'bridging mechanisms'" between the national and the supranational levels in the European context without necessarily acknowledging the latter's dependence on the former in terms of legitimacy in a normative, delegation sense.[71] National legitimating mechanisms, however, do not merely bridge; they *frame.* They define, in terms of political and legal culture, the normative boundaries for the exercise of legitimate authority while also establishing mechanisms to scrutinize policymaking within those boundaries—sometimes legally but always politically. These mechanisms enable, in particular, the supervision of "the slippery character of the functionally broad legal bases" in the European treaties[72]—those that authorize either the harmonization of national laws in furtherance of market integration (Articles 94–95 TEC/Articles 114–115 of the Treaty on the Functioning of the European Union [TFEU]) or, more generally, the adoption of measures needed to attain

---

70. German Lisbon Decision (2009), para. 301 (emphasis added) (citing "Article 5.1 sentence 1 and 5.2 TEU Lisbon; see also Article 1.1, Article 3.6, Article 4.1, Article 48.6(3) TEU Lisbon; Article 2.1 and 2.2, Article 4.1, Article 7, Article 19, Article 32, Article 130, Article 132.1, Article 207.6, Article 337 TFEU; Declaration no. 18 in Relation to the Delimitation of Competences; Declaration no. 24 Concerning the Legal Personality of the European Union")

71. Walker (2006d), 320 (internal citation omitted).

72. Weatherill (2005), 18.

"one of the objectives of the Community [for which] this Treaty has not [otherwise] provided the necessary powers" (Article 308 TEC/Article 352 TFEU). By providing a framework for policing these capacious and necessarily flexible legal bases, national oversight mechanisms provide an institutional means for reconnecting the resulting denationalized regulatory output to national structures. In doing so, this oversight allows that output to be "experienced" as democratically and constitutionally legitimate in some evolving yet "culturally legible" sense.[73]

For this reason the existence of national oversight mechanisms, from an administrative perspective, should not be understood as either anomalous or a sign of crisis in the European system.[74] Rather, it has been precisely through their development over time that European public law has worked toward a reconciliation, however imperfectly, between the largely functional (although often also political) demands for policy solutions at the supranational level and the continued dominant cultural attachment to national institutions as expressions of constitutional self-government in the European system. Moreover, consistent with the administrative character of European governance, these national oversight mechanisms serve primarily the function of legitimation (in the sense of democratic connection, identity expression, reason-giving, and accountability) as opposed to control.

Perhaps more than with any other instance of administrative governance, in fact, the integration context demonstrates the spectral rather than dichotomous nature of the distinction between legitimation and control. In the integration context, for example, there exists a good deal of formal control in the adoption of the treaties themselves, as the enabling legislation for European governance. Moreover, on an ongoing basis, there is control in those regulatory domains where the Member State executives have preserved unanimous

---

73. Walker (2006b), 355 (using the term "cultural legibility," commenting on Lindseth (2006)). On the relationship between public law and the cultural "experience" of democratic and constitutional legitimacy, see generally Lindseth (2002), (2004), (2005a), (2005b), and (2006). This historiographical theory is an adaptation of Thompson (1994), 222: "[H]istorical change eventuates ... because changes in productive relationships are *experienced* in social and cultural life, refracted in men's ideas and their values, and argued through their actions, their choices and their beliefs" (emphasis in original). Rather than focusing on changing productive relationships, as Thompson did, historians of public law should focus on how changing structures of public governance have been "experienced" in relation to historically rooted ideas and values of legitimate government inherited from the past.

74. See, e.g., Majone (2005), 64 (describing the imposition of national constraints on supranational autonomy as "the symptom of a deeper crisis: a growing mistrust between the member states and the supranational institutions").

voting in the Council (e.g., in tax harmonization). Finally, and most importantly, there is at least *shared* control exercised by the Council when it engages in collective oversight of the supranational policy process more generally. This occurs through its influence on agenda-setting, approval of legislation under qualified-majority voting, or intervention in the policy process through its committee structures, whether via the Committee of Permanent Representatives of the Member States (COREPER), or the comitology system.[75]

But the emergence of this form of shared oversight rather than individualized control is in fact of critical historical importance. Certain national leaders—Charles de Gaulle, most prominently—deeply resisted this loss of direct control, which led directly to the conflicts of the 1960s (the empty chair and the Luxembourg Compromise), which in turn prompted the emergence of the elaborate committee system for supervising regulatory power exercised by, or delegated to, the Commission (see Chapter 3). But what is important to recognize is that, much less than securing a national veto over supranational policy making, these developments in fact marked the definitive shift away from national control toward shared national executive oversight in European public law, and hence the acknowledgment of a measure of supranational regulatory autonomy, if not legitimacy.[76]

This particular history is later echoed, as we shall see in Chapters 4 and 5, both in the context of national *Kompetenz-Kompetenz* jurisprudence,[77] as well as in more recent discussions in the Convention on the Future of Europe with regard to a so-called red card procedure for national parliamentary scrutiny of subsidiarity.[78] This recurring tension between control and legitimation points to a central feature of European governance: The power of control, in the strongest sense, could not be retained by the individual Member States without in fact defeating the very purpose of supranational delegation in the first place.[79] It points to the fact that "the connecting thread"

---

75. See, e.g., Chapter 3, nn. 162–182 and accompanying text.

76. See Chapter 3, nn. 140–160 and accompanying text.

77. See Chapter 4, nn. 175–179 and accompanying text.

78. See Chapter 5, nn. 245–254 and accompanying text.

79. This would later be explicitly recognized by the German *Bundesverfassungsgericht* in its Maastricht Decision of 1993, a decision often misunderstood as hostile to integration. See Chapter 4, n. 178 and accompanying text. The German Maastricht Decision was deeply sensitive to integration's grounding in the postwar constitutional settlement. See generally, Chapter 4, nn. 166–183 and accompanying text; see also Lindseth (2003b).

in much of the institutional contestation in European integration over the last several decades has been

> the risk that one source of [supranational] legitimacy, its capacity to solve problems effectively in some circumstances where it is judged right to lift decision-making out of the exclusive grip of State-centred political actors, will be contaminated by undue deference to another source of its legitimacy, the democratic processes within the individual Member States.[80]

Consequently, "ensuring the effectiveness of the EU . . . and hence output efficiency" has required "insulating the supranational institutions from Member State control. It is only through their independence that supranational institutions are in a position to promote any Community interest, or to ensure reciprocal respect for the EU bargain."[81] It is precisely for this reason that European public law has attempted to translate the identifying feature of postwar administrative governance—the institutional separation of regulatory power from democratic and constitutional legitimation—into a workable supranational form.

Of course, relinquishing specific control should not be equated with the desire to establish complete supranational autonomy, certainly not in a constitutional sense. "Here, autonomy can only be understood—as is usual regarding the law of self-government—as an autonomy to rule which is independent but derived, [that is,] accorded by other legal entities."[82] Managing the tension between regulatory autonomy and derivative legitimacy has deeply shaped the national-supranational relationship in Europe over time, not just judicially (in the national *Kompetenz-Kompetenz* jurisprudence, to be sure) but also, perhaps more importantly, politically. As one integration historian has found, the desire to manage this tension manifested itself from the very earliest years of integration, when the Member States worked to establish "ever more complex administrative structures to ensure that they were both as well informed as possible about the way in which policy debates within the Community were evolving and could maximize the impact of their desiderata within [those] debates."[83] This effort to reinforce their role as

---

80. Weatherill (2005), 33.

81. Menon and Weatherill (2002), 119 (internal citation omitted).

82. German Lisbon Decision (2009), para. 231.

83. Ludlow (2009), 195.

political principals has evolved, as two political scientists have more recently described, into a range of "specialist mechanisms" by which Member States "co-ordinate their European policies and . . . manage their inputs into EU decision-making." [84]

It must be acknowledged, as well, that the Member States established certain institutions—the ECJ and the European Parliament (EP), most importantly, but also the European Commission—to serve some kind of legitimating functions on the supranational level. And in many respects these bodies have admirably served these functions and, as a consequence, have been rewarded with broader oversight responsibilities in the supranational policy process. Nevertheless, the persistence and growth of national as opposed to supranational oversight mechanisms reflects an important legal-cultural fact: These supranational bodies, in the eyes of many if not most Europeans, are ultimately inadequate in themselves for the purposes of specifically *democratic* and *constitutional* legitimation. Neither the Commission, the EP, nor the ECJ are understood to embody or express the capacity of a cohesive political community to rule itself through institutions historically constituted for that purpose. This is an empirical reality in European political and legal culture, one with deep historical roots that must be accounted *for*, both in terms of its origins and effects, rather than dismissed or argued *against*.[85] It is through the framework of national oversight—exercised most intensely through national executives, and more episodically through national high courts and national parliaments—that supranational policy processes are experienced, I maintain, as ultimately "under control" democratically and constitutionally, even if not necessarily "controlled" by any single entity or body.[86]

A final point must also be stressed, one of particular relevance to European legal and constitutional theory. Undoubtedly, as we will see below (particularly in Chapter 4), Europeans remain for the most part deferential to relatively

---

84. Kassim and Menon (2003), 130, citing Kassim et al. (2001), and Kassim et al. (2000).

85. Cf. Rittberger (2005), 33, critiquing the "democratic deficit" literature for its focus on redefining the "standards" by which European governance might be measured (e.g., Majone (1998)) rather than asking why perceptions of a democratic deficit exist and what impact these then have on institutional design in the EU. Scholars must take the national-supranational relationship as it is, not as they might wish it to be, in order to judge where European governance is and whither it is tending. It is not Eurosceptical to point this out. Cf. Charlemagne (2009b); Nosemonkey (2009); Stuart (2009).

86. Cf. Everson (1995), 190, citing Moe (1987); see also Majone (1994a), 29, citing same article.

autonomous exercises of supranational regulatory power, just as they are relatively accepting of increasingly autonomous forms of administrative governance on the national level. This is reflected in the largely uncontested way that national legal systems absorb the vast majority of European norms, with most individuals unaware of their supranational origins.[87] Nevertheless, the persistence and growth of national oversight mechanisms, particularly over the last two decades, suggest a deep resistance in political and legal culture to the recognition of any autonomous democratic and constitutional legitimacy or originality for European governance apart from national "delegations." This fact presents itself most acutely at critical moments of decision—in referenda over European treaties, for example, or in related exercises of constitutional review. This cultural reality has served as a background constraint on integration that cannot be dismissed or theorized away, even if the temptation to do so is great, perhaps because such attitudes seem normatively objectionable from the perspective of some idealized form of autonomous "deliberative" democracy or constitutionalism "beyond the state."

Scholars and, perhaps more importantly, judges on the ECJ have generally misinterpreted Europeans' relatively strong deference to the functional demands of integration as an acceptance of a kind of constitutional supremacy of supranational law over national law, including national norms of constitutional character.[88] Support for this view among legal scholars has typically flowed from an excessive focus on the functional autonomy of European supranationalism at the expense of the broader legitimating framework within which it operates.[89] One observer summarized the conventional view at the close of the 1990s: "The classical literature on the constitutionalisation of Community law has described how the case law of the Court developed a constitutional infrastructure with individual and fundamental rights, enforcement mechanisms, an institutional rule of law (e.g., separation of powers) and an autonomous and hierarchical legal order."[90]

---

87. Of course, there are exceptions, like the "metric martyrs" campaign in Britain, but such controversies are miniscule compared to the actual scope of supranationally generated norms. See Metric Martyrs Defence Fund, http://www.metricmartyrs.co.uk/ (last visited July 5, 2009).

88. See generally Alter (2001).

89. For an exhaustive and nuanced analysis of the interface between national constitutions and European law, but one in which the European constitutional perspective is ultimately foregrounded at the expense of the national, see Wouters (2000).

90. Poiares Maduro (1998), 8.

Conspicuously absent from this "constitutional infrastructure," however, has been democratic legitimacy, even as the ECJ made some relatively unpersuasive gestures in that direction, in efforts to maximize both its own role as well as that of the European Parliament in institutional disputes at the supranational level.[91] The legitimating practices at the core of this study suggest, however, the extent to which national legal elites look upon the absence of ultimate democratic legitimacy as a fundamental gap in the ECJ's constitutionalizing jurisprudence. National high court decisions of the last two decades, for example, are not interesting simply because they suggest how, "from a national constitutional perspective, the Court of Justice is just one more EU institution that, in principle, could act *ultra vires* under the colour of interpreting the Treaty."[92] Rather, they are exemplars of a type of cultural resistance to the perceived inadequacies of integration in terms of democratic and constitutional legitimacy classically understood. The reservation of the so-called power of *Kompetenz-Kompetenz* by these courts (explored in detail in Chapter 4) has, by its terms, been designed to preserve core values of national democracy in the face of integration's evident functional demands, all consistent with the postwar constitutional settlement, a task that the ECJ has been singularly unwilling to undertake.

Like the principle of subsidiarity that came to the foreground of European public law in the same decade (the 1990s), *Kompetenz-Kompetenz* operates less as a validity norm (i.e., one designed to police a rigid system of rules) than quintessentially as a "resistance norm" that functions "as a 'soft limit' that may be more or less yielding depending on the circumstances."[93] This national

---

91. See Case 138/79, *SA Roquettes Frères v. Council*, 1980 E.C.R. 3333, 3360 (resolving a legal basis dispute in part by reference to the "fundamental democratic principle that the peoples should take part in the exercise of power through the intermediary of a representative assembly"); see also Case C-300/89, *Commission v. Council*, 1991 E.C.R. I-2867, I-2900 (*re* the appropriate legal basis for the adoption of the titanium dioxide waste directive). This reasoning, however, begs the question of whether the European "peoples" collectively constitute a *demos* for purposes of collective self-government, or whether such democratic legitimacy continues to reside at the national level. See, e.g., Lindseth (1999), 672–83. Cf. also the Opinion of Advocate General Poiares Maduro, 26 Mar. 2009, n. 5, in Case C-411/06, *Commission v. Parliament and Council*, not yet reported, http://eur-lex. europa.eu/LexUriServ/LexUriServ.do?uri=CELEX:62006C0411:EN:HTML#Footref5 (last visited Nov. 3, 2009) ("To accept a general principle of preference for a legal basis which maximises the participation of the European Parliament in the decision-making process would be tantamount to altering the institutional and democratic balance laid down by the Treaty.").

92. Kumm (2006b), 530.

93. Young (2000), 1594. For more detail, see this Introduction, nn. 62–65 and accompanying text.

jurisprudence, coupled with the increasing activism of national parliaments over the same period (see Chapter 5), can be understood as a cultural rejection of the full-blown conception of "an autonomous and hierarchical legal order,"[94] at least with regard to its central but nevertheless most tenuous concept: the "supremacy" of European over national law.[95] In this regard, the distinction advanced by the Spanish *Tribunal Constitucional* in its 2004 ruling on the now-defunct Constitutional Treaty, between the "supremacy" of the national constitution and the "primacy" of European law only within its treaty-defined "scopes of application," is highly suggestive of the current state as well as the likely future direction of European public law.[96] It stands in defiance of those who had earlier argued, in the heady days of European constitutionalism of the late 1980s and early 1990s, that "[t]there is simply no nucleus of sovereignty that the Member States can invoke, as such, against the Community."[97]

Much less than being "ever more threadbare" as expressions of "state-centered democratic legitimation,"[98] nationally grounded oversight mechanisms have expanded over the last two decades precisely because supranational power is perceived as *delegated*—that is, derived from national legal orders—and, as such, demands some form of national legitimation. These mechanisms have developed to overcome what is best understood, not as a *democratic deficit*, but as a *democratic disconnect* in European governance. It is a disconnect between the exercise of supranational regulatory power and its ultimate sources of legitimacy on the national level.[99] By seeking to overcome that disconnect, European public law has sought to reconcile, in democratic and constitutional terms, the increased penetration of supranational regulatory norms with the persistence of domestic legal orders as the culturally privileged loci of legitimacy in the European system.

---

94. Poiares Maduro (1998), 8.

95. Claes (2007), 4–5.

96. See DTC 1/2004, at part 4 (ruling on the constitutionality on the Treaty establishing a Constitution for Europe), http://www.tribunalconstitucional.es/es/jurisprudencia/restrad/Paginas/DTC122004en.aspx (last visited Nov. 10, 2009). See also Avbelj (2008b), 19.

97. Lenaerts (1990), 220. On the persistence of this view among European constitutionalists, see, e.g., Schütze (2009), 9.

98. Walker (2003b), 199.

99. See Chapter 5, nn. 228–230 and 292–294 and accompanying text. See also, this Introduction, n. 67 and accompanying text.

ONE

Situating the Argument
Legal History, Institutional Change, and Integration Theory

※ 1.1 Administrative Governance as an Alternative Analytical Framework

European integration has always been "a novelty in want of a convincing label."[1] From its inception in the 1950s, a whole range of observers—scholars, lawyers, judges, public officials both national and supranational—have puzzled over how best to characterize European governance in legal terms.[2] The classic poles in the debate have long been familiar. Is Europe emerging as a new kind of "federal" polity, in which supranational institutions possess their own autonomous constitutional legitimacy over and above the Member States that created them? Or has Europe remained something of an "international organization"—albeit of an extraordinarily powerful type—in which intergovernmental negotiation and national self-interest continue to predominate?[3]

A half century of integration history, along with corresponding legal, political, and scholarly debate, have not yielded definitive answers to these questions, at least not explicitly. Indeed, by the end of the 1990s, it seemed that many analysts had given up trying to answer them at all. They largely

---

1. Grimm (1997), 229; see also Hooghe and Marks (2008), 108 ("The EU ... escapes labels .... Perhaps no field has spawned so much conceptual innovation as European integration; no field is so uncertain about what it is that needs to be explained.").

2. See, e.g., Schuman (1953a), 6–7 (discussing the nature of European supranationalism under the rubrics of "federalism" and "international individualism"); see also Vignes (1956), 11–15 (discussing European governance under the rubrics of, inter alia, "federalism," "technocracy," and "international administration").

3. See, e.g., McCormick (2007), 13 ("the EU is generally cast as either a treaty organization among states or a federal state writ large"); Dowding (2000), 126 ("The EU may, under some definitions, be an international organization, but it has many features of a federal state"); Burley and Mattli (1993), 41 (the EU "remains something well short of a federal state [but] has become something far more than an international organization of independent sovereigns").

accepted the proposition that the European legal order was, for lack of a better word, "*sui generis*,"[4] with a "multilevel" institutional complexity that the traditional poles in the debate could neither adequately capture nor describe.[5] The struggle then became, for the normatively inclined at least, to develop new and more complex theories of autonomous "European constitutionalism beyond the state."[6] This exercise produced so many different possibilities, however, that it arguably brought the supranational constitutional concept to the breaking point.[7]

This struggle over concepts and labels has not been simply an intellectual exercise divorced from any real consequence. It has reflected, rather, a broader political, legal, and cultural struggle—one that persists in Europe to this day—over how best to come to terms with what European institutions *are* (and *have been*), as well as what they might realistically *become* in the future—all in relation to what it means, precisely, to be "European" within this broader institutional framework.[8] The intensely political nature of this quest has been especially clear in the contentious battles of the last decade, first over the now defunct Constitutional Treaty, which French and Dutch voters rejected in separate referenda in 2005, and then over the seemingly more modest Treaty of Lisbon, which seemed to run the risk of meeting the

---

4. See, e.g., Walker (2005), 585 (noting the "fairly widespread belief or intuition as to the *sui generis* quality of the EU legal order") (emphasis in original) (citation omitted); MacCormick (1999), 106 (describing the nature of the supranational legal order, following the case law of the European Court of Justice, as "*sui generis*") (emphasis in original); Majone (1998), 6 ("we are still groping for normative criteria appropriate to the *sui generis* character of the European Community") (emphasis in original). This characterization could be said, however, to return to a view originally articulated in the 1950s. See Haas (2004 [1958]), 33–34, citing van Houtte (1955). For further engagement on the sui generis character of European governance, see, this chapter, nn. 127–128 and accompanying text.

5. For a succinct summary of the emergence of the "multilevel" approach to understanding integration, see Kohler-Koch and Rittberger (2007), 7–9; and Pollack (2005), 382–85. For a more detailed discussions, see Hooghe and Marks (2001) and (2008); Bache and Flinders (2004); and Bernard (2004).

6. See, e.g., Weiler and Wind (2003).

7. See Avbelj (2008a).

8. In this latter regard, see the stimulating reflections of Haltern (2007), 50 ("European discourse . . . is now fascinated by the question of who we are . . . by contested notions of identity. Therefore, we will have to inquire what meaning we read into Union law, and how this act of reading and understanding interacts with our beliefs about ourselves, and our ends"). For a brief overview of the literature on European identity, see Strumia (2009), 154–60.

same fate following its rejection by Irish voters in 2008 (not to mention its continued uncertain status in several Member States well into 2009).[9]

My first foray into these discussions came in an article published in 1999, in which I advanced the idea that the system of governance in the European Union (EU) might best be understood as "administrative" in character.[10] In the decade since, my administrative characterization has often been misunderstood, by European scholars especially, perhaps in part because of the quite different valence that Europeans and Americans have historically given to the notion of "administration."[11] In particular, my characterization has been misread as a suggestion that European governance is somehow "limited" and "specialized,"[12] even entirely "non-political,"[13] rather than being broadly and "deeply political" as it undoubtedly is.[14] My 1999 article in fact stressed how the jurisdiction of administrative bodies had often been depicted as technical in order to justify the delegation of power but that this depiction has never altered the essentially political character of the

---

9. The prospects for the Treaty of Lisbon considerably brightened in June 2009, when the European Council agreed on a series of "guarantees" paving the way for an Irish revote in fall 2009, which the "Yes" side won decisively. And then the German *Bundesverfassungsgericht* upheld the constitutionality of the treaty, albeit subject to a requirement that new implementing legislation be adopted to strength national parliamentary oversight of the German government's European policy (accomplished in September 2009). Nevertheless, uncertainty persisted: The presidents of Poland and the Czech Republic, both Eurosceptics, refused to sign their countries' instruments of ratification until the outcome of the second Irish referendum was known. Although the President of Poland, Lech Kaczyński, soon signed the treaty following the Irish victory, the President of the Czech Republic, Vaclav Klaus, did not. Eventually, however, even Klaus capitulated, following a decision of the Czech Constitutional Court on November 3, 2009, reiterating its earlier holding that the treaty was constitutional under national law. See Press Release, The Treaty of Lisbon Is in Conformity with the Constitutional Order of the Czech Republic and There is Nothing to Prevent its Ratification, http://www.usoud.cz/clanek/2144 (last visited Nov. 3, 2009).

10. See Lindseth (1999); see also Lindseth (2001), (2003a), (2005a). For a similar view, see Phelan (2002). On the relationship of my work to the later emerging Global Administrative Law Project, see, this chapter, n. 109.

11. Curtin (2009), 38, citing Rutgers (2000).

12. See de Búrca (2008b), 8 (arguing that "[t]he depiction of the EU as an expert agency writ large, with specialized limited 'administrative' functions delegated to it by internally democratic states which remain the primary source of its legitimacy is increasingly strained and difficult to defend"), citing, inter alia, Lindseth (1999).

13. Curtin (2009), 37, citing Lindseth (1999).

14. Hofmann and Türk (2007), 267; however earlier (ibid., 264), these authors suggest that I maintain the opposite, again citing Lindseth (1999), conflating me with Ipsen (1993).

power itself, in the sense of dealing with questions of values or the allocation of scarce resources, the very core of politics.[15]

Claims regarding the limited or specialized nature of European institutions are usually traced back to an older German literature of the early 1970s represented by the work of Hans Peter Ipsen.[16] Ipsen viewed integration, as one gloss has put it, as a kind of "*Zweckverband*, a regulatory agency or fourth branch of government which fulfils clearly specified functional goals and hence offers no room for political discretion."[17] Although my position has sometimes been conflated with Ipsen's,[18] my interpretation has always emphasized the inevitable—indeed, the intended—diffusion and fragmentation of political discretion in administrative governance, again in the sense of dealing with questions of value and the allocation of scarce resources in relative autonomy throughout the system.

Scholars have also associated my administrative characterization with the interpretation advanced in the 1990s by Giandomenico Majone,[19] whose extraordinarily influential work on integration as a "regulatory" regime has been called a "notable successor" to Ipsen's earlier interpretation.[20] I share with Majone the view that the nature and legitimacy of European power can best be measured against standards derived from modern administrative governance.[21] Nevertheless, I have differed significantly with Majone in my understanding of what those standards in fact demand, at least in legal and

---

15. See Lindseth (1999), 687–88, see also Lindseth (2001), 157 n. 51. Indeed, I would fully agree with Curtin (2009), 38, that politics and administration are deeply intertwined, joining "elected executives and administrators . . . together in the pursuit of sound governance."

16. See Ipsen (1972); see also Ipsen (1993).

17. Kohler-Koch and Rittberger (2007), 4, citing Ipsen (1972); see also Hofmann and Türk (2007), 264, citing Ipsen (1993). As Christian Joerges has succinctly described: "While wishing to root technocratic rationality in the EEC, at the same time, [Ipsen] wanted to restrict its sphere of action: the Communities were to confine themselves to administering questions of 'knowledge', but leave truly 'political' questions to democratic and legitimated bodies." Joerges (2003), 190–91 (elaborating on Ipsen's description of the three European communities as "purposive associations of functional integration" [*Zweckverbände funktionaler Integration*]), citing Ipsen (1972), 1045. A much fuller discussion of the phrase *Zweckverbände funktionaler Integration*, with lengthy definitions of the component terms, can be found at Ipsen (1972), 196–200. My position, however, arguably comes much closer to that set out in Vignes (1956).

18. Hofmann and Türk (2007), 264, citing Ipsen (1993) and Lindseth (1999).

19. See, e.g., de Búrca (2008b), 8 n. 14; see also Majone (1994a), (1996), (1998).

20. Walker (2005), 595.

21. See generally Majone (1998); see also Majone (2001a) and (2005), 36–38.

constitutional terms.[22] Majone's work of the later 1990s seemed to view technocratic autonomy, supranational or otherwise, as relatively unproblematic from a legitimacy standpoint, leading him to overlook the role of (particularly national) legitimating mechanisms in the integration context. Although his recent work has taken a more nuanced position,[23] my contributions have more explicitly and consistently stressed the incapacity of supranational institutions to legitimize themselves apart from mechanisms of national oversight.

The final misunderstanding of my administrative interpretation requires a somewhat more detailed response. It is reflected in the idea, advanced for example by Carol Harlow, that my approach seeks to force European institutions into a framework of "strict separation of powers" inspired by the purported model of the United States.[24] Admittedly, in perhaps typically American fashion, my work maintains a distinction between the "administrative" and the "executive," contrary to the prevailing practice in Europe, which often conflates the two.[25] I generally use the term "executive" only to refer to the political summit of the state (chief executives and cabinet members), whereas I use the administrative label more generally to refer to the diffuse, complex, and fragmented regulatory sphere both within and beyond the state. There are in fact sound reasons to keep the two categories distinct, as I try to spell out below.

The particular sense in which I apply the administrative label to integration—as well as my understanding of the mechanisms of legitimizing integration as a form of administrative governance—is drawn from a reading of longer-term developments throughout the North Atlantic world, including the United States

---

22. See, e.g., Lindseth (1999), 657–59, 684–91, and 696.

23. See, e.g., Majone (2005), 39–40; but see also Majone (2002), 335 (arguing for the recognition of an autonomous "regulatory estate" in a system of European governance reconceptualized as a "mixed polity").

24. Harlow (2002), 173.

25. See, e.g., Curtin (2009). Certainly there is conflation in American political discourse as well (individual presidencies are called "administrations," and agencies are understood—unless they are "independent"—to be within the "executive branch"). But it has long been a feature of American public law to distinguish between the President as chief executive and the subordinate administrative sphere, a distinction that arguably emerged in the Progressive era and consolidated itself under the New Deal. See, e.g., Goodnow (1900); and Landis (1938). Even if the distinction captures a basic socioinstitutional reality, it remains deeply contested on the normative-legal level in the United States. See, e.g., Calabresi and Yoo (2008) (advocating the "unitary executive" theory); and Strauss (2007) (opposed).

and Europe. This historiographical perspective stresses two overarching and somewhat contradictory trends. The first occurred over the course of the nineteenth century: the ascendance of centralized elected assemblies—parliaments and the like—which became the core institutions of representative government in democratizing nation-states of the North Atlantic.[26] (Of course, full democratization, defined in terms of extension of suffrage to all adult citizens equally, regardless of economic status, religion, race, or gender, would only come much later.)[27] The second development in some sense emerged out of the first, and was born of an increasing recognition over the late nineteenth and early twentieth century that these assemblies, along with traditional executive and judicial bodies, were increasingly unable "to deal with modern problems."[28] Deeply functional in character, this second development was by no means confined to the United States (as Chapter 2 will describe). Rather, throughout the North Atlantic world functional pressures led to the diffusion of normative power away from those same historically constituted bodies, including the political summit of the executive, into an increasingly complex and variegated administrative sphere, in order to address the challenges that modern industrial and later postindustrial society posed.[29]

To the extent that my perspective reflects an American-inflected historiographical theory, its inspiration is not "strict separation of powers" per Carol Harlow but rather something much more diffuse and nonlegal—what one American historian has recently called the "divided and dispersed organization of governance" in the United States.[30] My outlook admittedly stands in contrast with an older European (notably German and French) tradition that

---

26. Cf. Eley (1995), 106–15.

27. For a useful summary for Europe, see Tilly (2003), 213–17 ("A Rough Map of European Democratization").

28. Landis (1938), 1.

29. For a suggestive overview of trans-Atlantic developments in "social politics," see Rodgers (1998). For corresponding shifts in law and legal thought, cf. Kennedy (2006). On the complex interplay between democratization, regulation, and administration in modern societies, see also Rosanvallon (1990), 276–80. Indeed, some argue that over the last quarter century this process has now led to the emergence of an "administrative space" decoupled from the nation-state entirely, not merely regional in character (as in the EU) but also "global" in many respects. See generally Kingsbury et al. (2005); see also Cohen and Sabel (2005), 767–68.

30. Novak (2008), 763. There is also a developing political science literature exploring the strains on representative institutions in an era of globalization (for a succinct overview, see Kohler-Koch and Rittberger (2007), 10), although that literature arguably suffers from lack of historical perspective. Indeed, from the moment of its constitutional consolidation (roughly in the mid-nineteenth century), centralized institutions of representative

sees unification, bureaucratic centralization under the "executive," and the ideal of administration as a *pouvoir neutre* above social divisions as "the very essence of the State."[31] In *Democracy in America*, Tocqueville grappled with the same contrast, distinguishing between two different types of "centralization," one governmental, the other administrative. He juxtaposed the "centralization of government" in the United States (notably in state legislatures and Congress) with its "decentralization of administration" that stood in stark contrast with continental European counterparts.[32]

Admittedly, the functional diffusion and fragmentation of administrative power in the twentieth century would prove to be a very different phenomenon from the nineteenth-century system of "local administration" in the United States that Tocqueville so admired. Nevertheless, his differentiation among two different kinds of centralization suggests why it is important not to conflate the "executive" and the "administrative." The political summit of the executive (chief executives primarily, along with cabinet ministers) should be understood as a manifestation of the "centralization of government" in a Tocquevillean sense, in that these offices enjoy historically constituted legitimacy as embodiments or expressions of the capacity of the people to rule themselves.[33] The administrative apparatus, by contrast, developed in response to much more functional concerns, with a legitimacy that is primarily instrumental and derivative.[34]

---

government in the nation-state were under strain by centrifugal social and political forces. For a recent historical reflection on the American case, see Mashaw (2009).

31. Mannori and Sordi (forthcoming), section 6.6 ("The Invention of Administrative Law"). William Novak describes the inability of "classic European social theory" (of Hegel, Marx, Weber, Durkheim, and their progeny) to deal adequately with the "characteristic sprawl of the American state." Novak (2008), 766. It should be added, moreover, that it has been a staple of German extreme conservatism, going back to Carl Schmitt in the interwar period and carried forward by his numerous followers, notably Ernst Forsthoff, in the postwar decades, to lament the interpenetration of state and society. See Müller (2003), 24, 33, and 73–74. But it is important to add (as Novak implicitly acknowledges later in his article) that there exists an alternative strain in specifically *European* social theory, associated with Foucault, that seeks to come to terms with the diffusion and fragmentation of normative power. See Novak (2008), 772, citing Burchell et al. (1991).

32. See "Political Effects of the System of Local Administration in the United States," in Tocqueville (1889 [1835]), 67–78.

33. See Chapter 2, nn. 108–109 and accompanying text.

34. In this sense, I would agree with the effort in Curtin (2009), chaps. 4 and 5, to draw a distinction between executive power in a "political" and "administrative" sense. However, in keeping with my more Tocquevillean framework, I denote the former as executive pure and simple, only referring to the later as administrative, without conflating them both under the label "executive."

My belief has always been that twentieth-century European governance, both within and beyond the state, has increasingly exhibited the seemingly more American characteristics of disaggregation, decentralization, and interpenetration of public authority and civil society.[35] Such characteristics, I would add, did not emerge only recently, as part of a "New World Order" flowing from globalization, as some argue.[36] Rather, the emergence of these characteristics is deeply tied to the development of administrative governance over the course of the twentieth century more generally—that is, the diffusion and fragmentation of normative power *away* from the constituted bodies of representative government.

There are, I admit, risks in using anything approaching an American baseline to understand European developments. On the one hand, the American model of constitutional federalism has often provided the inspiration for the dominant, but ultimately inapt constitutional narrative of integration in European legal theory over the last several decades.[37] On the other hand, historians of integration have long critiqued explanations of integration propagated by American social scientists from the 1950s to the 1970s (notably neofunctionalist theory) as being responsible for a whole series of distortions and misunderstandings of integration that they believe are at least in part still with us today.[38] And in part to answer these concerns, I try to draw on specifically European integration historiography throughout this study, which helps to show that the diffusion and fragmentation of normative power is part of the evolution of modern governance more generally, including European governance, and thus is hardly limited to the American case.[39]

Integration historians are themselves beginning to stress these longer term trends, for example questioning the "historical innocence" of those political scientists who see the emergence of fragmented governance as

---

35. See Novak (2008), 763; cf. also Maier (1975); and Lodge (2008), 285.

36. See generally Slaughter (2004).

37. For a path-breaking critique, see generally Avbelj (2008b), especially at 14 (describing Weiler (1991), later incorporated into Weiler (1999a), as "the cornerstone, almost a sort of Bible of the EU constitutional narrative"). For a more recent, constitutional-federal analysis built on the American comparison, see Schütze (2009).

38. See, e.g., Milward (1995); see also van der Harst (2008), 5 (describing integration theory from the 1950s to the 1970s as "not only a-historical but also a-European, since dominated by American political scientists").

39. Cf. Bartolini (2005).

something that emerged only out of "'the ruins of the 1970s.'"[40] There is indeed a much deeper history to the "leaky" container of the modern regulatory state, certainly stretching well back into the nineteenth century.[41] Much less than being the all-powerful Westphalian entity of lore, the modern state as instrument of rule has been engaged in a nearly constant struggle to assert its purported "sovereign" prerogatives in the face of social, economic, and political change—the movement of people, goods, money, and ideas, etc.[42] Over the course of the twentieth century, these dynamic pressures made themselves felt not just in war but also in peace, continuing to strain if not break down several received legal and institutional boundaries from the state's seemingly more *Rechtsstaat* or rule of law past.

My interpretation of integration as *administrative, not constitutional* flows directly from this understanding of the state's history, particularly over the nineteenth and twentieth century.[43] In this way, it extends on certain well-known readings of integration history advanced by Alan Milward, undoubtedly the most important integration historian of the last three decades.[44] Milward has argued that integration is "one more stage in the long evolution of the European state."[45] His various studies of postwar Western Europe, however, have not generally explored the relationship between the emergence of administrative governance and the process of European integration. Milward's only suggestion in this regard can be found in a brief but still illuminating paragraph in the introductory chapter of his major work on the early years of integration, *The European Rescue of the Nation-State* (1992). "Integration [as pursued in the 1950s] was not the supersession of the nation-state by another form of governance as the nation-state became incapable," Milward writes. Rather, it was

---

40. Kaiser (2007), 2, quoting Hirst (2000), 19; see also, e.g., Scott (2002), 60–61 (marking the advent of "governance" to "the oil shock of the early 1970s and the accompanying fiscal crises"). For a succinct summary of the "preoccupation with crises of governability, overload, and legitimacy" in the social science literature in the 1970s (both left and right), see Goetz (2008), 258–60, citing, e.g., Offe (1972); Habermas (1976 [1973]); Brittan (1975); and King (1975).

41. Bright and Geyer (2002), 65; see also Lodge (2008), 285.

42. For a similar view, Sheehan (2006). See also Rodgers (1998).

43. See the Introduction, nn. 47–51 and accompanying text.

44. See, e.g., Milward (1984), (1992), (1993), (2000 [1992]), (2002), and (2005).

45. Milward (2000 [1992]), x.

the creation of the European nation-states themselves for their own purposes, an act of national will. This is not surprising, because in the long
run of history there has surely never been a period when national government in Europe has exercised more effective power and more extensive
control over its citizens than since the Second World War, nor one in
which its ambitions expanded so rapidly. Its laws, officials, policemen,
spies, statisticians, revenue collectors, and social workers have penetrated
into a far wider range of human activities than they were earlier able or
encouraged to do. If the states' executive [read "administrative"] power is
less arbitrarily exercised than in earlier periods, which some would also
dispute, it is still exercised remorselessly, frequently, in finer detail and
in more directions than it was. This must be reconciled in theory and in
history with the surrender of national sovereignty.[46]

There are, as Milward implies but does not explore, important linkages to
be drawn between the development of the modern administrative state in
postwar Western Europe and the process of European integration. Both
depended on a combination of a seeming *fusion* of normative power in the
national executive and a *diffusion* of power into a complex and far-reaching
administrative sphere. The core of Milward's argument is that the extension of
this phenomenon to the Community level in the 1950s actually reflected the
"will of the European nation-state to survive as an organizational entity."[47] The
same claim can also be made, I would suggest, with regard to the institutional
changes generally associated with the rise of administrative governance on
the national level, particularly the extensive shift in normative power to the
executive and technocratic sphere with the establishment of the welfare state
after 1945. Both forms of governance—national and supranational—were
reflective of a conscious effort by major political actors to reinforce the nation-
state by making it a more effective agent in the promotion of public welfare.

The present study seeks to add a legal dimension to Milward's historiographical insight, by focusing on something that Milward's more political-
economic analysis elides: public law and institutions. Milward asserts that
the durability of European integration resulted from it "rest[ing] so firmly on
the economic and social foundations of post-war political change." His analysis looks, however, only to "changes in the political economy of the post-war

---

46. Ibid., 18.

47. Ibid., 223.

state" and not to changes in the legal-institutional mechanisms through which the resulting public-policy choices were formulated or implemented.[48] When Milward has discussed the "bundle of policies" that all Western European states pursued in the postwar era (social welfare programs, agricultural protection, employment policies, industrialization policies), no mention is made of the broader, arguably transnational constitutional choice to expand executive power through legislative delegation, subject to expanded judicial review.[49] And thus when *The European Rescue of the Nation-State* ultimately reaches the question of specific institutional arrangements in the Treaty of Rome of 1957—which amounted to a further delegation of normative power to national executives (only now working in concert at the supranational level)—Milward in fact spends only two pages discussing them.[50]

To add a legal dimension to Milward's analysis, however, necessarily redirects our attention to the cultural dimension of institutional change. Neither European integration nor the broader diffusion and fragmentation of normative power of which it is a part would have been institutionally durable, I maintain, without a parallel transformation in understandings of legitimate governance on the national level in Europe over the middle third of the twentieth century.[51] As we shall see in Chapter 2, these understandings began to emerge (laboriously) out of the constitutional struggles of the interwar period—the so-called "crisis of parliamentary democracy"[52]—and received a dramatic push from the disaster of 1933–1945. The unexpected result of these struggles was the constitutional stabilization of the modern administrative state in Western Europe in the aftermath of World War II, a not inconsiderable historical achievement after decades of political and social crisis, total war, and genocide.[53] With this stabilization, the Western European state became,

---

48. Ibid.

49. See Milward and Sørensen (1993), 5–6.

50. Milward (2000 [1992]), 217–18.

51. See generally Lindseth (2004).

52. Although I draw this label from Ellen Kennedy's translation of Carl Schmitt's *Die geistesgeschichtliche Lage des heutigen Parlamentarismus* (see Schmitt (1985 [1926])) I explicitly reject Schmitt's interpretation of the nature of that crisis as well as his views on whether and how it could be surmounted. See generally Lindseth (2004); additionally, see, this chapter, nn. 110–111 and accompanying text, as well as Chapter 2, nn. 129–130 and accompanying text. For further discussion of the crisis of the nascent European democracies in the interwar period (of which Schmitt's theories were merely one expression), see Mazower (2000 [1998]), 5–27, as well as Chapter 2, nn. 6–64 and accompanying text.

53. Lindseth (2004), 1412–15.

in addition to being a phenomenal consumer and redistributor of material resources, a producer of legal norms on a scale far surpassing anything envisaged before. This dramatically augmented regulatory capacity allowed the various states of Western Europe to confront the many challenges—social, political, and economic—that postwar reconstruction presented, something undoubtedly essential to the success of the welfare state in the subsequent decades.

In redirecting our attention to the importance of a shared postwar constitutional settlement of administrative governance, I do not mean to deny more particular variation among national political systems (e.g., parliamentary vs. presidential) or among particular national histories.[54] Rather, the analytical approach taken here is simply meant to capture an overarching process within which much of the systemic and historical variation was occurring after 1945.[55] Although West Germany and France are at the forefront my analysis (as the historic "motors" of integration), the postwar constitutional settlement also manifested itself in such seemingly outlier countries as Britain, which did not share their immediate constitutional experiences of dictatorship and did not follow their lead into European integration in the 1950s.[56]

❦ 1.2 Delegation as a Normative-Legal Principle

Paralleling the emergence of this new kind of administrative state—and in fact linked to it—was the creation of the supranational bodies of European integration benefiting from precisely the transfers of authority that postwar constitutions authorized. Indeed, national constitutions would specifically permit reallocations of governing authority on both the national[57]

---

54. See, e.g., Huber and Shipan (2002), 215–18; see also Craig and Tomkins (2006); Verhey et al. (2008).

55. Cf. Huber and Shipan (2002), 226–28.

56. The transnational replication of the postwar constitutional settlement of administrative governance—albeit with variations owing to particular national histories—may perhaps be understood as an example of what organizational theorists call institutional "isomorphism." Rittberger (2005), 18 ("isomorphism is a process which forces one unit in a 'population' of institutions to resemble other units that face the same set of environmental conditions"), citing DiMaggio and Powell (1991). See also Radaelli (2000).

57. See Chapter 2, nn. 73–81 and accompanying text.

and supranational or international levels,[58] in the interest of postwar stabilization and interstate cooperation. Over the coming half century, supranational institutions in Europe would in fact take on an increasing share of the regulatory capacity in certain critical domains (notably relating to trade and ancillary fields, but also in the protection of human rights). By some controversial estimates, the normative power of European institutions would eventually surpass even that of the administrative states on which they were modeled and built.[59]

Delegation provided the legal framework, even if not always consciously articulated, to rationalize this state of affairs. It allowed regulatory power to be transferred while mediating legitimacy through the constituted bodies of the nation-state. Delegation thus linked (at least in law) the manifold exercises of regulatory power back to the "centralization of government" in a Tocquevillean sense—that is, the parliament—as the strongly legitimated legislative principal inherited from the nineteenth century. Over time, the legislature's legitimacy would be complemented by an increasingly democratically legitimated chief executive, along with the courts acting as mechanisms to protect basic constitutional and legislative commitments through judicial review—the dynamic combination of which provided the essential elements of the postwar constitutional settlement.

As we shall see in Chapter 2, however, antiliberals from the interwar period, most importantly Carl Schmitt, saw delegation as little more than a legal fiction, a holdover from a dying bourgeois-liberal *Rechtsstaat* of the nineteenth century. Eventually this skepticism toward delegation would

---

58. See Chapter 2, n. 68 and accompanying text, and Chapter 4, nn. 88–91, 96–97, and 109–111 and accompanying text. These constitutional innovations stand in sharp contrast to the situation after World War I, where forms of national and international delegation were both highly contested. For forms of national delegation, see Lindseth (2004), 1354–85. As to international delegations, consider the history of the League of Nations. See Pedersen (2007).

59. This is admittedly a deeply contested claim in its strongest form. Recall how, in 1988, Jacques Delors predicted that by 1998, "80 percent of economic, and perhaps social and fiscal policy-making" would be of EU origin. "This prediction has become a fundamental 'factoid' in discussions of the EU—often cited as 80 percent of lawmaking *in all issues* in Europe *already* comes from Brussels. Yet recent academic studies demonstrate that the actual percentage of EU-based legislation is probably between 10 and 20 percent of national rulemaking." Moravcsik (2005c), 364–65 (emphasis in original; citations omitted). See also O'Brennan and Raunio (2007a), 5 (referring to Delors' comment, "[r]esearch has shown this share to be much lower, even when including domestic laws that were in some way 'inspired' by the EU"). Regardless, it is safe to conclude that a *significant* portion of the total normative power exercised in European Member States can be traced to supranational delegations in one form or another.

come from other quarters as well, several distinctly more relevant for our purposes. Jean Monnet, for example, would recall in his *Memoirs* how, at the close of the first phase of the Schuman Plan conference in 1950, the Belgian representative objected to the term "merger of sovereignty" in the memorandum of understanding on institutional questions, favoring instead "delegation of sovereignty." "That argument is over," Monnet responded. "'Merger' is the word."[60] And so it seemed to the federalist Monnet, not merely linguistically but in point of fact. Indeed, Hans Peter Ipsen, who by temperament and Nazi past was arguably much closer to Schmitt than Monnet,[61] also would come to view the transfer of power to the supranational level as a *Gesamtakt staatlicher Integrationsgewalt*, a "comprehensive act of integration of governmental authority," not merely a delegation of power from the national level.[62]

In contemporary discussions of European governance, in fact, it is not uncommon to see the word "pooling" used to describe the Council of Ministers acting by qualified-majority voting, rather than the term delegation. [63] Although this language echoes perhaps more Monnet (or even Ipsen) than Schmitt, much contemporary scholarship on integration nevertheless reflects the latter's deep questioning of the very idea delegation to describe trends in modern governance.[64] Given the dramatic accumulation of normative power at the supranational level in Europe over the last half century, along with the resulting complexity of Europeanized administrative

---

60. Monnet (1978), 333.

61. Joerges (2003), 182–84 and in particular n. 92 (describing Ipsen's Nazi activities and the affinity of his work in the interwar and wartime periods to that of Schmitt).

62. Ipsen (1972), 61–62.

63. This book does not follow the convention among international relations (IR) specialists that distinguishes between supranational "pooling" of sovereignty and outright delegation. See Rittberger (2005), 5; see also Moravcsik (1998), 67 (referring to the Council of Ministers acting by a qualified-majority as a "pooling" rather than as a "delegation" of sovereignty). From the perspective of historical public law, this is a distinction without any essential difference apart from the nature and scope of the delegation. Whether normative power is given to a supranational body such as the Commission, the European Court of Justice, or the European Parliament—what IR regards as "delegation"—or to an intergovernmental body such as the Council of Ministers, even when acting by qualified majority—what IR regards as "pooling"—there is still a transfer of normative power *out of the national parliamentary realm* (i.e., a delegation). Consequently, this study uses the term *delegation* in the public-law sense to refer to both phenomena. See Chapter 3, nn. 65–68 and accompanying text.

64. See, e.g., Eberlein and Grande (2005) (describing the EU's regulatory regime as "beyond delegation"). For a detailed discussion, focusing particularly on the work of Charles Sabel, see generally the Conclusion.

governance, some commentators have found it simply implausible to assert that national bodies could still claim to act in some manner as the constitutional principals in the European system, or that supranational institutions operate as mere agents exercising delegated regulatory power.[65]

These views, however, ignore a critical dimension of the notion of delegation as it took on its recognizably modern legal function in the middle-third of the twentieth century.[66] Delegation was never merely—or even primarily—an empirical descriptor but rather, much more importantly, a normative-legal principle, one that allowed the diffuse and fragmented forms of administrative governance in the postwar decades to be experienced as culturally legitimate even as actual regulatory power shifted elsewhere.[67] Similar to the role that the concept of subsidiarity would serve in the integration context later in the century, delegation emerged as what we could fairly call a *resistance norm*.[68] Essential to the process of reconciliation, a resistance norm both recognizes the compelling nature of functional change, yet seeks to limit that change politically and legally in light of inherited cultural conceptions of legitimate governance.

On the national level, the notion of delegation, as well as the principal-agent relationship it normatively implied, in fact tolerated significant administrative autonomy (in European countries usually de facto, though eventually even de jure, with the proliferation of independent regulatory bodies on the national level in the final two decades of the century).[69] Nevertheless, the notion of delegation provided the legal-cultural justification for the establishment of a whole range of mechanisms—political oversight by cabinet

---

65. See, e.g., Cohen and Sabel (2005), 773–79; see also Everson (1999), 294 ("In the effort to establish new links between politics, society, and the market place, European regulatory institutions have become the focus for an evolving European market polity bearing little or no relationship with conventional statal [*sic*] polities. Clearly, in such a setting, traditional transmission-belt means of securing democratic accountability of a burgeoning European 'market administration' are somewhat obsolete. With no hint of legislative pre-determination and the substantive goals of regulation in ongoing doubt, administrative law simply has no single existing democratic mandate to protect."). For a slightly different but still skeptical take on fitting European governance into a delegation/principal-agent model, see Curtin (2007).

66. Lindseth (2001), 158–59.

67. See Lindseth (2001), 157–58; (2002), 139–143; as well as (2006), 107–111, from which the following discussion is drawn. For a particularly stark, recent example of misreading of delegation as an empirical descriptor, see Curtin (2007), especially 524–25.

68. See Young (2000). For more detail, see Introduction, nn. 62–63 and accompanying text.

69. See Chapter 3, nn. 185–186, and accompanying text.

ministers, legislative vetoes, judicial review, as well as more recently increased outside participation in, and transparency of, regulatory processes. These have all been designed to manage that administrative autonomy in a democratic and constitutional direction, promoting the sense of political and legal accountability and connection, if not actual control.

Rarely do these mechanisms prevent the exercise of delegated authority outright. Rather, consistent with the notion of delegation as a resistance norm, they simply serve to raise the costs to the agent of using that power,[70] while having the added benefit of simultaneously reducing the information costs to the legislative principal, thus enabling more effective oversight. As we shall see in the empirical chapters that follow, national oversight has developed in European public law to serve similar functions, raising the costs of enacting supranational rules on the one hand, while disgorging information and thus managing supranational normative autonomy in a democratic and constitutional direction (at least in a culturally recognizable sense) on the other.

Contrary to the expectations of some readers, this study will focus less on, though certainly not ignore, delegation of authority among or within supranational bodies, for example, under the comitology system,[71] or to European agencies.[72] Such structural dimensions of European governance have garnered a great deal of attention in recent years,[73] including attention given specifically to the complex mechanisms of accountability at the supranational level.[74] The purpose here, however, is not to analyze internal management or controls within the Commission,[75] or the manifold connections between the supranational administrative apparatus and national

---

70. Cf. Stephenson (2006) and (2008).

71. See, e.g., Bergström (2005); see also Bergström et al. (2007); Héritier and Moury (2009).

72. See, e.g., Saurer (2009); Kelemen (2005) and (2002); Scott and Trubek (2002); Chiti (2000).

73. See, e.g., the articles collected in *West European Politics* 31(4) (2008), "Special Issue: Towards a New Executive Order in Europe?"; see also, e.g., Franchino (2007); Pollack (2003); Menon and Weatherill (2002); and Majone (2001b).

74. See, e.g., the articles collected in the *European Law Journal* 13(4) (2007), "Special Issue: Accountability in EU Multilevel Governance"; see also, e.g., Harlow (2002); Bergman (2000); and Joerges and Neyer (1997).

75. This is an especially important question after the collapse of the Santer Commission, followed by the Kinnock reforms. See generally Lindseth et al. (2008), 41–64; see also Cini (2007), chaps. 2–3; Kassim (2004).

administrations in the implementation of European regulatory programs.[76] These are obviously important developments, all consistent with the need to reduce information costs and improve oversight in the extraordinarily dense system of modern Europeanized administrative governance. But, for the most part, even European constitutionalists find it difficult to dispute the fundamentally administrative character of these dimensions of European governance.[77]

My aim, rather, is to argue that the *entire* process of integration should be understood as an extension of administrative governance generally. It reflects the diffusion of normative power away from the historically constituted bodies of representative government on the national level, a process then legitimized on the basis of *delegation* as a historically constructed normative-legal principle. From this perspective, speaking of European governance as "constitutional," or in the process of "constitutionalization" (particularly with regard to its administrative law)[78] becomes a "category mistake."[79] Using this sort of language, in effect, elevates European governance implicitly to a level of autonomous constitutional *legitimacy* commensurate with its autonomous regulatory *power* and in so doing ignores or distorts the historical dynamic that has so profoundly contributed to the "politics of Eurocratic structure" over time.[80]

Genuinely constitutional government in the fullest sense of the term has remained, in political and legal culture, the preserve of national executive, legislative, and judicial bodies, whereas European governance, with all its extensive regulatory power, is something else—something that again is best understood as *administrative, not constitutional.* No doubt scholars will continue to use constitutional terminology to describe the accumulating European legal and institutional order—old habits are hard to break.[81] But what this study seeks to show is that, in doing so, they risk confusing regulatory power and constitutional legitimacy. Only by keeping the categories of

---

76. See generally the contributions in Weatherill (2007); Hofmann and Türk (2006); Kassim et al. (2001) and Kassim et al. (2000).

77. This was anticipated, for example, in Weiler et al. (1995), 26 (advancing the term "infranational" to describe these aspects of European governance). For a critique, see Lindseth (1999), 659–60, n. 128.

78. See, e.g., Everson (1999).

79. See Somek (2003), 708; see also Moravcsik (2005a).

80. Kelemen (2002).

81. Most recently, see, e.g., Curtin (2009); Konstadinides (2009).

power and legitimacy analytically distinct can we fully understand the historical dynamic that has animated European institutional design over the last half century. Most importantly, this includes the convergence of European public law around the legitimating structures and normative principles of the postwar constitutional settlement. In this regard, it is critical also that we not conflate the administrative character of the EU with executive power writ large.[82] Again, in doing so, we risk losing the ability to distinguish between the democratically and constitutionally legitimated bodies on the national level (including the political summit of the national executive) and the diffuse and fragmented manifestations of regulatory authority in the administrative sphere, both within and beyond the state. Only by making these various distinctions can we begin to confront, both in law and fact, the extraordinarily dense and complex system of Europeanized administrative governance on surer analytical ground.[83]

Coming from a slightly different direction, some readers may also find it surprising the extent to which the analysis below focuses relatively less on (although again certainly does not ignore) one of the more prominent expressions of national legitimation in European public law—the requirement of unanimous Member-State ratification of the European treaties and their amendments.[84] The importance of this requirement was brought home once again, of course, by the Irish rejection of the Treaty of Lisbon in 2008, as well as by the earlier French and Dutch rejections of the Constitutional Treaty in 2005. The inability of European public law to disconnect itself from its treaty character has been, for some observers at least, a troubling reflection of Europe's inability to achieve its rightfully autonomous "constitutional" status.[85] But the key point to emphasize here is that even this treaty character can and should be understood in terms of administrative governance, as an instrument of extending delegated authority from the national to the supranational level. The variety of ratification procedures mandated by national

---

82. Again, see, e.g., Curtin (2009); see also Curtin and Egeberg (2008).

83. See generally the Conclusion. Despite my evident conceptual differences with Curtin (2009), I recognize that her book is among the most serious and comprehensive recent efforts to come to terms with the complexity and density of European governance and is thus deeply worthy of admiration.

84. This requirement is usually the point of departure in, if not sole focus of, discussions by legal scholars of the relationship between the national and supranational orders in Europe. See, e.g., Wouters (2000), 28–29; see also Claes (2007), 3, 7.

85. See, e.g., Habermas (2008).

constitutions points to the fact that the true locus of primary legislative power in Europe—in the enabling treaties themselves—remains ultimately grounded in state-centered institutions and processes.[86] Even the bodies historically responsible for drafting treaty amendments, the intergovern-mental conferences (IGCs), have had a predominantly state-based cast. In short, the treaties are best understood as mechanisms to delegate normative power, akin to a *loi-cadre* on the national level (or a *traité-cadre* as some observers have called it).[87]

My primary focus, however, goes beyond these initial acts of delegation to the framework of legitimation once the delegation has occurred. These seemingly more technical legal and institutional developments—executive, legislative, and judicial—are well known to legal scholars and social scien-tists specializing in integration. Consequently, I do not claim to offer new details about their operation here. What I do hope to offer, however, is an analytical narrative explaining their historical origins and growth as an inte-grated legal whole, reflecting the convergence of European public law around the legitimating structures of the postwar constitutional settlement. Aspects of administrative governance have undoubtedly evolved over the last half century. In the European context, in particular, not only has there been increasing autonomy from hierarchical executive influence,[88] but there has also been an increasing judicialization of policy making as normative power has diffused and fragmented both within and beyond the state.[89] Nevertheless, the legitimating mechanisms of the postwar constitutional settlement have, in their broad outlines, remained remarkably stable, achieving the status of an enduring institution of governance in their own right. In terms of social theory, the postwar constitutional settlement arguably proved essential in the transition from the *Rechtsstaat* of the late-nineteenth and early-twentieth centuries to the *Sozialstaat* after 1945—and it will continue to play a role in

---

86. This was a point stressed and reinforced by the *Bundesverfassungsgericht* in its Lisbon Decision, when the Court demanded that any changes to the treaties under the simpli-fied revision procedure or passerelle clauses under the Treaty of Lisbon still be subjected to national parliamentary approval. German Lisbon Decision 2009, paras. 409–14.

87. Majone (2005), 7; see also, Chapter 3, nn. 113–115, and accompanying text.

88. Cf. Cohen and Sabel (2005). See also Goetz (2008), 266–67 (adding nuance to this claim).

89. See Kelemen (2009) and (2006).

legitimizing whatever form of supranational administrative governance ultimately emerges from the process of European integration.[90]

"Multilevel" is a label that political scientists and historians increasingly use to describe this form of governance.[91] Along with the related rubrics of network governance, pluralism, and even "experimentalism,"[92] the multilevel approach arguably brackets out a number of important questions regarding the distribution of legitimacy resources that this study specifically seeks to address. Not only do these various rubrics avoid "the question of ultimate authority"[93]—at least in a political-cultural sense—they also "tend to over-stress the autonomy and separateness of the constitutional orders, national and European respectively."[94] The national and supranational realms should not be understood as merely "'two different, but equally legitimate, perspec-tives'" on the integration process.[95] The implication of that view is that European integration operates, in effect, as a system of "agents without principals."[96] In such a system, neither national nor supranational institu-tions have particular claims of legitimacy superior to the others but rather are simply operating in some kind of pluralist dialogue—perhaps a "delibera-tive polyarchy," in the famous language of Cohen and Sabel.[97] The best one can hope for in such a situation is "institutional balance" or some kind of open-ended and diffuse accountability but not actual democratic legitimacy or connection in a historically recognizable sense.[98]

Although this may often be true as a functional and even political matter, it ignores the cultural dimension, which deeply shapes perceptions of what the ultimate ends of integration's institutional balance and account-ability should be. It is precisely *because* the national level in the EU retains

---

90. See McCormick (2007).

91. On the political-science side, see Kohler-Koch and Rittberger (2007), 7–9; Pollack (2005), 382–85, and more generally Hooghe and Marks (2001), (2008). On the historiographical side, see, e.g., Kaiser (2007). For a call for greater cooperation among political scientists and historians in the development of this framework, see Kaiser (2008).

92. See Sabel and Zeitlin (2008).

93. Claes (2007), 5.

94. Ibid.

95. de Witte (1991), 22, quoted in Poiares Maduro (1998), 31.

96. See Lindseth (2006); see also Cohen and Sabel (2004), 164–65; Dehousse (2008), 794–95.

97. See generally Cohen and Sabel (1997); see also Cohen and Sabel (2004), 164–75. For further discussion, see the Conclusion, nn. 28–60 and accompanying text.

98. Cf. Curtin (2009), 45, 55; see also Curtin (2007); Harlow and Rawlings (2007); Dehousse (2008).

the superior legitimacy resources in a cultural sense that European governance cannot be merely a "deliberative polyarchy" without a principal or principals (a point I take up in much greater detail in the Conclusion to this study). Rather, it is on the basis of their superior legitimacy resources that the several Member States can plausibly claim, at critical moments of decision, to serve as the ultimate democratic and constitutional principals in the European system, to which accountability and institutional balance are ultimately directed. This remains true despite the undoubted complexity of the regulatory network the Member States have created through integration.[99]

From the perspective of legitimacy, integration is not so much multilevel or polyarchical as it is "polycentric," something "deeply rooted in the history of [the European] continent."[100] The capacity for ultimate democratic and constitutional legitimation of European governance remains distributed among the constituted bodies of the several Member States; no similar capacity has yet migrated to the EU level. Even as functional pressures further drive the diffusion and fragmentation of regulatory power (and blur many received legal boundaries besides), the nation-state retains significant legitimacy advantages as expressions of collective self-government within national political communities. Representative institutions on the national level may functionally operate as plural nodes in a complex, multilevel or polyarchical regulatory network. But in cultural terms, the imbalance in legitimacy resources in European governance ensures that national constitutional bodies are perceived as the *privileged* nodes in that network, even as the functional demands of integration often run counter to that privileged status. This polycentric and imbalanced distribution of legitimacy resources—what the Conclusion will call *polycentric constitutionalism*—is then operationalized, legally and politically, through the mechanisms of national oversight discussed in Chapters 3 through 5. Because constitutional legitimacy is distributed *among* the constituted bodies of the Member States, supranational institutions remain administrative, not constitutional. Even as European institutions exercise significant and often autonomous regulatory power, they exist in a political-cultural sense in a derivative, delegated, agency relationship with their polycentric constitutional principals on the national level.

---

99. Cf. Somek (2009).

100. Majone (2005), 173, citing Polanyi (1951) and Jones (1987). See also Besselink (2006); Bartolini (2005).

My emphasis on delegation, as well as my references to the Member States as principals and supranational bodies as agents, may lead some readers to view my approach as merely an extension of a social science literature that uses similar terminology to describe the manner in which supranational authority has been institutionalized over time.[101] Viewing it as such an extension would be a mistake without clearly distinguishing constructivist and rational-choice choice approaches to institutional analysis.[102] Rational-choice institutionalism undoubtedly offers a compelling theory (often inspired by the analysis of the American administrative state) of why the Member States might have opted for supranational delegation as a tool of governance. Most importantly, rational-choice approaches theorize that the Member States have sought, as multiple principals, to reduce the transaction costs of their cooperation and enhance the credibility of their treaty commitments by delegating significant normative authority to relatively autonomous supranational bodies as their agents.[103] The problem with this rationalist interpretation, however, is that it often treats the choice for delegation in general (and for supranational delegation in particular) as a choice made *outside of time*, born of a logic without a normative legal and political history of its own.[104]

---

101. See, e.g., Pollack (2006a), (2005), (2003); Franchino (2007), (2005), (2004), (2002), (2001); Thatcher and Stone Sweet (2003); Kelemen (2002); Bergman and Damgaard (2000); Bergman (2000); Moravcsik (1998); and Majone (1998), (1996).

102. For more detail on the distinctions in the variants, see Hall and Taylor (1996). Specifically in the context of European integration, see Meunier and McNamara (2007), 4–7; Pollack (2005), 362–68; Schneider and Aspinwall (2001).

103. See, e.g., Moravcsik (1998), 9 (arguing that Member State decisions to delegate to the supranational level in the European Community "are best explained as efforts by governments to constrain and control one another—in game-theoretical language, by their effort to enhance the credibility of commitments"); see also Majone (2005), 64; and Menon and Weatherill (2002), 117. For succinct overviews of this literature, see Pollack (2005), 376–78; and Kassim and Menon (2003), 125–33.

104. Cf. Knudsen and Rasmussen (2008), 57 ("Delegation-agency theory . . . works with a relatively static view of time."). For example, Moravcsik (1998), 74, refers to "straightforwardly enforceable" delegation rules at the national level, in supposed contrast to the supranational context. The rules on delegation in the major states of Western Europe, at least in the third of a century prior to the advent of integration, were anything but "straightforwardly enforceable." See Lindseth (2004). Moreover, the complex mix of control/oversight mechanisms that emerged from this period of institutional breakdown would have a direct bearing on the institutional politics of both the postwar welfare state as well as European integration in the 1950s and after. More encouraging in this regard is Moravcsik's recent statement—that "[t]he justification for delegation and insulation of modern policymaking is not simply pragmatic, but deeply normative,"

Constructivist approaches, by contrast, take that normative history more seriously, paying much closer attention to the specifically cultural dimension in the process of institutional change. This implies, in the context of integration, an effort to understand why delegation came to be seen as an appropriate foundation for supranational governance in the 1950s and after. By tracing the emergence of this "logic of appropriateness,"[105] one should seek to understand how and why notions of hierarchical control necessarily gave way, over time, to looser forms of oversight as an acceptable means of legitimating diffuse and fragmented forms of administrative decision making.[106]

Despite these differences, both the rational-choice and constructivist approaches ultimately share one core premise with this study: that political action is constrained and shaped over time by historically constructed *institutions*. The concept of an institution is generally capacious enough to include not merely formal systems of rules but also informal procedures and settled modes of conduct (in short, enduring legitimating structures such as those described in this study).[107] The purpose of history as a scholarly discipline, and more particularly of legal history, should thus be to help trace the microfoundation of these structures—that is, "how and why they emerge, develop, or die out within any group," something that, in its complexity and variability among contexts, often appears to political scientists as "problematic" and "somewhat mysterious."[108]

---

see Moravcsik (2007), 50—a view clearly open to, as well as compatible with, the normative-legal history spelled out in this study.

105. Cf. Rittberger (2005), 18, describing the "logic of appropriateness," citing March and Olsen (1989), 23, and March and Olsen (1998), 951. See also March and Olsen (2009).

106. See, e.g., Chapter 3, nn. 140–160, Chapter 4, nn. 175–179, and Chapter 5, nn. 245–254 and accompanying text. From a theoretical standpoint, Giandomenico Majone has attempted to describe "two logics of delegation," one to agents subject to forms of control, and the other to "fiduciaries" or "trustees," who are given much greater degrees of effective and legal independence. See Majone (2001b); see also Franchino (2002) (critically elaborating Majone's claim). Integration historians have also begun to focus on the challenges of control in the context of integration, notably with regard to the emerging committee structures of the 1960s. See Ludlow (2009); Knudsen and Rasmussen (2008); see also Kaiser (2008), 307–08.

107. This definition is drawn from North (1990), 3–5. Other common definitions are those of March and Olsen (1998), 948 ("a relatively stable collection of practices and rules defining appropriate behavior for specific groups of actors in specific situations") and Hall (1986), 19 ("the formal rules, compliance procedures, and standard operating practices that structure the relationship between individuals in various units of the polity and economy").

108. Stone Sweet (2000), 8. The same point could be made about "preferences"—i.e., why particular historical actors value one course of action over others in particular contexts

The present study hopes to provide some of this additional normative-historical depth to our understanding of the logic and mechanisms of supranational delegation in Europe—indeed, perhaps in other bodies outside the nation-state that also exercise some measure of delegated normative power.[109] Delegation has served, I maintain, as the key legitimating connection in European public law over time. It has linked the "remarkably resilient" sources of democratic and constitutional legitimation inherited from the nineteenth century[110]—most importantly embodied in national legislatures—with the reality of diffuse and fragmented administrative governance that emerged in the twentieth, first nationally, then supranationally. By providing the normative justification for national oversight mechanisms, delegation sought to surmount the gap that Schmitt would claim was "insurmountable"—that is, the fundamental instability in the legal and political boundaries between legislative, executive, and adjudicative power, categories that he believed would inevitably devolve to the national leader to exercise.[111]

This study thus seeks to demonstrate that the notion of delegation in an administrative sense ("conferral" in the language of the European treaties), as well as the principal-agent relationship it normatively implies, have contributed directly to a similar reconciliation of the various dimensions of institutional change in integration—functional, political, and cultural.[112] The concept of delegation has often gone unarticulated in European public law, or has been discounted in favor of claims of constitutional originality for the supranational level. Nevertheless, delegation continues to provide the legal-cultural foundation for the imposition of a similar range of legitimating mechanisms over European governance.

---

at different points in time. See Katznelson and Weingast (2005), 2 ("We know too little about preferences, where they come from or how they are generated.").

109. The general phenomenon of administrative power beyond the state is now the focus of the so-called Global Administrative Law (GAL) project at New York University, which has garnered a good deal of attention among public law scholars in recent years. See generally the Global Administrative Law Project, http://www.iilj.org/GAL/default.asp (last visited Jan. 29, 2008); see also Kingsbury et al. (2005); and Global Administrative Law Bibliography (2005), 372 (listing Lindseth (1999) as a forerunner of the emerging literature). For a description of a competing project, using the concept of "international public authority" as its touchstone, see von Bogdandy (2008).

110. See Eley (1995), 110 (referring to "the constitutional frameworks fashioned [throughout Europe] in the 1860s" as "remarkably resilient").

111. Schmitt (1938 [1936]), 204. See Chapter 2, nn. 47–65 and accompanying text.

112. See the Introduction, nn. 37–38 and accompanying text.

Supranational institutions, these practices suggest, are not constitutionally original or autonomous, the result of some kind of *Gesamtakt staatlicher
Integrationsgewalt*,[113] or perhaps, alternatively, some kind of "sedimentary
'living' constitution."[114] The fact that the dominant narrative of integration
has been so deeply attached to the idea of constitutional originality may
explain why integration legal theory has been on the "wrong track" for so
long.[115] These practices reflect, rather, integration's deep dependence on
national institutions for democratic and constitutional legitimation, through
oversight mechanisms derived from the postwar constitutional settlement,
just as in the administrative state.

✺ 1.3 The Importance of National Antecedents

In its specifically normative-historical ambitions, this study also hopes to
serve as another kind of corrective, this time for certain strains in the institutionalist literature on integration that discount or neglect national antecedents, particularly those relating to the legal and institutional history of
delegation and administrative governance on the national level.[116] As one
historical sociologist has written, "the world is always *already* institutionalized. Change unfolds on historically specific terrain."[117] If the notion of
path dependence means anything to institutionalist explanations (as it purportedly does),[118] it should mean that we must try as best we can to establish

---

113. See this chapter, n. 62 and accompanying text.

114. Curtin (2009), 9.

115. Avbelj (2008b), 28. On the notion of "constitutional narrative," see the Introduction, n. 53
and accompanying text.

116. See Moravcsik (1998), which, although not explicitly institutionalist in theoretical orientation, nevertheless begins its historical analysis of the establishment of Europe's "quasi-
constitutional institutions" with the negotiation of the Treaty of Rome and largely
ignores the experience of the ECSC or underlying national models. See also Stone Sweet
and Sandholtz (1998), 2 ("We do not explain the founding of the [Community], but
rather its institutional development. Our starting point, therefore, is the Treaty of
Rome."). Another example is Curtin (2009), 9 (employing the "geological metaphor" of a
"sedimentary constitution" over time, arguing that "[t]he issue of time is clearly crucial,"
albeit without exploring the importance of national antecedents).

117. Clemens (2003), 446 (emphasis added). Put another way: "Institutions are what
persist from one day to the next; they are what hold the present to the past." Rubenfeld
(2001), 37.

118. Immergut and Anderson (2008), 354–55, discussing Pierson (2004).

historical context *first*—in all its normative-empirical complexity—*before* the impulse to theorization takes over.[119] In other words, one cannot understand the institutional contours of European integration *after* the 1950s without some effort to come to terms with the founding of integration *over the course* of the 1950s. And perhaps more importantly, one cannot understand the institutional choices made with regard to integration over the course of the 1950s (indeed, up to the present) without some appreciation of the legal-historical developments prior to the 1950s—that is, the emergence of the postwar constitutional settlement of administrative governance as a normative *institution* in its own right—which would be essential in shaping the subsequent institutionalization of supranational administrative governance in the postwar decades.

Integration historiography has, to its credit, never ignored the foundational period and is also increasingly adding a measure of theoretical sophistication to its analyses.[120] Moreover, some younger political scientists, notably Craig Parsons and Berthold Rittberger, have also begun to push the analytical perspective of the institutionalist literature back to the founding of the European Coal and Steel Community under the Treaty of Paris of 1951, with the specific aim of understanding the role of ideas and beliefs in shaping institutional design.[121] Their focus has been twofold. For Parsons, it has been on the emergence of the so-called "Community model"—that is, on integration by way of strong supranational institutions exercising some degree of autonomous regulatory power.[122] For Rittberger, it has been on how a "legitimacy deficit" arose from the very founding of integration as a consequence of supranational delegation, and how these beliefs shaped the power of such institutions as the European Parliament.[123]

---

119. Perhaps this impulse explains why Alan Milward once called the social-science literature on integration "a piquant but watery soup through which the historian hunts in vain for solid scraps of nutriment." Milward (2000 [1992]), 20. On the potential for cross-fertilization and cooperation between historical and rational-choice approaches to the study of institutions and preferences, see generally Katznelson and Weingast (2005).

120. See generally Chapter 3, and sources cited; see also Kaiser (2006), (2008), (2009), as well as Rasmussen (2009). For an effort to push the perspective further back into the administrative history of nation-states in the interwar period (albeit seen primarily through the prism of international cooperation rather than the emergence of administrative governance), see Badel et al. (2005).

121. Parsons (2003); Rittberger (2005).

122. Parsons (2003), 9.

123. See Rittberger (2005), 52–57.

These efforts are deeply welcome but could be supplemented in important ways. First, additional insight is needed into the origins of the ideas that Parsons and Rittberger identify as salient in the normative struggle over integration in the 1950s. Parsons, for example, did not see that an important part of the attraction of the Community model was its grounding in the separation of regulatory power and legitimacy that was a cornerstone of the constitutional settlement of administrative governance in the postwar decades.[124] Rittberger, on the other hand, asserted that "the model of representative, parliamentary democracy" has been "the template which [has] guide[d] political elites' responses to the perceived legitimacy deficit."[125] But he did not explore how prior transformations in that model, particularly in relation to the challenges posed by administrative governance (especially from the 1920s to the 1950s), affected the design of supranational institutions and their legitimating mechanisms over the last half century.

Part of the problem with both authors is that they have tended to limit their analysis to overtly expressed ideas and thus have failed to scrutinize how models of legitimation may be revealed in broader normative structures and institutions in the postwar decades.[126] As a consequence, their work does not really break with the more general tendency to view European governance as sui generis and institutionally without historical antecedents.[127] This is in line with the currently prevalent descriptions of European governance in the social science literature—"functional association of states; multi-level system of governance; transnational network of governments"—which, as Giandomenico Majone has remarked, "by their lack of historical

124. See Parsons (2003), 20 (suggesting, but not exploring, this relationship by stating the community model prevailed because of its ability to "connect to established elements of their environment" and "to already established norms").

125. Rittberger (2005), 199.

126. The same critique might be directed at Jachtenfuchs et al. (1998); see also Jachtenfuchs (2002). In Rittberger's case, this lack of attention to broader institutional practices prevents him from understanding the full import of the recourse to legitimation strategies relying increasingly on national parliaments in the 1990s and 2000s. See Chapter 5, nn. 199–202 and accompanying text.

127. Bartolini (2005), 116 ("It is often maintained that the history of nation-state political structuring . . . is not relevant when one deals with the process of European integration, given that the EU is a special case, a unique development, and a *sui generis* process. Therefore, according to this view, not much can be learned from its historical antecedents.").

references seem to take for granted the uniqueness of the Community model."[128]

Majone warns against coining ahistorical abstractions like "multilevel governance" to explain complex phenomena like integration, reminding us that "Occam's razor prescribes not to introduce new terms unless they actually improve our understanding of the processes and phenomena under investigation." He also notes that "[e]arly federalists like Jean Monnet . . . did not envisage a 'multilevel' system as the ultimate goal of European integration."[129] The virtue of administrative governance as an alternative analytical rubric (along with the associated theory of functionalism, as we shall see below)[130] is that both were very much on the minds of integration's advocates in the 1950s as they set out to build supranational regulatory institutions.[131] Indeed, as we shall see in the chapters that follow, the willingness of the Member States, and more particularly their parliaments, to bind themselves to norms produced by relatively autonomous regulatory entities at the supranational level (at least in certain specified domains) was a direct consequence of this political-cultural environment on the national level.

---

128. Majone (2002), 320. Recent trends in integration historiography, unfortunately, also adopt the multilevel rubric as a means of describing the transnational interactions suggested by the archival research. For a detailed overview, see Kaiser (2008), 306–09.

129. Majone (2005), v.

130. See Chapter 2, nn. 29–40 and accompanying text.

131. See, e.g., Chapter 3, nn. 18–32 and accompanying text; cf. also Chapter 4, n. 90 and accompanying text.

TWO

The Interwar Crisis and the Postwar Constitutional Settlement of Administrative Governance

THE WORKS OF THE BRITISH HISTORIAN Alan Milward have rightly dominated historical interpretation of the earlier years of European integration.[1] Among their many virtues is the explicit way in which they confront a core contradiction in the integration historiography: On the one hand, scholars have stressed "the surrender of national sovereignty" as central to the process of integration; on the other hand, as Milward points out, the postwar state in Western Europe, with its vast array of "laws, officials, policemen, spies, statisticians, revenue collectors, and social workers ... penetrated into a far wider range of human activities" than it ever had been able to do before.[2] A concrete example of this contradiction can be seen in the treatment of state-directed economic planning at the national level in the postwar period, the most prominent example being the Monnet Plan in France. Although scholars often see this "as the very symbol of post-war national resurrection in Europe," Milward again notes that "the architect of that plan, Jean Monnet, is also revered by European federalists as 'the father of Europe,' and Robert Schuman, the architect of the Treaty of Paris, was a firm supporter of the Plan."[3] How could this be?

This seeming contradiction—between support for a vast increase in the power of the state at home and the decision in favor of supranational delegation in certain limited domains in Europe—is much less puzzling once we realize that these choices are related not merely at the level of economic policy, something examined in detail by Milward. Rather, they are also linked at the level of institutional change within the nation-state itself, something the existing historiography has largely overlooked. The constitutional stabilization of delegation and administrative governance both on the national and supranational levels emerged out of a period of intense

---

1. See Chapter 1, nn. 44–50 and accompanying text.

2. Milward (2000 [1992]), 18.

3. Ibid., 16–17.

historical struggle stretching back at least to the end of World War I. During this period, the balance among legislative, executive, and judicial authority was fundamentally reworked, in response to intense functional demands as well as profound political turmoil. Most importantly, in this atmosphere, many questioned the forms and meaning of representative democracy, a process that in several leading countries ultimately led to a tragic choice in favor of dictatorship.

✹ 2.1 The Crisis of Parliamentary Democracy and Lessons Learned

The political turmoil of the interwar period was intimately bound up with the challenges of war and economic and social crisis. Europe's first experience with the demands of total war from 1914 to 1918, as well as the challenges of postwar reconstruction and reconversion to a peacetime economy thereafter, placed an extraordinary strain on the conventional constitutional division of powers throughout Europe. As Milward himself notes at the outset of *The European Rescue of the Nation-State* (1992), the experience of 1914 to 1918 required the European nation-state "to undertake feats of organization on a scale far greater than anything it had previously attempted," while at the same time forcing the state "to call on the allegiance of its citizens to a degree which it had not previously attempted." The sacrifices that the state demanded of Europe's citizens in World War I would not have been possible, he continues, "without an extension of the state's obligations to them, nor without the changes in the political system which that implied." Political instability in the interwar period flowed directly from the fact that "[f]ew European nation-states found themselves able . . . successfully to make the transition to a new form of governance securely founded on the larger pattern of obligations."[4]

Milward does not expand on what precisely this "new form of governance" entailed, at least in legal or institutional terms. But these generalizations nevertheless provide a useful point of entry into the political and constitutional struggles of the interwar period, as well as their social and economic underpinnings, out of which a new form of governance did indeed emerge after 1945.

Over the course of the 1920s and into the 1930s, the key constitutional question confronting Europeans was this: What should be the role of

---

4. Ibid., 4.

representative institutions, notably parliaments, in a state confronted by public demands for economic and social intervention on a scale never before seen in peacetime? To many political actors and scholarly observers alike, the appropriate response was reasonably clear: Fundamental changes in the constitutional distribution of powers would be necessary. Most importantly, national parliaments—whose generalist character and cumbersome deliberation had fit nicely with the seemingly more limited, liberal state of the nineteenth century—would now need to cede broad normative powers to the executive and emergent technocratic spheres, just as they had during the war in the interest of national defense.[5]

The irony, of course, was that "the Paris peace settlement [also] saw parliamentary democracy enthroned across Europe," built on "an overwhelming mistrust of executive authority," seen as the bulwark of the many autocratic regimes that had just collapsed.[6] The immediate postwar period was a "heady" time in which "the jurist was king," with the likes of Hugo Preuss in Germany and Hans Kelsen in Austria playing key roles in drafting postwar democratic-parliamentary constitutions.[7] Nevertheless, it was also a time of "chaos and confusion," hardly a propitious moment for the creation of durable parliamentary regimes where only rudiments and outlines had previously existed.[8] As Carl Schmitt would later observe, "the majority of states" (his particular focus was on Germany, France, Britain, as well as the United States) had found it increasingly necessary in the interwar period to "simplify" the procedures normally required for the adoption of legislative rules so as to remain "in harmony with the constant changes in the political, economic, and financial situation."[9] The shift in extensive normative power to

---

5. Lindseth (2004), 1355, n. 39.

6. Mazower (2000 [1998]), 4, 8.

7. Ibid., 7.

8. Ibid.

9. Schmitt (1938 [1936]), 200. This statement applied equally well to the Italian case. Charles Maier described what he called the "corrupting *trasformismo*" of constitutional government as pursued by the Fascists in late 1922: "Socialists excepted, the Chamber remained generally compliant before Mussolini and quickly endorsed a grant of 'full powers' for a year, supposedly on the informal assurance that the executive grant would be used only for trimming the bureaucracy or rationalizing tax laws. Only a few speakers complained; as one Socialist deputy pointed out, however, the system of bypassing parliament with decree legislation had been accepted since the war." Maier (1975), 344; see also Merlini (1995), 30 (describing the grant of "full powers" to the Salandra government in May 1915 as part of a "radical upheaval" in the "constitutional substance of the Italian form of government," which would "repeat [itself] seven years later, with the advent of fascism").

the executive was, in Schmitt's estimation, the principal instrument of this simplification.[10]

As Schmitt accurately noted, through the 1920s and into the 1930s, it was not just in Germany but also, in the victorious countries such as France, Britain, and the United States that one saw ever-broader concentrations of legislative and adjudicative authority in the executive branch. Indeed, the emergency legislation adopted during World War I often served as a kind of constitutional model for each successive enabling act (*Ermächtigungsgesetz, loi d'habilitation*). These legislative acts would transfer to the executive, in some degree or another, the necessary powers to address the perceived crisis of the moment (inflation, currency stabilization, economic depression). In Germany, moreover, recourse to the emergency powers of the Reich President under Article 48 of the Weimar Constitution reinforced this process. Although Article 48 was originally understood as conferring authority on the President only to address civil strife, it evolved into an excuse for the executive to exercise wide-ranging legislative powers.[11]

It was also under the Weimar Republic that a small group of German constitutional theorists, most notably Heinrich Triepel and Fritz Poetzsch, began to argue that legislative ordinances issued by the government under an enabling act—*Rechtsverordnungen*—were not only subject to the political control of the *Reichstag* but also the judicial control of the courts. Both Triepel and Poetzsch recognized that one of the main challenges of modern governance was to define a workable legal distinction between legislative and executive power. Triepel and Poetzsch were thus critical of both the extraordinary scope and the substantive indeterminacy of the delegations under the Weimar enabling acts.[12] They reasoned that if the constitution assigned legislative competence to the people's elected representatives, the *Reichstag* could not transfer that authority to another organ without calling into question both the constitution itself and its distribution of powers.[13]

---

10. Schmitt (1938 [1936]), 200. See also Mazower (2000 [1998]), 20 (describing "constitutional revisions to strengthen the executive" through authorized delegation in Poland in 1926, Austria in 1929, Spain in 1931, Estonia in 1933 and 1937, and Lithuania in 1935).

11. Lindseth (2004), 1360.

12. See, e.g., Poetzsch (1921).

13. In the reports of Triepel and Poetzsch at the convention of German jurists (*Deutscher Juristentag*) in 1922, the central question on the agenda was whether it would "be advisable to include new rules in the Reich constitution on the boundaries between legislation [*Gesetz*] and regulatory ordinances issued by the government [*Rechtsverordnung*]."

These critical views of the Weimar practice of wholesale delegation were not widely shared, however; rather, delegation was often viewed as a cornerstone of republican governance in a modern administrative state.[14] And yet, even with such shifts in power, the Weimar Republic was unable to achieve sufficient political stability to develop credible long-term solutions to the many problems confronting it. It is perhaps unsurprising, then, that the emergency powers of the Reich President under Article 48 of the Weimar Constitution assumed an increasingly important role in the production of legislative norms over the course of the 1920s, at critical junctures serving as a mechanism to overcome blockages in the *Reichstag* concerning central issues of economic policy.[15] Indeed, by the early 1930s, Article 48 became the purported constitutional foundation (aided greatly by Schmitt's theories) for extraparliamentary and eventually unadulterated antiparliamentary government in Germany.

Fom 1930 to 1932, political circumstances (the absence of a coherent majority in the *Reichstag*) forced the Brüning cabinet to govern using presidential decree powers under Article 48. But unlike the dictatorial governments that came immediately after (those of Papen, Schleicher, and then disastrously Hitler), the "semi-parliamentary" Brüning cabinet scrupulously submitted decrees to the *Reichstag* for post hoc control as required by the constitution. Thus, Brüning could claim to enjoy at least the toleration, indeed even the tacit support, of a negative parliamentary majority that included the Social Democrats, which repeatedly refused to annul the submitted decrees.[16] Brüning argued "in later years that his resort to government by decree did not suspend parliamentary control but merely changed its form."[17] This claim is less far-fetched than one might think, given its similarity to approaches being tested elsewhere,[18] as well as its anticipation of

---

See Triepel (1922) and Poetzsch (1922). For a discussion of the contributions of Triepel and Poetzsch to the proceedings, see Mößle (1990), 25.

14. For greater detail on Germany and France in the interwar period, see Lindseth (2004), 1361–81; for interwar Britain, see Lindseth (2005b), 663–76.

15. See, e.g., Steuernotverordnung des Reichspräsidenten, v. 7.12.1923 (RGBl. I S.1177); see also Scheuner (1967), 257–66. A list of presidential acts by emergency decree in the early Weimar period can be found in Poetzsch (1925), 141–47.

16. See Patch (1998), 72–117.

17. Patch (1998), 115.

18. In France, for example, Article 1 of Law of Aug. 3, 1926, *Journal Officiel de la République Française ("J.O."), Lois et Décrets*, Aug. 4, 1926, p. 8786, conferred decree powers on the government through the end of the year to undertake administrative reforms to shore up

forms of post hoc parliamentary oversight (e.g., vetoes and "laying" procedures) that would develop after 1945 throughout Western Europe.[19] One
might reproach Brüning for his deviation from the practices of "normal"
parliamentarism.[20] But that criticism ignores how "normal" parliamentarism
was under severe strain throughout interwar Europe, to the point that it was
difficult to discern precisely what "normal" parliamentarism was under the
circumstances.

One element in the interwar political and legal discourse, however,
rejected such shifts in power entirely, precisely on the grounds that they violated idealized, essentially Lockean conceptions of parliamentary democracy inherited from the past.[21] In 1926, the French Socialist Léon Blum argued
that the emergent practices of "full powers" (*pleins pouvoirs*) and "decree
laws" (*décrets-lois*) were "not only a violation of the Constitution, but a violation of national sovereignty, of which you [the members of parliament] are
the representatives, but not the masters and which you do not have the right
to delegate to others but yourselves."[22] Coming from the opposite end of the
political spectrum, Lord Hewart, the Lord Chief Justice of England, famously
published a book in 1929 provocatively entitled *The New Despotism*, in
which he argued that delegation of legislative and adjudicative powers to the
executive in the modern administrative state posed a grave threat to the "two
leading features" of the British constitution, "the Sovereignty of Parliament
and the Rule of Law."[23]

Both Blum and Hewart, however, would eventually capitulate in the face
of functional realities. In Blum's case, he would in fact seek decree powers for
his Popular Front governments in June 1937 and April 1938. And in the
debate over his 1937 request, Blum conceded that constitutional practice
had evolved: "Questions of *pleins pouvoirs*, in effect, are questions of constitutional law, but they are above all, as you well know, questions of confidence"
in the executive.[24] In Hewart's case, his position reportedly mellowed following the publication of the report of the Committee on Ministers' Powers

---

state finances, subject to the submission of the decrees to the parliament within three
months of their promulgation.

19. See this chapter, nn. 92–95 and accompanying text.

20. See, e.g., Gusy (1994), 274.

21. See the Introduction, n. 58 and accompanying text.

22. *J.O., Chambre des députés, débats*, July 7, 1926, p. 2773.

23. Hewart of Bury (1929), 17.

24. *J.O., Chambre des députés, débats*, June 15, 1937, p. 1979.

in 1932.[25] This was one of the more famous bodies in the historical development of UK administrative law, formed in 1929 directly in response to Hewart's critique.

The general conclusion of the Committee's report was "that the system of delegated legislation is both legitimate and constitutionally desirable for certain purposes," as a consequence of pressures on parliamentary time, the technicality of regulatory subject matters, the need for flexibility in the face of unforeseen contingencies, and even the need for regulatory experimentation.[26] The Committee thus rejected the sweeping denunciations of *The New Despotism*, finding that such criticisms, rather than destroying the case for delegation, simply demonstrated "that there are dangers in the practice; that it is liable to abuse; and that safeguards are required."[27] The legal and political formula for the legitimation of delegated legislative and adjudicative power in the future, the Committee suggested, would be some combination of direct legislative oversight of administrative action, ministerial responsibility, and corporatist participation in regulatory decision-making, as well as judicial review of executive and administrative actors exercising delegated power.

The Committee on Ministers' Powers included representatives of all parliamentary parties in order to bolster the report's credibility in the face of growing parliamentary discomfort with the purported excesses of "bureaucracy."[28] Among the members was Harold Laski, professor of political science at the London School of Economics and a leading exponent of "functionalist" approaches to the nascent administrative state. Functionalism emerged as an *idée-force* among a number of academics in the interwar period, particularly in the English-speaking world. These scholars viewed the task of apportioning power in the modern state in the face of functional demands as "neither one of law nor of formal logic, but of expediency."[29] Britons like Laski, Ivor Jennings, and William Robson, as well as Americans like James Landis and Felix Frankfurter, were at the intellectual forefront of what was, in effect, a transatlantic scholarly "style."[30] Deeply influenced

---

25. Committee on Ministers' Powers (1932); thanks to David Dyzenhaus for alerting me to Hewart's softened position following the publication of the Committee's report.

26. Committee on Ministers' Powers (1932), 51–52.

27. Ibid., 54.

28. For examples of expressions of that discomfort, see Willis (1933), 39.

29. See Willis (1935), 75.

30. See generally Loughlin (2005).

by pragmatism, the functionalist approach proceeded on the assumption that formal constitutional categories inherited from the past, most importantly "separation of powers," would necessarily need reform for the state to respond adequately to an array of social needs. The influence of functionalist thinking was evident, for example, in the report of the Committee on Ministers' Powers itself: "The truth is," the report asserted, "that if Parliament were not willing to delegate law-making power, Parliament would be unable to pass the kind and quantity of legislation which modern public opinion requires."[31]

Similar pressures were being felt by all interwar parliaments—indeed all legislatures throughout the North Atlantic world, the U.S. Congress of course included. In particular, there was an intense desire to avoid the perceived pathologies of legislative policy making, in which an excessive number of potential "veto players" (to use modern terminology)[32] undermined the capacity of formulating effective policy at all. The French conservative Raymond Poincaré, in the midst of one of his country's many postwar financial crises (this one in 1924), argued, for example, that legislative delegation was necessary to avoid the interest group blockages that inevitably inhibited parliamentary decision-making. "Why not admit it," Poincaré asserted, "any measure of simplification threatens certain interests,"[33] which in turn were easily mobilized to prevent parliament from making any moves that were disadvantageous to them. Thus, if the solution to the crisis required a legislative "discussion as a whole, we will not succeed. However, I want to succeed."[34] Hence his call for delegation.

Just over a decade later, James Landis, committed New Dealer and later dean of the Harvard Law School, would capture another element behind functionalist thinking in terms that would have resonated with many European observers: its pragmatic, problem-solving impulse. For Landis, the reordering of structures of governance was, he famously wrote, a consequence of "the inadequacy of a simple tripartite form of government to deal with modern problems."[35] The belief that functionalist pressures were acting as a solvent on received legal categories and structures, however, was not the

---

31. Committee on Ministers' Powers (1932), 23.

32. See Tsebelis (2002).

33. *J.O., Chambre des députés, débats,* Feb. 6, 1924, p. 511.

34. *J.O., Chambre des députés, débats,* Jan. 26, 1924, p. 287.

35. Landis (1938), 1.

exclusive preserve of domestic public law theorists, whether in Europe or the United States. This line of thinking soon migrated out of public law into the realm of international relations theory, finding inspiration in the work of an emergent class of transnational and eventually international functionaries— men such as Arthur Salter, who worked closely with Jean Monnet during World War I on interallied supply boards and later at the League of Nations, as well as others like Leonard S. Woolf and G. D. H. Cole.[36]

The academic voice for this form of international functionalism was the Romanian-born British theorist David Mitrany. Mitrany advanced the view that functional pressures would also eventually erode the boundaries of "national sovereignty" just as it had "separation of powers" before them, in a way that might promote new forms of pragmatic international cooperation. Mitrany first applied the functionalist label to international cooperation in a series of lectures at Yale in 1933.[37] A decade later, inspired by his reading of the New Deal experience, Mitrany would publish his famous pamphlet, *A Working Peace System: An Argument for the Functional Development of International Organization* (1943).[38] This work would eventually become the foundational text for this line of thinking in the European integration con- text over the subsequent decades.[39] "[T]he situation at the end of this war will resemble that in America in 1933, though on a wider and deeper scale," Mitrany wrote. "And for the same reasons the path pursued by Mr. Roosevelt in 1933 offers the best, perhaps the only, chance for getting a new interna- tional life going."[40]

It is important to stress, however, that just as functionalism was not the exclusive preserve of domestic public law theorists in the interwar period (witness Mitrany), it was also not the sole property of the intellectual left in the Anglo-American world. Not all who called for the functional reordering of the state, for example, would have shared in the belief, articulated by Landis, that the process of functional change must nevertheless "preserve those elements of responsibility and those conditions of balance that have distinguished Anglo-American government."[41] Far from it: Erstwhile

---

36. See Dubin (1983), 493.

37. See Mitrany (1933).

38. Mitrany (1946 [1943]).

39. For a summary, see Griffiths (1999), 191–94.

40. Mitrany (1946 [1943]), 30.

41. Landis (1938), 1.

economics professor and Portuguese dictator Antonio Salazar described the world in 1934 as a "great laboratory," in which "'the political systems of the nineteenth century are generally breaking down'" in the face of the need to adapt "'institutions to the requirements of new social and economic conditions.'"[42] In light of these functional pressures, Salazar was "convinced that in twenty years, if there is not some retrograde movement in political evolution, there will be no legislative assemblies left in Europe."[43]

Of course, even in the dictatorial regimes that emerged in the interwar period—be they authoritarian in Portugal, fascist in Italy, or national-socialist in Germany—legislative assemblies clung to life if not power. But in dictatorships they persisted only as hollowed out hulks with no real function at all—certainly not as instruments of legitimation (that function was ultimately vested in the person of the national leader). Rather, in these emergent interwar dictatorships, legislative assemblies persisted as mere window dressing, as "the tribute that vice customarily pays to virtue," to borrow a contemporaneous description from an American historian.[44]

The most articulate exponent of this form of extreme-right marginalization of the legislature was of course Carl Schmitt himself. Schmitt well understood, as noted earlier, the domestic consequences of functional pressures for interwar regimes throughout Europe: Whether conventionally labeled as parliamentary democracies or as dictatorships, he maintained, all were struggling to remain "in harmony with the constant changes in the political, economic, and financial situation."[45] And like Mitrany, although more ominously, Schmitt sensed the international-relations consequences of functional pressures on the continued viability of nation-states as economic and political units.[46]

In 1938, Schmitt contributed an article (originally published in Germany in 1936) to a collection of essays in honor of France's great comparative law scholar, Edouard Lambert, using this as an opportunity to disseminate to a wider audience his writings in Germany on "the recent evolution of the

---

42. Quoted in Mazower (2000 [1998]), 28.

43. Mazower (2000 [1998]), 28.

44. Becker (1943 [1940]), 203.

45. Schmitt (1938 [1936]), 200; see this chapter, n. 9 and accompanying text.

46. See Joerges (2003), 177 (describing Schmitt's theory of the *Großraum* in relation to "the erosion of the territorial state, a harbinger of the necessity to adapt international law to the factual restructuring of international relations and the replacement of classical international law by norm systems which one would call governance structures today").

problem of legislative delegations."[47] His basic argument was that, in the aftermath of World War I, developments in Germany, France, Britain, and the United States *all* reflected a similar breakdown in the constitutional bound-ary between legislative and executive power, to the obvious benefit of the latter. Only in Germany, however, had this process reached its logical conclu-sion, completely eliminating any semblance of "separation of powers," opting instead for a true system of "governmental legislation."[48]

Schmitt seemed well aware of his dependence on euphemism to soften the image of the Nazi regime in Germany. He believed that "the pejorative word dictatorship" should be avoided in the description of the German system after 1933. That system, in his view, simply vindicated the thinking of Aristotle and Thomas Aquinas about the proper locus of legislative power in the prince (i.e., the executive), demonstrating the superiority of these Aristotelian and Thomist notions "over the concepts of legislation and of constitution peculiar to separation-of-powers regimes."[49] Schmitt thus sug-gested that this return to reputedly traditional forms of governance in Europe was inevitable among all industrialized nations. Schmitt reasoned that there was simply "an insurmountable opposition between the concept of legisla-tion in a parliamentary regime and the evolution of public life over the course of the last decades," which demanded not the legislature's deliberation over general norms, but the executive's decisive action in concrete cases.[50]

Since the early 1920s Schmitt himself had been oscillating, as one com-mentator puts it, "between an emphasis on the significance of a legally ungrounded political decision and an emphasis on an inviolable deep legal structure."[51] For much of this period, this deep structure still had certain minimal separation-of-powers features in Schmitt's mind (for example, in the scope of executive authority vis-à-vis the *Reichstag* under Article 48).[52] And in his *Verfassungslehre* (1928), Schmitt could still seemingly lament the breakdown in the distinction between legislative statute and

---

47. Schmitt (1938 [1936]), 200; for the original German article, see Schmitt (1936).

48. Schmitt (1938 [1936]), 205.

49. Ibid., 201, 210.

50. Ibid., 204.

51. Balakrishnan (2000), 193; cf. also Bates (2006) (discussing the relationship between deci-sionism and institutionism in Schmitt's thinking over the course of the 1920s and early 1930s).

52. Balakrishnan (2000), 156, 163 (discussing Schmitt's position in *Legality and Legitimacy* (1932)).

administrative measure.[53] Nevertheless, in the final years of Weimar, Schmitt increasingly saw this distinction as unsustainable in light of functional pressures.[54] With the Nazi seizure of power, Schmitt was willing to abandon this distinction entirely, accepting the fusion of complete authority in Hitler as national leader, taking refuge in purportedly Aristotelian and Thomist justifications in order to do so. But in practice what Schmitt was accepting was the collapse of the distinction "between a law and an SS memo," which eventually led him, as one of his biographers nicely put it, into "a politico-theoretical cul-de-sac."[55] Leaving aside its colossal criminality and brutality, "the Hitler regime," as one of its foremost historians has noted, "was inimical to a rational order of government and administration" of any kind. "Its hallmark was *systemlessness*, administrative and governmental disorder, the erosion of clear patterns of government, however despotic."[56]

It would take the disaster of World War II to help Germany out of this disastrous dead end, even pushing someone as retrograde as Schmitt himself toward recognizing the imperative of reconciling parliamentary democracy with the demands of modern administrative governance. Toward the end of 1944, Schmitt wrote another piece—*Die Lage der europäischen Rechtswissenschaft [The Plight of European Jurisprudence] (1943/44)*[57]—that in certain respects can be viewed as a companion to his earlier contribution on the subject of delegation from 1936. Schmitt traced some of the same ground he had in the earlier piece—the acceleration of legislation after 1914, the "ever new and broader" delegations of legislative power in the postwar period[58]—and again he stressed how all industrialized countries had experienced a similar phenomenon "regardless of whether they were belligerents or neutrals, victors or vanquished, parliamentary states or so-called dictatorships." As Schmitt wrote, "the compulsion for legal regulations to accomodate [*sic*] the tempo of changing conditions was irresistible."[59]

Absent, however, from Schmitt's 1944 essay was the smug confidence of his 1936 piece in the German solution to the problem of delegation. This is

---

53. Schmitt (2008 [1928]), 110, 191.

54. Balakrishnan (2000), 147–48.

55. Ibid., 200, 199.

56. Kershaw (2008 [1993]), 35 (emphasis in original).

57. Schmitt (1990 [1944]).

58. Ibid., 50.

59. Ibid., 52.

perhaps understandable in light of the disaster that Germany had brought upon itself and millions of others in Europe and elsewhere as a result of the choices it made in 1933. Schmitt in 1944, surrounded by evidence of that German-inflicted catastrophe, now cited with approval Heinrich Triepel's efforts in the early 1920s to bring attention to the dangers of unchecked delegation.[60] He also cited Lord Hewart's "warning" in *The New Despotism* (although he claimed that it had been ignored, even in Britain), and wrote of the necessity for "a sense for the logic and consistency of concepts and institutions" and "the minimum of an orderly procedure, due process, without which there can be no law." He even wrote of the need for "a recognition of the individual based on mutual respect."[61]

The challenge facing Europe after 1945 was indeed to learn the lessons of the interwar period, although we would be justified in our skepticism of Schmitt's seeming reversal in 1944 in light of the hope he had invested in the constitutional principles of the Third Reich in the 1930s. In some sense, by 1944 Schmitt had simply gone to the opposite extreme, anticipating Hayek in issuing warnings of the dangers of "the increasing motorization of the legislative machinery" and "of this dissolution of law under the avalanche of ever more legislation."[62] Schmitt had not really let go of the view that delegation ultimately must lead to dictatorship, as he argued in 1936; rather, he simply no longer celebrated that process as the "triumph" of an older constitutional tradition in Europe.[63] As Schmitt quite rightly understood, the functional demands of modern governance required broad forms of legislative delegation, and this would remain as true after 1945 as it did after 1918.

It was precisely for this reason that postwar Europe was not going to follow the path that Schmitt now implicitly advocated, which was to abandon delegation as a form of governance altogether. Instead, the challenge was to find a way to make delegation work within the context of liberal-democratic institutions, to surmount what Schmitt had claimed in 1936 was "insurmountable." After 1945, the concentration of both legislative and

---

60. Ibid., 50; on Triepel's efforts in the early 1920s, see this chapter, nn. 12–13 and accompanying text.

61. Schmitt (1990 [1944]), 52, 67.

62. Ibid., 67. The seemingly Hayekian tone should perhaps not surprise us, although more accurately we should be speaking of a Schmittian tone in Hayek's later work, whose debt to Schmitt scholars have only barely begun to explore. See, e.g., Cristi (1984); Scheuermann (1997); see also McCormick (2007), 45, 83–85, nn. 20 and 21.

63. Schmitt (1938 [1936]), 210.

adjudicative powers in the executive and administrative spheres would continue to be a defining characteristic of governance throughout Europe, as it would in the United States. However, the process of postwar constitutional settlement would not be exclusively shaped by functional demands; instead, recalling Landis in 1938, it would seek some measure of "balance" and "responsibility,"[64] two elements woefully lacking in Schmitt's conceptions from the 1930s.

❦ 2.2 Elements of the Postwar Constitutional Settlement

As Landis's suggestion from 1938 anticipated, traditional considerations derived from understandings of the historic nature of the legislative, executive, and judicial branches in the state (now reinvigorated in light of the horrors of 1933–1945) would deeply influence the terms of the final settlement of administrative governance. Most importantly, there would be renewed attention to the necessity for safeguards in the executive's exercise of delegated legislative authority. In Britain, for example, there would be revived interest in the recommendations of the Committee on Ministers' Powers, leading to changes in parliamentary controls over delegated legislation and, eventually, heightened judicial review. And in France and West Germany, in reaction to their interwar and wartime experiences, the drafters of postwar constitutions would give special attention to the boundary between legislative and executive power, searching for ways to reinforce the constitutional position of the executive without sacrificing the democratic functions of the legislature or the protection of human rights.

Thus, contrary to Carl Schmitt's claims in 1936, the demands of modern governance and "the concepts of legislation and of constitution peculiar to separation-of-powers regimes"[65] would not, at least over the intermediate term after 1945, prove as contradictory as he predicted. Rather, in the decades after the end of World War II, Western European public law seemed to achieve what Schmitt had asserted was impossible only ten years before.

---

64. See this chapter, n. 41 and accompanying text.

65. Schmitt (1938 [1936]), 210.

Delegation and the Legislative Function Redefined

The major constitutional accomplishment in Western Europe after 1945, apart from the development of increasingly effective judicial mechanisms for the protection of individual rights, would be the discovery of a workable balance between traditional parliamentarism and the broad displacement of legislative power out of the parliamentary realm and into the executive and administrative spheres.[66] First and foremost, this required significant adjustments in the constitutional authority of legislatures to delegate normative power. In the postwar period, elected assemblies lost their preeminence both as institutions of norm production and as mechanisms of democratic legitimation (although certain core functions—in taxation or the definition of individual rights—would be retained in both regards, as we shall see below). The executive and administrative spheres—that is, cabinet-level politicians and their technocratic subordinates—in turn gained a much greater role in the production of regulatory norms, pursuant to general "framework laws" (*lois-cadres*) and other forms of enabling legislation adopted by the legislature. In the postwar constitutional settlement, parliamentary oversight, while not unimportant, became a decidedly secondary source of democratic legitimation, overtaken in nearly all countries (Denmark and Italy perhaps excepted)[67] by the leadership of the chief executive—what the postwar West Germans would aptly call "chancellor democracy" (*Kanzlerdemocratie*). Finally, an "internationalist spirit" pervaded Western Europe's postwar constitutions, several of which included provisions that explicitly authorized delegation of certain powers to international organizations.[68]

---

66. In fact, in the postwar era, there was a direct connection between postwar human rights regimes and the constitutionally permissible nature and scope of delegation. See this chapter, nn. 116–119 and accompanying text.

67. Regarding Denmark, see Chapter 5, nn. 115–118 and accompanying text. As for Italy, despite its notoriously powerful parliament and party system, it is arguably only a partial exception to this phenomenon. First, its constitution provided for extensive forms of delegated normative power (see this chapter, nn. 73 and 93 and accompanying text), authority that would be of critical importance to Italy's participation in European integration through the 1980s. In addition, Italy has arguably been moving "towards a more prime ministerial form of government since 1992." Raunio and Hix (2000), 152. On changes made to augment the coordinating function of the office of the prime minister over the last two decades, see Chapter 3, n. 186.

68. Claes and de Witte (1998), 173 (describing the "internationalist spirit" of the postwar Dutch constitutional amendments). For greater detail on the prevalence of these sorts of provisions in the postwar constitutions of Western Europe, see de Witte (1998), 282–86; and Claes (2005), 85–86. See also Chapter 4, nn. 88–90 and accompanying text.

To better understand the transformation in the role of the legislature in the postwar administrative state, it might be useful to recall a famous statement of Jean Monnet describing his powers as the head of the French planning commissariat, which he led prior to assuming the presidency of the High Authority of the European Coal and Steel Community (ECSC) in 1952. Monnet recognized that, in "administrative terms," the planning commissariat was "not capable of giving an order to anyone"[69]—that is, it had no direct regulatory authority of its own. Rather, it was a purely technocratic body of ambiguous institutional standing that, as one historian describes, "depended heavily on [its] powers of persuasion, on command of the economic data," but which otherwise lacked "a powerful position in making public policy."[70] The real authority to achieve public policy goals, both in law and politics, lay with the government and the ministries. But one cannot understand the full import of Monnet's statement without appreciating one additional key fact: *Even the government and the ministries* were largely powerless to implement the plan without the broad delegations of legislative authority from parliament that became common in the postwar era. In other words, the postwar political project of "modernization"—that is, technocratic planning under the hierarchical authority of the executive—depended above all on legislative delegation.[71] Delegation of normative power was the foundational element of the postwar constitutional settlement.

Given, however, the experiences of several major countries with essentially unchecked transfers of power in the interwar period (which ultimately provided the legal foundation, if not the political-cultural cause, for their devolution into dictatorship),[72] many of the new constitutions of postwar Western Europe seemed to take a restrictive approach to delegation. Article 76 of the postwar Italian constitution, for example, states: "The exercise of the legislative function may not be delegated to the government if the principles and guiding criteria have not been established and then only for a limited time and for specified ends."[73] Article 80(1) of the West German Basic Law of 1949 authorized the executive to issue *Rechtsverordnungen*

---

69. Hearings, Conseil Economique, Jan. 18, 1950, quoted in Kuisel (1981), 247.

70. Kuisel (1981), 247.

71. Cf. Corbel (1969), 216–21, describing how planning emerged out of a "parliamentary regime in crisis," of which one of the elements was "the resignation of the Parliament as a legislative organ."

72. Lindseth (2004).

73. Costituzione art. 76, translated in Camera dei Deputati (1990), 91.

(regulatory ordinances with the force of law) but, in a similar vein, required that the enabling legislation specify the "content, purpose, and scope" (*Inhalt, Zweck, und Ausmaß*) of the executive's normative authority.[74] This provision reflected the efforts of the Office of the Military Governor of the United States (OMGUS) to interject nondelegation principles articulated by the United States Supreme Court over the prior decades into postwar West German constitutional politics.[75]

What emerged in the postwar constitutional jurisprudence of the German Federal Constitutional Court (the *Bundesverfassungsgericht*) was not an inflexible, absolutist nondelegation doctrine—by its terms, Article 80(1) in fact *authorized* delegation—but rather a more subtle approach. The Court generally tried to uphold regulatory statutes by interpreting their provisions in a manner conforming to the constitutional requirements of Article 80(1) (an approach known in German as *verfassungskonforme Auslegung*).[76] To discipline this inquiry, the Court relied on a variety of related analytical formulas to constrain the executive's normative autonomy while nevertheless allowing the delegation to proceed. These included: the *Vorhersehbarkeitsformel*, which focused on whether the content of any future regulation was foreseeable from the statute itself; the *Selbstentscheidungsformel*, which focused on whether the legislature had itself decided the limits of the regulated area as well as the goals of the regulation; and the *Programmformel*, which focused on whether the statute had defined with sufficient clarity the regulatory program.[77]

---

74. Lindseth (2004), 1393. The official English translation of the Basic Law of the Federal Republic of Germany [hereinafter Basic Law] is available at https://www.btg-bestellservice. de/pdf/80201000.pdf (last visited April 29, 2010).

75. Mößle (1990), 55; Lindseth (2004), 1393. The American example also made itself felt in the writings of law professors: Perhaps the most influential commentary on the question of delegation in the early 1950s, by Bernhard Wolff (a leading professor of law and member of the Federal Constitutional Court until 1956), made explicit reference to the American jurisprudence. According to Wolff, the enabling legislation must specify "the program, the state-political, legal-political, social-political goal (*das staatspolitische, rechtspolitische, sozialpolitische Ziel*), which in English is expressed by the difficult-to-translate terms *policy* or *standards*." Wolff (1952), 197; for a discussion see Mößle (1990), 32–33; and Lindseth (2004), 1393–94.

76. See generally Lüdemann (2004), 27.

77. See generally BVerfGE 55, 207, 225–44 (1980) (describing in detail the history and tradition that had developed since the 1950s in which the Court endeavored to find implicit limitations on legislative delegations which, on their face, open-endedly authorized the promulgation of regulations by the executive).

Article 13 of the French Constitution of 1946 was, in form, even more restrictive than Article 80(1) of the Basic Law, if not outright prohibitive: "The National Assembly alone shall vote the laws [*la loi*]. It cannot delegate this right."[78] In practice, however, this seemingly unambiguous prohibition was interpreted in manner not unlike its Italian and German counterparts— in a pragmatic way authorizing delegation but subject to limitations as to determinacy and subject matter (with individual rights deemed particularly within the legislative domain).[79] The sweeping language of Article 13 did, however, make the postwar practice of broad delegation somewhat more embarrassing for the French government, leading to an ingenious solution: The French legislature simply redefined by statute the boundary between legislation and regulation.[80] The "law of August 17, 1948," as it was commonly known, declared that henceforth a whole range of matters previously understood to be within the legislative domain were "by their nature" actually of "a regulatory character" and therefore could be dealt with in the future by governmental decree, even if the decrees modified or rescinded existing statutory law.[81]

This was a typically functionalist law, which paid relatively little heed to prior formal categories of legislation and regulation but rather reworked those concepts to meet the new functional demands placed on the state for increased efficiency and public welfare. Managerial and purportedly technical imperatives predominated.[82] What is perhaps most telling about this statute, however, are not its substantive provisions but the way in which the French government enacted it. To stress its political importance, the government charged a special cabinet committee of prominent ministers—a

---

78. When quoting the constitution of October 1946, this study uses the translation of the French Press and Information Service contained in Foundation for Foreign Affairs (1947), app. X; see also Lindseth (2004), 1400.

79. Lindseth (2004), 1400–03.

80. Law No. 48–1268 of Aug. 17, 1948, *J.O., Lois et Décrets*, Aug. 18, 1948, p. 8082. See also Pinto (1948).

81. Law of August 17, 1948, arts. 6–7.

82. The regulatory domains included: the organization of public services, whether under state control or subsidized by the state, as well as of other public establishments; the limitation or elimination of staff positions; the organization of nationalized enterprises or other establishments of a commercial or industrial character under the control of the state; rules regarding public assistance and other forms of welfare; conditions for the issuance of loans by the Treasury; the regulation of the securities markets; the equalization of exchange rates; price controls; the regulation of energy usage; and the allocation of raw materials and industrial products.

conseil de gouvernement—with the task of presenting the bill to the Assembly. Included on the committee were several once or future prime ministers of France, including Robert Schuman (also the future foreign minister at the time of the Schuman Declaration in 1950 initiating the process of European integration). His strong political support for the law of August 17, 1948, which was then followed by a whole series of executive decrees[83] as well as even more ambitious enabling acts (*lois-cadres*),[84] reflects how Schuman was intimately involved with building the postwar administrative state at home even before he took up the cause of integration in Western Europe—a political trajectory he shared with the chief of the planning commissariat, Jean Monnet.[85]

The increasing pervasiveness of legislative delegation in Western Europe signified a shift in the role of national parliaments. Beyond acting as the democratic representative of the "people" or "Nation" as a whole (the function nineteenth-century constitutional doctrine assigned to them), the new function of parliaments was more instrumental—to yield a stable executive and to empower it with the necessary means to govern—and only then, somewhat secondarily, to supervise the exercise of executive and administrative authority. Postwar constitutions circumscribed the power of parliaments to censure individual ministers or governments, in the interest of governmental stability. In Germany, the key innovation in this regard was the so-called "constructive" vote of no confidence set forth in Article 67 of the Basic Law, which authorized the *Bundestag* to remove a chancellor only on a vote of an absolute majority to elect a successor government (individual ministers could not be removed).[86]

In France, it would not be until after 1958, with the advent of the semi-presidential Fifth Republic, that analogous provisions reinforcing executive power vis-à-vis parliamentary factionalism would be inserted into the constitution.[87] Long before de Gaulle's return to power, however, the legitimacy of the *régime d'assemblée* of the French Fourth Republic had collapsed, and not simply among Gaullists.[88] The transformation in the constitutional role

---

83. Maleville (1954).

84. See, e.g., Law of July 11, 1953, *J.O., Lois et Décrets*, July 11, 1953, p. 6143; Chapus (1953).

85. See this chapter, n. 3 and accompanying text.

86. See Basic Law, art. 67.

87. Lindseth (2004), 1407–08.

88. See the discussion of the changing attitudes of prominent scholars on the noncommunist left in Duhamel (1980), 206–208.

of the legislature vis-à-vis the executive was clear in the *travaux préparatoires* of the French constitution of 1958: "In the contemporary political context, the functions of the government necessarily include the power to enact provisions of a general scope"—that is, legislative provisions—whereas the "true mission of the Parliament is to monitor governmental policy" but, implicitly, not to define the details of that policy itself.[89] The drafters of the French constitution of 1958 also effectively constitutionalized the distinction between legislation and regulation in the law of August 1948, to the decided advantage of executive power.[90] Like the earlier statutory redefinition in August 1948 (as well as the numerous *lois-cadres* it enabled), the 1958 constitution was a "recognition *de jure* . . . of [the] legislative role of the government."[91] Moreover, even in strictly legislative domains, the French parliament after 1958 could also delegate its authority to the government to issue legislative ordinances for a limited period, subject to post hoc approval or nullification by the legislature.[92]

This sort of post hoc legislative role in regulatory power was not atypical of the sort of mechanisms found in other postwar administrative states. Under Article 77 of the Italian constitution, for example, the government could adopt emergency legislation by decree-law subject to post hoc review by the parliament.[93] In the Federal Republic of Germany, it was common practice for the *Bundestag* to reserve a right of veto over regulations (and the Federal Constitutional Court relied on the existence of such veto rights to uphold broad delegations of normative authority to the government adopted under Article 80(1) of the Basic Law).[94] In the United Kingdom, where the doctrine of parliamentary supremacy persisted after the war (and therefore

---

89. Jérôme Solal-Céligny, "Projet d'exposé des motifs de l'avant-projet de Constitution soumis au Comité consultatif constitutionnel le 29 juillet 1958," in Comité national chargé de la publication des travaux préparatoires des institutions de la Ve République (1987), 1:524.

90. See the discussion of Articles 34 and 37 of the 1958 constitution in Lindseth (2004), 1405–06.

91. Chapus (1953), 1003.

92. See art. 38.

93. Costituzione art. 77, translated in Camera dei Deputati (1990), 92.

94. *See*, e.g., BVerfGE 8, 274 (319–22). For a discussion of the court's view, see Currie (1993), 233. Under Article 80(2) of the Basic Law, the upper house of the German Parliament, the *Bundesrat*, also retains a right of veto that applies where certain specified interests of the several states of the federation *(Länder)* are implicated, regardless of the terms of the enabling legislation. This parallels the special rights of the *Bundesrat* vis-à-vis European legislation that falls into the constitutional domains of the *Länder*. See Chapter 4, n. 212 and accompanying text.

judicial enforcement of nondelegation principles was out of the question), this sort of post hoc parliamentary review of delegated legislation—"statutory instruments" in English legal parlance—became the primary means of legislative oversight and legitimation of regulatory power in the executive.[95]

One might question, as many did, the actual effectiveness of such mechanisms. In the ten years between 1944 and 1954, for example, the counsel to the Speaker of the British House of Commons found that the committee charged with scrutinizing delegated legislation examined 6886 instruments but called the attention of the House to only 66.[96] Rather the reality, to use the words of one member of the House from a little more than a decade later, was that the legislature had "surrendered most of its effective powers to the Executive."[97] It is to the executive, then, that we must now turn, to get a fuller sense of the contours of the postwar constitutional settlement, in particular the partial but significant shift in democratic legitimacy out of the legislative realm.

Technocracy and the Leadership of the National Executive

Underlying the shift in legal authority from the legislature to the executive was a secondary, although still important, political-cultural change. It was rooted in transformed understandings of the proper realm of politics belonging to the representative legislature and that of purportedly nonpolitical expertise (scientific, economic, financial, or organizational) belonging to a separate, technocratic sphere under the executive's hierarchical supervision or control. In some sense, "a major imperative" of the postwar constitutional settlement was to "depoliticize" policymaking, to borrow the phrase used by Michel Debré when, as newly installed prime minister in January 1959, he

---

95. Statutory Instruments Act, 1946, 9 & 10 Geo. 6, c. 36; see also Statutory Instruments Regulations, 1947, SI 1948 no. 1; and Statutory Instruments (Confirmatory Powers) Order, 1947, SI 1948 no. 2. On the similar mechanisms established to scrutinize European legislation after British accession in 1973, see Chapter 5, nn. 96–99 and accompanying text.

96. Carr (1955), 1050. On the similarly small percentage of European legislation subject to active scrutiny in the United Kingdom, see Chapter 5, nn. 108–109 and accompanying text.

97. 738 Parl. Deb., H.C. (5th ser.) (1966) 479 (statement of Richard Crossman, M.P.).

presented the first government of the Fifth Republic to the National Assembly.[98]

This desired depoliticization depended, of course, much less on an actual transformation of political questions into technical ones than on their displacement into the executive and administrative realms without altering their true nature.[99] In this sense, the notion of technocratic depoliticization provided a kind of ideological cover for the new regime, even as the difficult questions of balancing competing interests, allocating scarce resources, and choosing among potentially competing values continued to present themselves, only now in executive and administrative rather than legislative forums. The detailed policy choices would no longer be legitimized through a parliamentary vote (at least not directly, except for the enabling legislation itself). Rather, they would depend on public support for the government of the day and, perhaps more importantly, on faith in the person of the chief executive, whether termed prime minister, president, or chancellor.

As Konrad Adenauer stressed in his memoirs (in a clear allusion to the constructive vote of no-confidence provision in Article 67 of the Basic Law),[100] the postwar constitution made it

> impossible to remove individual ministers by a vote of no confidence, thus making it harder for the Federal Chancellor to fulfill his mandate. If the parliament disapproved of the policy of the Federal Chancellor, it was not to be allowed to remove the minister in question, but should have to table a vote of no confidence against the Federal Chancellor himself.[101]

The reader should note several telling aspects of this passage. First, there is the reference to chancellor fulfilling "*his* mandate." The meaning is unmistakable: The political mandate no longer belonged to the parliament as a whole (as it did in more classical republican conceptions of parliamentarism prevalent under Weimar), nor did it belong to the government collectively; rather, it belonged to the head of government—the chancellor himself. A similar implication can be drawn from the phrase "if the parliament disapproved of the policy *of* the Federal Chancellor." Again, policy goals were not

---

98. Merle (1962), 51.

99. The notion of displacement is taken from Honig (1993); cf. also Müller (2003), 85–86, discussing Lübbe (1962).

100. See this chapter, n. 86 and accompanying text.

101. Adenauer (1966), 122–23.

to be defined in parliament, nor even by the government collectively, but rather by the chancellor himself—the policy was *his*.

This passage strongly reflects Adenauer's understanding that, although the Basic Law reestablished a representative, parliamentary system of government in the western zones of occupation, that system was above all a *Kanzlerdemokratie*—a "chancellor democracy"—one dominated by the head of government. As a British political scientist pointed out in the early 1990s: "Each Bundestag election since 1949 has been a 'chancellor election' (*Kanzlerwahl*), in that the parties have entered the election as two rival groups, each with its own chancellor candidate."[102] The same statement could well be made about the plebiscitary character of parliamentary elections in other major democracies of Western Europe (Italy, until recently, perhaps excepted). This development is indicative of what might be called the semi-"presidentialization" of the parliamentary system, which was explicit in the French case in 1958 and implicit in the British and West German cases in the postwar decades.[103]

Max Weber had a term for this sort of regime—"plebiscitary leadership" democracy[104]—one that he hoped would take hold in Germany after 1918. In this view, the executive was best positioned to manage the domestic bureaucracy while also projecting national power on the international level. There was thus both a domestic administrative and international relations component to Weber's understanding, a combination of functions with perhaps disparate historical roots that would converge in the postwar decades.[105] The role of parliament in this scheme would also fundamentally change. Apart from the production of general legislative norms, the primary political role of parliament would be to train charismatic political leaders capable of exercising plebiscitary executive power, while also acting as an additional check on bureaucratic domination.

The entire French constitution of 1958 was arguably premised on this ideal of executive leadership, casting the President of the Republic as an

---

102. Southern (1994), 27. See also Amphoux (1962), 374–86 (stressing "le caractère plébiscitaire des élections en Allemagne fédérale").

103. Lindseth (2004), 1409.

104. See Weber (1978 [1922]), 2: 1451–59 ("Plebiscitary Leadership and Parliamentary Control," in "Appendix II: Parliament and Government in a Reconstructed Germany (A Contribution to the Political Critique of Officialdom and Party Politics)"). This appendix originally appeared in the *FAZ* in a series of articles in 1918.

105. See generally Chapter 3.

arbitre, or guide in policymaking.[106] A provision of the West German Basic Law, however, gave the chancellor even more explicit powers in this regard: Under Article 65, the West German chancellor had so-called *Richtlinienkompetenz*, or the sole authority to define "the general policy guidelines" for the government. Article 65, when combined with the greater political security that flowed from the constructive vote-of-no-confidence provision of Article 67 (and therefore also from the explicit constitutional identification of the government's collective responsibility and policy with the person of the chancellor), was a potentially powerful weapon, particularly in the hands of a strong-willed chancellor like Adenauer. (This authority, as we shall see, would play a direct role in Adenauer's effort to advance the cause of European integration in West German politics in the 1950s.)[107]

The German label "chancellor democracy" captures a basic attribute of postwar governance throughout most countries in Western Europe—not just on the continent but in the United Kingdom as well: Not only did the executive take on the predominant role in defining the real substance of policy but the executive now also became, in critical respects, the focus of the democratic aspirations of the people, displacing the role that traditional conceptions of parliamentary democracy had assigned to the elected legislature as a body. Parliaments retained an important role in democratic legitimation, of course, because the head of the executive could not govern without a working parliamentary majority.[108] In this sense, the parliament and the head of the executive in postwar Western Europe came to share responsibility for the democratic legitimation of administrative power in the modern welfare state—parliament for the formation of the government and for legislation, the head of the executive and the cabinet for the hierarchical political supervision of the administrative-technocratic sphere. Together they provided the necessary degree of connection between the burgeoning administrative apparatus and the "people" as a whole so that the postwar

---

106. "Allocution de M. Michel Debré, garde des Sceaux, ministre de la justice," before the *Conseil d'Etat*, August 27, 1958, in Comité national chargé de la publication des travaux préparatoires des institutions de la Ve République (1987), 3:265.

107. See Chapter 3, nn. 123–125 and accompanying text.

108. In Denmark, there has been a prevalence of minority governments (or, intermittently, weak coalition governments) since the 1950s. Nevertheless, "Cabinet responsibility" is "formally enshrined in the constitution," which "means that the Government must seek a working majority in Parliament and in its committees. If unable to work with a majority, it must resign." Fitzmaurice (1979), 205. For further details on the Danish system and its impact on European integration, see Chapter 5, nn. 114–133 and accompanying text.

administrative state could still be understood as democratic in some historically recognizable sense. This sharing of the function of democratic legitimation, in other words, proved critical to the reconciliation of administrative governance with older notions of "democratic consultation, scrutiny and control," as Aneurin Bevan put it in the 1950s.[109]

Courts as Commitment Mechanisms: Collective Democracy and Individual Rights

The judicial branch, however, would also play a key role in this process of reconciliation. Given the growing regulatory and interventionist ambitions of the welfare state, administrative agents came to enjoy a significant degree of effective independence from political oversight, as a consequence of organizational complexity if not also of formal legal right.[110] There was thus a rational-choice logic behind an increase in judicial review, because this agency autonomy undermined the capacity of hierarchical political control and thus created the need for an alternative kind of "commitment mechanism" to ensure compliance with legislative and constitutional requirements.[111] Judicial oversight served this purpose, even as the activities of the courts were normally rationalized in terms of the protection of separation of powers and individual rights, consistent with the constitutionalist ethos of the postwar period.

In its first decision applying Article 80(1) to a proposed legislative delegation, the German *Bundesverfassungsgericht*, for example, stated: "the Basic Law in this as in other respects reflects a decision in favor of a stricter separation of powers."[112] The Court expressed concern that parliament was abdicating its legislative role to the government through excessive or indeterminate delegation, something to be guarded against in light of the experience with the collapse of the Weimar Republic in 1932 and 1933. In the Court's view, it ultimately fell to judges to police the boundary between legislative and executive power in the postwar constitutional settlement. Under Articles 76 and 77 of Italy's postwar constitution, a similar policing function

---

109. Bevan (1953), 144.

110. See generally Braibant (1993).

111. See Lindseth (2005b), 683–85.

112. BVerfGE 1, 14 (60), translated in Currie (1993), 218.

was conferred on the Italian Constitutional Court.[113] And although the drafters of the French constitution of 1958 saw the balance between legislative and executive power differently from their German or Italian counterparts—hence the constitutionalization of the legislation-regulation distinction in the constitution of the Fifth Republic[114]—they charged the newly established Constitutional Council with essentially the same function, albeit with a different bias. According to Michel Debré, the Council was created as "a weapon" to ensure "against the deviation from the parliamentary regime" as it was constitutionally redefined in favor of the executive in 1958.[115]

The question of separation of powers in the postwar period, however, intersected in interesting ways with the question of individual rights. Under the so-called *Wesentlichkeitstheorie*, or "theory of essentialness," the West German *Bundesverfassungsgericht* sought to protect what it believed to be the "essential" functions of the parliament: the adoption of any legislative norms that might have an impact on constitutionally guaranteed rights or some other fundamental aspect of public policy. In a series of cases beginning in the late 1950s, the Court determined that the Basic Law, rather than authorizing delegation to the executive to adopt norms in these domains, required that the legislature, as the privileged representative of the nation as a whole, formulate the controlling rules in the enabling legislation itself (the so-called *Vorbehalt des Gesetzes*, or domain reserved to legislation).[116] The aim was to define those normative responsibilities that the legislature could not surrender to the executive, thereby ensuring the legislature's position in the postwar system of separation of powers. Similar interpretations were given to several provisions of the postwar Italian constitution (particularly those relating to criminal law), which were seen as creating an analogous *riserva di legge*.[117] And in 1953—five years prior to the establishment of the

---

113. See generally Volcansek (2000), chap. 3.

114. Lindseth (2004), 1405–06.

115. "Allocution de M. Michel Debré," in Comité national chargé de la publication des travaux préparatoires des institutions de la Ve République (1987), 3:260.

116. The leading decision was BVerfGE 7, 282 (302, 304), discussed in Currie (1993), 219; see also Lindseth (2004), 1395–96.

117. See, e.g., C. Cost., sent. n. 26/1966. Some areas, such as criminal law, are subject to an "absolute" *riserva di legge*, whereas other domains are subject to a "relative" requirement not unlike the American nondelegation doctrine, demanding only that national statutory law "indicate with sufficient specification the presuppositions, characters, content and limits" of the authority delegated outside the legislative sphere. Ibid.; for further elaboration, see Pittaro (1980), 479.

French Constitutional Council—the *Conseil d'Etat* (France's supreme administrative court) opined that "certain matters are reserved to legislation," in particular those relating to the rights and liberties that the preamble to the 1946 constitution now incorporated by reference.[118] This jurisprudential principle would persist beyond the establishment of the Fifth Republic in 1958.[119]

The connection in German, French, and Italian public law between the maintenance of the democratic system and the protection of individual rights is hardly surprising given the experience of these countries with dictatorship and the resulting violation of human rights on a mass scale prior to 1945.[120] German constitutional law, again unsurprisingly, was the most specific and demanding: The so-called "eternity clause" of Article 79(3) of the Basic Law quite explicitly drew the connection between protection of "human dignity" and democratic separation of powers. This article prohibited any amendment to either Article 1 or 20 of the Basic Law—the former recognizing the inviolability of human dignity and the enforceability of listed constitutional rights as positive law against all branches of government, and the latter establishing West Germany as "a democratic and social federal state" with all public authority emanating from the "people" through elections, with powers separated between the executive, legislative, and judicial branches.[121] The Basic Law further provided for the establishment of a Federal Constitutional Court to act as the ultimate judicial guarantor of these democratic structures and individual rights.

Even in an outlier country such as the United Kingdom, however, the judicial courts eventually became increasingly more protective of rights, particularly in the field of administrative law, thus suggesting the pervasiveness of the constitutionalist ethos throughout Western Europe in the postwar decades.[122] But this checking function, rather than merely focusing on rights, also served a legitimating function as well, smoothing the way for the dramatic increase in state intervention into society. In the interwar period, functionalists like Harold Laski had roundly criticized the British courts for

---

118. Commission de la fonction publique, avis. no. 60.497, 6 février 1953, in Gaudemet et al. (1997), 64; see also Lindseth (2004), 1402.

119. See the discussion of Articles 34 and 37 of the 1958 constitution in Lindseth (2004), 1405–06.

120. Cf. Moravcsik (2000c).

121. Basic Law, art. 79(3), for a discussion, see Lindseth (2004), 1388.

122. Lindseth (2005b), 683–84; Lindseth (2004), 1350, 1410–11.

hiding behind the formal categories of the common law to protect the prerogatives of private property and for being insufficiently attentive to the broader welfare purposes of interventionist legislation. Laski had called for a method of statutory interpretation "less analytical and more functional in character; it should seek to discover the effect of the legislative precept in action so as to give full weight to the social value it is intended to serve."[123] In the postwar decades British administrative law would eventually recognize the need for a balance between "private right and public advantage" and "fair play for the individual and efficiency of administration," as a special parliamentary committee would put it in 1957,[124] in a manner much more consistent with earlier functionalist demands.

✹ 2.3 Mediated Legitimacy and the Conditions for Constitutional Stability in the Two Postwar Eras

The process of constitutional settlement of the administrative state from the 1920s to the 1950s arguably paralleled the more general socioeconomic and sociopolitical stabilization throughout Western Europe over the same period. The American historian Charles Maier described this process in his seminal essay, "The Two Postwar Eras and the Conditions for Stability in Twentieth-Century Western Europe."[125] In that rightly famous piece, Maier asserted that "[b]oth postwar periods . . . formed part of a continuing effort at stabilization, a search that was sufficiently active and persistent (and rewarded finally with sufficient success) to comprise a major theme of twentieth-century Western European history."[126] According to Maier, the major sociopolitical achievement of this period was the incorporation of "a large enough segment of the working classes" into the political and economic order of modern capitalism. This achievement paralleled, Maier believed, "the major sociopolitical assignment" of the nineteenth century, which was "the incorporation of the middle classes and European bourgeoisie into the political community."[127]

---

123. Committee on Ministers' Powers (1932), Annex V, 137.

124. Committee on Administrative Tribunals and Enquiries (1957), 2.

125. Maier (1987).

126. Ibid., 161.

127. Ibid., 184.

Maier's analysis further suggested (albeit without significant elaboration) that this process of stabilization also had an important constitutional dimension: "The institutional device for the nineteenth century was parliamentary representation [while] the institutional foci for the twentieth-century achievement included trade unions, ambitious state economic agencies, and bureaucratized pressure groups."[128] Maier's work has had much to say about the political economy of corporatism in the twentieth century, but he has generally avoided any systematic analysis of the legal and constitutional underpinnings of the "ambitious state economic agencies" within which much of the corporatist negotiation at the core of his analysis was supposed to be taking place. The aim of this chapter has been to show that, just as Maier may fairly speak of the major sociopolitical achievement of twentieth-century Europe as being the incorporation of the interests of labor into the economic and political order of modern capitalism, the counterpart to this achievement in constitutional culture was the reconciliation of delegation and administrative governance with the principles of representative government developed over the course of the nineteenth century.

It was only after this constitutional reconciliation that Maier's "ambitious state economic agencies" could effectively operate in a newly stabilized and self-confident political and legal system, a process that undoubtedly reinforced the socioeconomic and sociopolitical stabilization that Maier has attempted to describe. In postwar administrative governance, all three historically constituted branches—the parliament, the government, and the courts—came to share responsibility for the democratic legitimation of administrative power in Western Europe. For Western Europeans struggling, as Alan Milward put it, for a "new form of governance" to meet the needs of the modern welfare state,[129] the legal and constitutional lesson of the prior decades was twofold: first, that executive and administrative power were essential to the welfare state's success; and second, that such power must be counterbalanced by parliamentary and judicial checks. The three traditional constitutional branches remained as separate *mechanisms of legitimation*—legislative, executive, and judicial—which allowed the postwar state to surmount what Carl Schmitt had asserted in the interwar period was "insurmountable."[130] This in turn allowed the diffusion and fragmentation of

---

128. Ibid.

129. See this chapter, n. 4 and accompanying text.

130. See Chapter 1, n. 111 and accompanying text.

normative power in the postwar administrative state to claim a democratic and constitutional legitimacy in a historically and culturally recognizable sense. Even as normative power diffused and fragmented outward, the branches of government that enjoyed constitutional legitimacy inherited from the past—whether democratic (i.e., executive or legislative) or judicial—became conduits through which the legitimacy of this power could be *mediated*. This sort of mediated legitimacy provided the foundation for a workable reconciliation of historical notions of representative government (which continued to regard the elected legislature as the cornerstone of self-rule) with the executive-technocratic reality of the administrative state after 1945.

THREE

Supranational Delegation and National Executive Leadership since the 1950s

THIS BRINGS US, then, to the inception of European integration in the 1950s. It would be within the national constitutional environment outlined in Chapter 2 that the advocates of Europe integration would attempt to translate a form of administrative governance, along with the basic elements of the postwar constitutional settlement, into workable supranational form. As we shall see in the chapters that follow, from its inception in the 1950s, European integration relied fairly heavily on mechanisms of mediated legitimacy—most importantly, on various forms of oversight by increasingly plebiscitary national executives—to establish the necessary connection between supranational regulation and historically constituted representative government on the national level. Eventually these mechanisms would also include judicial review by national high courts as well as scrutiny by national parliaments, all in the interest of furthering the integration project.

The process of European integration began, in a formal sense, with the Schuman Declaration of May 9, 1950. By its own stirring language, the primary purpose of integration was to render "war between France and Germany . . . not merely unthinkable, but materially impossible." This goal would be achieved by placing all "Franco-German production of coal and steel . . . under a common High Authority, within the framework of an organization open to the participation of the other countries of Europe." By "pooling" coal and steel production in this way, it was hoped that the participating countries would lay the "common foundations for economic development as a first step in the federation of Europe," something that would "change the destinies of those regions which have long been devoted to the manufacture of munitions of war, of which they have been the most constant victims."[1]

The Schuman Declaration should be taken at its word—its most important goal was to promote peace among historically warring states, most

---

1. Schuman Declaration (1950).

notably France and Germany. And yet, even as this overarching aim would provide impetus for integration well into the future, historians have discerned other purposes behind the Schuman Plan as well. For Germany, the aim was nothing less than normalization after the horrors of 1933 to 1945, by anchoring the Federal Republic firmly in the West. For France, the goals were arguably more material: "The Schuman Plan was called into existence to save the Monnet Plan," Alan Milward has argued.[2] He is referring here to France's postwar need—well understood by Jean Monnet, the Schuman Plan's principal author—to find some way of gaining better access to the German resources, the cornerstone of the postwar plan for French economic modernization.[3]

Milward's political-economic argument regarding Monnet's aims, however, could just as easily be restated in terms of postwar public law developments: The Schuman Plan set in motion the necessary *legal process* of supranational delegation to allow the public welfare goals of the Monnet Plan to be realized supranationally, as soon as it became clear that these goals could not be secured through purely national administrative means. The Treaty of Paris of 1951, which established the European Coal and Steel Community (ECSC), emerged as a kind of supranational counterpart to the national delegations effectuated, for example, by the law of August 17, 1948.[4] Just as Monnet's modernization plan for the postwar French economy ultimately required legal instruments delegating authority on the national level (the law of August 17, 1948), so too did Monnet's supranational plan for the modernization of the European coal and steel industries (as expressed in the Schuman Declaration).

The need for ongoing national executive legitimation of this supranationally delegated power was not, however, something that Monnet himself initially recognized as integral to integration's eventual success. At the outset of the negotiations of the Treaty of Paris, Monnet gambled on the willingness of national executives to acquiesce in a supranational system built primarily on technocratic autonomy, which he viewed as functionally necessary to overcoming the impediments of national sovereignty. This gamble, however,

---

2. Milward (1984), 475.

3. See also see Fransen (2001), 82 ("the limits that national boundaries posed on French modernization were directly related to Monnet's proposal for the [ECSC]"); Rittberger (2005), 77; Sheehan (2009), 156–58. In addition, see Monnet (1978), 277.

4. See Chapter 2, nn. 80–84 and accompanying text.

is one that Monnet would lose, not on functional grounds per se, but on political and cultural ones, as we shall see in the sections that follow.

Monnet was of course not so much a functionalist theorist as a functionalist man of action. Academic observers like David Mitrany, the person most responsible for importing interwar functionalism into international relations theory in the postwar period,[5] would in fact look to Monnet as a model of the sort of international actor driving the functionalist process forward.[6] So too would Mitrany's "neofunctionalist" heirs such as Ernst Haas and Leon Lindberg, who would undoubtedly be much more influential in the subsequent interpretation of the integration phenomenon.[7] All these men shared a profound faith in "the leading role of the technocrat" in advancing the process of international cooperation (Monnet being the chief exemplar).[8] The same would of course be true of Walter Hallstein, West Germany's principal negotiator on integration questions throughout the 1950s and later the first President of the European Commission after its establishment under the Treaty of Rome of 1957.

According to Robert Marjolin, who variously worked with Monnet and Hallstein in the early years of integration (and was a French member of the Hallstein Commission in the 1960s), both Monnet and Hallstein adhered to a set of understandings that would later be refined into a more positive theory of integration by the neofunctionalists.[9] Both believed, for example, that the process of integration, once commenced in certain limited domains, would necessarily "spill over" into other domains according to its own inexorable logic (*Sachlogik* in the language of Hallstein).[10] Both men also hoped that, over time, the existence of supranational institutions and processes would promote a shift in popular loyalties away from national institutions to the supranational level.[11] According to this logic, as Ernst Haas would later put it

---

5. See Chapter 2, nn. 37–40 and accompanying text.

6. See this chapter, n. 24.

7. The key neofunctionalist texts in the integration context were Haas (2004 [1958]) and Lindberg (1963).

8. Haas (2004 [1958]), xxv (Preface, 1968 ed.); see also ibid., xix.

9. Marjolin (1989), 265–66; see also Hallstein (1972). For more recent historical analysis of the influence of neofunctionalist theory on Hallstein and his staff, see White (2003); but see also the questionable conclusions of Warlouzet (2008), ascribing neofunctionalism to Marjolin and federalism to Hallstein. Although the latter is no doubt true, the former is doubtful.

10. Schönwald (2001), 164.

11. In addition to Haas (2004 [1958]), see, e.g., Haas (1963).

in 1968, national executives would be compelled to follow "the gradual, the indirect, the functional path toward political unity," giving "the economic technician . . . the shelter of the politicians' support."[12]

As this chapter will show, however, supranational technocratic autonomy did not emerge in quite the way that Monnet, Hallstein, or their theoretical allies like Haas had predicted. Rather, an unexpected historical contingency intervened, in the person of Charles de Gaulle, whose "[c]harisma and national self-assertion" were soon recognized as "the worst enemies of this [purportedly functionalist] process."[13] By the mid-1960s, as we shall see, de Gaulle was pursuing a policy of open hostility to what he called the "technocratic, stateless and irresponsible Areopagus,"[14] analogizing the European Commission of Hallstein to the supreme council of ancient Athens. De Gaulle's hostile attitude to Hallstein's pretensions for the Commission, along with the Commission's own overreaching (arguably born of faith in functionalist and neofunctionalist claims),[15] eventually led to the decisive political crisis in mid-1965, in the policy of French noncooperation known as the *chaise vide* (or "empty chair"), which we will explore in detail below.

This crisis would take six months to resolve, in the famous Luxembourg Compromise of January 1966. The historical consequence of the Luxembourg Compromise, while undoubtedly a turning point in the construction of national executive leadership in the integration process, was also ambiguous. On the one hand, it deeply undermined the autonomy of the technocratic Commission as a political actor, at least vis-à-vis the Council of Ministers, which cemented its leading role as the central political institution of integration.[16] On the other hand, as we also shall see, even as the Luxembourg Compromise consolidated national executive leadership, it also undermined the right of individual Member States to control the legislative process through a national right of veto (a by-product of unanimous voting). Contrary to the older, conventional view that the Luxembourg Compromise established a national right of veto, scholars today understand the crisis as merely

---

12. Haas (2004 [1958]), xx (Preface, 1968 ed.).

13. Ibid., xxvi (Preface, 1968 edition).

14. Referring to de Gaulle's famous September 9, 1965, press conference, in which he called the Commission an "*aréopage technocratique, apatride et irresponsable.*" See Ludlow (2006a), 73; see also Schönwald (2001), 157.

15. Schönwald (2001), 162–64; see generally White (2003); see also Ludlow (2006b), 84.

16. This thesis has been most persuasively advanced by N. Piers Ludlow in a series of contributions. See, e.g., Ludlow (2001), (2006a), and (2006b).

formalizing the emergent practice of consensus politics in the Council.[17] As such, the Luxembourg Compromise proved to be the definitive step in solidifying a system of shared *oversight* through a system of committees and other structures specifically designed to constrain the Commission's policymaking autonomy.

To understand the origins of these developments, however, one must again look back to the interwar period, as well as across the Atlantic—not just to interwar functionalism of the Anglo-American variety, but to the New Deal as a model for the likes of committed Europeanists like Jean Monnet.

3.1 A New Deal for Europe?: Technocratic Autonomy, the Treaty of Paris, and the Need for a National Executive Role

John Gillingham, an American historian of European integration, has stressed the New Deal as a background model for the integration program of Monnet in the 1950s: "The essential elements of [Monnet's] policy"—the creation of an explicitly supranational High Authority with an unprecedented degree of regulatory power capable of binding national governments—"underscore the importance of the New Deal inspiration."[18] Monnet wanted nothing less, in this view, than "a New Deal for French, and European, industry and planned to launch and land it with the help [of a] handful of like-minded men who wielded decisive power in the post war world."[19]

A reader might fairly ask whether this is merely an analytical conceit on Gillingham's part, an effort to deny the originality of the integration enterprise and impose on it an American model. There may be some truth in that assertion, but one should not allow it to obscure the acknowledged transatlantic inspirations, at least on the institutional level, for what became the European Communities. The only body mentioned in the Schuman Declaration was an independent technocratic body, the so-called High Authority,

---

17. See this chapter, nn. 158–160 and accompanying text. See also Baquero Cruz (2006) and Golub (2006); Ludlow (2001), 250–51. On the continuation of consensus politics up to the present, see Hayes-Renshaw and Wallace (2006), 310 ("Our data set on explicit voting in the Council over the past decade indicates the repeated preference of Council negotiators for reaching decisions by consensus on the 70% or so of decisions that are subject to a QMV legal base.").

18. Gillingham (1991), 232; see also Fransen (2001), 92.

19. Gillingham (1991), 368.

a name specifically intended to evoke the functional administrative agencies on the New Deal model (like the Tennessee Valley Authority).[20] Paul Reuter, a French law professor and member of Monnet's drafting team, would recall later how he "knew a bit of the American system," the principal virtue of which, in his view, was how it conferred on "independent men" the power to exercise a variety of functions, "be they 'quasi-judicial,' administrative, even economic.... When I proposed [this formula] to Monnet, using the American term 'Authority,' he accepted it immediately."[21]

The New Deal inspiration was, of course, more explicit in the earlier theoretical work of functionalist advocates like David Mitrany.[22] There is no evidence that Mitrany's functionalist theorizing influenced Jean Monnet directly[23] (if anything, the evidence points to Monnet as a model for Mitrany).[24] Nevertheless, the direction of influence is really beside the point. From an institutional standpoint, what the New Deal offered to both men was a seeming

---

20. Cohen and Madsen (2007), 186.

21. Reuter (1979 [1977]), 2:67. See also Monnet (1978), 296–97; Lynch (1988), 120, citing 81 AJ 152, Elaboration de la proposition du 9 mai 1950 ("It was Paul Reuter who [proposed] the form of a supranational High Authority whose decisions would be binding on governments.").

22. See Chapter 2, nn. 37–40 and accompanying text; see also Majone (2001a), 258–59.

23. Monnet does not mention Mitrany in his memoirs. See Monnet (1978). Nor do Jean Monnet's two major biographers, Duchêne (1994), and Roussel (1996).

24. Monnet was in fact a leading exemplar of a type of international cooperation, dating back to interallied supply and transport boards during World War I, which Mitrany would later come to characterize as "functionalist" in a series of lectures at Yale in 1933. See Mitrany (1933). During the interwar period, Mitrany became associated with several international actors and theorists who became leading proponents of this sort of cooperation, including Leonard S. Woolf, G. D. H. Cole, and in particular Arthur Salter, a British economist who had worked extensively with Monnet on these boards both during World War I and II, as well as at the League of Nations. See Dubin (1983), 493. These boards were charged with allocating shipping tonnage and other resources among the allies in the interest of the overall war effort. Monnet reportedly advocated a proposal (which was ultimately rejected) to have the boards evolve into "'an international council ... with full authority (*pleins pouvoirs*) to direct a general pool of tonnage'"—that is, a fully autonomous supranational regulatory body. "Conférence des Alliés, 1. Section des Importations et des transports maritimes. Décisions prises au cours des séances de Commission des 29, 30 Novembre et 1 Décembre 1917," 3 Dec. 1917, F12/7802, AN, as quoted and translated in Fransen (2001), 24; see also Monnet (1978), 66–69. The notion of *pleins pouvoirs* (or "full authority") was a term of art in interwar French public law to refer to fully autonomous normative power. See Lindseth (2004), 1377–81. But see Duchêne (1994), 38 ("there was no question of international authority over governments"). For Monnet's similar efforts at the outset of World War II, see Fransen (2001), 72–74; see also Gillingham (1991), 369 (noting that the High Authority "was meant to be run as Monnet imagined the wartime boards of American industry had been").

model of technocratic governance freed from legal limitations inherited from the past ("separation of powers" in the American case, "national sovereignty" in the case of European integration). The "whole trend of modern government," according to Mitrany, was toward policies and institutions "along the lines of specific ends and needs, and according to the conditions of their time and place, in lieu of the traditional organization on the basis of a set constitutional division of jurisdiction of rights and powers." The emergence of "specific administrative agencies" of the New Deal-type was, according to this functionalist view, "the peculiar trait and indeed the foundation of modern government," whose purpose and power was being "determined less by constitutional norms than by practical requirements." Mitrany thus called for harnessing this functionalist dynamic in service of peaceful change among states, allowing New Deal-type administrative governance to "do internationally what it does nationally"[25]—a call that Monnet would arguably heed seven years later.

There was, however, a strong measure of irony in the inspiration drawn from the New Deal model, at least insofar as supranational technocratic autonomy was concerned, functionally demanded or otherwise.[26] Although New Dealers had themselves understood Roosevelt's program of the 1930s, both in terms of policy and institutional design, to be fundamentally driven by functional demands,[27] they were also acutely aware of the importance that Roosevelt himself had placed on hierarchical political direction, with the President at the summit of the expanding regulatory apparatus. Regardless of what Roosevelt thought of fostering administrative independence as a practical matter, he was clearly hostile to it as a matter of law: Presidential control was critical to his vision of administrative politics, and he pursued that goal with consistency.[28] If advocates of integration paid more heed to this aspect of the American experience in the 1930s, they might have been more prepared for the assertions of national executive leadership that were to come in the process of integration from the 1950s onward.

---

25. Mitrany (1946 [1943]); quotations in this paragraph come from 27, 28, and 34.

26. Certainly Hallstein believed in the functional necessity of supranational autonomy. See Schönwald (2001), 162–64.

27. See, e.g., Chapter 2, n. 35 and accompanying text.

28. See, e.g., Humphrey's Executor v. United States, 295 U.S. 602 (1935). On this and other bases, American legal conservatives today cite Roosevelt as an advocate of the "unitary executive" theory *avant la lettre*. See Calabresi and Yoo (2008), chap. 32.

Reuter himself would later acknowledge how the proposal for a High Authority in the Schuman Declaration stood "in a disquieting solitude."[29] The High Authority's independence "was in some sense a desperate solution," because, as he put it, there was "neither a European parliament, nor government, nor people" on which to build an integrated polity or market (what today we would see as the institutional expression of the "no *demos*" problem). Reuter argued that the only way "to build Europe without Europeans" was "to address ourselves to independent personalities,"[30] whose decisions would then be binding on national governments. Thus, in the original French proposal the High Authority was to serve, in effect, as a kind of autonomous regulatory agency of an extraordinarily novel type, one that possessed normative power delegated from national parliaments but which would otherwise be freed from having its decisions legitimized by subsequent national oversight (notably through the national executive).[31]

In this sense, what the Schuman Plan was seeking constituted a decisive break with administrative governance on the national level in Western Europe.[32] Indeed, the original insistence of Monnet on an independent, supranational regulatory authority was among the major reasons for the British government's refusal to pursue the negotiations on the terms proposed by the French government in May 1950.[33] The United Kingdom's refusal to participate, however, would prove ironic in many respects. British qualms over supranationalism in the ECSC were in fact shared not only by elements within the French government itself,[34] but also, more importantly, by the

---

29. Reuter (1953), 51.

30. Ibid., 51-52; see also Reuter (1979 [1977]), 67.

31. Cf. Vignes (1956).

32. According to Rittberger, "given the lack of any prior experience, there was no 'blueprint' as to who this new supranational institution should be accountable to." Rittberger (2005), 78. Nevertheless, Monnet had something of a track record in seeking this kind of supranational regulatory autonomy. During World War I, he attempted to gain supranational *pleins pouvoirs* for interallied supply boards, on which he sat as France's representative. See this chapter, n. 24.

33. One historian has referred to "a fundamental clash of assumptions between the British and the French," the former not opposed to a coal and steel community in principle but favoring only one based "on the principle of inter-governmental cooperation," whereas the later sought a "'supra-national' authority, the establishment of which would involve a surrender of sovereignty by member states." Bullen (1988), 206. See also Bullen (1989), 326 (referring to one of the features of British policy as "the refusal to relinquish the sovereign authority of Parliament to supranational bodies"); as well as Milward (2002), chap. 3.

34. See Lynch (1988), 123 (describing the views of the French finance minister, Petsche); Milward (2002), 76 (describing views of Petsche as well as those of Bidault (former foreign

Benelux governments, led by the Dutch.[35] Although the Dutch agreed to join the negotiations, they worked tirelessly—and with some success, as it turned out—to transform the ECSC into something much closer to the sort of intergovernmental body that Britain would have preferred.[36] Meeting in early June 1950, the Benelux countries agreed on a negotiating position that would accept the establishment of a "board" (the administrative terminology is telling[37]) comprised of personalities designated by the national governments, serving for a sufficiently lengthy period of time to ensure their independence as a practical matter.[38] Attached to the board would be a body composed of producer, labor, and consumer groups—what the treaty would call the "Consultative Committee"—which would be largely powerless but would nevertheless symbolize the desire to institutionalize some form of social interest representation at the Community level.[39] Perhaps most importantly, the Benelux countries agreed that together they would press for the establishment of both a Council of Ministers to oversee the High Authority's activities in a political sense, as well as a Court of Justice to oversee its activities in a legal or judicial sense.[40]

Consequently, the Benelux position from the outset contrasted sharply with the views of the French delegation (under Monnet's leadership), which insisted on the total institutional independence of the High Authority. France was

---

minister) and Mayer (justice minister)); see also Parsons (2003), 61 (similarly negative views held by Buron (Economic Affairs), Louvel (Industry and Trade), and Bacon (Labor)).

35. Rittberger (2005), 78–79.

36. According to Bullen, the adoption of the so-called "Dutch formula" in fact "was considered as raising the possibility of Britain belatedly joining the negotiations on the basis that further dilutions of supra-nationalism would be possible." Bullen (1988), 208; but see Milward (2002), 64, quoting Roger Stevens, head of Economic Relations Department, to Ernest Bevin: "'[The Dutch formula] is still far removed from any concept which Ministers would be prepared to accept'"; see also Milward (2002), 73, criticizing Dell (1995).

37. Advocates of the ECSC would use a similar administrative terminology in their description of the High Authority. See Philip (1951), 14 ("The principal function of this international board of experts will be to supervise prices.").

38. The story of the institutional negotiations over the Treaty of Paris has been extensively described elsewhere and need only be summarized here. The following discussion is based on the accounts set forth in Küsters (1988) and Spierenburg and Poidevin (1993), 9–24 (Spierenburg led the Dutch delegation in the negotiations). These accounts are broadly in accord with Monnet (1978), 331–33, and Reuter (1953), 52–53, as well as Milward (1984), 409.

39. Treaty of Paris, arts. 18–19. This, too, built on similar initiatives at the national level. See Lindseth (2004), 1412–13.

40. See also Rittberger (2005), 97.

only willing to contemplate the establishment of a quasi-parliamentary assembly composed of representatives from national parliaments, which would have no legislative function in the traditional sense. Rather, consistent with shifting views on the proper role of legislatures in the modern administrative state,[41] the Assembly would be able to "control" the High Authority (in the French sense of the verb *contrôler,* meaning to check or to monitor, not the English sense of specific policy direction). This would be accomplished through a right of censure by a supermajority of two-thirds, after the High Authority's issuance of its annual report.[42] This form of limited parliamentary supervision was all that Monnet included in the initial draft treaty presented to the other participating states as the sole basis for further negotiations.[43]

A compromise on institutional questions subsequently emerged in the summer of 1950 that aggregated the various elements of the Benelux and the French positions. On the one hand, several leading provisions of the Treaty of Paris of 1951 would seem to reflect the French position that the sine qua non of supranationalism was the autonomy of the High Authority from national control.[44] Article 9 provided that the members of the High Authority were to "exercise their functions in complete independence, in the general interest of the Community;" they were neither to "solicit nor accept instructions from any government or any organization."[45] Not only did Article 9 require members of the High Authority to "abstain from all conduct incompatible with the supranational character of their functions," it added that each Member State was obligated "to respect this supranational character and not to seek to influence the members of the High Authority in the execution of their duties."

---

41. See, e.g., Chapter 2, n. 89 and accompanying text.

42. Rittberger (2005), 98–99. This constituted a break as well from the model of consultative "talking shop" parliamentary assemblies in such postwar bodies as Council of Europe or the Western European Union (WEU). See ibid., 1–2 and 80.

43. Küsters (1988), 79; Spierenburg and Poidevin (1993), 16–17. Milward argues, based on notes of a conversation between British officials and members of the Belgian delegation, that "[h]ad Belgium understood in advance the nature and contents of the working document which was to be drawn up by Monnet and his associates as the sole initial basis for negotiations, it would 'in all probability' have taken the same attitude as the United Kingdom and refused to negotiate from that basis." Milward (2000 [1992]), 64.

44. Schuman (1953a), 7.

45. Treaty of Paris, art. 9. For English quotations of the original Treaty of Paris, this study uses the translation published by the High Authority of the ECSC. See Treaty Establishing the European Coal and Steel Community (1951).

On the other hand, as Robert Schuman would himself later recognize, one could not speak of the supranational independence of the High Authority under Article 9 without noting that it was exercised only "within the limits of the Treaty."[46] These limits were not merely substantive (the High Authority's regulatory powers in principle extended only to the coal and steel industries and not to the general economy). They were also organizational and procedural, reflecting significant concessions to the Benelux position. The most important concession involved the High Authority's relationship with the "Special Council of Ministers," or simply the "Council," the body composed of government ministers (i.e., representatives of national executives at the supranational level), whose establishment Monnet originally opposed.[47]

Formally speaking, under the terms of Article 26 of the Treaty of Paris, the Council of Ministers was not to exercise any oversight or control function over the High Authority at all—this was, in principal, left to the parliamentary Assembly. Rather, according to Article 26, the Council existed simply to "harmonis[e] the action of the High Authority and that of the Governments, which are responsible for the general economic policies of their countries." Nevertheless, the more specific provisions of the treaty specified a whole range of domains in which the High Authority could not act without first consulting with, or, more importantly, gaining the agreement of, the Council of Ministers.[48] Perhaps most importantly, Article 95 of the Treaty of Paris provided that only the Council, acting by unanimity, could authorize the High Authority to act in "cases not provided for in this Treaty" but which nevertheless appeared necessary to fulfill the goals of the common market.[49]

---

46. Schuman (1953a), 7.

47. See this chapter, nn. 36–43 and accompanying text and nn. 57–65 and accompanying text.

48. For an exhaustive analysis, see Prieur (1962), 73–81. For example, only the Council in the first instance, acting by unanimity, could establish consumption and allocation restrictions in times of serious shortages in production of coal, steel or related products (Treaty of Paris, art. 59 (2)) and only where the Council could not decide did the High Authority gain the power to make these allocations (art. 59 (3)). For other examples, see art. 54 (unanimity required to authorize "works or installations" to increase production or lower production costs); art. 50(2) (two-thirds majority required to raise the 1-percent levy on the production of coal and steel). And in the area of noncompliance by a Member State with its obligations under the treaty, only the Council, acting by a two-thirds majority, could authorize the High Authority to impose sanctions on the recalcitrant state. Treaty of Paris, art. 88.

49. Treaty of Paris, art. 95.

The formal reservation of these so-called spillover issues ran directly contrary to neofunctionalist theory in the 1950s.[50] Unlike functionalists, neofunctionalists openly admitted that at least the initial decision to delegate was the by-product of a highly political rather than merely functional/technical calculation of "need."[51] But like the functionalists, neofunctionalists still saw the driving force behind any *subsequent* expansion of the supranational regulatory competences to be the purportedly neutral imperatives of functional problem-solving (the *spillover* effect). The scope of spillover was supposed to be determined by supranational technocrats, operating in relative autonomy from political control by national executives, and in alliance with subnational economic interests committed to expanding integration. Article 95 of the Treaty of Paris, by contrast, vested the power to control spillover directly in the national executives, sitting in the Council of Ministers.

It is true that many of the more onerous voting requirements that the treaty imposed, particularly several requiring unanimity in the Council, were in fact designed to inhibit Member State control and promote the High Authority's independence in the pursuit of the treaty's common market goals in the areas of coal and steel.[52] And in the vast majority of cases the Council's powers were limited to simple majority authorizations or mere consultations.[53] The latter included the High Authority's powers in such key areas as fixing maximum or minimum prices;[54] or the suspension of any special assistance or subsidies to, as well as charges on, domestic coal and steel enterprises by national governments.[55]

Nevertheless, even if the limitation of Council involvement to mere consultation seemed to restrict its supervisory powers, the very existence of the Council constituted a major deviation from a purist understanding of supranational autonomy as expressed in Article 9. One need only look to the range

---

50. Most importantly, Haas (2004 [1958]).

51. Haas (1964), chaps.1–2.

52. For example, where the treaty granted the High Authority a measure of discretion to take action in a particular field (for example to establish a system of production quotas in the case of a decline in demand (Article 58 (1)), or to declare a serious shortage which would give rise to the imposition of consumption or allocation controls by the Council, Article 59 (1)), the treaty sometimes allowed the Council to override the High Authority refusal to take action, but only by a unanimous vote. See also Article 61, regarding the establishment of maximum or minimum prices.

53. See Prieur (1962), 79–80.

54. Treaty of Paris, arts. 60–61.

55. Convention on the Transitional Provisions, sec. 11.

of obligations on the part of the High Authority to consult with and/or obtain the agreement of the Council of Ministers[56] to recognize that the general statement contained in Article 9—that the members of the High Authority were neither to "solicit nor accept instructions from any government or any organization"—was not, in fact, a blanket or unqualified assertion of the complete normative autonomy of the High Authority.

Thus, in the process of institutional compromise, it was the French negotiating team (led by Monnet) that clearly made the largest concessions on the question of the High Authority's autonomy. The Benelux countries did, however, offer Monnet a degree of cover: They agreed to the High Authority's supranational independence *in form*—hence the language of Articles 9 and 26—but only with the understanding that, as Monnet put it in early July 1950, "the concrete translation of this principle can nevertheless be modified, and without doubt improved."[57] The French, German, and Italian delegations could, based on Article 26, still regard the Council simply as a kind of liaison body between the High Authority and national governments.[58] Nevertheless, the panoply of treaty requirements for the High Authority to consult with and/or obtain the agreement of the Council reflected the success of the Benelux countries in subjecting the High Authority to some form of national executive influence.[59]

One historian, Hanns Jürgen Küsters, has argued that the negotiations over institutional questions in the summer of 1950 involved a fundamental conflict concerning the very nature of supranationalism in the ECSC, a conflict centering around the source of the High Authority's powers and, therefore, the proper means for its supervision.[60] On the one side, there was Monnet, who asserted that the source of the High Authority's power were the national parliaments, the representatives of national sovereignty. From this

---

56. See this chapter, n. 48.

57. Spierenburg and Poidevin (1993), 20, citing "Réunion du Comité des chefs de délégation sur les questions institutionnelles 5 juillet" (Fondation Jean Monnet); see also Monnet (1978), 331–33.

58. See this chapter, nn. 47–48 and accompanying text. Nongovernmental advocates of the ECSC took essentially the same view. André Philip, in a pamphlet supporting the Schuman Plan put out by the European Movement, argued that the existence of the Council "does not affect in any way the general structure of the organisation, nor does it posses any power of control over the Authority itself, which remains a truly supranational authority, a federal cabinet for coal and steel." See Philip (1951), 17.

59. See this chapter, n. 48.

60. Küsters (1988), 83; see also Spierenburg and Poidevin (1993), 20.

perspective, the High Authority's legitimacy flowed from the parliamentary transfer of sovereign authority itself, and the only appropriate oversight should be by the Assembly composed of national parliamentary representatives; no subsequent national executive oversight was necessary or appropriate. On the other side, there were the Benelux countries, which asserted that national governments were the source of the High Authority's power because it operated under a mandate derived from a treaty concluded by the governments. From this perspective, continuing governmental oversight (indeed, even in some instances, actual control) was in fact both warranted and desirable.

According to the theory advanced in this study, however, these apparently conflicting positions are largely compatible. What France and the Benelux countries were emphasizing were different elements of administrative legitimation at the heart of the postwar constitutional settlement.[61] In the aftermath of World War II, the legitimacy of administrative action depended, in the first instance, on a lawful legislative enactment—a *loi-cadre*, if you will. In the case of the ECSC, that *loi-cadre* took the form of a treaty (a *traité-cadre* as Giandomenico Majone puts it),[62] a novel form of enabling legislation to be sure, but one which had the same legal effect as traditional forms of enabling legislation on the national level: the delegation of regulatory power. The fact that this enabling legislation—the treaty—was drafted by governmental and technocratic representatives for subsequent parliamentary approval is hardly surprising: The same officials played a similarly predominant role in legislative drafting on the national level in the postwar decades.[63] Just as on the national level, moreover, although parliamentary approval was necessary in the first instance to effect the delegation under the "legislation," once that delegation occurred, the focus of legitimation shifted to the national executive, through its hierarchical political responsibility for the administrative sphere (only now that sphere extended outside the confines of the nation-state).

Ultimately the Benelux countries prevailed upon Monnet to recognize that the success of the ECSC negotiations depended on the creation of a Council of Ministers to oversee (and sometimes even control, in the case of

---

61. Cf. Rittberger (2005), 105–107.

62. Majone (2005), 7.

63. See the quotation from Chapus (1953), 1003, Chapter 2, n. 91 and accompanying text ("enabling acts are merely the recognition *de jure* . . . . of [the] legislative role of the government").

spillover issues)[64] any High Authority actions that might implicate a national government's domestic political responsibility.[65] As a matter of public law, however, what national executives really achieved with the Council of Ministers was in many respects an extension of *their own* domestic policy-making autonomy relative to parliamentary and interest group opposition in the administrative state. As Paul Reuter stressed in his 1953 treatise on the ECSC, the effort to free norm production from such national level parliamentary interference was one of the central aims of supranational delegation. According to Reuter, the Council of Ministers was not a traditional diplomatic conference that reached agreements that were then subject to domestic constitutional procedures, notably subsequent parliamentary approval, in order to gain legal effect. Rather, the Council was "an organ of the Community to which the States [read: 'national parliaments'] have transferred certain competences."[66] This transfer further meant, in Reuter's estimation, that even where the Council was to act by unanimity (for example, regarding spillover issues under Article 95), the normative action had been "withdrawn from the competence of the Member States [again, read: 'national parliaments'] and their constitutional rules [would] no longer apply."[67]

The spillover provision in Article 95 had the effect of again further expanding the domestic policymaking autonomy of national executives. National governments could now unanimously agree among themselves, without having to go back to their national parliaments to gain the ratification of a treaty amendment, in order to effectively stretch the competence of the High Authority to regulatory questions related to, but outside of, the area of coal and steel.[68] Moreover, what this signified, as a matter of Community norm production and public law, was the complete identification of the national regulatory interest with the policy goals defined by the national executive, unencumbered by other forms domestic legal or constitutional

---

64. See this chapter, n. 49 and accompanying text.

65. Spierenburg and Poidevin (1993), 20; see also Rittberger (2005), 81.

66. Reuter (1953), 63.

67. Ibid.

68. The equivalent of art. 95 in the Treaty of Rome (art. 235) would be exploited in precisely this manner to expand the competence of the EEC in the 1970s and 1980s. See Chapter 4, nn. 82–84 and accompanying text. However, this use of art. 235 would also be regarded as constitutionally problematic by national courts. See, e.g., the German attitude in the so-called Maastricht Decision (Chapter 4, n. 183 and accompanying text), as well as that of the Danish Supreme Court (Chapter 4, n. 184).

control.[69] This, of course, was a central characteristic of administrative governance as it had emerged on the national level in the postwar decades.[70]

What the ECSC negotiations also perhaps proved was the fundamental impossibility of separating the purportedly *technical* from the *political*.[71] The basic premise of the Benelux call for the establishment of a Council of Ministers was that technical decision-making at the Community level would inevitably impinge on political questions of values or the allocation of scarce resources, for which political oversight would be necessary.[72] Organizational questions were thus intimately bound up with the intergovernmental effort "to determine as far as possible the extent and direction of national gain and loss before the High Authority began to function."[73] Given the legal framework within which the High Authority was supposed to operate, it is hardly surprising, as Alan Milward concluded from his examination of the archival evidence, that it did not subsequently act "as a neutral functional regulator as [the neofunctionalists] claimed."[74] Despite the language in Articles 9 and 26 on the relationship between the High Authority and the Council of Ministers, in its details the treaty in fact established a highly institutionalized process of essentially intergovernmental politics (of which the High Authority's power to make regulatory initiatives was simply one element). The organs of the ECSC arguably came into existence in the legal form they did "precisely

---

69. As we shall see in Chapter 5, none of the original six Member States established effective mechanisms of the national parliamentary scrutiny over supranational delegation in the 1950s or 1960s. The first Member States that would establish such mechanisms (indeed, from the moment of their accession) would be Denmark and the United Kingdom in 1973. Although quite different in their method of scrutiny and the stringency of direct control, the Danish and British models of parliamentary scrutiny would come to serve as models of all future entrants, as well as for the original six Member States, which would eventually dramatically upgrade their scrutiny mechanisms in the 1980s and 1990s.

70. See Chapter 2, nn. 101–103 and accompanying text.

71. Monnet struggled to exclude purportedly technical questions from the early phase of the ECSC negotiations, believing these were better left until a later stage, and perhaps even until after the treaty itself had been ratified, when the High Authority could appropriately take them up. See Spierenburg and Poidevin (1993), 17. Volker Berghahn reports that, "[w]hen Monnet saw Adenauer on 23 May 1950 for preliminary talks in the capital of the Federal Republic, he advised the chancellor 'not to send technical experts, if possible, but [to select] as delegates personalities who thought in European terms and who had a wide economic horizon to prevent that the Schuman Plan was filibustered (*zerredet*) with problems of a technical kind.'" Berghahn (1986), 121.

72. Spierenburg and Poidevin (1993), 20; Rittberger (2005), 96.

73. Milward (1984), 498; Rittberger (2005), 96, 102–103.

74. Milward (2000 [1992]), 15; see also Alter and Steinberg (2007).

because the issues involved could not be reduced to the merely functional level."[75]

The difficult task of reconciling political rather than merely technical differences—that is, those involving the distribution of costs and benefits among the negotiating countries—required a different kind of legal and institutional framework. In this sort of framework, national executives would be compelled to place their weight, and their legitimacy, behind the seemingly technical deals that were struck over economic substance. As we shall see in the next section, this role for national executives would become even more pronounced with the establishment of the European Economic Community under the Treaty of Rome in 1957.

3.2 Toward National Executive Control?: Negotiating the Treaty of Rome

The functionalist advocates of integration in the 1950s no doubt underestimated the genuinely political character of the ECSC's regulatory activities and, therefore, the need for national governments to institute mechanisms of political supervision through the Council of Ministers. Nevertheless, the emphasis the functionalists placed on the technical character of the Community problem-solving corresponded to reality in at least one important sense: In the coal and steel context, precisely because it was broadly *perceived* to involve regulatory issues of a largely technical or functional nature, supranational delegation was less *politically* problematic, requiring little or no parliamentary involvement.[76] Although knowledgeable insiders recognized otherwise—as the detailed provisions of the Treaty of Paris suggested—this seemingly technical character of coal and steel regulation helped to neutralize political opposition to the adoption of the Treaty of Paris when it was presented to national parliaments.[77]

---

75. Milward (2000 [1992]), 15.

76. On the growing distinction between the technical and the political in the allocation of authority between governments and parliaments in the postwar period, see Chapter 2, nn. 80–92 and 98–99 and accompanying text. Also telling was the fact that none of the national parliaments established any form of effective scrutiny procedures after the adoption of the Rome treaties. See Chapter 5, nn. 68–79 and accompanying text.

77. In the debate over the Treaty of Paris in the French National Assembly, for example, a Gaullist deputy complained that French sovereignty was being "abandon[ed] . . . to a stateless and uncontrolled technocracy." Jacques Soustelle, *J.O., Débats parlementaires*,

The same sort of stratagem was unavailable, of course, once the process of European integration shifted from such a narrow and seemingly technical realm to one that went to the very heart of the nation-state's traditional political responsibilities: national defense and control of the armed forces. No matter how well-intentioned a response to the difficult question of German rearmament, the French proposal for a European Defense Community (EDC) in the fall of 1950, culminating in the signing of the proposed EDC Treaty in May 1952, quickly revealed the limits of political support for supranational delegation. No place was this more true than in France itself. The long domestic political agony for the EDC Treaty, ending only with its definitive rejection by the French National Assembly in August 1954, would cast a shadow over European integration for the remainder of the decade. More importantly, this debacle suggested that the more overtly political the policy domain (such as defense), the greater the political demands for direct control by strongly legitimated national leaders.[78] The supranational "Commissariat" (the EDC's version of the High Authority), as the French sociologist Raymond Aron would note a few years later, depended "neither on an elected Assembly nor on an organized State" and would represent a political community of a tenuous "historical or moral reality."[79] Given the highly political nature of national defense, the measure of technocratic autonomy that the High Authority enjoyed at the head of the ECSC—and perhaps even more importantly, the *supranational* character of that technocratic autonomy—could not be transferred to the EDC Commissariat, even one operating under the supervision of a Council of Ministers, without giving rise to profound political misgivings at the national level.

---

assemblée nationale, Dec. 6, 1951, p. 8881. However, a center-right supporter of the ECSC could offer the more comforting argument that the High Authority was "merely the organ for the administration of common rules," with delegated normative powers subject to the detailed and precise terms of the treaty. Alfred Coste-Floret, *J.O., debats parlementaires, assemblée nationale*, Dec. 6, 1951, p. 8854. Outside of those strictly delimited and largely technical realms, Coste-Floret implied, national governments and parliaments retained the full prerogatives of sovereignty. For a discussion of the parliamentary debates, see Mason (1955), 22–23.

78. In his otherwise insightful discussion of the EDC debate in France, Parsons does not explore how the nature of the EDC made supranational delegation so much more controversial as a matter of principle, which in turn made it impossible to forge a political majority supportive of extending the community model to defense. See generally Parsons (2003), chap. 2.

79. Aron (1956), 4–5.

The French National Assembly's rejection of the EDC Treaty in August 1954 would have consequences not merely for the process of European integration in the 1950s but also for the future of the French Fourth Republic as it limped toward its demise in 1958. On the national front, the EDC question revealed "the conflicts and stalemates of French domestic politics" that would ultimately undermine France's *régime d'assemblée* completely by 1958.[80] The precariousness of the governing majorities in 1953,[81] which relied on the votes of both anti-EDC Gaullists and those of the pro-EDC center-right, compelled a succession of French governments to put off any final political decision over the fate of the treaty.[82] Thus, the French national executive was effectively compelled to follow the converse of Pierre Mendès France's famous dictum—to govern was decidedly *not* to choose.[83] Indeed, it was only in the domestic arena, and only in the seemingly more technical areas of economic policy, that the center-right governing majorities in France at the time were able to agree on forms of delegation that would enable credible policymaking to occur at all.[84]

On the supranational front, the rejection of the EDC by the French National Assembly in 1954 would directly influence both the substantive scope and institutional form of the so-called relaunch of European integration in the mid-1950s. The term "relaunch" is admittedly subject to some controversy ("myth," Alan Milward has derisively called it, "nurtured by federalists and other advocates of political unification as an end in itself").[85]

---

80. Rioux (1987), 201.

81. Perhaps most emblematic of the problem was the power vacuum from May 21, 1953, when the Mayer government resigned, until June 26, 1953, the date of Laniel's investiture, when France was left without a government due to a lack of a coherent majority in the National Assembly.

82. According to Jean-Pierre Rioux: "The simple fact is that whereas the majorities favourable to the EDC—and who made governments—were increasingly fragile, their opponents— who brought down governments—remained as determined and active as ever. Thus a government's only hope of survival lay in shelving the EDC treaty." Rioux (1987), 204.

83. Perhaps not surprisingly it was a Mendès France government that would allow the treaty to come to a vote in August 1954.

84. See Chapter 2, nn. 80–84 and accompanying text; see also Lindseth (2004), 1398–1402.

85. Milward (2000 [1992]), 119. The problem with the label is that it implicitly gives too much credit to the efforts of Jean Monnet and his close collaborator, Paul-Henri Spaak, the Belgian foreign minister, and too little to the persistence of the Dutch government, and more specifically its foreign minister, Johan Willem Beyen. From the early 1950s onward, Beyen and the Dutch government had been pursuing the goal of what would become the cornerstone of the future EEC: the customs union among the Member States of the ECSC. See generally ibid., chap. 4. The Dutch government had in fact made the inclusion of the

Despite Milward's economically oriented dismissal of the notion, the term still retains an important measure of validity on the level of institutional politics. The Treaty of Rome of 1957 would retain the quadripartite organizational form of the ECSC (a national executive Council of Ministers, a supranational technocratic body now called the "European Commission," a parliamentary Assembly, and a Court of Justice).[86] But there would also be one major substantive difference between the institutional structures of the new European Economic Community (EEC) and the old ECSC: The legal balance of power in the EEC would shift formally and decisively toward the Council of Ministers, which gained the final say in most aspects of legislative norm production at the Community level.

The success of the negotiations leading to the Treaty of Rome thus would turn not merely on its economic merits, as Milward emphasizes, but also on the conscious effort on the part of key political actors to manage the entire institutional question in the direction of national executive control and strictly limited supranational technocratic autonomy. Throughout this process, the notion of supranationalism as a federal constitutionalist ideal would be studiously avoided,[87] in favor of a supranationalism of a more functional, instrumental character. It would be a supranationalism that accepted a measure of autonomous authority at the Community level but only to police the compliance of Member States with their agreements over economic substance. Otherwise, the supranationalism of the new EEC was designed to preserve the freedom of action of national executives that had been so strenuously achieved at the national level in the constitutional stabilization of administrative governance in the postwar decades. In this sense, the Member States recognized that certain commitment institutions—the European Commission, the Court of Justice—would be instrumentally necessary, not as the foundation of a future federal Europe, but as guarantors of

---

customs union the price of Dutch adherence to the EDC, and when that project died in 1954, the Dutch continued to press—successfully, as it turned out—for its realization on its own terms. In other words, European federalists such as Monnet and Spaak less *relaunched* the process of European integration in the mid-1950s than they *retreated* to the substantive economic terrain of the customs union, already well prepared by the Dutch.

86. The Treaty of Rome also established an "Economic and Social Committee," akin to the ECSC's Consultative Committee, for the representation "of various categories of economic and social activity." Treaty of Rome, art. 193. The committee was, like its ECSC counterpart, largely powerless, enjoying at best only the right to be consulted on certain questions.

87. Gillingham (2003), 44 and 49, quoting Marjolin (1989).

the narrowly defined policy goals of economic and market integration set forth in the Treaty of Rome.

This reliance on a functionalist, instrumental supranationalism (cloaked as much as possible in the guise of political intergovernmentalism) manifested itself in the earliest stages of the relaunch. In the joint memorandum prepared by the Benelux governments calling for the establishment of a customs union (circulated in advance of the conference of ECSC foreign ministers in June 1955 in Messina, Italy), no mention was made of the idea of supranationalism or of a High Authority. Rather, the memorandum spoke only of "'common authorities'" or an "'organism,'" with the remaining institutional questions to be left to the intergovernmental conference responsible for drafting the treaty.[88] The purpose of such vagueness was to avoid "awaken[ing] the strong anti-supranational sentiments in France and elsewhere," as well as to facilitate "the adherence of the other governments to the basic idea of organizing a conference on the issues raised by the Benelux."[89]

At the Messina meeting itself, rather than a decision in favor of an intergovernmental conference directly, the ECSC foreign ministers decided first to refer the Benelux proposal to an ad hoc interministerial committee of high level officials. Paul-Henri Spaak, the Belgian Foreign Minister, would serve as chair. Although the Spaak Committee engaged in sensitive political discussions of the substantive and institutional framework for future intergovernmental negotiations, the committee's seemingly technocratic composition allowed it to be portrayed domestically, particularly in France, as primarily "a group of experts."[90] The report produced by the committee[91] also followed a similarly functionalist/technocratic strategy on institutional questions, placing emphasis on substantive policy goals (such as a customs union) and only then making mention of the new Community institutions "of which the competences will be clearly defined."[92]

Like the Benelux memorandum, the Spaak Report studiously avoided even mentioning the idea of supranationalism or a High Authority, opting

---

88. See generally Harryvan and Kersten (1989), 150–51, citing BZ, II, 913.100, No. 139 ("Memorandum des Pays Benelux aux Six Pays de la C.E.C.A.").

89. Harryvan and Kersten (1989), 151; cf. Pescatore (1981), 165 (speaking of the desire of the negotiators at the future intergovernmental conference "to appease the demons that [the EDC] had aroused").

90. Moravcsik (1998), 116.

91. Spaak Report (1956).

92. Ibid., 23.

instead for the name European Commission, an even more functionalist and administrative sounding term. In the determination of what the competences of the organs of the new common market should be, the Spaak Report distilled out three broad "principles" to guide future intergovernmental negotiators. These principles are suggestive of the delicate political issues that the question of supranational delegation presented, as well as the degree of hierarchical (national-executive) control each required.

First, the Spaak Report stated that, in the absence of an as-yet-unattained convergence of monetary, budgetary, and social policies among the six Member States, the institutional distribution of powers in the new economic community must reflect the following basic distinction: "[Q]uestions of general economic policy" were to "remain the reserved domain of the governments" of the Member States, whereas "problems" associated with the "functioning" of the common market would to be delegated to the Community level.[93] This political/functional distinction suggests a desire to reassure those who might fear that the EEC would become the foundation for an open-ended transfer of political competences to the supranational level.

Second, the report asserted that certain regulatory domains specifically required a measure of supranational autonomy from intergovernmental control. The least problematic example was "the application and control of competition rules" (antitrust) which, after all, would be "in the interest of the producers themselves," who would benefit from the rapidity and legal certainty of a common supranational mechanism.[94] More audaciously, the report stated that the Member States could not realistically rely on intergovernmental mechanisms to enforce "the execution of engagements taken by the States or the administration of safeguard clauses" for the simple reason that a requirement of unanimity would permit either a national veto or at least an unacceptable round of political dealing (*marchandages*). Rather, the credibility of the policy commitments made under the treaty would require "the creation of an organ endowed with its own power and with a common responsibility."[95]

The third principle outlined in the Spaak Report was perhaps the most revealing of the delicate institutional issues ahead. The report asserted that, even though most questions of general law and policy would remain the

---

93. Ibid., 24.

94. Ibid.

95. Ibid.

province of national institutions, certain of these laws and policies would nevertheless have "such a decisive impact on the functioning of the market" that the creation of some kind of "common institution" would be warranted to make proposals to national governments (through the Council of Ministers) to adopt measures to "coordinate" them. Indeed, such coordination could be "so indispensable to the functioning and the development of the market" that the treaty might have to dispense with the rule of unanimity in the Council of Ministers "in strictly enumerated cases or after the passage of a determinate period."[96]

The third principle quite rightly suggested, in other words, that functional questions could not be easily separated from political ones, and that the construction of a common market was not simply a matter of the straightforward creation of a customs union or other forms of sectoral integration. Rather, it would require significant harmonization among national laws and policies in related domains. Although no autonomous supranational body should have the right to *impose* such harmonization, the report asserted that such a body—the Commission—should still have the power of initiative at least to *propose* it—the infamous "Community model."[97] Moreover, the Commission's harmonization proposals should not in every case require the unanimous support of all Member State governments in the Council of Ministers. Although unanimity would remain "the rule,"[98] the report stated that in certain cases the Council of Ministers should be able to adopt harmonization measures through qualified-majority voting, in the overall interest of achieving a functioning common market.

The three institutional principles enunciated by the Spaak Report well anticipated the central problems that would confront the negotiators of the Treaty of Rome over the course of the next year. On the one hand, the Spaak Report's overall institutional discussion (which was actually quite limited) adhered closely to functionalist language in describing the Commission's responsibilities.[99] On the other hand, it also made quite clear that the authority of the Commission under the Community model would inevitably overlap to a great degree with political questions close to the core responsibilities of

---

96. Ibid.

97. See generally Parsons (2003), 9, 97 (describing the institutionalization of the "community model").

98. Spaak Report (1956), 25.

99. The report, for example, spoke of the Commission primarily "administering the treaty and overseeing the functioning and the development of the common market." Ibid.

the Member States. In other words, the report suggested that a kind of political supranationalism was, to a certain extent, unavoidable in order to achieve the goals of market integration. It was, nevertheless, primarily an instrumental, nonideological supranationalism—that is, one not motivated by any teleological supranational federalism, at least not overtly. But it was also a supranationalism that necessarily had to cloak itself in the functionalist language of technocratic administration for fear of the political consequences.[100] Additionally, it was a supranationalism that required a dramatically augmented role for national executives through the Council of Ministers, in order to distinguish it from the institutional system of the ECSC.

This did not mean, however, that the effort to strike the right balance in the treaty between the Council's and Commission's relative functions would be easy. The task was given over to a group of nationally designated legal experts—the *groupe juridique*—which was responsible for drafting the institutional and legal provisions in the Treaties of Rome.[101] The legal group clearly recognized, based on the political decisions made at higher levels, "that the central institution would henceforth be the Council, in the hands of which would be largely concentrated the power of political decision, as well as the legislative function."[102] Nevertheless, in its capacity as principal drafter of the institutional provisions, the legal negotiators paid a great deal of attention to "the articulation between the right of initiative of the Commission and the right of decision of the Council."[103] Given the ultimate decisional power in the Council, the *groupe juridique* inserted a provision designed to

---

100. As Robert Schuman would write in 1953: "The competence of these supranational institutions applies, then, to technical problems rather than to functions that involve the sovereignty of the state." Milward (2000 [1992]), quoting Schuman (1953b), 23.

101. The major questions of policy were the responsibility of the other two main negotiating groups, for the common market and atomic affairs respectively. The legal group was assembled originally as a drafting group (*groupe de rédaction*) responsible for putting into legal forms the agreements over political and economic substance made by the other groups. It took on, however, a key role in the actual negotiation of the institutional provisions. See generally Pescatore (1981). The deference that the political negotiators gave to the *groupe juridique* on institutional questions (its proposals, always presented unanimously, were never rejected) was arguably a harbinger of the sort of deference that would be characteristic of legal neofunctionalism that took hold in integration in the 1960s. See generally Burley and Mattli (1993).

102. Pescatore (1981), 168.

103. Ibid., 169.

protect, at least, the Commission's unfettered discretion in making legislative proposals.[104]

Outside the *groupe juridique,* by all accounts the negotiations over the Treaty of Rome were guided by the notion "that supranationality should be no more than what proved minimally necessary" to achieve the common market.[105] This approach was certainly consistent with the basic tenor of the Spaak Report. Keeping supranationality to a minimum, however, also placed an even greater burden on the treaty negotiators "to write into the treaty text the maximum possible detail of the actions which must be taken in the future."[106] This also meant a significant degree of variation across issue areas as to the nature and scope of supranational delegation, depending on the importance of a particular regulatory domain to powerful national interests.[107] There would, in other words, be no uniform "legislative" process, as one might expect in a "federal" government, but rather procedural variation that one typically finds across administrative agencies depending on the regulatory domain.

The forms of supranational delegation in the Treaty of Rome fell broadly into three categories: delegation to the Commission, acting as a relatively autonomous supranational technocratic body (e.g., in the formulation or enforcement of competition policy); delegation to the Council of Ministers acting quasi-supranationally in its own right through qualified-majority voting (QMV); and delegation to the Council of Ministers acting unanimously, thus effectively delegating the normative power to each particular national executive but only if each reached agreement to act in concert with

---

104. Article 149 thus provided that, as long as the Council had not acted, the Commission remained free to alter its proposal at any time. By contrast, for the Council to amend a proposal of the Commission, Article 149 required unanimity of the Member State representatives. In this respect, the legal group borrowed from the model established by the ECSC Treaty, in which a Council unanimity requirement was actually often used to augment the normative autonomy of the Commission (although the Council still retained the ultimate power of decision in most cases, in striking contrast to the Treaty of Paris). See this chapter, n. 52 and accompanying text.

105. Milward (2000 [1992]), 210.

106. Ibid.

107. Moravcsik (1998), 8. This could be understood as a manifestation of the "politics of bureaucratic" structure articulated by Moe (1989) in the American case. For a recent, explicit application of Moe's analytical approach to European integration, see Kelemen (2002).

the other Member State executives.[108] The treaty also introduced a distinction between a "regulation"—which would be "binding in its entirety and directly applicable in all Member States" without the necessity of further national implementing action—as well as a "directive"—which would be binding on Member States only "as to the result to be achieved," leaving "to national authorities the choice of form and methods" of implementation (parliamentary legislation, administrative regulation, etc.) (originally Article 189; later Article 249 of the Treaty Establishing the European Community [TEC] and now Article 288 of the Treaty on the Functioning of the European Union [TFEU]).

A leading member of the *groupe juridique* recalled later that the legal negotiators recognized how the "normative acts having a direct effect would in reality be sorts of *lois communautaires*" but that "such an expression had no chance of being accepted."[109] Thus, "we decided . . . to lower the terminology one notch and to speak of 'regulations,' an expression that would be more acceptable in the Member States."[110] Regulations were generally the specified legal instrument to be used in those relatively narrow realms in which the treaty authorized the Commission to exercise fully autonomous regulatory power (although the Council also possessed the power to adopt regulations in some circumstances, such as agriculture).[111] Directives were generally the instrument to be used in those much more politically delicate situations, such as harmonization of national laws and policies in the creation of the common market under the old Article 100 (Article 94 TEC/Article 115 TFEU), where the normative power was delegated to the Council acting unanimously on a proposal from the Commission. Because directives left implementation to

---

108. Even where negotiators attempted to specify rules directly on the face of the treaty—for example, prohibiting new customs duties among the Member States as a step in the creation of the customs union (as Article 12 of the Treaty of Rome would in fact do)—this too effected a kind of supranational delegation. In these circumstances, the delegation would not be to the Commission or Council, but rather to the European Court of Justice, which was given the responsibility of interpreting, on a case-by-case basis, the legal meaning of these purportedly unambiguous treaty provisions. See Case 26/62, *Van Gend & Loos v. Nederlandse Administratie der Belastingen*, 1963 E.C.R. 1. The treaty also introduced an additional layer of national control by mandating that, in certain areas, the Commission should formulate its proposals in conjunction with a committee composed of national officials (for example, in transport and monetary policy under Articles 83 and 105).

109. Pescatore (1981), 171.

110. Ibid.

111. Treaty of Rome, art. 43(2).

national institutions, this also reintroduced the possibility of a limited, post hoc role for national parliaments in Community norm-production: Directives falling within the constitutional domain of the legislature at the national level would, in theory, require national implementing legislation (rather than, say, an executive decree).[112]

For Andrew Moravcsik, an American political scientist, aside from the "precise and nearly automatic schedule for the reduction of internal tariffs" among the Member States, the Treaty of Rome was primarily "a 'framework' document, describing institutional procedures through which rules would be elaborated rather than specific rules themselves."[113] The choice of words is apt, calling to mind the notion of a *loi-cadre,* or framework law, the preferred instrument for the delegation of normative power in the final years of the French Fourth Republic.[114] One integration historian has been more explicit: "[T]he Rome Treaty was very much a 'traité cadre'—a framework document that provided the mechanisms for cooperation but left up to later decision-makers the choice of what policies should flank the basic customs union."[115] Indeed, this is a good working description not merely of the Treaty of Rome but also of most forms of enabling legislation in the modern administrative state. The purpose of enabling legislation, both national and supranational, was not to make rules but rather to confer power on other institutions to make rules,[116] subject to statutory guidelines and control procedures that would operate as commitment mechanisms to ensure a stream of policy choices in line with the original delegation.

These supranational delegations to the Community, and more particularly to the Council of Ministers, can only be understood as legal-historical products of their time; that is, as further examples of how the legislature had "surrendered most of its effective powers to the Executive," just as in the domestic

---

112. However, even in those cases, national parliaments would still be bound, under Community law, by the Council of Ministers' collective agreement as to "the result to be achieved" by the directive, thus constraining the parliament's normal legislative pre-rogatives. The European Court of Justice would in fact later hold that directives could have a direct effect in certain circumstances, despite the absence of national imple-menting legislation, thus effectively circumventing the limited, post hoc role of the national parliaments in implementing directives. See this chapter, nn. 169–172 and accompanying text.

113. Moravcsik (1998), 152.

114. See Chapter 2, nn. 88–92 and accompanying text.

115. Ludlow (2006a), 3; see also Majone (2005), 7 (using the same term).

116. See Rubin (1989), 380–85 (describing "transitive" versus "intransitive" legislation).

administrative state.[117] This legal-historical background helps to contextualize the institutional structure of the Community, which as Moravcsik has rightly put it, "severely restrict[ed] formal participation in decision-making by most domestic actors other than the executive. Issues that were once handled by domestic parliaments and publics" were now subject to the secret bargaining of national executives within supranational institutions.[118] Thus, "the so-called 'democratic deficit' . . . is not a coincidental characteristic of the [Community]; it is an integral part of the [Community's] institutional design."[119] Moravcsik concluded from this insight that the process of European integration in this way "strengthen[ed] the state."[120] His real point should be, however, that European integration built on a strengthening *administrative* state as it emerged in the postwar decades, dominated by national executives and their technocratic subordinates.[121]

The West German negotiating experience demonstrates this point well, while also taking us back to some of the central elements of the *Kanzlerdemokratie* established under the Basic Law of 1949.[122] In the mid-1950s, with the relaunch of negotiations over a customs union underway, Adenauer encountered resistance to the Community model of integration (especially from Ludwig Erhard, his economics minister and political rival). To overcome that resistance, Adenauer drew directly on his constitutional *Richtlinienkompetenz*,[123] issuing a guidance memorandum to his ministers that stated: "[A]s a general principle of our policy we have to carry out the Messina resolution resolutely and without qualification. . . . The integration of the Six is to be promoted by all conceivable methods . . . . I ask you to regard the above as a guideline for the Federal Government's policy (as in Article 65

---

117. Chapter 2, n. 97.

118. Moravcsik (1994), 3.

119. Ibid. In a more recent piece, Moravcsik again draws the linkage between the administrative state and European integration, arguing that European institutions are afflicted with no more a democratic deficit than are constitutional nation-states. See Moravcsik (2002); see also Moravcsik (2004). However, this argument ignores a key distinction between administrative governance nationally and supranationally—the absence of a recognized, democratically legitimate political superior in the latter case to oversee the activities of the supranational administrative apparatus.

120. Moravcsik (1994), 3.

121. For further elaboration of this idea, see Phelan (2002).

122. See generally Lee (1995).

123. See Chapter 2, nn. 106–107 and accompanying text.

of the Basic Law) and to act accordingly."[124] In the end, in the constitutional and political context in which West Germany found itself in 1956 and 1957, it was "the Chancellor's position and power within the Cabinet" that determined West Germany's European policy.[125]

The constitutional and political situation of the French chief executive at the end of the Fourth Republic contrasted sharply. Under the 1946 constitution, the French prime minister lacked anything approaching the same constitutional prerogatives as his West German counterpart. Indeed, it was precisely *because of* the precarious institutional position of French governments in the middle 1950s that France became the wild card in the negotiations over European integration (witness the collapse of the EDC in 1954). After his unexpected investiture as prime minister following the parliamentary elections of January 1956, the French socialist leader Guy Mollet, a committed integrationist, was forced to resort to subterfuge in order to pursue a pro-European policy without inciting strong political opposition at home[126] (which, given the constitutional weakness of his office, he could not control). As Mollet would later complain, the instability of the Fourth Republic had made it practically impossible, "in the face of our partners, of our allies or of our adversaries, . . . to hold to any engagements whatsoever, [or] to establish a durable policy."[127]

---

124. Adenauer (1967), 254–55, as translated in Lee (1995), 54, n. 32.

125. Lee (1995), 51; cf. Milward (1984), 390 (describing how, regarding the negotiations of the Treaty of Paris, "without Adenauer's autocratic imposition of his own foreign policy on the Federal government [the French] proposals would surely have not been made"); see also Rittberger (2005), 91 (quoting Milward). Ann-Christina Lauring Knudsen also sees Adenauer's constitutional authority as decisive in the negotiations of the Common Agricultural Policy in the early 1960s. Knudsen (2001), 136 ("The principle of Richtlinienkompetenz meant that the Chancellor had the last word in deciding Federal policy matters.").

126. Parsons (2002), 69–72. Mollet consistently portrayed the Spaak Committee, for example, as merely an expert body, rarely mentioning its workings in meetings with other ministers, much less acknowledging the committee for the political forum it in fact was. Once the intergovernmental negotiations opened in Brussels in June 1956, Mollet tried to control tightly both information regarding, as well as influence over, the French negotiating strategy, relying heavily for this purposes on his own staff, led by his *chef de cabinet*, Émile Noël. Moravcsik (1998), 116. Also playing important roles were Maurice Faure, who led the French delegation in Brussels, and Alexandre Verret, who chaired the interministerial liaison committee on the common market. Bossuat (1995), 28.

127. "Procès-verbal de la commission du suffrage universel de l'Assemblée Nationale, 1er juin 1958," in *Documents pour servir a l'histoire de l'elaboration de la constitution du 4 octobre 1958* (1987), 1:155. For this reason, Mollet broke with his own party (to considerable personal political damage to himself over the long term) and decided to support de

De Gaulle's subsequent policy successes in areas that had bedeviled his Fourth Republic predecessors (notably in economic reform and trade liberalization) arguably owed to "the power of the Fifth Republic presidency" and to his stronger domestic position.[128] Looking back on Mollet's approach to the negotiation of the Treaty of Rome, however, one can see elements that anticipated the governing style of the Fifth Republic, albeit without the formal backing of constitutional provisions. Mollet broke with "the normal decentralized procedures of the Fourth Republic, whereby a weak central executive devolved initiative to individual ministries,"[129] which were often treated as separate political fiefdoms by coalition partners. Moreover, Mollet's success in pushing through the Treaty of Rome was also at least partly due to his consistent ability to portray integration as essentially an economic question and therefore largely technical in character; consequently, the treaty passed the National Assembly after relatively unproblematic political debate.[130] The "technical" character of the Treaty of Rome, however, masked its great political import, particularly on questions of tariff reduction and customs union. As we shall see, Gaullists would later maintain that the institutional weakness of the French executive under the Fourth Republic undermined Mollet's capacity to negotiate a treaty sufficiently respectful of France's sovereign prerogatives—which de Gaulle of course equated with national executive control over supranational policy decisions.

※ 3.3 From Control to Oversight: the Luxembourg Compromise, the European Council, and Beyond

Control may have been what de Gaulle sought in his institutional challenge to the Community in the 1960s, but it is not what he achieved. When he assumed the presidency of the newly established Fifth Republic in 1959, de Gaulle understood the economic benefits of integration, most importantly the Europeanization of agricultural protection. But he was also deeply hostile to some of the more supranational elements of the treaty, particularly the progressive shift to qualified-majority voting (QMV) over the course of

---

Gaulle's domestic constitutional proposals in May 1958, which would lead to the establishment of the semi-presidential regime of the Fifth Republic.

128. Moravcsik (1998), 181.

129. Ibid., 116.

130. Ibid.; see also Parsons (2003), 114–15.

the "transition period" lasting 12 years (divided equally into three parts).[131] De Gaulle would later assert that, to accept QMV after "we had decided to take destiny into our own hands" at home would leave France "exposed to the possibility of being overruled in any economic matter whatsoever, and therefore in social and sometimes political matters" as well.[132]

"For his first four years in power," however, de Gaulle "confounded those who expected an immediate clash."[133] It would not be until the controversy over the French veto of the British application in January 1963 that Gaullist obstructionism would overtly manifest itself. In the interim, as the historian Piers Ludlow has written, "far from casting off all supranational shackles and proclaiming France's total freedom from external constraints," de Gaulle pushed hard for the common agricultural policy (CAP), which included delegating "considerable powers of initiative and oversight [of Member State implementation] to the European Commission. Gaullist France seemed as committed to the Community game as any of its partners."[134] The battle over QMV did not come, in fact, until 1965, the final year of the second stage of the transition period. The timing was not coincidental, because the beginning of the third stage also marked the shift to QMV in many key policy domains.

The particular provocation for the Gaullist challenge would not be the shift to QMV itself, however, but the Hallstein Commission's announcement of a proposal for CAP financing that included increased powers for the Commission, independent funding for the Community ("own resources"), as well as a broadened budgetary role for the European Parliament.[135] These proposals reflected, as the historian Matthias Schönwald has suggested, Walter Hallstein's particular mix of functionalist *Sachlogik* and federalist idealism when it came to matters European.[136] Hallstein viewed the Commission in distinctly political terms, as the institutional foundation of an eventual federal union at the European level. He believed, according to Schönwald,

---

131. Parsons claims that Mollet had intentionally sought to "fool the French Assembly, with weak initial Commission powers and majority voting that increased over the transition period to be like that of the ECSC." Parsons (2003), 113.

132. de Gaulle (1965), as translated in Teasdale (1993), 568.

133. Ludlow (2006a), 5.

134. Ludlow (2006a), 5 (internal citations omitted).

135. For summaries of the Commission's proposals, see, e.g., Palayret (2006), 52–53; Ludlow (2006b), 81–86; Schönwald (2001), 167–69; Vaïsse (2001), 204–05.

136. Schönwald (2001), 159–64. For more on the mixture of federalism and functionalism in Hallstein's thinking, see Wessels (1995).

that "[h]istory had shown that—as a rule—the delegation of power to independent institutions marked the beginning of such a process."[137]

This historical rule was apparently at least in part derived from the work of Heinrich Triepel, Hallstein's university teacher in 1920s Berlin, who studied the emergence of the federal German state out of the seemingly more confederal Reich constitution of 1871.[138] Hallstein's focus on Triepel's historical theory of federalism ignored, however, Triepel's less well known but perhaps more pertinent writings under Weimar regarding delegation in an era of administrative governance.[139] Although unaware of Triepel's writings, de Gaulle chose to view integration from a similarly "administrative" perspective, and this clearly fed his hostility to supranational technocratic autonomy without continuing hierarchical-political (i.e., national executive) control. The Commission was, from this perspective, principally a technocratic body "without any political legitimacy" that "should therefore be at the service of governments."[140]

Given the increased Commission autonomy that he associated with QMV, de Gaulle believed that an eventual confrontation with the Commission was "sooner or later, inevitable."[141] But de Gaulle's understanding of the Commission's ultimate dependence on national executives arguably differed only in degree, not in nature, from views prevailing in other Member States. On this critical question, historians have found no "crude five-to-one split between France and its partners [as] is often suggested."[142] Rather, in the years leading up to the empty chair crisis, other Member States, notably Germany, made it known that they too generally viewed the Commission's role as subordinate to and supportive of the Council.[143] In the midst of the negotiations over the eventual fusion of the High Authority with the commissions of the EEC and the European Atomic Energy Community (Euratom), Germany argued that the Council of Ministers "could be more accurately compared to a national Government than could the European Commission."[144]

---

137. Schönwald (2001), 164.

138. Again, this is the implication of Schönwald (2001), 159–64.

139. See Chapter 2, nn. 12–13 and accompanying text.

140. Vaïsse (2001), 199 ; see also Palayret (2006), 49; Schönwald (2001), 170.

141. de Gaulle (1965); see also Schönwald (2001), 157.

142. Ludlow (2006a), 46.

143. Ludlow (2009), 191.

144. Ludlow (2006a), 46, quoting CMA, I/16/64, Council minutes, 25 Mar., 1964.

A year earlier, the Member States (again led by Germany—the Commission's purported ally in the later confrontation with de Gaulle) also began usurping the Commission's agenda-setting role by issuing "action plans."[145] This shift toward Council control over the agenda intensified over the decade, to the point that, as one historian has put it, the "once-confident helmsmen" (the Commission) was "reduced to relaying plans devised in national capitals rather than in Brussels," thus losing "its role as the main arbiter of the Community agenda."[146] Repeated controversies over the course of the 1960s—British accession, CAP financing, as well as QMV—demonstrated that as soon as the issues "became political as opposed to technical, Commission influence melted away."[147]

After the initially maladroit announcement of its CAP financing proposals to the European Parliament (without consulting the Council), the Hallstein Commission receded to sidelines of the ensuing crisis, playing a largely marginal role in its resolution. In some sense, the Commission's inability to move beyond its subordinate role to the Council demonstrated how much the postwar functionalists had miscalculated in believing that a supranational technocratic body could effectively operate without "some over-all political authority above it," as early functionalists had hoped for such organizations.[148] The earlier experience with the Organization for Economic Co-operation and Development (OECD), which loomed in the background of institutional politics in the European Community in the 1960s, had provided the first demonstration of this point. As a purely technocratic body, the OECD had evolved into nothing more than "a forum for registering international agreements made elsewhere, increasingly of a minor kind."[149] In contrast with the OECD, the European Community emerged as it did—with national executives providing essential political leadership within the

---

145. Ludlow (2006a), 38–39.

146. Ibid., 210.

147. Ibid., 209.

148. Mitrany questioned what he called "the habitual assumption . . . that international action must have some over-all *political authority* above it" (his emphasis); rather,

    it is the central view of the functional approach that such an authority is not essential for our greatest and real immediate needs. The several functions could be organized through the [enabling] agreement, given specifically in each case, of the national governments chiefly interested, with the grant of the requisite powers and resources.

    Mitrany (1946 [1943]), 45.

149. Milward (1984), 207 (referring to the OECD's forerunner, the Organization for European Economic Co-operation [OEEC]).

Council—as "a total rejection of integration within [the] particular political framework" exemplified by the OECD.[150] Integration required national executive leadership.

And yet, while the OECD experience demonstrated the inherent weaknesses of a purely technocratic body unable to forge genuine political deals, it also suggested the dangers of individual national control over supranational policy making. As a traditional intergovernmental body, OECD member states retained the right of veto. And thus, in the negotiations leading to the Luxembourg Compromise in January 1966, the OECD was specifically invoked by other national leaders "as a spectre of the paralyzing effects of rights of veto."[151] In this sense, integration required national leadership, but not necessarily individualized national *control*.

From a public law perspective, the issue driving the empty chair crisis was thus not *whether* the policy agenda would be managed by the Member States (all Member States believed it should), but *how* it would be managed—whether unilaterally by a single Member State exercising a veto under a unanimity regime, or collectively by the Council using consensus politics, albeit in the shadow of QMV. The particular policy struggles behind the empty chair crisis—between, say, French insistence that CAP financing be resolved ahead of all other issues (to its satisfaction, of course), and Germany's increasing calls for "balanced progress" or "synchronization" of the Community policy agenda[152]—can be seen in this light. For those favoring synchronized policy development—in effect, the five Member States apart from France—the choice between national control versus shared oversight was obvious. This was especially the case given the way that France had dominated the policy agenda since the British veto in January 1963.[153] For the French, these policy questions intersected with genuine concerns over legitimate governance. De Gaulle feared the move to QMV in the third stage would strengthen the position of the Commission—"this embryonic technocracy, for the most part foreign"[154]—which would no longer need to satisfy each and

---

150. Milward (1984), 209.

151. Harryvan and van der Harst (2001), 186.

152. Oppelland (2001), 231–33, 242; Ludlow (2006a), 24, 69, 108; Palayret (2006), 49, 51; Türk (2006), 119; Coppolaro (2006), 223; see also Bergström (2005), 58.

153. See generally Ludlow (1999); see also Ludlow (2006b), 87; Palayret (2006), 59–60.

154. de Gaulle (1965), translated in Teasdale (1993), 568.

every Member State in order to see its legislative proposals adopted in the Council.[155]

As de Gaulle's own advisers had made clear to him in early 1965, however, the likelihood of this occurring in practice was relatively small given the prevalence of consensus politics in the Council.[156] Nevertheless, it was precisely because French interests were not at serious risk that one must conclude de Gaulle was motivated primarily by constitutional principle.[157] For the other Member States, however, functional considerations—the need for a more efficient and balanced (but still nationally managed) supranational process of policy development—led them to favor shared oversight via the Council.

In this struggle between control and oversight, de Gaulle's position clearly did not prevail, contrary to the manner in which the results of the empty chair crisis are conventionally remembered. The Luxembourg Compromise only codified the traditional practice of consensus politics in the Council, a strong norm to be sure, but not the *révision d'ensemble* ("complete overhaul") of the QMV provisions in the treaty that was the stated goal of the French government.[158] As a matter of both law and subsequent practice within the Council, the Luxembourg Compromise did not lay the foundations for a

---

155. So long as Member State amendments to a Commission proposal could only be made upon a unanimous vote under art. 149, the Commission would enjoy an effective veto over Member State changes, "unless by some extraordinary chance, the six states were unanimous in formulating an amendment." Thus, de Gaulle sought to exploit the crisis to remove "certain mistakes and ambiguities in the Treaties," notably the shift to qualified-majority voting at the beginning of the third stage. de Gaulle (1965), translated in Teasdale (1993), 568–69.

156. Palayret (2006), 54.

157. Rather than, say, concerns derived from domestic interest-group politics: see Palayret (2006), 45–46, 58–59, criticizing Moravcsik (2000a), (2000b), and (1998); see also Palayret (2006), 65–66; Vaïsse (2001), 213–14. Moravcsik goes so far as to argue that the French government had not exercised its right to delay the transition to the second stage in 1961–1962 because at that moment de Gaulle was pursuing a strategy of deception in Europe to secure an agreement on the CAP on terms most favorable to French agricultural interests. Moravcsik (1998), 186–87; but see Lieshout et al. (2004) (deeply critical of Moravcsik's methods, sources, and conclusions on this point); see also Pine (2008).

158. Palayret (2006), 63. The Compromise provided only that, where "very important" national interests were at stake, "the Council will endeavour, within a reasonable time, to reach a solution that can be adopted by all"—leaving it to the French to insist, in isolation, that this meant an obligation to continue discussions "until unanimous agreement has been reached." See *Bulletin of the European Economic Community* (Bull. EEC), Mar. 1966 , 8–10, reprinted in Palayret et al. (2006), 325 (app. 2).

"veto culture" as is often supposed,[159] much less a "second European constitution" apart from the original Treaty of Rome itself.[160] The events of late 1965 and early 1966 simply marked the *reassertion* of an older set of ground rules for European integration which had manifested themselves first in the negotiations of the Treaty of Paris and then in actual operation of the ECSC over the course of the 1950s: Community norm-production needed to be mediated in some way through national executives, just as in the administrative state.

This outcome nevertheless still defied the predictions of the neofunctionalists, who had foreseen a Commission-led, technocratic process of spillover from one domain to the next, inexorably driving the process of European integration forward beyond its original core mandate.[161] The emergent structure of shared national executive oversight through the Council—which "corresponded neither to the more ambitious federal dreams [of Hallstein] nor to the intergovernmentalism of the French President"[162]—was in fact deeply tied to the diffusion and fragmentation of normative power in an era of administrative governance. At the European level, below the Council summit, there developed a dense and complex system of oversight committees—the most important being the Committee of Permanent Representatives of the Member States (COREPER), the Council's own permanent bureaucracy in Brussels. COREPER, in turn, included numerous subcommittees and working groups of national officials operating at the supranational level. There also emerged so-called "management committees," which operated in some sense as a conduit between the Council and the Commission, to oversee powers delegated by the former to the latter, particular under the CAP.[163] Later supplemented by so-called "regulatory committees" and other variants, these bodies served as the forerunners of what would become the comitology system that is now widely used across most regulatory domains at the supranational level.

---

159. Teasdale (1993), 570. See Golub (2006) for a detailed empirical critique of this claim; see also Baquero Cruz (2006), 259–62; Ludlow (2001), 250–51.

160. Cassese and della Cananea (1992), 86. For a subtle critique of the claim that the Luxembourg Compromise in some manner revised the constitutional law of integration, see Baquero Cruz (2006), 265–75.

161. This contradiction is something that neofunctionalist theorists themselves were compelled to recognize. See, e.g., Haas (1971).

162. Ludlow (2001), 257.

163. Bertram (1967); see also Bergström (2005), 77–78; Vos (1999a), 20–21.

Historians are only beginning to pay close attention to the emergence of the committee system.[164] What they are finding is a development that reflects the changing "nature of European politics from foreign affairs to domestic affairs," in which "[c]ommittees came to function as a broad and diverse interface between the European administration and the national administrations."[165] Undoubtedly, "the early EEC did necessitate some national sacrifices in terms of total national autonomy," but these sacrifices were always counter-balanced by mechanisms designed to "ensure that the member-states retain[ed] enough leverage . . . to direct the overall evolution of the integration process."[166] Even if the Member States could not exercise particular *control* in a plenary administrative-law sense, they could still *oversee* the process of integration in a way that satisfied their desired ends.

The Merger Treaty of 1965 gave a formal legal basis to COREPER's emerging role.[167] It also effected another change of a perhaps more symbolic nature, although one no less interesting for our purposes. In replacing the High Authority with a single Commission for the three European Communities (ECSC, EEC, and Euratom), the Merger Treaty deleted the old Article 9 of the Treaty of Paris, which referred to the "supranational character" of the High Authority.[168] The new provision—Article 10 of the Merger Treaty—also specified that the members of the unified Commission would, "in the general interest of the Communities, be completely independent in the performance of their duties." However, in contrast with Article 9 of the Treaty of Paris, Article 10 of the Merger Treaty tracked the language of the Treaty of Rome, dropping the word "supranational" in its description of these duties. It stated, rather, only that the members of the Commission should "refrain from any action incompatible with their duties," and that "[e]ach Member State undertakes to respect this principle and not to seek to influence the members of the Commission in the performance of their tasks." As a consequence of this change, the sole mention of the "supranational" character of European integration (in Article 9 of the Treaty of Paris)—a word studiously avoided in the

---

164. See Ludlow (2009) and (2005); Knudsen and Rasmussen (2008).

165. Knudsen and Rasmussen (2008), 60.

166. Ludlow (2009), 201.

167. Treaty Establishing a Single Council and a Single Commission of the European Communities, April 8, 1965, J.O. 152/1 (July 13, 1967), art. 4, reprinted in Treaties Establishing the European Communities (1987).

168. See this chapter, n. 45 and accompanying text.

Spaak Report as well as the Treaty of Rome—was now removed from the positive treaty law of European integration entirely.

Of course, the deletion of a word did not change the character of the Commission itself, which remained, in certain limited domains and for certain recognized instrumental purposes, an autonomously supranational body (something even more true for the European Court of Justice [ECJ]). Nevertheless, the elimination of the old Article 9 of the Treaty of Paris symbolized the basic political reality of European integration in the 1960s, which, insofar as the policy process was concerned (as opposed to, say, adjudication), was a distinctly more nationally managed than supranational phenomenon. Indeed, despite the battles over QMV in the empty chair crisis of 1965, unanimity remained the rule in perhaps the most politically delicate aspect of European integration—the issuance of directives to harmonize national law and policies under the old Article 100 of the Treaty of Rome (Article 94 TEC/Article 115 TFEU). It would not be until the adoption of the Single European Act (SEA) of 1986 that the Member States would finally extend the use of QMV to the adoption of harmonization directives in completion of the internal market (Article 100a, later Article 95 TEC/Article 114 TFEU).

But from a legal standpoint, even under the old Article 100, unanimity in the Council still effected a delegation of legislative power out of the national *parliamentary* realm. The beneficiary of that delegation was each particular national executive, operating in conjunction with its fellow national executives in the Council of Ministers. The ECJ would reinforce this concentration of authority in 1974, when it held that, in disputes between private individuals and public authorities at the national level, the provisions of the directive adopted by the Council could have direct effect in national law without the adoption of national implementing legislation.[169] The conditions that the Court laid down—that the directive be unambiguous in its terms and the time limit for implementation had passed—simply gave national executives, through the Council, the opportunity to impose a collective legislative decision on the national parliament despite the limited, post hoc powers of transposition that national parliaments were supposed to enjoy under the Treaty of Rome, specifically the old Article 189 (Article 249 TEC/Article 288 TFEU).[170] Eventually, this power would be expanded to include the

---

169. Case 41/74, *Van Duyn v. Home Office*, 1974 E.C.R. 1337.

170. This judicial circumvention of the role of national parliaments in Community law-making was in some sense presaged by the United Kingdom's accession to the Community two years before. The accession legislation adopted by the British parliament—the European

enforcement of similar directives against decentralized authorities within the state, such as municipalities,[171] or public service providers,[172] regardless of whether national law gave the national executive this sort of normative authority in purely domestic circumstances.

The year 1974 also marked an even more important institutional reinforcement of national executive power at the supranational level, one with significant long-term effects for political oversight in the Community. At the initiative of French President Valéry Giscard d'Estaing and German Chancellor Helmut Schmidt, the national chief executives formed themselves into the "European Council," a body initially outside the confines of treaty law,[173] to serve as a forum for the chief executives to decide on the future direction of integration policy. Distinguished from the regular meetings of government ministers within the Council of Ministers, the European Council assembled in (then) semi-annual summit meetings. The purpose was not legislative, as with the Council of Ministers, but rather to provide overall guidance to Europe's supranational policy process—a sort of informal, but politically potent, *Richtlinienkompetenz* on the supranational level.[174]

From the old federalist standpoint associated with Walter Hallstein, the European Council might appear as another reversal of the progress toward integration, a view that assumed that the most important measure of such progress was the degree of supranational normative autonomy in Community decision-making. The more persuasive historical interpretation (that of Alan Milward) is that, "rather than reversing the process of European integration," the establishment of the European Council "actually signifie[d] a wish to extend Community decision-making to new areas in response to changes in national policy objectives arising from the fundamental change in economic

---

Communities Act, 1972 Eliz. 2, c. 68—provided that, as a general matter, the implementation of Community directives into British law would be done by way of *statutory instrument* and not by parliamentary legislation. Ibid., sec. 2(2). Thus, on accession to the Community, the British parliament relinquished its right to vote on the form and content of the implementation of most directives, limiting its powers, rather, to scrutiny mechanisms similar to the procedures established for delegated legislation under the Statutory Instruments Act of 1946. Compare Chapter 2, nn. 95–96 and accompanying text, with Chapter 5, nn. 96–99 and accompanying text.

171. Case 103/88, *Fratelli Costanza SpA v. Commune di Milano*, 1989 E.C.R. 1839, paras. 30–31.

172. Case C-188/89, *A. Foster and Others v. British Gas plc*, 1990 E.C.R. I-3313, paras. 18–20.

173. The European Council would not be formally established until the Single European Act of 1986.

174. See Chapter 2, nn. 106–107 and accompanying text.

circumstances of the western European countries after 1974."[175] The establishment of the European Council suggested that, with end of the three decades of steady postwar expansion (the *trentes glorieuses*), European integration would need the political backing and direction of the national chief executives. Technocratic policy development in the Commission (the old Community model), even under ministerial supervision in the Council of Ministers, would not be enough; some form of plebiscitary leadership by heads of state or government was required. The European Council served that purpose, translating into workable supranational form the semi-"presidentialization" that had earlier stabilized administrative governance at the national level.[176]

The long-term consequences of the establishment of the European Council would be profound for the institutional life of the Community. The meetings of the European Council (now four times per year) have become the political focal points of the EU's annual calendar. As one commentator prosaically described, "[t]he dates of its meetings ... mark the rhythm of the Union's various activities in the way religious feast days marked the rhythm of daily life in medieval Christiandom."[177] Behind the rituals, however, there is real political decision-making and a not inconsiderable record of achievement. Jacques Delors, Commission President from 1985 to 1995 (during which European integration made major strides and, indeed, the European Union itself came into being in 1993), has written that "it has become evident that the European Council plays—and should continue to play—an irreplaceable role in the recurrent efforts to develop a politically integrated Europe."[178] Two leading integration scholars, in a 2002 study, noted how "the European Council has, for over a quarter of a century, fixed the agenda of the Union, especially as the EU has moved beyond the specific tasks laid down in the original treaties. Nothing decisive has been initiated without its approval."[179]

In this effort, the European Council has had recourse to another institution—the "Presidency"—that in some sense has served as its bridge to the Council of Ministers. Individual Member State executives held the Presidency on a

---

175. Milward and Sørensen (1993), 24–25.

176. See Chapter 2, nn. 103–107 and accompanying text; cf. Lindseth (2003a), 372.

177. de Schoutheete (2006), 57.

178. Jacques Delors, Forward to de Schoutheete and Wallace (2002).

179. de Schoutheete and Wallace (2002), 10.

rotating six-month basis, chairing both the meetings of the European Council and the various formations of the Council of Ministers, as well as the dense system of subcommittees and working groups within COREPER.[180] The Presidency has been the Member States' primary vehicle for agenda-setting at the supranational level, again contrary to the purported Community model envisioned in the 1950s. All of this "was accomplished without changing the formal prerogatives laid down in the Treaty. . . . By the mid-1980s, the Presidency had become the central managing force in the Council, coordinating the agendas of the various Councils, committees, and working groups," again "at the expense of the Commission."[181] Indeed, when the Member States finally extended the use of QMV to the harmonization of laws in completion of the internal market under Article 100a of the Single European Act in 1986 (Article 95 TEC/Article 114 TFEU), they compensated with a decision in 1988 to require each incoming Presidency to draft a "comprehensive work program,"—in effect, an intergovernmentally determined agenda— a requirement formalized in the Council's rules of procedure in 1993.[182]

The shift from national executive control to oversight at the Community level over the course of the 1960s to the 1980s should not be viewed in isolation from other developments in administrative governance generally.[183] This shift also coincided, it should be noted, with much greater toleration of diffusion and fragmentation of normative power at the national level (subject to forms of oversight from the center), a development deserving of much greater normative-historical inquiry.[184] British "quangos" and French *autorités administratives indépendentes*, for example, emerged as prominent mechanisms of national governance over the same period.[185] Aspects of this phenomenon manifested themselves in Germany as well, where the complexity of modern administration began to overwhelm the old notion of a hierarchically controlled "chancellor democracy," leading some commentators

---

180. The Treaty of Lisbon, of course, introduces a permanent President of the European Council, on a two-and-a-half year term, renewable once. See art. 15(5) TEU post-Lisbon. As to the various configurations of the Council, aside from Foreign Affairs, Member States will still hold the presidency on the basis of rotation. See art. 16(9) TEU post-Lisbon.

181. Tallberg (2006), 48.

182. Ibid., 50.

183. See generally Egeberg (2008).

184. Cf. Raunio and Hix (2000), 146–47, citing Majone (1994b) and (1996).

185. For a very useful summary, see Marcou (1995), 59–60.

to speak instead merely of a "coordination democracy," in which the chancellor served only as a policy manager at the center of a highly pluralist institutional network.[186]

Historical understanding of the relationship between these national and supranational developments remains underdeveloped. But there is no denying the basic identity of changes in the nature of administrative governance both nationally and supranationally. As one study has stressed, by the mid-1960s it was already apparent that Community policy processes had become "so demanding and complex that it was impossible for [the Member States] to act with a single voice."[187] "[T]heoretical notions of member state control" did not map easily onto the deeply "blurred" emergent policy processes: "the member states were still there" but were "represented by a myriad of national officials in an increasingly functionally divided Council, and the Council's work was increasingly dispersed among sectoral councils, subcommittees, and working groups within COREPER.[188] "This was a development toward a European political system that began in earnest within a few years of the EEC Treaty's entering into force,"[189] but its effects are still very much with us today.

---

186. Padgett (1994), 18–19, n. 19; see also Mayntz (1980), 140. In Italy, moreover, there was a parallel move toward greater coordination from the center (in the famous Law No. 400 of August 23, 1988). Legge 23 agosto 1988, No. 400, "Disciplina dell'attività di Governo e ordinamento della Presidenza del Consiglio dei Ministri," http://www.governo.it/Presidenza/normativa/legge2308_400.html (last visited Feb. 2, 2008). Ironically, given Italy's experience in the postwar decades of highly decentralized coalition governments, this law in fact served to significantly *augment* the power of the prime minister (*il presidente del consiglio dei ministri*). Nevertheless, the net effect was similar, transforming the national chief executive into the role of policy coordinator, marking an important convergence—albeit from the opposite direction—of the Italian system with those elsewhere in Western Europe. It also had important bearing on subsequent improvements in the coordination and implementation of supranational law within the Italian Republic. Legge 23 agosto 1988, No. 400, Art. 5(3)(a); for further discussion, see Furlong (1996), 39.

187. Knudsen and Rasmussen (2008), 60.

188. Ibid., 65.

189. Ibid.

FOUR

Supranational Delegation and National Judicial Review since the 1960s

WE NOW TURN TO THE JUDICIAL DIMENSION of the postwar constitutional settlement, and for this we need to focus primarily on national judicial review of supranational action. For some readers this may seem a surprising choice: Why not focus on the European Court of Justice (ECJ)? The ECJ has certainly loomed large in integration history, in many respects reflecting the desire to translate the judicial dimension of the postwar constitutional settlement into supranational form. But that translation failed in one important respect: On the national level, courts and other court-like *juridictions administratives* served as mechanisms of mediated legitimacy over administrative institutions that, on the one hand, possessed extensive rulemaking and adjudicative powers but, on the other, had no corresponding democratic and constitutional legitimacy of their own. The ECJ, by contrast, has never really viewed its principal function as one of constraining the normative autonomy of Community institutions, despite their lack of autonomous democratic and constitutional legitimacy. Rather, the ECJ has actively sought to promote that autonomy—including, most importantly, the Court's own—in the interest of developing a more effective mechanism for policing Member State commitment to the goals of integration.

Although the ECJ's approach may be understandable in terms of building an autonomous "constitutional infrastructure" for integration,[1] it is in deep tension with the normal judicial role in the postwar constitutional settlement of administrative governance. This is particularly the case as to the enforcement of the permissible scope of supranational delegation. By contrast, the national high courts (including supreme *juridictions administratives* like the French *Conseil d'Etat*) are accustomed to hearing purely national challenges to regulatory actions or legislative delegations for violating constitutional

---

1. Poiares Maduro(1998), 8. See the Introduction, n. 90 and accompanying text.

limitations on the transfer of authority.[2] Indeed, over the course of the postwar decades several national high courts (the German and the Italian, most notably) had gone very far in defining the substantive "reserve" of normative power that needed to be retained in the legislative domain (*Vorbehalt des Gesetzes* in German, *riserva di legge* in Italian) consistent with the reestablishment of representative democracy, separation of powers, and the rule of law in the aftermath of dictatorship.[3]

Thus, the national courts possessed the conceptual tools to police the bounds of supranational delegation in the interest of democracy. Of course, the ECJ could have borrowed these tools, but it chose not to do so. Although the Court often took seriously its role as the guarantor of supranational legality under the treaties, it was deeply reluctant to enforce limits on supranational delegation. As a consequence, over time, this critical task would necessarily fall to the national high courts. Being judicial bodies themselves— indeed ones imbued with an equally strong sense of mission in the enforcement of rights and powers (see Chapter 2)—the national high courts were not encumbered by some of the legal-cultural inhibitions that constrained national executives vis-à-vis the ECJ. In any event, the national executives in the Council, at least relative to their national parliaments, were often collectively the beneficiaries of ECJ decisions, expanding the scope of their policy making discretion at the supranational level, even if that discretion had to be shared with their fellow national executives in the Council.[4] And perhaps more importantly, under the prevailing legal culture of the postwar decades, open resistance by national executives to the work of courts, whether national or supranational, was clearly frowned upon.[5]

---

2. See, e.g., Chapter 2, nn. 112–119 and accompanying text. Indeed, in Germany, one commentator has claimed that "the striking down of statutes on delegation grounds is considered a normal event that frequently occurs." Kischel (1994), 239.

3. See Chapter 2, nn. 116–117 and accompanying text.

4. See, e.g., Chapter 3, nn. 170–172 and accompanying text.

5. Cf. Weiler (1991), 2428 (explaining Member State deference to ECJ rulings in terms of "the deep-seated legitimacy that derives from the mythical neutrality and religious-like authority with which we invest our supreme courts"). An anecdote from the first decade of the existence of the European Economic Community (EEC) suggests the strength of these inhibitions. In 1966, in the midst of the so-called "turnover tax struggle," the German federal government ordered German customs officials to disregard a decision of the ECJ because it conflicted "with well-reasoned arguments of the federal government." July 7, 1966 (IIIB.4–V 8534-1/66), *Der Betrieb* (1966), 1160, quoted in Alter (1996), 475. This attempt to assert the normative supremacy of the national executive over the Court provoked a campaign by German legal scholars and the Association of German Exporters against the government's order, culminating in official questions to the government in

In eventually taking on the role of judicial oversight of the scope of supranational delegation, however, the national high courts were not without inhibitions of their own—most importantly, a deep-seated judicial reluctance to interfere with policy choices that did not implicate clear questions of law or subjective rights. It is no doubt true that, in reviewing the constitutionality of the various European treaty changes in the 1990s and 2000s, several national high courts would claim a power of *Kompetenz-Kompetenz*; that is, the ultimate authority to define the limit of supranational competences relative to the Member States. But—and this too must be stressed— even the most ambitious of the national high courts in this regard (say, the German, the Danish, or the Czech) would do so *only after* clearly establishing that their fundamental approach would continue to be one of *deference* to the political choice in favor of European integration. Indeed, in Germany, the *Bundesverfassungsgericht* eventually acknowledged that this deference was constitutionally mandated as an aspect of "the principle of openness towards European law" (*Europarechtsfreundlichkeit*) under the Basic Law.[6] Earlier case law had made clear, as we shall see below, that such openness should include broad deference to the ECJ itself as the designated judicial mechanism for ruling on the validity of Community acts and in ensuring compliance by the Member States with their supranational commitments in the treaties and secondary Community law.[7]

But as the Danish Supreme Court would make plain in 1998, "the national courts cannot be deprived of their right to examine the question of whether a particular EC legal act exceeds the limits for the transfer of sovereignty brought about by the Act of Accession."[8] The ultimate purpose of this sort of

---

parliament as to how to reconcile the order with the principles of the *Rechtsstaat*. Meier (1994); see also Alter (1996), 476. For further discussion, see Alter (2001), 80–87.

6. German Lisbon Decision (2009), paras. 225 and 240.

7. See this chapter, nn. 129–130 and accompanying text.

8. *Carlsen and Others v. Rasmussen*, Case I-361/1997 of 6 Apr. 1998, 1998 UfR 800, reprinted in Oppenheimer (1994/2003), 2:191. (Due to the original Danish "no" on the Maastricht Treaty and subsequent procedural issues, the Danish Supreme Court did not rule on the constitutionality of the Treaty of Maastricht until 1998. For a succinct summary, see Claes (2006), 514–15.) One might say that *Carlsen* was an implicit rejection, on national constitutional grounds, of a strong reading of the principle contained in Article 292 of the Treaty Establishing the European Community (TEC), subsequently Article 344 of the Treaty on the Functioning of the European Union (TFEU), which provides that the "Member States undertake not to submit a dispute concerning the interpretation or application of this Treaty [now simply "the Treaties"] to any method of settlement other than those provided for therein."

ultra vires review was not merely to police the boundaries of supranational competence. Rather, it was to determine whether and under what circumstances supranational delegation imperiled "the constitutional assumption of a democratic system of government" on the national level.[9] The Polish Constitutional Tribunal, in its 2005 ruling on the constitutionality of Polish accession to the European Union (EU), similarly held that "the delegation of competences" cannot occur "to such an extent that it would signify the inability of the Republic of Poland to continue functioning as a sovereign and democratic State."[10] The Czech Constitutional Court, in its 2008 ruling on the constitutionality of the Treaty of Lisbon, put the same point this way: "[T]he transfer of powers of Czech Republic bodies cannot go so far as to violate the very essence of the republic as a sovereign and democratic state governed by the rule of law."[11]

It may be tempting to dismiss these holdings as the product of judicialized hostility to the integration project in otherwise Eurosceptical countries—the residuum of the excessive nationalism of the German Maastricht Decision of 1993. But that would also be wrong. As Julio Baquero Cruz has observed in a recent analysis of the legacy of the German Maastricht Decision, "the decision has never been overruled, the mark it has left on EU law is deep, and the ideas behind it are very much alive."[12] This is reflected most importantly in decisions of other national high courts into the present decade, which suggested that the reservation of *Kompetenz-Kompetenz* had become well-settled constitutional law. For example, the *Tribunal Constitucional* of Spain, not a country known for its Euroscepticism (judicial or otherwise), held in 2004 that European law only prevails within the scope of "the competences

---

9. *Carlsen*, Case I-361/1997, as reprinted in Oppenheimer (1994/2003), 2:191. The *Bundesverfassungsgericht* stressed a similar obligation to protect democracy in the German Maastricht Decision, defining the national judicial role as ultimately ensuring "that a living democracy is maintained in the Member States while integration proceeds." See *Brunner v. European Union Treaty* (the "German Maastricht Decision"), Cases 2 BvR 2134/92 and 2159/92 of 12 Oct. 1993, BVerfGE 89, 155, [1994] 1 C.M.L.R. 57, reprinted in Oppenheimer (1994/2003), 1:527–75; quotation at 33 I.L.M. 388, 421 (1994). This study uses the International Legal Materials (I.L.M.) translation because it is superior to the Common Market Law Reports (C.M.L.R.) translation found in Oppenheimer (1994/2003).

10. K18/04, 11 May 2005, *Polish Membership of the European Union (Accession Treaty)*, para. 8, excerpted and translated in Craig and de Búrca (2008), 372.

11. Pl. ÚS 19/08, 26 Nov. 2008, *Treaty of Lisbon Amending the Treaty on European Union and the Treaty Establishing the European Community*, para. 97, http://angl.concourt.cz/angl_verze/doc/pl-19-08.php (last visited June 11, 2009).

12. Baquero Cruz (2008), 391.

attributed to the European Union;" otherwise European law explicitly incorporates the national right of *Kompetenz-Kompetenz* (which the Court found was "proclaimed unmistakably" in the treaty).[13]

To gain a better sense of how and why these national high courts felt it necessary to police for themselves these outer limits on supranational delegation, some historical context is needed. For that, we do indeed need to begin with the ECJ, in order to get a better sense of the increasingly supranationalized legal environment in which the national high courts were operating from the 1960s onward.[14]

✻ 4.1 The European Court of Justice and Judicially Sanctioned Spillover

Beginning in the early 1960s, enterprising litigation strategies pursued by private actors—not to mention frankly constitutionalist understandings of the integration process advanced by judges on the ECJ—transformed the Court into perhaps the most effective supranational agent of integration, certainly more autonomous than the European Commission. This transformation depended, however, on the ECJ overcoming a critical legal obstacle. By the express terms of the original treaties (most importantly the Treaty of Rome), only the Member States or the European Commission had standing before the ECJ to seek a declaration of a Member State's noncompliance with its obligations, under the so-called infringement procedure of the old Articles 169–170 of the Treaty of Rome (Articles 226–227 of the Treaty Establishing the European Community [TEC], subsequently Articles 258–259 of the Treaty on the Functioning of the European Union [TFEU]). Thus, on these sorts of politically sensitive claims, the treaty seemed to make access to the Court a political question for national executives or the Commission.

Not long after however, in the famous *Van Gend & Loos* decision of 1963,[15] the Court recognized, de facto, private-party standing for similar types of

---

13. DTC 1/2004, at part 3, http://www.tribunalconstitucional.es/es/jurisprudencia/restrad/Paginas/DTC122004en.aspx (last visited July 7, 2009).

14. The purpose of this discussion is not to retrace the milestones of the ECJ's "constitutionalizing" jurisprudence in the 1960s and 1970s (direct effect, supremacy, implied powers, etc.), which other scholars have quite ably explored from both a legal and political science perspective. See, e.g., Weiler (1991); Stone Sweet (2004).

15. Case 26/62, *Van Gend & Loos v. Nederlandse Administratie der Belastingen*, 1963 E.C.R. 1.

claims under the preliminary reference procedure of the old Article 177 (Article 234 TEC/Article 267 TFEU). In giving private parties standing to challenge Member State compliance with their obligations under supranational law, the Court vastly increased the reach of its review function. No longer would it be dependent on the political gatekeeping of the other Member States or the Commission. Rather, it could now take cases stemming from the strategic legal calculations of individual litigants in national courts, along with those of lower national judges. *Van Gend & Loos* was an effective invitation to lower national courts, as one American political scientist put it, "to circumvent the restrictive jurisprudence of higher courts, and to re-open legal debates which had been closed, and thus to try for legal outcomes of their preference for policy or legal reasons."[16]

Robert Lecourt, the French judge on the ECJ widely credited as the principal author of *Van Gend & Loos,* would later admit that among his primary concerns was "the extreme vulnerability of the Community's legal order if it could only rely on sanctioning through the censure of a long and insufficient infringement procedure."[17] A new reading of the Court's preliminary reference jurisdiction was essential, in his view, to bolster the review function of the Court, inadequate by the terms of the original treaties. As he put it in *Van Gend & Loos:* "The vigilance of individuals concerned to protect their rights amounts to an effective supervision in addition to the supervision entrusted by [the infringement procedure] to the diligence of the Commission and of the Member States." The decision further stated: "A restriction of the guarantees against infringement . . . by Member States to the procedures under Article 169 and 170 would remove all direct protection of the individual rights of their nationals." More importantly, Article 169 and 170 would be "ineffective," if recourse to them was made "after the implementation of a national decision taken contrary to the provisions of the Treaty."[18] By recognizing the standing of private parties to bring compliance claims by way of preliminary reference, the ECJ opened the door to extensive supranational judicial intervention into national legal orders.[19]

---

16. Alter (1996), 466; see also Alter (2001), 3.

17. Lecourt (1991), 360, as translated in Alter (2001), 15.

18. 1963 E.C.R. at 13.

19. Contrast the Court's approach in this context to its hostile attitude toward private-party standing to challenge the legality of Community action under the old Article 173 (Article 230 TEC/Article 263 TFEU). See this chapter, nn. 34–40 and accompanying text.

This judgment (as with all others of the ECJ) was issued per curiam, which meant that outsiders did not understand how deeply contested it in fact was within the Court itself, with four judges reportedly voting for and three against the final version.[20] Nevertheless, the expansive interpretation of the Court's preliminary reference jurisdiction would provide the procedural foundation for the articulation of the major substantive "constitutional" doctrines of Community law—direct effect and supremacy—the latter also based on a creative interpretation of the "duty of Community loyalty" under the old Article 5 of the original treaty (later Article 10 TEC/Article 4(3) TFEU). It also became the basis for the imposition of a whole range of procedural and remedial requirements within national legal systems designed to promote the effectiveness of Community law. The consequences are well known among lawyers and judges who are regularly involved in European legal matters, as one commentator succinctly described:

> When faced with Community law, the [national] judge must apply different standards of interpretation and construction, he must review legislation and administrative action even in circumstances where applicable national law would not allow him to do so. Sometimes he must even offer remedies which simply are not available under national law. . . . In States where the primary legislature, for instance, is still considered, in law, to be sovereign and immune from judicial review, this no longer holds true within the scope of Community law. Where Community law is at stake, primary legislation loses its immunity from judicial review by ordinary courts. In addition, in the realm of Community law, courts have the competence to grant interim relief against the Crown, even if that was unheard of before. Likewise, the State is no longer immune from actions in damages even for legislative wrong and even in those States which are still immune outside the sphere of Community law.[21]

Undergirding this extensive case law was a method of treaty interpretation—the so-called *teleological method*. This approach was based on the idea that "an ever closer union among the peoples of Europe" (as set out in the preamble to the Treaty of Rome) constituted the very purpose—the *telos*—of European integration, which justified interpretations of the treaty most

---

20. Rasmussen (2008), cited in Kaiser (2008), 308.

21. Claes (2006), 5–6.

conducive to its achievement. The related notion of *effet utile* took the teleo-logical method to the level of individual provisions, holding that "once the purpose of [a particular treaty] provision [was] clearly identified, its detailed terms [would] be interpreted so 'as to ensure that the provision retains its effectiveness.'"[22] The Court used the teleological approach and *effet utile* to overcome textual obstacles, ambiguities, or silences in the treaties to achieve the aims of integration as the judges understood them, looking to what they regarded as the "spirit" and "general scheme," and not just the "wording" of the treaty.[23] On this basis, as one judge would later claim, the drafters of the Treaty of Rome purportedly built a "preference for Europe" into "the genetic code transmitted to the Court."[24]

The teleological method and *effet utile* are now so closely identified with the ECJ that observers often overlook their essentially functionalist charac-ter. It was born of the same jurisprudential mindset that rationalized the restructuring of the administrative state (and unprecedented intervention into society) from the 1920s to the 1950s. In interwar Britain, for example, Harold Laski called for a similar method of statutory interpretation "less analytical and more functional in character," which "should seek to discover the effect of the legislative precept in action."[25] Robert Lecourt, whose 1931 doctoral dissertation reflected the strongly functionalist spirit of the inter-war period,[26] would later argue that instrumental-functional concerns should guide all legal interpretation: Law was inherently "in the service of an objec-tive," he argued in his book *L'Europe des juges* (1976), and "[t]he goal is the engine of the law."[27]

The functionalist interpretation of the Court's jurisdiction under the pre-liminary reference mechanism overshadowed, however, what was supposed to be the ECJ's primary role: acting as a supranational *juridiction administrative* on the model of the French *Conseil d'Etat*, established to control the legality

---

22. Fennelly (1997), 674, quoting Case 9/70, *Grad v. Finanzamt Traunstein*, 1970 E.C.R. 825, 837, para. 5.

23. See, e.g., 1963 E.C.R. at 12.

24. Mancini and Keeling (1994), 186.

25. See Chapter 2, n. 123 and accompanying text.

26. Lecourt (1931), 282–83 (describing the *action en réintégrande*—designed to reestablish possession of property after violent dispossession—as "a remarkable example of a purely judicial construction necessitated by equity and practical circumstances in the face of textual silence or imprecision," guided by the "same principle [on which] our entire law rests ... the interdiction of violence").

27. Lecourt (1976), 305; see also Alter (2001), 20.

of regulatory action taken by Community institutions, not the Member States.[28] In this regard, the treaties quite expressly gave private parties standing to invoke the jurisdiction of the Court, with its judicial authority directed at the Commission and Council. In this respect it was indisputable that treaties created a "new legal order," as the Court famously claimed in *Van Gend & Loos*, although it was not necessarily the one defined by Lecourt.[29] Given the largely executive and technocratic character of the new Community as envisioned by Monnet and his team in 1950–1951 (including Maurice Lagrange, a member of the French *Conseil d'Etat* and later the first Advocate-General on the ECJ), it was only natural that a tribunal would be established at the Community level to enforce legality against administrative power in its new supranational guise.[30] The French socialist André Philip, in a pamphlet supporting the Schuman Plan published by the European Movement in 1951, expressed the typical view of the Court and its role: The new ECJ had been explicitly "modeled on the French Council of State (*Conseil d'Etat*), an administrative institution which has in fact ensured the protection of private interests and individual liberties for more than a century."[31]

Although the ECJ would generally take seriously the protection of certain individual rights in the Community regulatory process,[32] the Court would take much more seriously its role in promoting the effectiveness of Community law in national courts through the preliminary reference procedure. On the one hand, the Court has been extraordinarily solicitous, even in the absence of a clear textual basis in the treaties, toward private party standing with regard to preliminary references—going so far, in fact, as to recognize entirely new causes of action (including state liability in *Francovich*)[33]— in order to maximize Member State compliance with their Community legal obligations. By contrast, even though the treaty text itself is more open to the

---

28. Treaty of Paris, art. 33; Treaty of Rome, art. 173. Both these articles grounded the four bases for judicial control directly on the four analogous bases in French administrative law (under the so-called *recours pour excès de pouvoir*, or action for breach of authority): lack of competence, infringement of an essential procedural requirement, infringement of the Treaty or of any rule of law relating to its application, and misuse of powers.

29. 1963 E.C.R., at 12.

30. Lagrange (1979 [1976]), 2:128.

31. Philip (1951), 38; see also Ministre des affaires étrangères (1951).

32. See generally Bignami (2005).

33. Cases C-6 and 9/90, *Francovich and Others v. Italy*, 1991 E.C.R. I-5357 (creating a damages remedy in national court for Member State failure to properly transpose Community directives into national law).

standing of private-party challenges to the legality of Community action (after all, this was supposed to be the Court's principal function), the Court has been extraordinarily restrictive in this context, even downright hostile.

The test for "individual concern" within the meaning of the old Article 173 (Article 230 TEC), formulated originally in the *Plaumann* case of 1963,[34] made it "literally impossible for an applicant *ever* to succeed" in a third-party challenge to the legality of a decision addressed to another person, "except in a very limited category of retrospective cases."[35] The Court further extended the restrictive *Plaumann* test to challenges to regulations as well.[36] Despite persistent criticism from scholars and recent calls for liberalization from among the ranks of the advocates-general,[37] the ECJ held firm, claiming that any alteration to the requirements for private-party standing to challenge Community action would require an amendment to the treaty.[38] (In fact, the new Article 263 TFEU partially eliminates the "individual concern" requirement, at least with regard to a "regulatory act . . . which does not entail implementing measures"—in those circumstances, the party need only show "direct concern.")[39]

The Court, of course, exhibited no similar hesitations toward expansively interpreting private-party standing to challenge Member State action in either *Van Gend & Loos* or *Francovich*, despite significantly weaker textual bases in the treaties. As Advocate-General Jacobs noted in *Unión de Pequeños Agricultores* in 2002 in calling for liberalization of standing under Article 230 TEC, the Court had always seemed willing to "extend the scope

34. Case 25/62, *Plaumann & Co. v. Commission*, 1963 E.C.R. 95.

35. Craig and de Búrca (2008), 512. In an otherwise excellent historical treatment, Vauchez (2008), 24, misreads the import of this restrictive standing jurisprudence as "an important guarantee given to the Member States that individuals would not intervene too often and too much in EC politics," rather than what it in fact was, an effort to augment the autonomy of supranational policy processes from particularist claims advanced in litigation.

36. Craig and de Búrca (2008), 517–20. The only exceptions are the antidumping, competition, and state aids contexts, where the Court could not avoid the clear mandate of the treaty to take a more liberal approach.

37. See, e.g., the Opinion of Advocate General Jacobs in Case C-50/00 P, *Unión de Pequeños Agricultores v. Council*, 2002 E.C.R. I-6677.

38. 2002 E.C.R. at I-6735-36, para. 45.

39. In a press release in November 2009 outlining the impact of the entry into force of the Treaty of Lisbon on the supranational judicial system, the ECJ indicated that this new language "eases the conditions for the admissibility of actions brought by individuals (natural or legal persons) against decisions of the institutions, bodies, offices or agencies of the European Union," indicating that the party need only show that "they are directly affected by it." See Court of Justice of the European Communities (2009), 3.

of judicial protection in response to the growth of powers of the Community institutions," but not here. He further pointed out that "to insulate potentially unlawful measures from judicial scrutiny cannot be justified on grounds of administrative or legislative efficiency."[40] Indeed, one could fairly argue that the lack of autonomous democratic and constitutional legitimation in the supranational policy process warrants *more, not less, liberal standing* for private parties challenging the legality of Community acts (again, this would be consistent with the ECJ's original purpose, as a supranational *juridiction administrative*).

The Court, however, has generally overlooked the legal implications of the executive-technocratic character of the Community's legislative process. The notable exceptions have come not from judges themselves but arguably from its advocates-general. In *Costa v. ENEL*,[41] the 1964 judgment in which the Court laid the groundwork for what would become the doctrine of supremacy of Community law, Advocate-General Lagrange was forced to acknowledge the executive-technocratic character of integration in order to join issue with views then emerging in West Germany on the constitutionality of integration.[42] These views questioned, as Lagrange put it, whether the Community "[o]ffers the citizens of the Federal Republic the fullness of the guarantees which are allowed to them by the constitution of the country, in particular because measures of a legislative nature may be taken within the framework of the Community by organs of a non-parliamentary nature (Council, Commission) in those cases where, by German law, they could only fall within the jurisdiction of Parliament."[43] To this, Lagrange countered:

> Community regulations, even the most important ones, are not legislative measures nor even, as is sometimes said, "quasi-legislative measures" but rather measures emanating from an *executive power* (Council or Commission) [emphasis in original] which can only act within the

---

40. Opinion of Advocate General Jacobs, 2002 E.C.R. at I-6715-17, para. 102 (4)-(5).

41. Case 6/64, *Costa v. ENEL*, 1964 E.C.R. 585, 600, Opinion of Advocate-General Lagrange. The role of the advocate-general is to represent the public interest in the litigation and to offer a recommendation to the Court as to how it is to decide. The advocate-general's opinions are published along with the Court's opinion and constitute a kind of persuasive authority about the state of the law. The office of advocate-general again reflects the influence of the French model on the ECJ (a similar office exists in both French civil and administrative justice).

42. See this chapter, nn. 102–105 and accompanying text.

43. 1964 E.C.R., at 604.

framework of the powers delegated to it by the Treaty and within the jurisdictional control of the Court of Justice. It is certainly true to say that the Treaty of Rome has, in a sense, the character of a genuine constitution, the constitution of the Community . . . ; but for the greater part the Treaty has, above all, the character of an "outline law" [*loi-cadre* in the original French] and this is a perfectly legitimate method where a situation of an evolutionary nature such as the establishment of a common market is concerned, in respect of which the object to be attained and the conditions to be realized (rather than the detailed rules for its realization) are defined in such a way that the generality of the provisions need not exclude precision: [W]e are still far from the "carte blanche" given to the executive by certain national parliaments.[44]

Lagrange was offering here a typically functionalist rationale for delegation of legislative power to executive and administrative bodies in the postwar decades.[45] There existed, he asserted, "a situation of an evolutionary nature"—the creation of the common market—which called for a *loi-cadre* that would, on the one hand, define general goals but, on the other, leave the elaboration of the "detailed rules" to "an executive power." All of this was "perfectly legitimate," Lagrange stated, as long as the enabling legislation defined sufficiently "the object to be attained and the conditions to be realized" so that the delegation would not amount to a legislative "carte blanche" (as had been so constitutionally problematic in the interwar period).[46] Moreover, within the scope of the delegation, Lagrange asserted, an executive-technocratic body ("Council or Commission") had to retain decisive influence, subject to judicial oversight by the Court.

In this description, Lagrange never really addressed the essence of the emerging German constitutional concern (which we will be taking up in greater detail in the next section).[47] The Basic Law of the Federal Republic authorized delegation to be sure, but only on the assumption that the counterbalancing *national* executive and judicial control mechanisms

---

44. 1964 E.C.R., at 604–05.

45. See also Lagrange's opinion of 14 June 1957 in Joined Cases 7/56 and 3-7/57, *Dineke Algera et al. v. Common Assembly of the European Coal and Steel Community*, 1957 E.C.R. 39, quoted in Curtin (2009), 44: "The Treaty is based upon delegation, with the consent of the Member States, of sovereignty to supranational institutions for a strictly defined purpose."

46. On the use of the phrase "carte blanche" to describe uncontrolled delegation in the interwar period, see Lindseth (2004), 1381 (quoting Carré de Malberg (1984 [1931]), 88).

47. See this chapter, nn. 102–105 and accompanying text.

would *themselves* possess some kind autonomous constitutional legitimacy sufficient to compensate for the shift in the locus of normative power outside the parliamentary realm. Lagrange's description of the delegated character of Community governance, accurate in the main though it was, simply begged the question of the constitutional legitimacy of the Community's denationalized executive, technocracy, and judiciary.

Lagrange's description in fact confused the *form* of controls with their necessary socio-constitutional *substance,* which led him uncritically to impute to Community institutions (and especially the Court) a legitimating function comparable to that of national constitutional bodies within the postwar administrative state. As he stated, in a striking passage:

> The citizens of the Federal Republic therefore do find within the Community legal system certain guarantees, in particular through review by the Court, which, albeit not identical, *are still comparable* to those which their own national system ensured (prior to the transfer of jurisdiction under the Treaty) by the existence of a more extensive supremacy in Parliament.[48]

The idea that a supranational court could substitute itself for a national parliament as a legitimating mechanism was, to say the least, extraordinary. It was arguably expressive of a profound faith in judges (even supranational ones) as guarantors of political order in the postwar era. And in this respect, Lagrange simply presaged what would become the Court's own conventional understanding by the 1980s: In the Court's famous phrase, the treaties were a "constitutional charter of a Community based on the rule of law,"[49] in which the Court itself served as the ultimate legitimating mechanism, free from mediation through any national constitutional body. The Member States, at least insofar as their Community obligations were concerned, would in the Court's eyes become mere "trustees of the common interest."[50]

In this reading of the Court's role, the ECJ had exclusive authority in declaring a Community law invalid,[51] a particularly problematic assertion in

---

48. 1964 E.C.R., at 605 (emphasis added).

49. Case 294/83, *Parti écologiste "Les Verts" v. Parliament,* 1986 E.C.R. 1339, 1365, para. 23; see also Opinion 1/91, 1991 E.C.R. I-6079, I-6102, para. 21; and Case C-2/88 *Imm., Zwartveld et al.,* 1990 E.C.R. I-3365, I-3373, para. 16.

50. Case 804/79, *Commission v. United Kingdom,* 1981 E.C.R. 1045, 1075, para. 30.

51. See, e.g., Case 314/85, *Foto Frost v. Hauptzollamt Lübeck-Ost,* 1987 E.C.R. 4199.

light of the future conflict over *Kompetenz-Kompetenz.*[52] In exercising this pre-rogative, the Court looked only to the functional demands of integration, hold-ing that any contrary national rules—including those of a constitutional nature—needed to give way.[53] Thus, as one commentator described the ECJ's outlook, "even the most minor piece of technical Community legislation ranks above the most cherished national constitutional norm."[54] At no time, how-ever, did the ECJ's case law take seriously, much less even explore, the legal implications of Community regulation "emanating from an *executive power* (Council or Commission) which can only act within the framework of the powers delegated to it by the Treaty and within the jurisdictional control of the Court of Justice," to recall the words of Advocate-General Lagrange in *Costa.*[55]

If we think counterfactually for a moment—imagining an ECJ more vigor-ous in its policing of the bounds of supranational delegation—we might expect decisions periodically striking down a piece of supranational legisla-tion on the grounds that it exceeded the scope of the power delegated to the supranational level. This has certainly not been uncommon on the national level under the postwar constitutional settlement.[56] But as two leading com-mentators would write in the mid-1990s, the Court had not seen fit, up to that point at least, to invalidate a piece of Community legislation "for pure and simple lack of competence."[57] The first decision in which it appeared to do so came in 2000, in the *Tobacco Advertising* judgment,[58] in what was some-times perceived as a delayed response to the German Maastricht Decision of the German Federal Constitutional Court in 1993.[59] However, for those who thought *Tobacco Advertising* portended more vigorous policing of

---

52. See this chapter, nn. 163–165 and accompanying text.

53. Case 11/70, *Internationale Handelsgesellschaft*, 1970 E.C.R. 1125, 1134 ("the validity of a Community measure or its effect within a Member State cannot be affected by allega-tions that it runs counter to either fundamental rights as formulated by the constitution of that State or the principles of national constitutional structure").

54. Weatherill (1995), 106.

55. See this chapter, n. 44 and accompanying text (emphasis added).

56. See, e.g., Kischel (1994), 239.

57. Weiler and Trachtman (1996–1997), 388; see also de Witte (1991), 3 ("the Court of Justice has, until now, never found the Community to be acting *ultra vires*").

58. Case C-376/98, *Germany v. Parliament and Council*, 2000 ECR I-8419 (striking down the tobacco advertising directive).

59. See this chapter, n. 166 and accompanying text; but see also Opinion 2/94, 1996 E.C.R. I-1759, discussed in this chapter, at nn. 184–186 and accompanying text, which clearly was in response to the *Maastricht Decision* of the German court.

Community competence by the Court (or by the Commission and Council, for that matter), they were soon disappointed. As one commentator concluded in 2005, "one need only scratch the legislative surface to reveal measures that seem questionable in light of *Tobacco Advertising* yet which even subsequently to that judgment have sailed through on the wind of unanimous support in the Council. *Plus ça change, plus ça reste la même chose.*"[60]

And none of this problematic legislation yielded a Court challenge of any significance on the question of the scope of the Community's competence. In fact, the reasoning of *Tobacco Advertising* was itself sufficiently ambiguous that six years later the Court could rather easily validate, using its long-established teleological and functional approach, a renewed effort by the Commission and Council to adopt a modified version of the same legislation as properly within the scope of supranational power.[61] The teleological approach, the Court's jurisprudence had already established, permitted the most capacious possible reading of the legislative bases in the treaty relating to the creation of the internal market. This inclination to expansive interpretation in turn permitted the Court to dismiss the idea that more specific, and substantively and procedurally more restrictive, legislative bases were controlling; nor did the Court need to confront the possibility that the treaties did not in fact delegate the legislative power to the Community in the first place.[62] The case law typically found, rather, that the functional demands of market integration overwhelmed other legal boundaries in the treaties.[63]

It has been through the Court's role under the preliminary reference mechanism that the Court has forged an objective alliance with private litigants to expand the Community's normative reach into unexpected corners of market regulation. This alliance manifested itself most clearly in the judicial enforcement of the free movement of goods provisions of the treaty—the

---

60. Weatherill (2005), 14.

61. Case C-380/03, *Germany v. Parliament and Council*, 2006 ECR I-11573.

62. See Lindseth (1999), 705–10 and 714–26.

63. The pillar structure introduced by the Treaty of Maastricht in 1992, with common foreign and security policy (CFSP) and justice and home affairs (JHA) outside the Community pillar, complicates this picture somewhat. Compare, e.g., Case C-176/03, *Commission v. Council*, 2005 E.C.R. I-7879 (holding that, although criminal law does not, as a rule, fall within the Community's sphere of competence, the Community does have an implied competence linked to a specific legal basis in the Community pillar and may therefore adopt appropriate criminal law measures) with Case 440/05, *Commission v. Council*, 2007 E.C.R. I-9097, para. 70 (holding that, "contrary to the submission of the Commission, the determination of the type and level of the criminal penalties to be applied does not fall within the Community's sphere of competence").

most fundamental aspect of the Community's "material constitution"[64]—in the face of contrary national restrictions and regulatory requirements.[65] But one could also discern its effects in the Court's enforcement of the other freedoms as well (the free movement of workers, services, and capital, as well as the right of establishment). By the 1990s, scholarly observers began to query whether this jurisprudence constituted the realization of the long-predicted spillover effect, which had been central to neofunctionalist theory of the 1950s and 1960s.[66] But contrary to the neofunctionalist predictions, it was the law that "function[ed] as a mask for politics, precisely the role neofunctionalists originally forecast for economics."[67] Indeed, recent historical research (notably of Antoine Vauchez but also of Morten Rasmussen) has uncovered the extent to which this was a conscious strategy of the Court in the 1960s, pursued by Robert Lecourt as well as other judges, clerks, and lawyers close to the ECJ.[68] In the effort to construct Europe, these supranational legal professionals viewed themselves, in effect, as "the institutionalized carriers of the European idea" in the face of political resistance or reluctance.[69]

---

64. Weiler (1999b), 354; see more generally Poiares Maduro (1998).

65. The key treaty provision, the old Article 30 (Article 28 TEC/Article 36 TFEU), prohibits the Member States from imposing "quantitative restrictions on imports" (i.e., quotas) and, more importantly, "all measures having equivalent effect," language specifically directed against nontariff barriers to the free movement of goods.

66. See generally Burley and Mattli (1993); on neofunctionalist theory and the spillover effect, see Chapter 3, nn. 50–51 and accompanying text.

67. Burley and Mattli (1993), 44.

68. See generally Vauchez (2008), and especially at 20, translating Lecourt (1964), 22:

> The legal method to unify Europe lies in the fact that EC law has the effect of multiplying relations, associations, transactions beyond borders, as well as of triggering narrow interrelations of activities, interests, and human relationships. The resulting interpenetration of populations cements *in concreto* a lively Europe become irreversible. Thereby, this process will necessarily call for a political coronation required by the very needs of the population ruled by this unique body of law.

> But it is important to add that lawyers within the Legal Service of the Commission also played a key role. See Vauchez (2008), 9–10, citing, inter alia, Rasmussen (2008). And the implications of the Court's activities were not lost on Walter Hallstein either. Vauchez (2008), 22.

69. Vauchez (2008), 16, citing the statement of Judge Donner (as quoted in Feld (1964), 116). Vauchez describes the increasing "transgression of the separation of political and judicial orders" following the French veto of the first British application for membership in 1963:

> This transgression . . . is also made by the director of the Commission's Legal service, Michel Gaudet: "while the statesmen discuss the political future of Europe, without sparing the weight of their authority and the fiery of their convictions, the lawyers of our six countries dedicate themselves to the *birth* of a European *law* which is discreet, yet full of promises" (underlined in the text, Gaudet (1963)). A couple of weeks later, ECJ

It was arguably this judicially led process of spillover that the national executives were reacting against, at least in part, when they expanded the scope of qualified-majority voting (QMV) in the 1980s as a means of restoring political control over internal market integration.[70] Today, the concept of spillover has seeped into the general political discourse (particularly in the debates over the Constitutional Treaty and the Treaty of Lisbon) and is now more prosaically described as "competence creep."[71] We should not overly minimize, however, the role of national executives even in this process of judicially sanctioned spillover or competence creep. Although the Court's decisions in particular cases cannot be explained in terms of ongoing national control,[72] the Court offered a normatively attractive option to national executives nonetheless: a uniform and centralized source of legal judgments consistent with free movement and market integration—goals to which the Member States had clearly committed themselves in the treaties.[73] Although certain Member State executives might sometimes find this process disruptive in particular corners of their own national law,[74] they ultimately

---

judge and former political leader Robert Lecourt went further, indicating ECJ's case-law as one of the possible fuel for a lasting European integration: "in times where the establishment of a political construction is at a standstill, the field is clear to accomplish other, certainly more modest, progresses but ... which might be determinant.... The practical Europe, which evolves under the influence of mere facts, could soon make political Europe inevitable." (Lecourt (1963), 31).

Vauchez (2008), 16 (all internal quotations translated by Vauchez).

70. See Lenaerts (1992), 110–11 (asserting that, post-1986, minimal harmonization combined with QMV were "better than the alternative of letting the judicial process continue to make the necessary policy choices incrementally.... In other words, Member States were led to prefer political legislation, even at the risk of being pushed into the minority on a vote concluding Council deliberations among the Member States, to a kind of 'creeping legislation' through the judicial process, to which they were completely external.")

71. See, e.g., Weatherill (2005).

72. For a succinct overview of the scholarly debate regarding the responsiveness of the ECJ to national control, prompted in particular by the work of Geoffrey Garrett in the early 1990s, see Pollack (2006b), 40 (describing how subsequent work has shown that "the Court has been able to pursue the process of legal integration far beyond the collective preferences of the member governments, in part because of the high costs to member states in overruling or failing to comply with ECJ decisions").

73. Cf. Moravcsik (1998), 9 (arguing that Member State decisions to delegate to the supranational level in the European Community "are best explained as efforts by governments to constrain and control one another—in game-theoretical language, by their effort to enhance the credibility of commitments").

74. See, e.g., the "turnover tax struggle" in Germany in the 1960s, discussed earlier, this chapter, n. 5. See also the discussion of the ECJ's recent tax jurisprudence in Graetz and Warren (2006).

acquiesced because it was so functionally suited to policing national compliance with supranational obligations.[75]

In short, resorting to case-by-case adjudication to overcome the complex and varied ways in which national rules might impede free movement turned out to be an ingenious way to avoid, at least initially, the more cumbersome political process (particularly under conditions of unanimity) of identifying domains for legislative harmonization and then achieving a difficult political consensus to remove those impediments.[76] As the political scientists Alec Stone Sweet and James Caporaso have shown, there is statistical evidence that preliminary references and legislative harmonization ("negative" and "positive" integration) operated symbiotically over time, with the Commission and Council using references to the Court as a kind of signaling mechanism to indicate the domains ripe for the adoption of a harmonization directive.[77]

Despite national executives' relative loss of direct control, there was much in the ECJ case law that they found favorable to their political position vis-à-vis potential domestic institutional obstacles. Perhaps most importantly, this case law created a means by which national executives could, under the guise of integration, effectively impose legislative decisions on national parliaments,[78]

---

75. Kelemen (2006), 105 ("member state governments have supported this approach because they doubt one another's commitment to implementation and seek to facilitate enforcement actions against noncompliant states"). Perhaps this explains the Member States' acquiescence to the damages remedy in *Francovich*. See this chapter, n. 33 and accompanying text.

76. The Court in fact contributed significantly to the effort to find a means of overcoming nontariff trade barriers without full harmonization, through its decision in *Cassis de Dijon* (Case 120/78, *Rewe-Zentral AG v. Bundesmonopolverwaltung für Branntwein*, 1979 E.C.R. 649). The Commission later exploited this decision as a basis for an approach to free movement based in minimal harmonization and mutual recognition of regulatory standards. For an analysis, see Alter and Meunier-Aitsahalia (1994); see also Lindseth (1999), 664–65.

77. See Stone Sweet and Caporaso (1998a) (finding a positive and significant statistical relationship between references and subsequent Community legislation); see also Stone Sweet and Caporaso (1998b). The study also found, importantly, that there was a nearly linear relationship between increases in intra-Community trade and Article 177 references, suggesting a direct linkage between the two.

78. See Chapter 3, nn. 169–170 and accompanying text. There were also corresponding developments within national constitutional law, augmenting executive power against the national parliament as a means of facilitating participation in European integration. The best example is the accession legislation adopted by the British parliament—the European Communities Act, 1972 Eliz. 2, c. 68—which provided that, as a general matter, the implementation of Community directives into British law would be done by way of *statutory instrument* (in effect, executive order) and not by parliamentary legislation.

as well as on decentralized bodies such as municipalities,[79] and even on public service providers.[80] The 1970s also saw other examples in which the ECJ quietly permitted the extension of the Council's legislative competences—for example, in the area of the free movement of workers (Article 48 of the Treaty of Rome; later Article 39 TEC/Article 45 TFEU), interpreting it to reach qualifications for educational grants, even though at the time educational policy was clearly outside Community jurisdiction.[81] Finally, the Court permitted the use of the spillover legislative authority under Article 235 of the Treaty of Rome, which was modeled on the old Article 95 of the Treaty of Paris.[82] Under Article 235 (later Article 308 TEC/Article 352 TFEU), the Council had power to adopt by unanimity, on a proposal from the Commission and after "consulting" the European Parliament, "appropriate measures" that were needed where "action by the Community should prove necessary to attain, in the course of the operation of the common market, one of the objectives of the Community and this [where] Treaty has not provided the necessary powers."

The old Article 235 amounted, in effect, to a reserve authority that could be deployed where the treaty proved insufficiently flexible for the Commission's and Council's purposes. Interestingly, this provision had been inserted into the treaty by the *groupe juridique,* specifically as a "corrective" to the "extreme casuism of the attributions of competence which characterize[d] the EEC treaty."[83] In this sense, a kind of functionalist,

---

Ibid., section 2(2) (subject to the exceptions set out in section 1(1), e.g., "to make any provision imposing or increasing taxation" or "to create any new criminal offence punishable with imprisonment for more than two years"). Thus, upon accession to the Community, the British parliament relinquished its right to vote on the form and content of the implementation of most directives, limiting its powers, rather, to scrutiny mechanisms described in Chapter 5, nn. 95–99 and accompanying text. Compare the Irish European Communities Act, more particularly section 3(2), which provides for implementation of Community directives by way of ministerial statutory instrument with minimal parliamentary control. In *Meagher v. Minister for Agriculture and Attorney General,* [1994] 1 I.R. 347, the Supreme Court of Ireland interpreted this provision to find that implementation of Community directives in could not be challenged under Article 29 of the Irish constitution, even if the statutory instruments fell within the legislative power vested exclusively in the *Oireachtas* (Irish parliament) under Article 15 of the constitution. For a discussion, as well as later case refining this holding, see Claes (2006), 636–37. See also Phelan (1997), 339.

79. Case 103/88, *Fratelli Costanza SpA v. Commune di Milano,* 1989 E.C.R. 1839, 1870–71, paras. 30–31.

80. Case C-188/89, *A. Foster and Others v. British Gas plc,* 1990 E.C.R. I-3313, paras. 18–20.

81. See Case 9/74, *Casagrande v. Landeshauptstadt München,* 1974 E.C.R. 773, 777–78, para. 2.

82. See Chapter 3, n. 49 and accompanying text.

83. Pescatore (1981), 172.

teleological flexibility was built directly into the Community's legislative process, giving the Council a legal basis to adopt Commission proposals in such areas as environmental policy and consumer protection before these areas were explicitly added to Community jurisdiction.[84] This sort of legislative spillover was politically palatable precisely because national executives—the principal mechanism of democratic legitimation in the postwar administrative state—maintained effective control over this portion of the Community's legislative output by way of unanimity. In this regard, the corrective of the old Article 235 was very much dependent on notions of executive leadership that were central to the postwar constitutional settlement.[85]

As we shall see below, however, the use of this legislative basis would also be among the central concerns of national high courts in the 1990s, once they turned their attention to the constitutional limitations, if any, on supranational delegation.[86] But first we must consider the attitudes of national high courts in the intervening decades. If a relatively autonomous, supranational adjudicative body proved functionally attractive to national executives during this period, it would prove nearly so to the national high courts over time. Prior to the 1990s, the national high courts quite successfully came to terms with the political choice in favor of integration, and more particularly with the compliance function delegated to the ECJ. In doing so, the national high courts helped to institutionalize a sort of *dualité de juridiction*—a dual court system—that was not unprecedented, paralleling the judicial acceptance of administrative justice on the national level, an essential historical precondition to the eventual constitutional settlement of administrative governance in the twentieth century.[87]

❦ 4.2 Defining National Judicial Deference to Supranational Delegation from the 1960s to the 1980s

Animating postwar constitutions in Western Europe was not merely a desire for national reconstruction. Rather, also imbuing these constitutions was an

---

84. For a summary, see Usher (1988), 30; see also Weiler (1991), 2444–47.

85. Perhaps for this reason, modern-day adherents to neofunctionalist theory, unlike their predecessors, recognize the role of national executives in ratifying the process of spillover. See, e.g., Stone Sweet (2004), 17–18.

86. See this chapter, nn. 183–186 and accompanying text.

87. See this chapter, nn. 131–144 and accompanying text.

"internationalist spirit," which would manifest itself in constitutional provisions that explicitly authorized delegation of powers to international organizations in the interest of peace.[88] This "openness toward international law" (*Völkerrechtsfreundlichkeit*), as Germans termed it,[89] was of course born of a very specific history. It reflected both a post-Nuremberg aspiration to protect a new range of human rights as well as a New Deal-type faith in the possibilities of international organizations as functional, technocratic problem-solvers.[90]

The Dutch constitution was emblematic of the most extreme adherence to this faith, textually open not merely to international delegations but also to the supremacy and direct effect of internationally produced regulatory norms in the domestic legal system.[91] But even in a country like Belgium, whose constitutional text was silent on international delegation until the 1970s,[92] the internationalist spirit was inescapable for national judges in the national legal system. Despite the lack of a secure textual basis, a constitutional rationale emerged over the course of the 1950s and 1960s to justify

---

88. See Chapter 2, n. 68 and accompanying text, citing Claes and de Witte (1998), 173; de Witte (1998), 282–86; and Claes (2005), 85–86.

89. See German Lisbon Decision (2009), para. 219.

90. Cf. Borgwardt (2005a), 239 ("While the jurisprudence underlying Nuremberg's charter was an unstable amalgam of natural law, common law, and traditional positivist reasoning, the tribunal's main contribution to postwar multilateralism was arguably its quasi-administrative, fact-finding role—another cherished objective of New Deal-style institutions"); see also Borgwardt (2005b), 401, 452–53.

91. A series of Dutch constitutional amendments in 1953 and 1956 made clear that international "agreements which, according to their terms, can be binding on anyone"—i.e., what Americans would call *self-executing agreements*—had primacy over both existing and subsequent national legislation. Claes and de Witte (1998), 173–75 (describing the insertion of Articles 65–66 into the Dutch constitution). As part of the same package of amendments, the Dutch constitution also recognized the direct effect of secondary normative decisions delegated to international organizations. Claes and de Witte (1998), 174 (describing Article 67 of the Dutch constitution). Moreover, as to European integration specifically, a 1962 judgment of the *Hoge Raad* (the supreme court of the Netherlands) recognized the authority of the ECJ by explicitly holding that a preliminary reference was required in order to determine whether provisions of the European treaties were self-executing within the scope of the direct effect and supremacy provisions of the Dutch constitution. Claes and de Witte (1998), 177 (citing *de Geus en Uitdenbogerd v. Robert Bosch GmbH et al.*, Hoge Raad, 18 May 1962, Nederlandse Jurisprudentie (1965), 115). The preliminary reference that gave rise to *Van Gend & Loos* (this chapter, n. 15) followed soon after. For additional background on the role of Dutch lawyers and judges promoting the idea of provisions of the Treaty of Rome as "self-executing" (particularly via the preliminary reference mechanism), see Vauchez (2008), 8–9.

92. See de Witte (2003), 354 (citing Belgian Constitution, art. 34—formerly art. 25*bis*—in French; my translation); see also Claes (2007), 15.

both supranational delegation and a kind of supremacy doctrine, in substance if not in name. This rationale derived from the treaty-making authority of the executive under the constitution, which was reconceptualized as superior to any contrary national rules (statutes and regulations).[93] This view, of course, depended on key elements of the postwar constitutional settlement: on the one hand, on the augmented legitimacy of the executive in representing the nation on the international level; on the other, on the transformed (and diminished) role of the legislature in the postwar constitutional system.[94] Parliamentary approval of treaties (and more particularly *European* treaties) came to be seen not as "an act of legislation" but simply as "an act of high oversight" (*une acte de haute tutelle*).[95] In other words, Belgian judges reevaluated the constitutional system in light of altered postwar understandings of separation of powers as well as integration's functional demands. In this way, they achieved their own kind of reconciliation between older legal categories and the newer institutional reality characterized by supranational delegation.

From the early 1960s onward, no constitutional system struggled more explicitly to achieve this sort of reconciliation than the German. As with other postwar constitutions in Western Europe, the West German Basic Law of 1949 was explicitly open to international delegation, as part of its more general *Völkerrechtsfreundlichkeit.*[96] Article 24(1) provided: "The Federation may by legislation transfer sovereign rights [*Hoheitsrechte*] to interstate institutions [*zwischenstaatliche Einrichtungen*]." *Hoheitsrechte*, it must be noted, is a term of art in German constitutional law, referring to "the form in which sovereignty is exercised," which "should not be confused with sovereignty itself, for which the German language has the different term of *Souveränität.*"

---

93. Claes (2006), 201, citing *mercuriales* by Ganshof van der Meersch (1968); and Ganshof van der Meersch (1969). A *mercuriale* is the speech given by the *procureur general* of the Belgian Court of Cassation (the supreme judicial court) at the beginning of the judicial term.

94. Compare Chapter 2, nn. 104–109 and accompanying text.

95. Ganshof van der Meersch (1968), 489. From this reconceptualization of the parliamentary role, Belgian judges moved rather easily to find that Community law prevailed over contrary national legislation or regulation. Claes (2006), 202–03, citing *Franco-Suisse Le Ski*, Belgian Court of Cassation, 27 May 1971, translated in Oppenheimer (1994/2003), 1:266. Subsequent decisions by Belgium's other two high courts (the *Conseil d'Etat* and the Court of Arbitration) confirm, however, that this supremacy does not prevail over the constitution itself, except insofar as the constitution explicitly permits it to do so. See de Witte (2003), 356–57.

96. For an overview, see de Witte (1998), 282–86 (emphasis in original).

Thus, the Basic Law did *not* permit "the transfer of a *portion* of *Souveränität* which remain[ed], indivisibly, with the German people," but it did permit the attribution of *Hoheitsrechte* "to international institutions, just as they [could] be attributed to the *Länder* institutions."[97] In other words, only normative power could be transferred, but the sovereign capacity for self-legitimation, embodied in the historically constituted bodies at the national level, necessarily remained.[98] Article 24, then, could be understood as an expression of the separation of power from legitimacy that was central to the postwar constitutional settlement of administrative governance.

Article 24 was not the only constitutional provision, however, of potential relevance to European integration in the Federal Republic. Several other provisions entrenched the principle of separation of powers—notably Article 20 (which, under the so-called "eternity clause" of Article 79(3), could not be amended)[99] and Article 129(3) (which declared "void" any purported grant to the executive a power "to issue provisions in place of statutes"). In the same spirit were the formal requirements for delegation of legislative power under Article 80(1), already described in detail in Chapter 2.[100] Taken together, these provisions potentially, although not necessarily, raised delicate legal issues for integration.

The problem, of course, was that integration entailed the extensive delegation of normative power to an institution dominated by national executives, the Council of Ministers, as Advocate-General Lagrange conceded in his opinion in *Costa*.[101] Even if the Basic Law authorized international delegation in the abstract, the question was whether the specific institutional structure of European integration, with its evident legislative empowerment of national executives through the Council, constituted a violation of the entrenched separation-of-powers provisions of the Basic Law. In the late 1950s and early 1960s, there was in fact "a fierce discussion in [the] German

---

97. de Witte (1998), 303 (citations omitted).

98. This is a point the *Bundesverfassungsgericht* would later make explicit in the German Lisbon Decision (2009), para. 232 ("there can be no independent subject of legitim[ation] for the authority of the European Union which constitutes itself, so to speak, on a higher level, without being derived from" the Member States).

99. See Chapter 2, n. 121 and accompanying text.

100. See Chapter 2, n. 74 and accompanying text.

101. See this chapter, nn. 41–46 and accompanying text.

legal literature as to whether German membership violated . . . German constitutional law."[102]

The German judiciary entered this debate famously in 1963, in a decision by the tax court in Rhineland-Palatinate (*Finanzgericht Rheinland-Pfalz*).[103] The *Finanzgericht* began by noting that the delegation of normative power to the Community (*qua* "executive organ") did not comply with the requirements in Article 80(1) of the Basic Law, which governed legislative delegations to the executive within the national constitutional system.[104] In deciding to refer the matter to the *Bundesverfassungsgericht*, however, the tax court further stressed the entrenched separation-of-powers principles in the Basic Law:

> Article 129(3) expressly prohibits the legislature from abdicating its legislative responsibility by excessively generous grants of power by allowing executive organs to alter or supplement statutes by regulation, or simply to issue regulations in the place of statutes. Articles 80 and 129 show the legislator's intention to restrict the law-making power, which is in practice indispensable to the executive, within the narrowest possible limits. Article 79(3) forbids infringement of the principle of separation of powers [through its reference to Article 20]. This emphasizes that the separation of powers is a principle of the highest importance, and that the limits of the exception contained in the Constitution itself [i.e., Article 80(1)] cannot be extended. There can be no doubt that to allow an executive organ to issue statutes [as European integration purportedly allowed] violates Article 79(3). Thus the Federal legislature's right to share its power with supra-national organisations is faced with an insuperable obstacle, where its exercise involves violating a fundamental constitutional principle such as separation of powers.[105]

When the *Bundesverfassungsgericht* finally responded to the reference in 1967, it relied heavily on Article 24 to uphold the constitutionality of

---

102. Claes (2006), 504, citing Mann (1972), 418ff; Hopt (1966); and Alter (2001), 71–80. It was to this legal literature that Advocate-General Lagrange was apparently referring in his opinion in *Costa*, discussed earlier, this chapter, nn. 42–43 and accompanying text.

103. *Re Tax on Malt Barley*, Case III 77/63, FG (Rheinland-Pfalz), 14 Nov. 1963, [1964] C.M.L.R. 130.

104. [1964] C.M.L.R. at 132–33.

105. Ibid., 135–36.

supranational delegation. "The Community itself is neither a state nor a federal state. It is a gradually integrating Community of a special nature, an 'interstate institution' in the sense of Article 24(1) of the Basic Law to which the Federal Republic of Germany—like many other member states—has 'transferred' certain sovereign rights."[106] The Court, in reaching this conclusion, also used terms suggesting a degree of autonomy for the Community that was the near polar opposite of the analysis of the *Finanzgericht:* "A new public authority was thus created which is *autonomous and independent* with regard to state authority of the separate member states. Consequently its acts have neither to be approved ('ratified') by the member states nor can they be annulled by them. The E.E.C. Treaty is as it were the *constitution of this Community.*"[107] The *Bundesverfassungsgericht* would never again describe the legal autonomy of the Community in such sweeping, seemingly constitutional terms.

Before the Court returned to the question of integration's relationship to the national constitutional order (in the famous *Solange I* decision of 1974),[108] another national high court—the Italian *Corte costituzionale*—entered the discussion in a way that would influence the subsequent development of the German case law. As in the Basic Law, the postwar Italian constitution contained a provision (Article 11) by which Italy agreed "on conditions of equality with other states, to the limitations of sovereignty necessary for an order that ensures peace and justice among Nations; it promotes and encourages international organizations having such ends in view."[109] In Italian constitutional law it was also well-settled that "'limitation' of sovereignty cannot become 'loss' of sovereignty,"[110] and that Article 11 only authorized a functional

---

106. BVerfG decision, 1 BvR 248/63, 1 BvR 216/67 of 18 Oct. 1967, [1968] 1 EuR 134, 135–36, as translated in Alter (2001), 78.

107. [1968] 1 EuR 134, 135–36, as translated in Alter (2001), 78 (emphasis added).

108. *Internationale Handelsgeselchaft mbH v. Einfuhr- und Vorratstelle für Getriebe und Futtermittel*, Case 2 BvG 52/71, BVerfGE 37, 271; [1974] 2 C.M.L.R. 540, 551 [hereinafter *Solange I*].

109. Costituzione art. 11, translated in Camera dei Deputati (1990), 72.

110. Cartabia (1998), 133, 134. The French *Conseil constitutionnel* has applied a similar formula to the interpretation of the authorization of "limitations" of sovereignty in the interest of international cooperation in Article 55 of the French constitution of 1958. C.C., dec. no. 76-71 of 29-30 Dec. 1976, *Parlement européen*, 74 I.L.R. 527, translated in Oppenheimer (1994/2003), 1:315 ("Since the Preamble to the Constitution of 1946, reaffirmed by the Preamble to the Constitution of 1958, states that subject to principles of reciprocity France agrees to limitations of sovereignty which are necessary for the organization and defence of peace, no provision of a constitutional nature allows all or part

curtailment but not a complete or even partial "alienat[ion]" of sovereignty to bodies operating under the joint authority of the participating states.[111] In a series of cases interpreting Article 11—stretching from *Frontini* in 1973[112] through *Granital* in 1984[113] and *Fragd* in 1989[114]—the Italian Constitutional Court upheld supranational delegation against formalist challenges (notably the claim that it unconstitutionally invaded the *riserva di legge*).[115] The Court also acknowledged that the Community legal order was separate from the national system, a political decision that Italian judges were bound to respect.[116] "The two legal orders are autonomous and separate," the Court stated in *Granital*, "even though there is co-ordination between them on the basis of the division of competences established and guaranteed by the Treaty."[117]

But the *Corte costituzionale* also alluded to the existence of certain "counter-limits" (*controlimiti*) to supranational normative autonomy and supremacy.[118] In a famous passage from *Frontini* (reiterated in the later cases), the Italian Constitutional Court warned that any "aberrant interpretation" of the treaty by which Community institutions might claim "an unacceptable power to violate the fundamental principles of our constitutional order or the inalienable rights of man" would compel the Court to "control

---

of national sovereignty to be transferred to any international organization"). For further discussion, see Claes (2006), 472–73.

111. de Witte (1998), 285 (referring to the general "doctrinal compromise" in "post-1945 Western Europe," of which Article 11 is a part). Article 11 may also be understood as an expression of the separation of power from legitimacy that was central to the constitutionalization of delegation as a means of governance.

112. Corte constituzionale, decision n. 183/73 of 27 Dec. 1973, *Frontini*, 18 Giur. Cost. I 2401; [1974] 2 C.M.L.R. 372; see also Oppenheimer (1994/2003), 1:629–40.

113. C. cost., decision n. 170/84 of 8 June 1984, *Granital*, Giur. Cost. I 1098; 21 *Common Market L. Rev.* 756 (1984) (with note by Giorgio Gaja); see also Oppenheimer (1994/2003), 1:643–52.

114. Corte costituzionale, decision n. 232/1989 of 21 Apr. 1989, *Fragd*, translated in Oppenheimer (1994/2003), 1:653–62.

115. *Frontini*, [1974] 2 C.M.L.R. at 383–84 (rejecting challenge to Community regulation because it failed to respect the *riserva di legge*, i.e., that portion of the legislative power which can only be exercised by the parliament under the Italian constitution). On the role of the *riserva di legge* in postwar Italian constitutional law, See Chapter 2, n. 117 and accompanying text.

116. *Frontini*, [1974] 2 C.M.L.R. at 385–87.

117. *Granital*, as translated in Oppenheimer (1994/2003), 1:647.

118. See de Witte (1998), 288–89; for further details on the origins of the *controlimiti*, see Claes (2006), 502–03.

the continuing compatibility of the Treaty with the above-mentioned fundamental principles."[119]

The German Constitutional Court would later pick up on the notion of counter-limits in its two seemingly contradictory *Solange* decisions of 1974 and 1986.[120] *Solange I* suggested an aggressive, ongoing role for the Court in reviewing the decisions of the ECJ—a direct attack not only on supranational supremacy but also, in some sense, on its legitimacy. The German Court stated that "as long as" the Community lacked "a democratically legitimated parliament," as well as genuine oversight over the Council and Commission as executive-technocratic policy-makers, and, finally, "a codified catalogue of fundamental rights" on par with national protections,[121] the *Bundesverfassungsgericht* would need to retain jurisdiction to review whether Community norms satisfied national constitutional requirements.[122] A decade of scholarly criticism (as well as suggestions by the Court itself that it was willing to revisit this holding)[123] ultimately led the Court to retreat from the full-blown implications of *Solange I*. But in reversing itself in *Solange II* in 1986,[124] the Constitutional Court did not reject the underlying principle of its earlier decision (notably relating to the nondemocratic character of supranational power). Rather, the Court found only that the protections of *individual rights* under Community law had advanced to the point that the Court would "no longer exercise its jurisdiction" in that regard.[125] But the Court also reiterated (alluding to "similar limits under the Italian Constitution") that the Basic Law could not permit Germany "to surrender by way of ceding sovereign rights to international institutions the identity of the prevailing constitutional order of the Federal Republic by breaking into its basic framework, that is, into the structure which makes it up."[126]

---

119. [1974] 2 C.M.L.R. at 389.

120. de Witte (1998), 289.

121. [1974] 2 C.M.L.R. at 551.

122. Ibid., 551–52.

123. See the so-called *Vielleicht* ("maybe") decision of 1979, *Steinike und Weinling v. Bundesamt für Ernährung und Fortswirtschaft—Vielleicht*, BVerfGE 52, 187, [1980] 2 C.M.L.R. 531; for a discussion, see Alter (2001), 94.

124. *Wünsche Handelsgesellschaft*, Case 2 BvR 197/83, BVerfGE 73, 339; [1987] 3 C.M.L.R. 225 [hereinafter *Solange II*].

125. [1987] 3 C.M.L.R. at 265.

126. [1987] 3 C.M.L.R. at 257, citing La Pergola and Del Duca (1985).

This is the essence of the constitutional concern of the postwar settlement, defined in light of the crisis of parliamentary democracy of the interwar period and the devolution of representative government into dictatorship.[127] Of course, European integration presented no threat of dictatorship, although it did significantly empower national executives and supranational technocrats in an otherwise highly complex and fragmented supranational regulatory process. Thus, for the time being, German and Italian allusions to counter-limits remained vague reservations that might never be activated. Nevertheless, the distinction drawn in *Solange II*—deference on issues of rights-protection but not on supranational interference with national democracy—would reappear in that court's holdings of the 1990s and 2000s.[128]

The core message of the 1980s, however—of both the German and Italian constitutional courts—remained strongly one of deference. As the *Corte costituzionale* stressed in *Granital:* "In relation to the sphere of application of [Community] regulations, municipal law forms an order which does not seek to superimpose its control over rules produced by the separate and autonomous Community system, even though the municipal legal order does guarantee the observance of those rules on national territory."[129] Similarly, as the *Bundesverfassungsgericht* would explicitly rule later in the decade (in the *Kloppenburg* decision), it was not the place of the national court to substitute its judgment (to use American administrative law terminology) for that of the supranational adjudicator without in effect denying German litigants their *gesetzlichen Richter* ("lawful judge") as guaranteed under the German Basic Law.[130]

This reference to the ECJ as "lawful judge" had broader and undoubtedly unintended historical resonance. More specifically, it linked the process of European integration to an important aspect of the constitutionalization of administrative governance on the national level.[131] In the historical

---

127. See generally Chapter 2; see also Lindseth (2004).

128. See this chapter, nn. 203–214 and accompanying text.

129. *Granital,* as translated in Oppenheimer (1994/2003), 1:649.

130. *Frau Kloppenburg v. Finanzamt Leer,* decn. 2 BvR 687/85 of 8 Apr. 1987, BVerfGE 75, 223; [1988] 3 C.M.L.R. 1, reprinted in Oppenheimer (1994/2003), 1:497–519, interpreting Article 100(1) of the German Basic law, prohibiting removal of cases from the "lawful judge" (*gesetzlichen Richter*).

131. *Kloppenburg* was not without irony specifically within the German context as well: Like the collection of constitutional provisions cited by the *Finanzgericht Rheinland Pfalz* in 1963 (see this chapter, nn. 104–105 and accompanying text, citing arts. 20, 79, 80,

development of such governance, a perennial concern was which sort of tribunal—one part of the administration itself, or one belonging to the ordinary judiciary—should serve as the "lawful judge" of administrative action.[132] Americans will recall how, in 1938, James Landis described the "widespread distrust" of the courts as one of the principal motivations behind the emergence of administrative governance in the United States.[133] He argued that "[t]he administrative process is, in essence, our generation's answer to the inadequacy of" both inexpert legislatures and generalist judges.[134] Similarly, in interwar Britain, the debate was not over *whether* administration should be subject to legal control but over *which judges* could best balance the often conflicting interests of private rights and public welfare—those sitting on the ordinary courts or those a part of some hypothetical hierarchy of administrative tribunals in the French tradition.[135]

The question of who is the "lawful judge" of integration in fact resonates with perhaps the most venerable principle in the history of French administrative law—*juger l'administration, c'est encore administrer*—"to judge the administration is still to administer." This principle serves as the foundation for the *dualité de juridiction* on which France has built its entire system of justice (ordinary versus administrative courts). It is an extension of the substantive principle that the actions of the state and its agents should governed by special rules (*règles dérogatoires au droit commun*) flowing from the state's duty to defend the general interest. These powers are distinct from those of private law, and this distinction in turn reflects the fact that the state and its

---

and 129), the Constitutional Court was now using a provision (art. 101) inserted into the Basic Law specifically in reaction to the abuses of the National-Socialist dictatorship, only this time not to oppose but to affirm the structures of European integration. The core purpose of Article 101 was the prohibition on extraordinary courts and only secondarily the removal of cases from the "lawful judge" (in order to specifically outlaw the Nazi abuse of removing actions to irregularly constituted tribunals—or worse). In the 1963 decision of the *Finanzgericht*, the Court cited the *Ermächtigungsgesetz* of 24 Mar. 1933, as well as the need to avoid "[t]he undermining and destruction of the rule of law for a second time . . . only by the courts opposing every attempt to interpret another inadequately circumscribed constitutional provision so as to weaken Article 79 (3) of the Constitution's protection of the principle of separation of powers." [1964] C.M.L.R. at 136.

132. Stolleis (2001), 215–18.

133. Landis (1938), 32–33.

134. Ibid., 46.

135. Lindseth (2005a), 126.

agents enjoy special powers (*pouvoirs exorbitants du droit commun*) beyond those enjoyed by individuals under private law.

Although these ideas are hardly unique to France, what sets the French tradition apart (certainly from the common law tradition) is the jurisdictional corollary that the state and its agents are therefore entitled to a separate judge, imbued with *le sens de l'Etat,* in principle giving priority to the general interest, operating in a system of tribunals distinct from the ordinary judicial courts. Under the modern formulation of this idea (famously elaborated by Jean Romieu, the *commissaire du gouvernement* in the seminal *Terrier* decision of 1903),[136] the determining jurisdictional factor should be the existence of a dispute concerning *le service public,* or "public service": "Anything concerning the organization or the functioning of public services," wrote Romieu, "constitutes an *administrative operation,* which is, *by its nature,* within the domain of the administrative court."[137]

The Community system of judicial remedies, especially the ECJ's seemingly exclusive interpretive jurisdiction under the preliminary reference procedure, arguably reflects an analogous principle—*juger l'intégration, c'est encore intégrer*—or at least the ECJ's case law would suggest as much. Because judicial review of Community law will have a direct impact on the success or failure of market integration on a supranational scale, the drafters of the treaties placed (so the argument goes) exclusive jurisdiction over treaty interpretation in an adjudicative body that was autonomously supranational, imbued with *le sens de la Communauté* (so to speak) and therefore reliably committed to the "Community interest."[138] For example, the ECJ's case law regarding which sort of bodies which should make preliminary references under the old Article 177 (Article 234 TEC/Article 267 TFEU) is not confined to those tribunals operating solely within the confines of the state. Rather, it extends to any body "acting under a degree of governmental supervision," whose decisions "may affect the exercise of rights granted by

---

136. C.E. 6 févr. 1903, *Rec.* 94, concl. Romieu. The *commissaire du gouvernement,* despite the misleading title, was in fact a totally independent magistrate, and after recent reforms in 2009 is now called the *rapporteur public.* It is charged with providing the *Conseil d'Etat* an opinion ("conclusions") as to the proper disposition of the case—often the only elaborated reasoning for the decision that is publicly disclosed beyond the often laconic "decision" itself (which is more akin to an "order" in the American system). This aspect of the role of the *commissaire du gouvernement/rapporteur public* can be roughly compared to that of the advocate general before ECJ. See, e.g., the discussion of the opinion of Advocate General Lagrange, this chapter, nn. 42–48 and accompanying text.

137. As quoted in Long et al. (1993), 68 (emphasis in original).

138. For a recent scholarly defense of this position, see Baquero Cruz (2008), 414–15.

Community law." In those circumstances, the Court finds, "it is imperative ... , in order to ensure the proper functioning of Community law, that the Court should have an opportunity of ruling on issues of interpretation and validity arising out of such proceedings."[139] Indeed, in defining the substantive reach of the doctrine of direct effect of directives, the Court has adopted a version of the "public service" criterion of French administrative law, holding that "a body, whatever its legal form," which is responsible "for providing a public service under the control of the State and has for that purpose special powers [*pouvoirs exorbitants* in the original French] beyond those which result from the normal rules applicable in relations between individuals," is subject to the terms of a directly effective directive.[140]

The *Kloppenburg* judgment of the *Bundesverfassungsgericht* in 1987, finding that the ECJ is the "lawful judge" of Community law within Germany, should be understood in light of the same instrumental concerns articulated by the ECJ—in effect, *juger l'intégration, c'est encore intégrer*. The authority of the ECJ as "lawful judge" derives, in the German court's view, from the *political* choice of the Member States to foster "co-operation between [their courts] and the Court of Justice of the European Communities," which in turn "contributes to the interpretation and application of Community law in as uniform a way as possible by all courts within the ambit of the EEC Treaty, in the interest of the Treaty objective of integration, certainty as to the law and equal application of the law."[141] But as the *Bundesverfassungsgericht* added, the ECJ "has not been given adjudicative power by the EEC Treaty to extend its jurisdiction limitlessly," and the Member States remain "the masters of the Community treaties."[142] Indeed, even in the French *dualité de juridiction* the administrative courts do not serve as the ultimate judge of the scope of administrative competence, at least relative to the judicial courts. Rather, in cases of conflict between the two orders of jurisdiction, the matter is referred to a conflicts tribunal (*Tribunal des conflits*), comprised of judges from both the supreme administrative and judicial courts, to rule on

---

139. Case 246/80, *C. Broekmeulen v. Huisarts Registratie Commissie*, 1981 E.C.R. 2311, I-2238, para. 16.

140. Case C-188/89, *A. Foster and Others v. British Gas plc*, 1990 E.C.R. I-3313, I-3348-49, para. 20. For further discussion, see de Witte (1995), 297–98.

141. *Kloppenburg*, [1988] 3 C.M.L.R. at 13, reprinted in Oppenheimer (1994/2003), 1:509.

142. [1988] 3 C.M.L.R. at 18, reprinted in Oppenheimer (1994/2003), 1:515–16.

the conflict.[143] These sorts of qualifications to the autonomous power of the "administrative" judge would take on greater importance in debates over *Kompetenz-Kompetenz* in the 1990s.[144]

It should perhaps be unsurprising that the French *Conseil d'Etat*, with its *sens de l'Etat* and not *de la Communauté*, would be the last holdout among national high courts in deferring to the primacy of Community law over subsequently adopted national norms.[145] The British courts, by contrast, proved surprisingly more accommodating (under implicit orders from Parliament),[146] as would the other high courts—judicial and constitutional—in the French system.[147] The *Conseil d'Etat*, too, would eventually end its resistance in 1989.[148] However, the terms of its acquiescence (at least as suggested in the opinion of the *commissaire du gouvernement* in the case, Patrick Frydman) were very much consistent with the line taken previously by the German and Italian constitutional courts, rooted ultimately in what was understood to be national constitutional requirements, not some new form of supranational constitutional legitimacy.[149] The fundamental basis of the decision was

---

143. Lindseth (1999), 731; see also Burdeau (1995), 202. For additional discussion, see the Conclusion, nn. 101–102 and accompanying text.

144. See this chapter, nn. 163–181 and accompanying text.

145. It is hard to generalize from one piece of evidence, but during my fellowship at the *Conseil d'Etat* in 1994–1995, I recall distinctly a private conversation with a senior member (then a section president) who expressed irritation with what this member viewed as the unnecessary supervisory role of the ECJ in matters involving some aspects of European law (an ever expanding category of cases). This person's irritation was in part driven by deep pride in the *Conseil d'Etat*'s established record in independently controlling the legality of administrative action in France.

146. See de Witte (1998), 290–91. For a collection of the British cases over the course through 1990, see Oppenheimer (1994/2003), 1:755–909.

147. See generally Alter (2001), 145–51 (analyzing the case law of the French *Cour de cassation* in the 1970s); and 159 (describing the *Conseil constitutionnel*'s acceptance in 1986 of direct effect and supremacy in line with the reasoning of the *Cour de cassation*).

148. C.E. Ass., 20 oct. 1989, *Nicolo*, *Rec.* 190, conclusions Frydman; translated in [1990] 1 C.M.L.R. 173; reprinted in Oppenheimer (1994/2003), 1:335–56.

149. The reasoning of the Irish Supreme Court was similar (see *Crotty v. An Taoiseach*, 18 Feb. and 9 Apr. 1987, [1987] I.R. 713; [1987] 2 C.M.L.R. 666; Oppenheimer (1994/2003), 1:595–627), although the Irish constitutional provision—Article 29(4)(3)—on which supremacy and direct effect were grounded was unusually sweeping in its terms. Article 29(4)(3) provides in pertinent part: "No provision of this Constitution invalidates laws enacted, acts done or measures adopted by the State necessitated by the obligations of membership of the Communities or prevents laws enacted, acts done or measures adopted by the Communities, or the institutions thereof, from having the force of law in the State." According to Monica Claes, this provision "was inserted because membership in the European Communities was considered inconsistent with several

Article 55 of the French constitution of 1958, another of the postwar provisions that opened national systems to international cooperation (in this case affirming the superiority of treaties over statutes, subject to reciprocity). In his conclusions, however, Frydman explicitly rejected the jurisprudence of the ECJ "which, as we know, gives Community law absolute supremacy over the rules of national law, even if they are constitutional."[150] Rather, he stressed the "expediency" of giving Community law primacy over subsequently enacted national legislation in the interest of integration,[151] while also dismissing the ECJ's "supranational way of thinking ... which [if correct] would quite certainly render the Treaty unconstitutional, however it may be regarded in the political context."[152]

As we shall see in the next section, tensions between national and supranational "ways of thinking" would become increasingly more intense in the 1990s, with the ambitious expansion of the normative reach of supranational institutions under the Treaty of Maastricht of 1992 (including an increase in the domains subject to qualified-majority voting). By the end of the 1990s, in fact, several leading national high courts had given a much clearer sense of the points at which they too could no longer defer to the ECJ, consistent with their obligation under the postwar constitutional settlement. The purpose of these decisions was to protect democratic structures on the national level, in a jurisprudence that would then be carried forward by several national high courts in the 2000s.

In articulating these limits, however, these national courts would also make clear that they would *not* apply an overly formalist nondelegation principle to European integration (which, as the *Finanzgericht Rheinland-Pfalz* demonstrated, would mean the "insuperable" unconstitutionality of the integration project itself).[153] They would keep in mind, as the German Lisbon Decision put it in 2009, that their constitutions and political systems now reflected an "openness towards European law" (*Europarechtsfreundlichkeit*).[154]

---

constitutional provisions and principles ... [s]uch as the retention of exclusive national legislative, executive, and judicial power [and] the sovereignty and independence of the State." Claes (2006), 524 and n. 105. Later case law questioned the sweep of Article 29(4) (3), however, in the area of abortion. For an overview, see Claes (2006), 526–31.

150. [1990] 1 C.M.L.R. at 190; Oppenheimer (1994/2003), 1:353.

151. See, e.g., [1990] 1 C.M.L.R. at 179 and 182; Oppenheimer (1994/2003), 1:341 and 344.

152. [1990] 1 C.M.L.R. at 190; Oppenheimer (1994/2003), 1:353–54.

153. See this chapter, n. 105 and accompanying text.

154. German Lisbon Decision (2009), paras. 225 and 240.

In this sense, the national high courts' approach would echo that of the United States Supreme Court to broad and perhaps constitutionally problematic delegations: When in the rare case such concerns have surfaced, rather than resorting to wholesale invalidation, U.S. judges have used these concerns as an interpretive constraint—that is, as a kind of counter-limit or "resistance norm"[155]—to avoid statutory constructions of administrative authority that amounted to "such a 'sweeping delegation of legislative power' that it might be unconstitutional."[156]

✹ 4.3 Defining the Limits of Strong Deference: *Kompetenz-Kompetenz* in the Constitutional Politics and Jurisprudence of the Last Two Decades

Looking back from the perspective of twenty years, the decade of the 1990s seemed to start promisingly enough for the "supranational way of thinking."[157] The ruling of the British House of Lords in *Factortame* in October 1990,[158] at least when compared to decisions of other national high courts later in the decade, led more than one commentator to conclude that a "high-water mark" of national judicial acceptance of the imperatives of integration had been reached.[159] The law lords' opinions suggested that a norm previously "considered central to the basic doctrine of UK constitutional law, the doctrine of parliamentary supremacy, turned out to be defeasible," or at least

155. Cf. Young (2000). For more detail, see the Introduction, nn. 62–63 and accompanying text.

156. Indus. Union Dep't v. Am. Petroleum Inst., 448 U.S. 607, 646 (1980), quoting A.L.A. Schechter Poultry Corp. v. United States, 295 U.S. 495, 439 (1935); see also Sunstein (2000), 316 ("Rather than invalidating federal legislation as excessively open-ended, courts hold that federal administrative agencies may not engage in certain activities unless and until Congress has expressly authorized them to do so. . . . As a technical matter, the key holdings are based not on the nondelegation doctrine but on certain 'canons' of construction.").

157. This chapter, n. 152 and accompanying text.

158. *R. v. Secretary of State for Transport, ex parte Factortame Ltd (No.2)*, 11 Oct. 1990, [1991] 1 A.C. 603, reprinted in Oppenheimer (1994/2003), 1:882–909. The entire *Factortame* saga, including prior decisions of the House of Lords and the ECJ, are also reprinted in Oppenheimer (1994/2003), 1:823–909.

159. MacCormick (1999), 98; see also de Witte (1998), 293.

highly malleable, in the face of integration's functional demands.[160] The ease with which the House of Lords manipulated the doctrine of parliamentary sovereignty to reach the desired result further suggested, at least to one observer, that "constitutional reservations to the full reception of Community law seemed confined to Germany and Italy and could appear more as symbolic gestures than as effective threats to the uniform application of EC law."[161]

That sanguine view unfortunately ignored important elements in the reasoning in *Factortame* itself. As Lord Bridge specified in his opinion, Parliament had only "accord[ed] supremacy to rules of Community law *in areas to which they apply*."[162] As a leading British commentator subsequently noted: "The problem being addressed here is often referred to as *Kompetenz-Kompetenz:* [W]ho has the ultimate authority to decide whether a matter is within the competence of the EC?"[163] Over the last two decades, the issue of *Kompetenz-Kompetenz* emerged as a major point of tension between national high courts and the ECJ. In the 1980s, the ECJ made clear that, in its view, the European treaties gave it *exclusive* jurisdiction to rule on the validity of a Community norm—which of course included the determination of whether or not it is within the scope of Community competence delegated under the treaties.[164] The decisions of several leading national high courts in the 1990s and 2000s would reveal, however, real discontent "with this arrogation of authority," particularly because "the ECJ has, as is well known, often reasoned teleologically and expanded the boundaries of Community competence in a manner

---

160. MacCormick (1999), 98. The House of Lords accomplished this feat primarily by reversing the traditional presumption that, where two Acts of Parliament conflicted, the later one was understood as an implied repeal of the earlier. This traditional presumption would no longer apply in the Community law context, and "[i]f Parliament ever wishes to derogate from its Community obligations [to which it committed in the European Communities Act 1972] then it will have to do so *expressly and unequivocally.*" Craig (2003), 419 (emphasis in original). Moreover, the European Communities Act 1972 itself would be read as impliedly conferring injunctive authority on the courts to achieve the ends of integration. Craig (2003), 418, citing [1991] 1 A.C. at 658–59 (opinion by Lord Bridge).

161. de Witte (1998), 293.

162. Craig (2003), 418, citing [1991] 1 A.C. at 659 (opinion by Lord Bridge) (emphasis added).

163. Craig (2003), 420.

164. See Case 314/85, *Foto Frost v. Hauptzollamt Lübeck-Ost*, 1987 E.C.R. 4199. For an overview of the case law, see Claes (2006), 562–69.

which has caused disquiet within some national legal systems, such as the German."[165]

Indeed, the German Federal Constitutional Court would squarely join issue on the question of *Kompetenz-Kompetenz* in its 1993 ruling on the constitutionality of the Treaty of Maastricht, upholding the treaty under the Basic Law but giving voice to this sense of disquiet.[166] The *Bundesverfassungsgericht* would then reiterate this line of thinking in an even more developed ruling issued in June 2009, upholding the Treaty of Lisbon but also laying out constitutional parameters governing supranational delegation and national democratic legitimation.[167] These two decisions can be seen as bookends on an era, prompted by a nearly continuous political process of treaty reform and ratification stretching over two decades. It was a process of constitutional politics that forced national high courts to focus on the national foundations of European integration and the limits of permissible supranational delegation. Perhaps more importantly, this line of cases would also signal a clear rejection of the full blown conception of constitutional "supremacy" of European over national law (echoing the position of the French *Conseil d'Etat* in 1989),[168] instead substituting a much more modest and constrained notion of "primacy."[169]

What has been poorly understood about this jurisprudence, particularly the line initiated by the *Bundesverfassungsgericht* in its Maastricht decision, is the depth of its grounding in the postwar constitutional settlement of administrative governance. Certainly much of the legal commentary on

---

165. Craig (2003), 420.

166. *Brunner v. European Union Treaty* (the "German Maastricht Decision"), Cases 2 BvR 2134/92 and 2159/92 of 12 Oct. 1993, BVerfGE 89, 155, [1994] 1 C.M.L.R. 57, reprinted in Oppenheimer (1994/2003), 1:527–75; see also 33 I.L.M. 388 (1994). This study uses the I.L.M. translation because it is superior to the C.M.L.R. translation found in Oppenheimer (1994/2003).

167. German Lisbon Decision (2009).

168. See this chapter, nn. 150–152 and accompanying text.

169. See the decision of the Spanish *Tribunal Constitucional* on the constitutionality of the Treaty establishing a Constitution for Europe, DTC 1/2004, at part 4 (distinguishing between the "supremacy" of the national constitution and the "primacy" of European law within its treaty-defined "scopes of application"), http://www.tribunalconstitucional.es/es/jurisprudencia/restrad/Paginas/DTC122004en.aspx (last visited Nov. 10, 2009); German Lisbon Decision (2009), para. 343 ("the primacy of Union law only applies by virtue of the order to apply the law issued by the Act approving the Treaties. As regards public authority exercised in Germany, the primacy of application only reaches as far as the Federal Republic of Germany approved this conflict of law rule and was permitted to do so."). See also Avbelj (2008b), 19.

these decisions in English has ignored this fact, often displaying a deeply mistaken interpretation of the historical underpinnings of the Court's reasoning.[170] My aim in this section is thus to draw out these legal-historical underpinnings in the postwar constitutional settlement more explicitly, culminating in the German Lisbon Decision of 2009, which is examined in greater detail below.

But we begin, of course, with the German Maastricht Decision of 1993. In terms of the linkage to the postwar constitutional settlement, the most important aspect of the ruling was the Court's emphasis on the national parliament's initial delegation of normative power to Community institutions through the treaty and the act of accession. From the Court's perspective, these acts provided the legitimating foundation upon which supranational norms could gain force in the domestic legal order. As with the delegation via an enabling act on the domestic level, the Court examined the shift in normative power to the supranational level using language that echoed its prior jurisprudence under Article 80(1) of the Basic Law. The Court thus inquired whether the German parliament had defined powers of the EU "foreseeably" and had "standardized them to a sufficiently definable level."[171] The Court, however, explicitly took a more lenient approach to the question of supranational delegation as compared to purely national delegations, in effect acknowledging the challenge posed by coordination among multiple principals.[172] The Court noted that "a Treaty under international law has to be negotiated between the contracting parties," and thus "the demands placed upon the precision and solidity of the Treaty provisions cannot be as great as those which are otherwise prescribed for a law by the parliamentary reservation [*Parlamentsvorbehalt*]"—i.e., the core of normative power that

---

170. See, e.g., Weiler (1995), 222 (claiming instead that the Court based its claim of ultimate *Kompetenz-Kompetenz* on a conception of democracy derived from Carl Schmitt). For an extended critique of this interpretation, see Lindseth (2003b). For variants on the Weiler interpretation that are suggestive of its influence in English-language scholarship, see, e.g., Stone Sweet (2000), 177 (stating that the decision "legitimizes the very source" of the purported democratic deficit in the Community: its "intergovernmental elements"); and Alter (2001), 107 (lamenting the decision's seemingly "nationalist tone," and puzzling over how it "created a constitutional limit on the transfer of national political authority to the EC level based on the inviolability of German democracy"). But see also Claes (2006), 608, n. 189 ("[w]hat is disturbing is the tone, rather than the content" of the decision); see also Baquero Cruz (2008), 391 ("[m]any years have passed and we may now be able to read the Maastricht-Urteil with more detachment and even learn something from it").

171. 33 I.L.M. at 422. Compare Chapter 2, nn. 74–77 and accompanying text.

172. I will return to this challenge in the Conclusion, nn. 10–13 and accompanying text.

parliament cannot generally delegate under the Basic Law.[173] There would be no return, in other words, to the formalist approach to nondelegation of the *Finanzgericht Rheinland-Pfalz* in 1963.[174]

The *Bundesverfassungsgericht* additionally noted that, once the delegation was made, the various national executives assembled in the Council of Ministers provided oversight for (and therefore an important degree of ongoing democratic legitimacy of) the Community's normative output—just as hierarchical oversight mechanisms by the executive helped to legitimize administrative governance at the national level.[175] The Court acknowledged that the shift away from unanimity in the Council since the mid-1980s (something extended in the Maastricht Treaty) meant that "the German Federal Parliament, and with it the enfranchised citizen"—that is, those bodies to whom the national executive was ultimately accountable—"necessarily lose some of their influence upon the process of decision-making and the formation of political will."[176] But the Court again stressed that the democratic legitimation of Europe's normative output "cannot be effected in the same way as it can with a State regime which is governed uniformly and conclusively by a State constitution."[177] "The imposition of unanimity as a *general* requirement would, by definition, give the will of the individual state priority over that of the inter-governmental community and would therefore bring into question the very structure of such a community."[178] The Court was unwilling to demand such individualized State control, in effect acknowledging the basic institutional realities that had prevailed in the Community since the 1960s (see Chapter 3). In part, the Court justified its acceptance of this degree of supranational normative autonomy by relying on rather conventional notions of technocratic expertise, as well as on the political

---

173. 33 I.L.M. at 422. On the notion of a normative domain "reserved" to the parliament, see Chapter 2, n. 116 and accompanying text.

174. See this chapter, n. 105 and accompanying text.

175. See 33 I.L.M. at 421–22 ("the exercise of sovereign powers is largely determined by governments. If Community powers of this nature are based upon the democratic process of forming political will conveyed by each individual people, they must be exercised by an institution delegated by the governments of the Member States, which are themselves subject to democratic control."). The Court stressed as well mechanisms for national legislative and *Länder* oversight that the constitutional amendments prompted by the Maastricht Treaty had added to the Basic Law. 33 I.L.M. at 425–26. We take up the question of national parliamentary scrutiny in Chapter 5.

176. 33 I.L.M. at 418.

177. Ibid.

178. Ibid., at 419.

incapacities of parliaments under electoral and interest group pressures—all common justifications for delegation under the postwar constitutional settlement.[179]

The Court's reasoning drew on the postwar constitutional settlement in one final, critical respect—the national judicial enforcement of constitutional bounds of permissible delegation. In the Court's view, it was ultimately the constitutional duty of the national judiciary to ensure that the normative power remained within the "standardized" boundaries defined in the treaty and act of accession. If a supranationally produced norm fell outside those boundaries, it "would not be binding within German territory," because the requisite initial democratic legitimation of the norm would be lacking.[180] "Accordingly, the German Federal Constitutional Court must examine the question of whether or not legal instruments of European institutions or governmental entities may be considered to remain within the bounds of the sovereign rights accorded to them, or whether they may be considered to exceed those bounds."[181]

In applying this analytical framework, the Court upheld the Treaty of Maastricht, in important part because it found the treaty "regulat[ed] to a sufficiently foreseeable degree the procedures for future exercise of the sovereign powers granted based on the parliamentary accountability provided for by the Act of Accession."[182] In reaching this conclusion, however, the Court scrutinized quite closely several provisions that, if construed in ways the Court deemed unacceptable, could negate the limits of Community competence defined by the legislature. In a famous passage clearly directed at the ECJ, the *Bundesverfassungsgericht* stated:

> If to date dynamic expansion of the existing Treaties has been based upon liberal interpretation of Art. 235 of the EEC Treaty . . . , [as well as] upon considerations of the implied powers of the European Communities, [and] upon interpreting the Treaty in the sense of the maximum possible exploitation of the Community's powers ("effet utile") . . . , [then] when standards of competence are being interpreted by institutions and governmental entities of the Communities in the future, the fact that the

---

179. Ibid., at 439 (discussing the independence of the European Central Bank).

180. Ibid., at 422–23.

181. Ibid., at 423.

182. Ibid., at 426.

Maastricht Treaty draws a basic distinction between the exercise of limited sovereign powers and amendment of the Treaty will have to be taken into consideration. Thus interpretation of such standards may not have an effect equivalent to an extension of the Treaty; indeed, if standards of competence were interpreted this way, such interpretation would not have any binding effect on Germany.[183]

Relatively quickly, the ECJ addressed the concern that the old Article 235 (Article 308 TEC/Article 352 TFEU) operated as a backdoor means to amend the treaty. In 1996, the Court of Justice issued an advisory opinion (*Opinion 2/94*) on whether the Community could accede, on the basis of Article 235, to the European Convention on Human Rights.[184] Like the *Bundesverfassungsgericht*, the ECJ stressed that the Community's ability to act was limited to only those "powers conferred upon it by the Treaty."[185] The ECJ then specifically stated that Article 235 "cannot serve as a basis for widening the scope of Community powers," and more particularly that it "cannot be used as a basis for the adoption of provisions whose effect would, in substance, be to amend the Treaty without following the procedure which it provides for that purpose."[186]

German concerns were not limited, however, to the potential misuse of the reserve legislative authority of the old Article 235.[187] Indeed, the decision of the *Bundesverfassungsgericht* to interpret the EC Treaty independently, without recourse to a preliminary reference, implied a limitation on the ECJ's claim to exclusive interpretative jurisdiction (in effect, supremacy) under the treaties.[188] In ruling on the constitutionality of the Treaty of Maastricht, the

---

183. Ibid., at 441.

184. Opinion 2/94, 1996 E.C.R. I-1759. The Danish Supreme Court would later take cognizance of this decision in dismissing a similar challenge to the constitutionality of the Maastricht Treaty, although the Danish court also alluded to past instances when "this provision may have been applied on the basis of a wider interpretation." See *Carlsen and Others v. Rasmussen*, Case I-361/1997 of 6 Apr. 1998, 1998 *UfR* 800, as translated by the Danish Foreign Office, reprinted in Oppenheimer (1994/2003), 2:189.

185. 1996 E.C.R. at I-1787.

186. Ibid., at I-1788.

187. On the "reserve" nature of Article 235, see this chapter, nn. 83–84 and accompanying text.

188. But see Claes (2006), 607–08 (claiming that the ECJ's exclusive interpretive authority is "not an issue of supremacy, but one of jurisdiction. The Court of Justice possesses this exclusive jurisdiction because the Member States have attributed it in the Treaties"); see also Claes (2006), 609 (describing how the "*Bundesverfassungsgericht* thus denied the

Bundesverfassungsgericht necessarily offered its own construction of the EC Treaty—a use, in the integration context, of the well-established principle of *verfassungskonforme Auslegung*—the preference for statutory interpretation consistent with the demands of the constitution.[189] (This principle is not unlike the nondelegation canons used by the United States Supreme Court to counter potentially problematic interpretations of statutory authority in the American administrative state.)[190] Other national high courts have also acted in a similar vein, if less confrontationally. In France, for example, the *Conseil constitutionnel* has used so-called "reservations of interpretation" to uphold aspects of European treaties—but only on the basis of particular interpretations it has specified.[191] This approach has also been specifically criticized in France as an encroachment of the ECJ's exclusive interpretive jurisdiction.[192]

These claims of an autonomous interpretive authority on the part of national high courts were part of a broader process of constitutional politics in the Member States. Most famous in this regard were the developments in Denmark: the initial "no" vote on the Maastricht Treaty in a first referendum in 1992, followed by a victory for the "yes" side in a second referendum in 1993. This reversal occurred, however, only after the Danish government extracted an agreement from the other Member States at the European Council summit at Edinburgh in late 1992 (the "Edinburgh Agreement") recognizing four Danish exceptions to make the treaty more acceptable to the Danish electorate.[193] These exceptions in effect imposed a series of nationally determined interpretations on the treaty, albeit through a political rather than a judicial process. The aim was exactly the same, however, as with judicially imposed *verfassungskonforme Auslegung* in Germany or "reservations

---

exclusive jurisdiction of the Court of Justice to decide whether a particular measure had been validly adopted or was invalid for lack of competence"). The refusal of the Constitutional Court to make a preliminary reference continues: see Baquero Cruz (2008), 396, discussing the Court's decision regarding the European Arrest Warrant, BVerfGE, 2 BvR 2236/04, judgment of 18 July 2005.

189. See Chapter 2, n. 76 and accompanying text.

190. See this chapter, n. 156 and accompanying text.

191. For an overview, see Phelan (1997), 238–39; see also 240–43 (asserting that, under reservations of interpretation, that the *Conseil constitutionnel* held that an absolute "delegation of control of the guarantee of the fundamental rights and liberties of citizens is unconstitutional"). But see Claes (2006), 629 (arguing that the passage in question "is not clear").

192. Luchaire (1992).

193. Edinburgh Agreement (1992). For a succinct summery, see Hansen (2002), 72–74.

of interpretation" in France. They sought to harness "the power of clarification and interpretation," as one commentator put it, in defense of core national constitutional values: "Clarifying how specific articles must (and must not) be interpreted can prove to be of great importance later on, and it must be seen as a way of controlling the extent of cooperation."[194]

The initial Danish "no" was followed by a near-rejection of the treaty in a French referendum, adding to the tense constitutional politics engendered by Maastricht. Nevertheless, no Member State would ultimately reject the treaty or its expansion of integration's functional reach (symbolized by the formal establishment of the EU in 1993). But in several countries, ratification of the Maastricht Treaty required constitutional amendments that restated the legal relationship between European integration and national constitutional orders (not unlike the Danish exceptions) in ways that were also clearly in tension with the ECJ's earlier unqualified claims of supranational normative autonomy and supremacy.

In France itself, for example, two provisions were adopted that went beyond what was strictly required by the ruling of the *Conseil constitutionnel* on the Maastricht Treaty.[195] A new Article 88–1 was inserted into the French constitution, which described how the Member States established supranational institutions solely "to exercise some of their powers in common." This was an effort to confirm in law, as one commentator put it, "that, when the European Community institutions exercise their powers, they are, constitutionally speaking, acting on behalf of the sovereign peoples of the Member States."[196] In a different provision (Article 88–4), the French constitution obligated the national executive to lay before the national parliament all proposals for legislation at the European level that, if presented nationally, would fall within the constitutionally defined legislative domain.[197] This provision

---

194. See Krunke (2005), 349 (also finding that the National Compromise "'close[d]' off possibilities with regard to Denmark which the Treaty offer[ed]" and that, from the perspective of ten years later, "it is clear that the Danish exceptions did actually have an effect on Danish European Union policy"). On the Danish National Compromise, see Chapter 5, n. 19 and accompanying text.

195. C.C., dec. no. 92–308 DC of 9 Apr. 1992, translated in Oppenheimer (1994/2003), 1:385–98.

196. de Witte (1998), 296. The Danish National Compromise included provisions to the same effect. See Krunke (2005), 344 (describing section B.2 of the compromise as affirming that "Community co-operation involves independent states which, in accordance with the founding Treaties, have freely decided to exercise their powers in common").

197. On the constitutional domain of the legislature, see Chapter 2, n. 90 and accompanying text. As we shall see in Chapter 5, n. 164 and accompanying text, the national

further allowed for the parliament to adopt resolutions to influence the negotiating position of the government in the supranational legislative process—a topic we take up in Chapter 5.

Germany inserted similar provisions under a new "Europe Article" of the Basic Law, Article 23, to augment national-parliamentary and *Länder* input into the supranational legislative process.[198] Article 23(1) defined, as one commentator put it, "express substantive limits to European integration"[199]— that is, that German participation in integration depends on its continuing commitment to "democratic, social, and federal principles, to the rule of law, and to the principle of subsidiarity," as well as on its guaranty of "a level of protection of basic rights essentially comparable to that afforded by this Basic Law."[200] Moreover, Article 23(1) specified (in terms that would take on great significance in the German Lisbon Decision of 2009)[201] that any future transfer of sovereign rights (*Hoheitsrechte*) to the EU had to be done by way of "a law" (*Gesetz*)—that is, by an act of the legislature; executive action alone, on the basis of the prior ratification of the treaties, could not suffice. Finally, this provision reiterated that German participation is also expressly subject to the rules regarding constitutional amendment in Article 79(2) as well as the "eternity clause" of Article 79(3), in order to prevent a situation where the original supranational delegation of *Hoheitsrechte* might be overtaken by subsequent developments (for example, ECJ interpretations expanding the scope of supranational authority).

This sort of constitutional specification of the delegated character of supranational authority did not, for the most part, alter the deferential approach of the German and French high courts. Nor should it have. For the remainder of the 1990s and into the 2000s, German and French judges continued to recognize that, within these (rather permissive) constitutionally defined limits, the supranational policy process continued to enjoy a significant margin of discretion on numerous questions to which national judges

---

parliamentary scrutiny procedures in Portugal and Finland adopted in the 1990s would be subject to a similar limitation.

198. See this chapter, n. 175, for discussion of these provisions in the German Maastricht Decision. Again, we take up the question of national parliamentary scrutiny in more detail Chapter 5 of this study.

199. de Witte (1998), 297.

200. German Basic Law, art. 23(1).

201. See this chapter, nn. 229–231 and accompanying text.

must defer.[202] Indeed, in the seemingly endless "banana" litigation, the German Federal Constitutional Court also made clear, as it had in the Maastricht Decision itself, that deference was generally required even on most questions of fundamental rights.[203] The Court's subsequent decision on the European Arrest Warrant suggested some limits to this deferential

---

202. For example, in a subsequent challenge to the replacement of the German mark with the euro (foreseen in the Maastricht Treaty as the third stage in the transition to monetary union), the *Bundesverfassungsgericht* expressly refused to interject itself into the process, recognizing that the law allocated the judgments in question to policymakers. *European Monetary Union Constitutionality Case*, Cases 2 BvR 1877/97 and 50/98 of 31 Mar. 1998, BVerfGE 97, 350, as translated in Oppenheimer (1994/2003), 2:258–69. The Court specifically found that the Maastricht Treaty had left "scope for economic and political assessment and forecasting," and that "[t]he Federal Government and Parliament assume responsibility for this in order to ensure the protection of financial property." BVerfGE 97, 368, translated in Oppenheimer (1994/2003), 2:262. It further held that compliance with the requirements of Article 23 of the Basic Law on parliamentary participation meant that "entry into the third stage of monetary union is legitimated on an adequate democratic basis." BVerfGE 97, 369, translated in Oppenheimer (1994/2003), 2:263. [In its judgment of May 7, 2010 (rejecting an application for a preliminary injunction to block German participation in the emergency loan to Greece), the *Bundesverfassungsgericht* specifically relied on this earlier ruling to hold that "[a]mong the constitutional organs, it is above all for the Federal Government to make such assessments [whether a loan to Greece is warranted in the circumstances of the financial crisis], which the *Bundesverfassungsgericht* can only control in a limited fashion (e.g., BVerfGE 97, 350, 376)." BVerfG, Case 2 BvR 987/10 of 7 May 2010, pt. B, para. 2(a), http://www.bundesverfassungsgericht.de/entscheidungen/rs20100507_2bvr098710.html (last visited May 8, 2010) ("Unter den Verfassungsorganen ist vor allem die Bundesregierung dazu berufen, derartige Einschätzungen vorzunehmen, die das Bundesverfassungsgericht nur eingeschränkt kontrollieren kann (vgl. BVerfGE 97, 350 <376>).")]

203. *Banana Market Organization Constitutionality Case*, Case 2 BvL 1/97 of 7 June 2000, BVerfGE 102, 147, 163–64, translated in Oppenheimer (1994/2003), 2:283 (referring specifically to both Article 23 of the Basic Law and its prior holding in *Solange II*, stating "constitutional complaints and references from courts are inadmissible *ab initio* if the statement of reasons for them does not show that the developments of European law . . . ha[ve] fallen below the necessary standard of fundamental rights. The statement of reasons or a reference by a national court or for a constitutional complaint which asserts an infringement by Community law of fundamental rights in the Constitution must therefore show in detail that the minimum protection of fundamental rights unconditionally required in the particular case is not generally ensured"). See also the German Maastricht Decision, 33 I.L.M. at 412 (stating "the European Court of Justice guarantees the protection of basic rights in each individual case for the entire area of the European Community," whereas "the Federal Constitutional Court can therefore limit itself to a general guarantee of mandatory standards of basic rights," citing *Solange II*, BVerfGE 73, 339, at 387). Those who ascribe the decision in the Banana litigation to the departure of the conservative author of the Maastricht Decision, Paul Kirchhof, from the *Bundesverfassungsgericht* (see, e.g., Alter (2001), ignore this earlier reaffirmation as well as the decisions in the EMU case (this chapter, n. 202) and TV Broadcasting Directive case (this chapter, n. 212), both of which were decided while Kirchhof was still on the bench. See also Claes (2006), 482.

attitude in the peculiar context of the extradition.[204] But the basic attitude of deference nevertheless remained intact. Indeed, a decision of the French *Conseil d'Etat* in February 2007 also took an approach that suggested the strong willingness to defer to supranational adjudication on most questions of rights.[205]

For those who see fundamental rights as the "chief responsibility" and "single most significant domain" of national constitutional jurisdictions,[206] deference in this area would seem surprising and perhaps somewhat anomalous in light of the Court's apparently more aggressive approach on questions of *Kompetenz-Kompetenz*. But this interpretation reflects a misunderstanding of the full nature of the judicial commitment function under the postwar constitutional settlement. This function stretches well beyond rights protection to questions of democracy and constitutional structure, that is, *mediated legitimacy*, as Chapter 2 concluded. And these latter functions arguably have a greater claim to being the "chief responsibility" and "single most significant domain" of national constitutional jurisdictions.

Indeed, for sound reasons relating to the incentives facing litigants and judges, these functions could not be deferred to the ECJ whereas rights protection in most cases could. The incentives for private litigants to vindicate

---

204. "Peculiar" because of the linkage the Court was able to draw between the complainant's status as a German citizen and freedom from extradition under Article 16(2) of the Basic Law. In a somewhat strained fashion, the Court saw this freedom as one of several citizenship rights "whose guarantee legitimises public authority in a democracy. The civic rights and duties that are connected with the possession of citizenship for every individual are at the same time constituent bases of the entire polity." BVerfGE 113, 2 BvR 2236/04, judgment of 18 July 2005, para. 67; official translation in English, http://www.bundesverfassungsgericht.de/entscheidungen/rs20050718_2bvr223604en. html. This reasoning had the effect of converting a rights case into one linked the Maastricht Decision's concerns over democracy protection, a stretch to say the least. In this regard, see the dissent opinion of Judge Gerhardt at para. 190 (regretting the majority's effort to draw "an intrinsic connection [between] the ban on extradition and citizenship as a status"). In any case, technically the judgment ruled only on the constitutionality of German implementing legislation of the framework decision on the European arrest warrant, rather than of the framework decision itself. In doing so, however, the Court engaged in its own interpretation of the framework decision, rather than refer the question to the ECJ. For a critical discussion, see Baquero Cruz (2008), 395–97.

205. CE Ass., 8 fév. 2007, *Arcelor*, http://www.conseil-etat.fr/ce/jurispd/index_ac_ld0706. shtml (in French) (last visited Nov. 14, 2007) (holding that, in challenges involving claims to rights violation in the implementation of Community law by way of administrative regulation, the *Conseil d'Etat* will look first to whether a corresponding right exists in Community law and if so, then refer the matter to the ECJ; if not, it will proceed to the constitutional rights claim itself).

206. Claes (2006), 595.

their fundamental rights are almost always strong regardless of the forum, national or supranational. Moreover, the judicial culture of the last half century has been generally very receptive to rights-based claims; thus a national high court could safely expect a supranational adjudicator to treat a rights-based challenge to supranational action in manner reasonably respectful of rights protection. By contrast, the incentives have been much weaker for litigants and (at least) supranational judges to protect mediated legitimacy or separation of powers through the enforcement of delegation constraints. In the parliamentary systems of Europe, the legislative majority (even a coalition) will usually be hesitant to oppose the government's support for a European measure except in rare circumstances.[207] Consequently, the incentive of other institutional players to mount a challenge is significantly weaker in the democracy-protection context, thus necessitating a more aggressive judicial role.[208]

As the Danish Supreme Court (the *Højesteret*) would later put it in its own Maastricht judgment of 1998,[209] the really difficult challenge for national high courts was not protecting individual rights but determining whether and how supranational delegation imperiled "the constitutional assumption of a democratic system of government" on the national level.[210] Similar concerns

---

207. The hesitance is squarely reflected in the behavior of national parliamentary scrutiny committees over the course of the 1990s and 2000s. See generally Chapter 5; see also Auel (2009).

208. The German Maastricht Decision of 1993 was itself a case in point: Rather than being maintained as an "institutional dispute" (*Organstreit*), which risked being inadmissible, the Court reached the institutional questions through an individual's complaint regarding a voting rights violation under Article 38 of the Basic Law. See de Witte (1998), 298 (discussing how the right to vote under Article 38 became, in the German Maastricht Decision, "a right *to participate, through the vote, in the legitimation of state power*") (emphasis in original); see also Claes (2006), 480 (arguing that the Court "bent existing case law as it stood so as to make the challenge admissible"). Later, in the German Lisbon Decision of 2009, the Court would recognize that, because *Organstreit* proceedings are subject to "the interplay of political forces," the Court relaxed the traditional prohibition on a party asserting the rights of another (in this case, a minority party asserting the rights of the *Bundestag* itself), finding this appropriate where the majority "does not wish to exercise its rights, in particular in relation to the Federal Government carried by it . . . , but also where the parliamentary minority wishes to assert rights of the Bundestag against the parliamentary majority that politically carries the Federal Government." German Lisbon Decision (2009), para. 205.

209. Due to the original Danish "no" on the Maastricht Treaty and subsequent procedural issues, the Danish Supreme Court did not rule on the constitutionality of the treaty until 1998. For a succinct summary, see Claes (2006), 514–15.

210. *Carlsen*, as reprinted in Oppenheimer (1994/2003), 2:191. The *Bundesverfassungsgericht* stressed a similar obligation to protect democracy in the German Maastricht Decision.

would be expressed by the Polish and Czech high courts in this decade.[211] Included in the democracy-protective judicial function, as the German Maastricht Decision had earlier made clear, was attention to the impact of integration on domestic constitutional divisions of powers, both vertical and horizontal, or at least those structures understood to relate directly to the democratic and constitutional character of the state itself.[212] Not all such structures necessarily fell into this category—some deeply held ones could apparently be remolded in the face of integration's functional demands (as the British case law seemed to suggest).[213] Of course, one must add into the calculus the historical propensity of the ECJ, functionally and teleologically, to downplay if not ignore supranational delegation constraints.[214] When all of this is taken into consideration, one begins to see why national high courts might regard the reservation of ultimate *Kompetenz-Kompetenz* as essential to preventing unacceptable interpretations of supranational authority that negate mediated legitimacy or the democratic nature of the original legislative delegation.

The Czech Constitutional Court, however, in its 2008 decision on the Treaty of Lisbon, also added an interesting measure of nuance to this discussion. It noted how "a spontaneous, undirected [i.e., functional] process" necessarily was transforming "politics, culture, social psychology and . . . law," including, perhaps most importantly, understandings of sovereignty.[215] Sovereignty is not so much "lost" in this functional process as it is remade

---

33 I.L.M. at 421 (defining the national judicial role as ultimately ensuring "that a living democracy is maintained in the Member States while integration proceeds").

211. See this chapter, nn. 10–11 and accompanying text.

212. Cf. *Television Broadcasting Directive Case*, Case 2 BvG 1/89 of 22 Mar. 1995, BVerfGE 92, 203, translated in Oppenheimer (1994/2003), 2:232–52. Although not a separation-of-powers case, it related more broadly to constitutional structure (in this case federalism). The decision provided a detailed explanation of the duties of the German federal government at the supranational level with regard to German *Länder*, which derived from the federal structure of the German republic on the national level.

213. See this chapter, nn. 158–161 and accompanying text. Cf. also Kumm (2006c), 297 (discussing the Italian approach as "refus[ing] to apply EU law only when it infringes on what it deems the essential contents of fundamental constitutional values, but does not generally give priority to specific constitutional rules").

214. See this chapter, nn. 62–63 and accompanying text.

215. Pl. ÚS 19/08, para. 101, http://angl.concourt.cz/angl_verze/doc/pl-19-08.php (last visited June 11, 2009).

through willing cooperation on the basis of shared values.[216] But, as the Czech court stressed, this transformation still cannot amount to "an unlimited transfer of sovereignty."[217] The challenge, then, was to define the boundary between acceptable transformation and unacceptable loss of sovereignty. The Czech court was alluding, in effect, to the difficult process of reconciliation in the process of defining the constitutional foundations of European integration.

The *Bundesverfassungsgericht*, in its own later ruling on the Treaty of Lisbon issued in June 2009, effectively followed the Czech court's lead by recognizing the necessary transformation of modern sovereignty in the face of functional pressures. The German Federal Constitutional Court noted how "[t]he Basic Law abandons a high-handed concept of sovereign statehood that is sufficient unto itself" in favor of one grounded in "voluntary, mutual commitment . . . which secures peace and strengthens the possibilities of shaping policy by joint coordinated action."[218] The Court further recognized how, pursuant to Article 23, "the Basic Law can be adapted to the development of the European Union."[219] Indeed, "derogations from the organisational principles of democracy applying on the national level" are permitted in the integration context, as in the administrative state before it, precisely "due to the requirements of a European Union."[220] The Basic Law does not demand, the Court later stated, "'structural congruence' . . . or even the correspondence of the institutional order of the European Union to the order that the principle of democracy of the Basic Law prescribes for the national level. What is required, however, is a democratic elaboration which is commensurate to the status and the function of the Union"[221]—that is, a reconciliation between

---

216. In its follow-up, 2009 ruling, the Court was even more emphatic, stating that, as long as the competences delegated to the EU are "exercised with [Czech] participation in a pre-agreed, controlled manner," this should not be seen as "a sign of the weakening of sovereignty, but, on the contrary, can lead to strengthening it in the joint process of an integrated whole." Pl. ÚS 29/09, para. 147, http://www.concourt.cz/clanek/GetFile?id=2150 (last visited Nov. 3, 2009), translated in Press Release, The Treaty of Lisbon Is in Conformity with the Constitutional Order of the Czech Republic and There Is Nothing to Prevent its Ratification, Brno, the Constitutional Court (3 Nov. 2009), http://www.usoud.cz/clanek/2144 (last visited Nov. 3, 2009).

217. Pl. ÚS 19/08, para. 109; more generally, see paras. 98–108.

218. German Lisbon Decision (2009), paras. 223 and 220.

219. Ibid., para. 230.

220. Ibid., para. 227.

221. Ibid., 266 (citations omitted).

integration's administrative character and its need for democratic and constitutional legitimacy mediated through national institutions.

Although the Court's references to "joint coordinated action" suggested a willingness to forego direct control over specific regulatory outcomes (at least those lawfully within the scope of the EU's jurisdiction), the Court nevertheless stressed that the constitutional demands of democracy on the national level necessarily imposed certain broad parameters within which the integration process must operate. Most importantly, the Court stated that the "eternity clause" of Article 79(3) "takes the disposal of the identity of the free constitutional order even out of the hands of the constitution-amending legislature. The Basic Law thus not only assumes sovereign statehood but guarantees it."[222] This meant, in the Court's view, that "the constitution-amending legislature" was constitutionally prohibited from joining, on its own accord, a European "federal state"; rather, only the German people directly could make such a decision, exercising its constituent power through a constitutional revision going beyond mere amendment (in effect, the replacement of the current Basic Law with a new constitution).[223] But the Court then made clear that, even as to this inviolable "sovereign statehood," it was referring to something that by definition was no longer "absolute" but rather deeply open to European integration as well as the broader functional-political dynamic it represents. This is a key subtlety in the Court's reasoning,

---

222. Ibid., para. 218. Halberstam and Möllers (2009), 1254, makes the puzzling claim that the Court's analysis of the Lisbon Treaty on the basis of the "eternity clause" is a misuse of Article 79(3). They reason that this provision was not meant "to preserve the sovereignty of the German state within the process of European integration," but rather "to prevent the German state from a new 1933, from a slow slippage into totalitarianism without an obviously illegal break." The latter is no doubt true, but the former assertion is a deeply questionable, for at least two reasons. First, the text is written, not surprisingly, in general terms and says nothing of "slippage into totalitarianism" per se. Rather, it speaks of prohibiting any act that would amend either Article 1 or 20 of the Basic Law—the latter establishing West Germany as "a democratic and social federal state" with all public authority emanating from the "people" through elections, with powers separated between the executive, legislative, and judicial branches—certainly language sufficiently capacious to reach integration. Second, the claim of Halberstam and Möllers that this application of Article 79(3) violated the purported original intent of the Parliamentary Council of 1949, which drafted the Basic Law, ignores a fundamental intervening event: the adoption of the new Article 23 in the aftermath of Maastricht, specifically subjecting European integration to the requirements of Article 79(3). See this chapter, nn. 198–202 and accompanying text.

223. German Lisbon Decision (2009), para. 228; on the people's right to exercise constituent power, see Article 146 of the Basic Law.

one that adds a great deal of flexibility to what might otherwise appear to be a rigid, Eurosceptical analytical framework.[224]

The core requirement of that framework, again like that of the Maastricht Decision before it, concerned democratic legitimation derived from the principle of "conferral" (*begrenzte Einzelermächtigung*, or "limited specific empowerment," to translate the more evocative German). According to the Court, "conferral"—that is, *delegation* in the postwar constitutional settlement—provided the essential linkage between European public law and its national constitutional foundations.[225] To give effect to this principle, the Court again followed the lead of its earlier Maastricht judgment, drawing directly from analytical formulas developed in the delegation jurisprudence of the postwar decades under Article 80(1) of the Basic Law.[226] This included both the *Programmformel* as well as again the *Vorhersehbarkeitsformel*, which we encountered previously.[227] Together these formulas are designed to ensure that the legislature defined the regulatory "program" in the enabling legislation in a sufficiently "predictable" or "foreseeable" manner,[228] thus preserving some semblance of democracy in a historically recognizable sense, even as actual regulatory power migrated elsewhere.

It was specifically as to the predictability requirement, in fact, that the Court found the basis to strike down elements of the legislation implementing the Treaty of Lisbon as unconstitutional (although not the Treaty of Lisbon itself). The Court was concerned that the provisions implementing the "simplified revision procedure" of Article 48(6) of the Treaty on European Union (TEU) post-Lisbon, as well as the "passerelle" clauses of Article 48(7)

---

224. See Schorkopf (2009), 1224.

225. German Lisbon Decision (2009), para. 234 ("the principle of conferral under European law ... [is] the expression of the foundation of Union authority in the constitutional law of the Member States.").

226. See this chapter, nn. 171 and 182 and accompanying text.

227. See Chapter 2, n. 77 and accompanying text.

228. The German Lisbon Decision stated that variously the "integration programme of the European Union must be sufficiently precise;" that there must be a "predetermined integration programme;" and that "the member states may not be deprived of the right to review adherence to the integration programme." German Lisbon Decision (2009), paras. 236, 238, and 334. The Court then added a requirement of predictability (*Vorhersehbarkeit*) in order to interpret the more specific demands on the legislature under Article 23 of the Basic Law. "The principle of democracy as well as the principle of subsidiarity, which is structurally demanded by Article 23(1)," together require, in the Court's view, that the transfer and subsequent exercise of sovereign powers in the European Union be "[substantively] restrict[ed] ... in a predictable manner." German Lisbon Decision (2009), para. 251.

TEU post-Lisbon (along with several other more specific provisions) did not fulfill the requirement under Article 23(1) of the Basic Law that any transfer of sovereign powers must be undertaken through a specific "law" (*Gesetz*). The general ratification of the treaty itself would not suffice for democratic legitimation, precisely because of the lack of foreseeability in how these provisions of the Treaty of Lisbon might be used in the future.[229]

Indeed, in the Court's view, the predictability requirement—"that the integration programme envisaged in the [treaties] can still be predicted and determined by the German legislative bodies"[230]—provided the foundation for the more general prohibition against supranational *Kompetenz-Kompetenz*. This prohibition was not just directed against the interpretive authority of the ECJ (as in the German Maastricht Decision) but also, perhaps most importantly, against the Union's legislative process. Implicitly this meant the national executives assembled in the Council, who might seek to maximize their own power by marginalizing national parliamentary involvement. Here, too, the Court expressed concerns about the reserve legislative authority in the treaty, which has become Article 352 TFEU post-Lisbon (the old Article 235 of the Treaty of Rome and subsequently Article 308 TEC). Because of "the undetermined nature of future cases of [Article 352's] application,"[231] the Court held that the German government may not support its use without seeking specific, prior statutory authorization from the legislature pursuant to Article 23 of the Basic Law. The treaty itself was constitutional, the Court ruled, but the preservation of democracy on the national level demanded an implementing law with significantly increased national parliamentary involvement.

---

229. German Lisbon Decision (2009), para. 311 ("The implications" of changes in policies under the simplified revision procedure, the Court stated, "are hardly predictable [*kaum vorhersehbar*] for the German legislature. Article 48(6) TEU post-Lisbon opens up to the European Council a broad scope of action for amendments of primary law."). See also ibid., para. 415. The Court applied the same standard to the passerelle provisions, stating that "the exercise of the general and special bridging clauses must be predictable at the point in time of the ratification of the Treaty of Lisbon by the German legislature." Ibid., para. 318. Because the shift from unanimity to qualified majority voting constituted "a Treaty amendment under primary law," antecedent legislation was required before the German government could support such a shift in the Council. The sole exception would be in those cases of "special bridging clauses [that] are restricted to areas which are already sufficiently determined by the Treaty of Lisbon." Ibid., para. 319–20.

230. German Lisbon Decision (2009), para. 322.

231. Ibid., para. 328.

The Court's sensitivity to national parliamentary prerogatives manifested itself in another line of reasoning as well: The claim that there are "[e]ssential areas of democratic formative action" whose transfer to supranational competence is particularly sensitive and potentially constitutionally problematic.[232] Echoing the Court's "theory of essentialness" (*Wesentlichkeitstheorie*) in the domestic administrative state,[233] the German Lisbon Decision signaled that there are "content-related limits to the transfer of sovereign powers" analogous to the statutory reserve (*Vorbehalt des Gesetzes*) that applies nationally.[234] But in noting these limits, the Court again made clear that the existence of this reserve did "not mean *per se* that a number of sovereign powers . . . can be determined from the outset or specific types of sovereign powers must remain in the hands of the state. . . . Political union means the joint exercise of public authority, including the legislative authority, which even reaches into the traditional core areas of the state's area of competence."[235] The Court acknowledged that the authority granted to supranational institutions is often capacious.[236] And in exercising that authority, German law accepts both that autonomy and even "implied powers."[237] Nevertheless, in those "[e]ssential areas of democratic formative action" there is a need for both

---

232. Ibid., para. 249. These domains included, according to the Court, criminal law, use of military or police force, control over the domestic budget, and family law, among others. See, e.g., ibid., paras. 249–260, and 347–69. The Court's list is hardly beyond criticism. See Schönberger (2009), 1209; Halberstam and Möllers (2009), 1250. Moreover, this aspect of the decision emboldened a group of Czech senators, supported by President Vaclav Klaus, to ask the Czech Constitutional Court to define a similar list of domains, as part of their last-ditch effort to prevent the Treaty of Lisbon from entering into force. The Czech Court specifically demurred, stating "it does not consider it possible, in view of the role that it plays in the constitutional system of the Czech Republic, that it should create such a catalog of nontransferable competences and authoritatively define 'the substantive limits for the transfer of competence' as the petitioner requests." Pl. ÚS 29/09, para. 111, http://www.concourt.cz/clanek/GetFile?id=2150 (last visited Nov. 3, 2009), translated in Press Release, The Treaty of Lisbon Is in Conformity with the Constitutional Order of the Czech Republic and There Is Nothing to Prevent its Ratification, Brno, the Constitutional Court (3 Nov. 2009), http://www.usoud.cz/clanek/2144 (last visited Nov. 3, 2009).

233. See Chapter 2, nn. 115–116 and accompanying text.

234. German Lisbon Decision (2009), para. 247. On the *Vorbehalt des Gesetzes*, See Chapter 2, n. 116 and accompanying text.

235. German Lisbon Decision (2009), para. 248.

236. Ibid., para. 231 ("supranational autonomy . . . is quite far-reaching in political everyday life" even as it must "always [be] limited [substantively]").

237. Ibid., para. 237 ("[t]his is part of the mandate of integration which is wanted by the Basic Law").

interpretive constraint and heightened oversight, both by national representative institutions and the Court, consistent with the demands of "living democracy" on the national level.[238]

There are undoubtedly many seemingly Eurosceptical aspects of the decision, particularly as to Germany's purported inability to join a European "federal state" under the current Basic Law, or the EU's lack of autonomous democratic legitimacy, especially but not exclusively through the European Parliament.[239] Nevertheless, the Court's ultimate reasoning, like that of the Maastricht Decision, was strongly deferential to the current realities of integration. Even if the Court alluded to the existence of an "inviolable" core of sovereignty and democracy protected by the national constitution,[240] the Court in turn gave these concepts such flexible interpretation that it is difficult to see how the vast bulk of integration activity might be affected by them in any significant way. Through this decision, the Court seemed to articulate a normative framework not of *validity* but of *resistance*, i.e., "a 'soft limit' which may be more or less yielding depending on the circumstances."[241]

It would thus be wrong to regard the Court's analysis, as former German Foreign Minister Joschka Fischer described it soon after, as simplistically binary, "based on a fiction of two separate spheres, which almost hostilely face each other." To Fischer, this ignored "the real challenge for politics and constitutional law . . . the process of interpenetration of these two spheres, which characterizes European reality."[242] To the contrary, the ruling appeared deeply cognizant of that reality. As another German commentator argued (in part in response to Fischer), the decision entailed "a serious attempt to rethink democracy for the age of major supranational decisions"—that is, democracy still grounded nationally but nevertheless confronted by the delegation of significant regulatory power to the supranational level. "If the political arena is being relocated . . . from the nation-state to Brussels," this commentator continued, "then it is only logical that the sphere of

---

238. Ibid., para. 351. The Court demanded, for example, a "narrow interpretation" of the EU's new competence in the area of criminal law in the interest of democratic and constitutional legitimacy, finding that, to the extent it might be interpreted as a "blanket empowerment" (*Blankettermächtigung*), antecedent legislation would be required for each unforeseen extension. Ibid., paras. 360 and 363; see also paras. 364–66.

239. German Lisbon Decision (2009), e.g., paras. 278–97.

240. Ibid., para. 216.

241. Young (2000), 1594. See the Introduction, nn. 62–63, and 93 and accompanying text.

242. Fischer (2009).

responsibility of the [national] parliament, which is elected to control the executive, should relocate too. That is exactly what the Federal Constitutional Court is demanding."[243]

The German Lisbon Decision, along with rulings of other national high courts over the last two decades, serve as reminders that, in the historical process of contestation over the institutional and legal direction of integration, national institutions enjoy a considerable advantage in what I have called *legitimacy resources*.[244] Despite the quite significant migration of regulatory power to the supranational level over the last several decades, these cases suggest that, in the legal-cultural domain at least, the national level retains ultimate constitutional legitimacy to define, and therefore to enforce if need be, the limits of supranational competence. The purpose is to maintain a historically recognizable system of constitutional democracy on the national level. For certain scholars, this may be a "bewildering description of the legal situation," a "conceptual and constitutional limbo,"[245] or a state of "perpetual deficiency" for integration that is unacceptable.[246] But the "double-bind" that these scholarly critics perceive[247]—whereby supranational bodies are allowed to exercise *significant* autonomous regulatory power as agents of the Member States but not *so much* as to eclipse the latter's democratic and constitutional character—would perhaps be less perplexing if more attention were paid to the legal-cultural foundations of integration in the postwar constitutional settlement of administrative governance.

The national high courts' approach to the legal complexities of integration intuitively draws from that settlement, suggesting the extent to which the EU is less sui generis than is often supposed, but rather a "new dimension to an old problem."[248] Cognizant of the separation of power and legitimacy, these courts are struggling to achieve a reconciliation in a spirit of deference but also of concern. They recognize "the requirements of a European Union"[249]—that is, the creation of an extensive and relatively autonomous supranational regulatory apparatus, albeit one that lacks democratic and

---

243. Darnstädt (2009).

244. See, e.g., the Introduction, nn. 31–32 and accompanying text; see also Chapter 1, nn. 98–99 and accompanying text.

245. Schönberger (2009), 1210.

246. Halberstam and Möllers (2009), 1252.

247. Schönberger (2009), 1210; Halberstam and Möllers (2009), 1251–52.

248. Lindseth (1999), 630.

249. German Lisbon Decision (2009), para. 227.

constitutional legitimacy of its own. But they also take seriously integration's purported foundation in "representative democracy" on the national level and seek to preserve it in a constitutionally meaningful way, despite delegation.[250] This is the essence of the struggle for reconciliation that has characterized the contestation over administrative governance since the postwar decades, now shifted to the realm of European integration.

---

250. Article 10 TEU post-Lisbon.

FIVE

Supranational Delegation and National Parliamentary Scrutiny since the 1970s

THE FINAL DIMENSION of the convergence of European public law around the legitimating structures of the postwar constitutional settlement involves national parliamentary scrutiny. Chapter 3 gave us a sense of how, for much of integration history, the primary job of overseeing supranational action in a political sense has fallen to the national executives in the Council. But we also know from Chapter 2 that, on the domestic level, the postwar constitutional settlement also entailed at least a residual role for national parliaments in overseeing delegated power. Thus, we might expect the development of similar oversight functions in European public law, consistent with the postwar constitutional settlement.[1]

In this regard, the core holding of the German Lisbon Decision of 2009—that Article 23(1) of the German Basic Law demands specific, antecedent legislation before the German government can vote in favor of using the simplified revision procedure, the passerelle clauses, or the reserve legislative authority under Article 352 of the Treaty on the Functioning of the European Union (TFEU)—should perhaps be unsurprising. Beyond these specific situations, however, the Court's otherwise far-ranging ruling provided little guidance regarding more routine national parliamentary scrutiny of European Union (EU) legislation. In its analysis, the Court alluded at one point to the role of the *Bundestag's* Committee on European Union Affairs, whose existence is now constitutionally guaranteed under Article 45 of the Basic Law.[2] But these references were not central to its decision.

This too, however, should not surprise us. As the Czech Constitutional Court noted in its own decision on the Treaty of Lisbon in 2008, except at the

---

1. Cf. Katz (1999), 25 ("The same parliamentary oversight and control that reconcile administrative actions with the norms of democratic government for purely domestic issues might be expected to perform the same function with decisions concerning the implementation of EU policies.").

2. German Lisbon Decision (2009), paras. 405 and 408.

outer constitutional margins of permissible delegation, supervising the exercise of supranational authority is "a priori a political question, which provides the legislature wide discretion."[3] Ultimately it is for the legislature itself, in conjunction with the national government, to determine politically what the specifics of ongoing national parliamentary oversight will be. As the Danish Supreme Court noted in its decision on the Maastricht Treaty in 1998:

> In so far as the EC Treaty is concerned, legislative powers have been transferred primarily to the Council, in which the Danish Government can exercise its influence and is answerable to the [Danish] Parliament. It is reasonable to assume that the Parliament has the task of considering whether participation by the Government in [further] EC integration should be conditional upon any additional democratic control.[4]

In short, oversight of policymaking within bounds of otherwise lawful supranational delegation is primarily a political and not a legal undertaking (as it also is, overwhelmingly, in the administrative state).[5] But the political character of national parliamentary oversight does not mean that judges have played no role in prompting the development of this scrutiny as a significant element in European public law over the last several decades. Certainly, as the German Lisbon Decision of 2009 suggests, the national parliamentary role responds to a broad constitutional imperative for democratic legitimation on the national level. Nevertheless, for the most part, the judicial impetus for national parliamentary scrutiny has been indirect, ironically involving not the national high courts but the European Court of Justice (ECJ).

By the later 1990s, several decisions of the ECJ had made it clear that the Court would not use the subsidiarity principle to protect national legal orders from questionable exercises of supranational legislative power.[6] Consequently, it became clear that subsidiarity would need enforcement by

---

3. Pl. ÚS 19/08, 26 November 2008, *Treaty of Lisbon Amending the Treaty on European Union and the Treaty Establishing the European Community*, para.109, http://angl.concourt.cz/angl_verze/doc/pl-19-08.php (last visited June 11, 2009).

4. Case I-361/1997, *Carlsen and Others v. Rasmussen*, 6 Apr. 1998, 1998 UfR 800, reprinted in Oppenheimer (1994/2003), 2:192.

5. Cf. Mashaw (2005); but see also Mashaw (2007).

6. See this chapter, nn. 32–39 and accompanying text.

other means, and for this an augmented national parliamentary role gained increasing attention. European scrutiny mechanisms had existed in certain countries (notably Denmark and the United Kingdom) as early as the 1970s. Nevertheless, it was not until after the vast expansion of supranational regulatory power in 1986 under the Single European Act (SEA), continuing through the effort to reform the democratic foundations of integration into the 2000s, that national parliamentary scrutiny would become a significant element of integration law and politics in other Member States. In the present decade, however, attention to the increased national parliamentary role in national systems eventually translated into significant changes in *supranational* law. The so-called subsidiarity early-warning mechanism of the Constitutional Treaty, now carried over to the Treaty of Lisbon, built directly on the national developments of the prior two decades.

Thus, to understand the evolution of national parliamentary scrutiny in European public law, one must follow two strands of development, one national, one supranational. But these histories are in fact intertwined. As a point of entry into that complex relationship, we begin in a somewhat unorthodox fashion—in the middle—looking to the pivotal changes occurring in European integration subsequent to the introduction of the principle of subsidiarity in response to the vast expansion in supranational regulatory power since 1986. One cannot understand why national parliamentary scrutiny developed as a feature of European governance without first appreciating the increasing penetration of European norms into national legal orders, as well as the failure of the ECJ to police that penetration under the principle of subsidiarity in any meaningful way.

🌺 5.1 The Pivotal Change: Subsidiarity and the Expansion of Supranational Regulatory Power After 1986

Subsidiarity made its first appearance in European public law in 1986, in provisions of the SEA on environmental regulation.[7] Then, under Maastricht, it became a general principle of European law through the insertion of Article 3b into the EC Treaty (later renumbered as Article 5 of the Treaty Establishing the European Community [TEC] and subsequently Article 5(3) of the Treaty

---

7. As amended by the SEA, art. 130r(4).

on European Union [TEU] post-Lisbon). The old Article 3b specified that beyond areas falling within the Community's "exclusive competence," such as the customs union, "the Community shall take action . . . only if and in so far as the objectives of the proposed action cannot be sufficiently achieved by the Member States and can therefore, by reason of the scale or effects of the proposed action, be better achieved by the Community." The insertion of this language was prompted directly by the quite dramatic expansion of supranational regulatory authority under the SEA as well as the equally dramatic upsurge in legislation in completion of the internal market under the 1992 program.[8]

Indeed, although the establishment of the European Union under the Treaty of Maastricht undoubtedly symbolized a new stage in the integration process, the key legal groundwork was laid in the SEA and more particularly in the adoption of qualified-majority voting (QMV) for harmonization directives for the internal market (originally Article 100a; later Article 95 TEC/ Article 114 TFEU). This step further diminished the Member State's capacity for direct national control of the Commission and left them, as one commentator put it, "in need of new instruments . . . , especially since the SEA had also extended the Community's sphere of action to new areas (worker health and safety, research and technology, and regional development, as well as environmental protection)."[9] In fact, it was fully expected that "the next few years would bring still further treaty amendments, and still new legislative competences for the Community."[10] Thus it was "no coincidence" that, in both further expanding QMV as well as extending the substantive reach of the EC Treaty itself (along with the adoption of the TEU), the Treaty of Maastricht would also "put subsidiarity in plain view, making it a central principle of [European] law."[11]

---

8. See European Commission (1985).

9. Bermann (1994), 345.

10. Ibid.

11. Ibid. Aside from its insertion into the TEU itself (in the Preamble as well as art. B, later art. 2) along with art. 3b (later art. 5) of the EC Treaty, the drafters at Maastricht would "emphasize the connection between subsidiarity and the expansion of the Community's powers" with language in "virtually every new treaty chapter" of the EC Treaty. The purpose of such language was, like the subsidiarity principle itself, to underscore "that the Member States continue[d] to exercise primary responsibility in these new Community spheres. This [was] the case with education, vocational training, culture, health, consumer protection, and industrial competitiveness, each of which the [Treaty of Maastricht brought] within the sphere of Community action." Bermann (1994), 346 (citations omitted).

Nor was it a coincidence that at the same historical juncture there would be increased attention (albeit more inchoate) to expanding the role of national parliaments as a source of democratic legitimation in the expansion of supranational regulatory authority.[12] However, the linkage between subsidiarity and national parliaments would not become fully clear until a decade later, first in the now-defunct Constitutional Treaty, then in the Treaty of Lisbon.[13] At Maastricht, the role of national parliaments would be recognized only in nonbinding declarations attached to the TEU,[14] although this would be developed later into a protocol attached to the Treaty of Amsterdam on the role of national parliaments.[15] The drafters inserted the subsidiarity principle itself, by contrast, directly into the body of the EC Treaty, even as its precise meaning, as well as the manner of its enforcement, remained an open question.

From the moment of its original appearance in European law in the mid-1980s, subsidiarity in fact "received surprisingly poor academic mention" because of its deeply ambiguous content, clarity, and utility as a workable legal principle.[16] Lord Mackenzie Stuart, a Scottish former President of the ECJ, expressed the conventional view in 1991: "To decide whether a given action is more appropriate at Community level, necessary at Community level, effective at Community level is essentially a political topic. It is not the sort of question a Court should be asked to decide."[17] This widespread skepticism with regard to the justiciability of subsidiarity did little to deter the Member States. Rather, they continued to look to subsidiarity as the *political* touchstone in their broader effort to ensure that, as the substantive reach of

---

12. In both the lead up to, and during the intergovernmental conferences (IGCs) that culminated in the Treaty of Maastricht, both the European Council (at length) and the Commission considered the role of national parliaments in their submissions. For a succinct summary, see Westlake (1996), 169–70.

13. See this chapter, section 5.3.

14. Following proposals by the United Kingdom and France at the Maastricht IGC, the TEU included Declaration No. 13 on the Role of National Parliaments, and Declaration No. 14 on the Conference of Parliaments ("Assises"). See Krekelberg (2001), 477 and 479; see also Corbett (1993), 61–62.

15. For a copy of the original Treaty of Amsterdam, see http://www.eurotreaties.com/amsterdamtreaty.pdf (last visited July 15, 2009). For the Protocol (No. 9) on the Role of National Parliaments in the European Union (1997), as part of the consolidated treaties (pre-Lisbon), see 2006 O.J. (C 321) E/227–28.

16. Bermann (1994), 332.

17. In European Institute of Public Administration (1991), as quoted in Weatherill (2005), 16.

European norms was expanded, supranational "decisions [would be] taken as closely as possible to the citizen," or at least this is how the new preamble to the TEU would put it, specifically adding "in accordance with the principle of subsidiarity."[18]

Subsidiarity received special emphasis in political discussions in those Member States most ambivalent about the direction of integration. Following the referendum defeat in Denmark in June 1992, for example, Danish parties drafted a national compromise that, inter alia, specifically looked to subsidiarity as a way for integration to "take greater account of different traditions and forms of organization in the individual Member States" (pairing this with calls for heightened transparency, regulatory simplicity, and national parliamentary scrutiny, among other concerns).[19] The conclusions of the European Council at its meeting in Lisbon soon after the Danish defeat, as well as those issued in Birmingham in October after the shockingly close victory in the French referendum, echoed this linkage. The Birmingham Declaration, as one contemporaneous observer put it, emphasized "elements . . . designed [not merely] to appeal in Denmark, but also to reticent backbenchers in the UK" who had yet to vote on the Maastricht Treaty.[20] These elements would include greater respect for cultural traditions, better information for national parliaments and the introduction of procedures to make enforcement of the principle of subsidiarity a reality.

The primary aim of the Danish national compromise, of course, was to specify the four exceptions to the Maastricht Treaty that Denmark demanded as the basis for a second Danish referendum.[21] But in acquiescing to these exceptions, the heads of state and government who reassembled at Edinburgh in December 1992 were acutely sensitive not just to the concerns of the Danish electorate or the "reticent backbenchers in the UK," but also to increasingly anxious public opinion throughout Europe. Thus, the Edinburgh Council took steps to realize the goals of its earlier Birmingham Declaration by conspicuously adopting a new set of subsidiarity guidelines that it paired with additional "measures to increase transparency and openness in the

---

18. For the TEU as originally adopted, see http://eur-lex.europa.eu/en/treaties/dat/11992M/htm/11992M.html#0001000001 (last visited July 17, 2009).

19. Danish National Compromise (1992); see also http://www.euo.dk/emner_en/forbehold/ (last visited June 15, 2009); for additional background see Krunke (2005), 343.

20. Corbett (1993), 69.

21. See Chapter 4, nn. 193–194 and accompanying text.

decision-making process of the Community."[22] The following year, the Commission, Council, and European Parliament took the Edinburgh guidelines one step further by entering into an interinstitutional agreement "on procedures for implementing the principle of subsidiarity."[23] The most important feature of this agreement, for our purposes, was the commitment of the Commission, in exercising its right of initiative under the treaties, to "take into account the principle of subsidiarity and show that it has been observed."[24] More specifically, the Commission agreed, as part of its explanatory memorandum for any proposal, to submit "a justification . . . under the principle of subsidiarity."[25]

Although the actual content of these procedural commitments remained extremely vague, they nevertheless suggested something important—that perhaps the key dimension of subsidiarity was in fact procedural, not substantive or even jurisdictional. Subsidiarity, understood procedurally, directed "the legislative institutions of the Community to engage in a particular inquiry before concluding that action at the Community rather than Member State level is warranted."[26] This further implied, in turn, a possible role for the Court of Justice, pointing to a kind of judicial review directed at verifying "whether the institutions themselves examined the possibility of alternative remedies at or below the Member State level."[27] Without "enmeshing [the Court] in profoundly political judgments that it [was] ill-equipped to make," the procedural dimension of subsidiarity suggested that the Court still needed to ensure that supranational institutions (and particularly the Commission) "structure[d] their discussion and focus[ed] their debate" specifically on questions of subsidiarity, which then "should promote a realistic assessment . . . of the costs and benefits of Community action and inaction alike."[28]

---

22. Edinburgh European Council (1992), 9. The European Council also specifically made reference to these new guidelines in its acceptance of the Danish exceptions as well. Ibid., 25.

23. Interinstitutional Agreement of 25 October 1993 between the European Parliament, the Council and the Commission on procedures for implementing the principle of subsidiarity, 1993 O.J. (C 329) 135 [hereinafter "Interinstitutional Agreement (1993)"].

24. Interinstitutional Agreement (1993), section II(1).

25. Ibid., section II(2).

26. Bermann (1994), 336.

27. Ibid., 391.

28. Ibid.

In its procedural dimension, the subsidiarity principle also implied a type of judicial review by the ECJ focused not on substantive policy judgments, but on the quality of reasoning of the decision maker. Just as we saw in Chapter 4, here too a parallel to an American-style administrative experience was arguably beginning to manifest itself. The procedural dimension of subsidiarity implied an obligation of reasoned decision making not unlike the obligation imposed on U.S. administrative agencies under the so-called *hard look doctrine*.[29] This sort of legal control reflected the idea that, "[i]n the administrative context, . . . a reviewing court promotes democratic legitimacy when it forces the agency, as an aspect of legality, to give sufficient reasons for its actions. . . . [T]he reviewing court must satisfy itself that the agency 'examine[d] the relevant data and articulate[d] a satisfactory explanation' for its normative output."[30] In theory at least, the Court would not need to substitute its judgment for that of the agency, as long as the agency could show that it engaged in a process of reasoned decision making, considering alternatives and explaining its decision.

If this is indeed the sort of judicial review that a proceduralized subsidiarity principle was supposed to entail, then it, too, was a manifestation of the changing nature of public law generally in an era of dense and complex administrative governance. No longer would the focus primarily be on rule-based analyses of validity or invalidity; rather, public law was shifting toward a balancing system of resistance norms, designed primarily to raise the costs of decision-making by imposing additional procedural burdens without necessarily drawing bright lines.[31] In the European context, however, this obligation of reasoned analysis, at least regarding subsidiarity, would not be *judicially* but rather *politically* imposed—that is, by the Member States themselves by way of the treaties and European Council, rather than by the ECJ by way of judicial decision. In significant part, this was due to the ECJ's unwillingness to acknowledge subsidiarity's procedural dimension. The Court's treatment of the subsidiarity principle in the 1990s and into the early 2000s demonstrated quite clearly that, as one commentator put it, it is sometimes

---

29. Greater Boston Television Corp. v. FCC, 444 F.2d 841, 851 (D.C. Cir. 1970) (footnote omitted), *cert. denied*, 403 U.S. 923 (1971) (describing "hard look" review). In Motor Vehicle Mfr. Ass'n v. State Farm Mut. Auto. Ins. Co., 463 U.S. 29 (1983), the Supreme Court "essentially endorsed 'hard look' review." See Strauss (1989), 539.

30. Lindseth (1999), 714, quoting *State Farm*, 463 U.S., at 43.

31. See, e.g., Young (2000), 1597; and also the Introduction, nn. 62–63 and accompanying text. See also Stephenson (2008) and (2006).

easier to insert language into a European treaty than it is to make it "matter" to the Court.[32] This was particularly the case where that language was designed to constrain supranational normative autonomy, contrary to what the judges (ahistorically) believed to be "the genetic code transmitted to the Court."[33]

Several cases before the ECJ in the late 1990s and early 2000s raised serious questions of subsidiarity, and in each the Court rejected demands for something approaching hard look review.[34] In the first case, the Court simply inferred, in the absence of any evidence, that the legislation satisfied the requirements of subsidiarity solely by virtue of the Council's decision to legislate.[35] In another, the Court relied exclusively on conclusory statements contained in the directive's recitals, finding somewhat sweepingly that "the Parliament and the Council did explain why they considered that their action was in conformity with the principle of subsidiarity."[36] In still another case, the Court found that compliance with subsidiarity could be "implicit" in the directive's recitals, without any detailed statement of reasons.[37] As one commentator concluded from these and other cases, the Court's approach "neatly sustained subsidiarity as a legal principle on paper while conceding much in practice to legislative discretion. Once it [was] determined that a competence to establish common rules exists, the political decision to

---

32. Bermann (1994), 335.

33. See Chapter 4, n. 24 and accompanying text.

34. See the Court's judgments regarding in Case C-84/94, *United Kingdom v. Council*, 1996 E.C.R. I-5755 [hereinafter *Working Time Directive*]; Case C-233/94, *Germany v. Parliament and Council*, 1997 E.C.R. I-2405 [hereinafter *Deposit-Guarantee Schemes*]; and Case C-491/01, *R. v. Secretary of State ex parte BAT and Imperial Tobacco*, 2002 E.C.R. I-11543. For a detailed critique of the first two decisions, see Lindseth (1999), 714–26; for a critique of the third, see Weatherill (2005), 15–16.

35. *Working Time Directive*, 1996 E.C.R. at I-5809, para. 47 ("Once the Council has found that it is necessary to improve the existing level of protection as regards the health and safety of workers and to harmonise the conditions in this area . . . , achievement of that objective through the imposition of minimum requirements *necessarily presupposes* Community-wide action.") (emphasis added). For a critique, see Lindseth (1999), 715–16.

36. *Deposit-Guarantee Schemes*, 1997 E.C.R. at I-2453, para. 28; see Lindseth (1999), 716. One might also note that the directive satisfied the rather perfunctory general reason-giving obligation under the old Article 190 (Article 253 TEC/Article 296 TFEU), at least as it was permissively interpreted by the Court. See Lindseth (1999), 692–93.

37. Case C-377/98, *Netherlands v. Parliament and Council*, 2001 E.C.R. I-07079, para. 33 [hereinafter *Biotechnological Inventions*].

exercise that competence seem[ed] *in practice* immune from judicial supervision."[38]

Thus, despite the evidentiary burdens that a proceduralized subsidiarity principle seemed to place on European institutions, the Court found it sufficient, as a leading casebook on European law put it in the midst of these decisions, for "the institutions merely to reach and to state a conclusion ... ; they [did] not apparently have to recite detailed evidence to support that conclusion—much less convince the Court that the conclusion is correct."[39] Indeed, these cases arguably reflected the Court's long-established, fundamentally constitutionalist mindset, which insisted on regarding the supranational legislative process as similar to that of a constitutional legislature on the national level—at least in so far as the judicial power to demand reasons was concerned. According to the ECJ, "it would be pointless to require [the legislature to provide] a specific statement of reasons for each of the technical choices made by it"[40]—which compares, in effect, to the sort of deference the U.S. Supreme Court gives Congress under the rational-basis test.[41] The irony, of course, is that the ECJ's jurisdiction to annul a piece of European legislation is based on the old Article 173 (later Article 230 TEC/Article 263 TFEU), which grounds its four bases for judicial control directly on the four analogous bases in French administrative law (under the so-called *recours pour excès de pouvoir,* or action for breach of authority).[42] The ECJ thus converted what should have been a form of administrative review (in theory more demanding) into a kind of loose constitutional oversight, for which deference to the "legislature" (rather than an administrative rulemaker) is great.[43]

The ECJ's permissiveness in the 1990s thus forced the Member States to specify for themselves what Europe's supranational judges would not—that to satisfy the requirements of subsidiarity, European institutions would need

---

38. Weatherill (2005), 15–16 (emphasis in original), discussing *BAT and Imperial Tobacco*, 2002 E.C.R. I-11543.

39. Bermann et al. (1998), 23.

40. *Working Time Directive*, 1996 E.C.R. at I-5816, para. 79.

41. United States R.R. Retirement Bd. v. Fritz, 449 U.S. 166, 179 (1980) ("[w]here, as here, there are plausible reasons for Congress' action, our inquiry is at an end. . . . [T]his Court has never insisted that a legislative body articulate its reasons for enacting a statute").

42. See Chapter 4, n. 28 and accompanying text.

43. Compare the Court's approach to standing and its test for "individual concern" from Case 25/62, *Plaumann & Co. v. Commission*, 1963 E.C.R. 95; see Chapter 4, nn. 34–40 and accompanying text.

to assemble an evidentiary record showing why supranational legislation was required in the particular case. The first step was the insertion of the Subsidiarity Protocol in the EC Treaty under the Treaty of Amsterdam of 1997, at the urging of France, Germany, and the United Kingdom, among other Member States.[44] The Amsterdam Subsidiarity Protocol provided, in pertinent part, that "[f]or any proposed Community legislation, the reasons on which it is based shall be stated with a view to justifying its compliance with the principles of subsidiarity and proportionality." It further specified that "the reasons ... must be substantiated by qualitative or, wherever possible, quantitative indicators."[45] The Protocol also harkened back to the conclusions of the Edinburgh European Council in 1992,[46] pairing rules on the implementation of subsidiarity with measures to increase transparency and openness in EU decision making. The Protocol obligated the Commission to "consult widely before proposing legislation and, wherever appropriate, publish consultation documents," as well as "to take duly into account" the burdens of the rules it was proposing on "national governments, local authorities, economic operators and citizens," which in turn should "be minimised and proportionate to the objective to be achieved." And finally, the Protocol obligated the Commission to issue an annual report to the European Council and the other European institutions on the application of the principles of subsidiarity and proportionality.

The Amsterdam Subsidiarity Protocol thus established the rudiments of an administrative-procedural code obligating the Commission to consult interests, assess impacts, and report to oversight bodies—all in order to exert influence over the Commission's exercise of its (increasingly more constrained) right of policy development and initiative. The elaboration of this administrative-type code took on even greater urgency in the reform environment following the resignation of the Santer Commission in 1999.[47] During that time, successive European Councils—at Lisbon in March 2000, Stockholm in March 2001, Gothenburg in June 2001, Laeken in December 2001, and Barcelona in March 2002—all called on the Commission to develop

---

44. Protocol (No 30) on the Application of the Principles of Subsidiarity and Proportionality (1997), 2006 O.J. (C 321) E/308 [hereinafter "Amsterdam Subsidiarity Protocol (1997)"].

45. Amsterdam Subsidiarity Protocol (1997), para. 4.

46. In fact, in para. 5, the Amsterdam Subsidiarity Protocol (1997) effectively codified the substantive guidelines laid down by the Edinburgh European Council in 1992. See this chapter, n. 22 and accompanying text.

47. See generally Lindseth et al. (2008), 41–46.

"a strategy for further coordinated action to simplify the regulatory environment." The Commission in turn, produced its now-famous *White Paper on Governance* in July 2001,[48] which committed the Commission to a program of improving the quality of EU legislation. Since 2001, the Commission has progressively introduced a detailed procedural system where each major policy initiative must include a consultation with stakeholders, an analysis of the measure's expected impact, and a justification of action at the EU level in accordance with the principles of subsidiarity and proportionality.

There is a good deal of skepticism toward the effectiveness of a proceduralized subsidiarity requirement in combating so-called *competence creep*, the colloquial term now used to refer to the old phenomenon of spillover. One observer has concluded, for example: "The Amsterdam Protocol may have prompted proceduralization of subsidiarity by requiring wider consultation and more explicit reasoning, but it is far from plain that any genuine change in institutional culture . . . has been achieved."[49] Commission compliance has been "on occasion at best perfunctory," often making "no serious attempt to substantiate" that a particular piece of legislation conforms to subsidiarity.[50] Others are more sanguine, citing anecdotal evidence from the Commission's annual *Better Lawmaking* reports that subsidiarity is having an impact.[51] But in any case, the real problem with enforcing subsidiarity may not be with the Commission but rather with the Council—that is, the national executives assembled at the supranational level:

> If a sufficient number of members of the Council—a qualified majority now, whereas unanimous support was previously required—are politically predisposed to the adoption of a particular measure, then appeal to subsidiarity under Article 5(2) [TEC/Article 5(3) TEU post-Lisbon] is no more politically likely to be sturdy enough to hold the line in the legislative process than insistence on the importance of attributed competence

---

48. See European Commission (2001), 23.

49. Weatherill (2005), 12.

50. Weatherill (2005), 11, citing, e.g., the preamble to Directive 2000/31/EC of the European Parliament and of the Council of 8 June 2000 on certain legal aspects of information society services, in particular electronic commerce, in the Internal Market, 2000 O.J. (L 178) 1.

51. Cooper (2006), 286.

pursuant to Article 5(1) [TEC/Articles 5(1) and (2) TEU post-Lisbon]. Substance outweighs constitutional nicety.[52]

Ultimately, it is this sort of distrust of the ability of supranational policy-makers, even under national executive oversight, that provides the essential backdrop for the emerging role of national parliaments in European integration over the last several decades—both under national and, more importantly, supranational law. The Treaty of Lisbon, following the lead of the now-defunct Constitutional Treaty of 2004, adds a significant new procedural element, the subsidiarity early-warning mechanism. This element enlists the aid of the national parliaments in the task of scrutinizing supranational policy formulation in the Commission, simultaneous with its consideration by the Council and European Parliament.[53] This mechanism reflects, in some sense, the realization that the existing players in the Community's rulemaking process "cannot be trusted" because they have "a self-interest in enhancing the scope of decision-making that is feasible at the EC level.... The EC system is, in short, not safe in the hands of the EC's own institutions"[54]— including, perhaps most importantly, the national executives assembled in the Council, as well as the ECJ.

The new early-warning mechanism will build on developments under national law over the prior two decades, which have significantly strengthened the legitimating (if not control) functions of national parliaments vis-à-vis national executives in the formulation of their EU policies. In the next section, we take up these national developments, tracing the emergence of the various models of scrutiny from the 1970s to the 1990s, focusing on the two leading competitors, the Danish "mandating" and the British "document-based" systems. We also consider the diffusion of these competing models among the Member States over the course of the 1990s and into the 2000s. And on the question of diffusion more specifically, it is important to note how variants on the Danish approach especially (which the *Højesteret* stressed in 1998)[55] would prove normatively attractive as newer Member States from the Nordic, Central, and Eastern European regions looked for

---

52. Weatherill (2005), 11.

53. For an overview, see Lindseth et al. (2008), 94–95.

54. Weatherill (2005), 17.

55. See this chapter, n. 4 and accompanying text.

ways to address persistent concerns over the seeming lack of democratic legitimacy in European integration in the 2000s.

※ 5.2 The Institutionalization of National Parliamentary Scrutiny under National Law since the 1970s

One cannot address the development of national parliamentary scrutiny of European affairs without first at least alluding to the so-called *deparliamentarization thesis*—the notion that integration has been a key causal factor in the declining role of national parliaments over the last half century.[56] In its weaker form, the thesis is descriptively unobjectionable. It simply points to the fact that integration has relied on the delegation of normative power out of the realm of national parliaments, just as in the administrative state. A more moderate version can be found in the work of some political scientists, who speak, for example, of "the deparliamentarization of national polities and the short-circuiting of democratic procedures of interest representation and procedures to ensure accountability."[57] But in its strongest form, what we might call its "legal variant" (because it has appeared in the works of influential legal scholars), the thesis is more problematic. From this latter perspective, integration has "perverted democracy" itself,[58] leading to "a neo absolutist process of decision-making" rooted in "an excessive empowerment of the executive."[59]

In whatever form, however, the thesis ultimately begs an important historical question: "deparliamentarization" measured against what standard, defined precisely when? The historical evidence we discussed in Chapter 2, for example, suggests an inverse historical relationship: The process of European integration was not the cause of deparliamentarization but rather was the beneficiary of a preexisting transformation of national systems in a

---

56. The deparliamentarization thesis has had its origins in the literature on executive-legislative relations on the domestic level, although in recent years it has been strongly linked to European integration. See, e.g., Börzel and Sprungk (2007); O'Brennan and Raunio (2007a); Rittberger (2005), 198–99; Damgaard and Jensen (2005); Raunio and Hix (2000); Anderson and Burns (1996).

57. Rittberger (2005), 199.

58. Weiler (1995), 233; see also Wincott (1998).

59. Curtin (1997), 48.

decidedly executive and technocratic direction. Indeed, important strands in the recent political-science literature seem to be moving toward a more sophisticated understanding this complicated historical relationship, in two interrelated respects.

First, political scientists are beginning to challenge, on historical grounds, the "gloomy picture" presented by strong advocates of the deparliamentarization thesis.[60] The revisionists have quite convincingly shown that, in the integration context, several Member States have in fact developed forms of parliamentary oversight that are often more advanced than the mechanisms that apply in purely national contexts with regard to delegated power.[61] Accompanying this process has been development of an institutional infrastructure, including the widespread creation of oversight committees within national parliaments. It has also included the creation of mechanisms for these bodies to exchange information and coordinate their activities at the supranational level, notably COSAC (the French acronym for the "Conference of Community and European Affairs Committees of Parliaments of the European Union").[62] Domestically, it has also included the expansion of committee staff, in some cases extending to the creation of a national parliamentary presence in Brussels itself, to monitor the complex structures of policy development within the Commission, Council, COREPER and its working groups, as well as the European Parliament.[63]

Second, and perhaps more importantly, some political scientists (most importantly Katrin Auel and her collaborators) are also beginning to develop more sophisticated frameworks to assess the function of national

---

60. Raunio and Hix (2000), 143.

61. See, e.g., Raunio and Hix (2000); Damgaard and Jensen (2005); Auel and Benz (2007), 59 ("in domestic politics, parliaments have suffered from an incremental downgrading due to the decline of clear political cleavages and the increasing need for expertise in public policy. In European politics they are increasingly confronted with a visible structural change as their legislative competencies are explicitly transferred to a higher level. They have reacted to this obvious loss of power by implementing institutional reforms"). For empirical evidence in support of these claims, see the comprehensive country and regional reports contained in Norton (1996c); Maurer and Wessels (2001c); Kiiver (2006); O'Brennan and Raunio (2007b); and Tans et al. (2007); see also Cygan (2001).

62. For greater detail, see Lindseth et al. (2008), 96–99.

63. See, e.g., Hölscheidt (2001), 126–27; Szukala and Rozenberg (2001), 233; Calussi and Grassi (2001), 277–78, 289; Blümel and Neuhold (2001), 328; see also Nordic EAC (2002), 18–19; Pratt (1998), 225, 229.

parliamentary scrutiny in relation to national EU policies.[64] This line of thinking is shifting away from the search for impact on specific policies (i.e., *power*
or *control* in a narrowly defined sense), which is almost impossible to assess.[65]
In fact, perhaps no form of oversight in the integration context more explicitly demonstrates the separation of regulatory power from the ultimate
institutional mechanisms of legitimation than national parliamentary scrutiny. Very much consistent with the historiographical and legal theory of
this study, these political scientists have persuasively analyzed national
parliamentary scrutiny of European policy as primarily a mechanism of
legitimation.[66] Their focus has been on the way in which scrutiny procedures,
both formal and informal, reduce "information costs" (to use the jargon of
principle-agent theory), improving the ability of legislators to develop an
understanding of the nature and consequences of European proposals while
also making the national executive's position on these questions more transparent. This in turn promotes more meaningful legislative input, which can
often be informal and within party structures (given the delicate balance
that members of the majority must often strike between supporting the
incumbent government and acting as a reliable conduit for citizen and interest-
group pressures). Thus, these analysts suggest that there is no necessary
correlation between the scope of formal scrutiny rights and parliamentary
capacity to legitimize the executive's EU policy.[67]

At the inception of integration in the 1950s, however, the parliaments of
the original six Member States showed relatively little systematic interest in
taking on these various roles in European matters, formally or otherwise.
The parliamentary function was primarily understood as one of ratifying the
treaty and then allowing the national executive to take the policymaking
lead, which was further seen primarily as an aspect of foreign policy.[68] There
was apparently little or no political pressure for detailed national-parliamentary
scrutiny of European policy in the early years of integration, which was not
yet perceived as having a major domestic regulatory impact (this would not
occur in earnest until the 1980s). In such an environment, where integration's

---

64. See, e.g., Auel (2006), (2007a), (2007b), and (2009); Auel and Benz (2005) and (2007); and
Auel and Rittberger (2006).

65. See generally Auel (2007b).

66. See Auel (2006), (2007a), and (2009); Auel and Benz (2005) and (2007); Auel and Rittberger
(2006); and Benz (2004).

67. For further detail, see this chapter, nn. 185–190 and accompanying text.

68. Maurer and Wessels (2001b), 429, citing Cassese (1982).

effect on domestic parliamentary power seemed minimal, a kind of supranational idealism could more easily take root. It would be reflected in "a feeling that national parliaments should not be deeply involved, but should encourage the rapid transfer of democratic control functions to the European Parliament."[69] Of course, at the time as well, the members of the European Parliament were appointed from the ranks of national MPs. But as we shall see below, the shift in 1979 to an independently elected (and therefore seemingly more autonomous) European Parliament was not the particular cause of heightened demands for scrutiny. Rather, what was more important was the increasing awareness of the domestic regulatory impact of European norms, particularly in the aftermath of the SEA and the flurry of legislation as part of the 1992 single market program. One observer has evocatively called this period "the awakening of national parliaments" ("*le réveil des parlements nationaux*").[70]

In the case of the French parliament in particular, noninterference for much of the earlier period was perhaps understandable given the national legislature's relatively degraded constitutional position under the Fifth Republic.[71] As late as the mid-1970s, French parliamentarians were said to view "with equanimity or indifference the transfer of its legislative powers to European Community institutions"[72]—although this would soon begin to change.[73] The parliaments of the Benelux countries were slightly more attentive to European matters, some even intermittently establishing committees to monitor European affairs, however these were often of an ephemeral importance.[74] More puzzling perhaps was the nonreaction of the Italian parliament, which under Italy's postwar constitution retained its "'centrality' and uniqueness," most importantly "in its law-making functions."[75] And yet

---

69. Fitzmaurice (1979), 203.

70. Magnette (2003), 83.

71. The French constitution of 1958 concentrated agenda-setting and, more importantly, normative power in the government; strictly limited the number of parliamentary committees and days in session; and, finally, enlisted a set of ancillary institutions—the newly established *Conseil constitutionnel*, as well as the venerable *Conseil d'Etat*—to police the boundary between legislative and executive power, in principle in favor of the latter. See Chapter 2, nn. 87–92 and 114–115 and accompanying text.

72. Rizzuto (1996), 47, citing Frears (1975).

73. See this chapter, nn. 140–146 and accompanying text.

74. Helpful chronologies on the establishment of scrutiny committees in the various Member States can be found in Norton (1996a), 180, and Maurer and Wessels (2001b), 437.

75. Furlong (1996), 37.

Italian MPs were hardly more active than their counterparts in other Member States.[76] The Chamber of Deputies relied on its foreign affairs committee structure rather than establishing a specific European oversight mechanism. In keeping with the idea of integration as foreign policy, the Italian parliament relied well into the 1980s "on periodic omnibus laws which gave wide delegated powers to the Government to enable it to deal with the detail of international [i.e., European] obligations."[77]

The German parliament, at least initially, seemed to struggle more explicitly with the challenge of obtaining European information from the government. Article 2 of the German act of accession of 1957 specified that the federal government "shall keep the Bundestag and the Bundesrat continually informed of developments in the Council." Moreover, if "a decision in the Council requires the making of a German Law"—i.e., a directive requiring transposition by way of statute—"or has immediate force of law in the Federal Republic of Germany"—i.e., a regulation or certain categories of decisions—then "notification should be made prior to the Council making its decision."[78] In the implementation of this provision, however, the *Bundesrat* and the *Bundestag* responded differently. The upper house established a committee devoted to European affairs in 1957 (the *Ausschuss für Fragen der Europäischen Gemeinschaften*). The *Bundestag,* by contrast, initially relied on the existing committee structure, though this proved inefficient and unwieldy. In the mid-1960s a committee of senior parliamentarians (*Integrationsältestenrat*) was established to coordinate referrals to other committees, but this body rarely met and eventually disbanded.[79]

It was only with the entry of Denmark and the United Kingdom into the Community in 1973 that more enduring models of parliamentary scrutiny would emerge on the national level. The entry of these countries also

---

76. The Foreign Affairs Committee of the Italian Senate established a subcommittee on integration in 1968, but this body's remit has been described as "fact-finding and consultative," with "minimal impact on parliamentary activities." Calussi and Grassi (2001), 276.

77. Furlong (1996), 38 (citing "law 1203 of 1957 relating to the ratification of the Treaty of Rome, laws 871 of 1965 and 740 of 1969 dealing with the transitional arrangements to the Common Market, similar *leggi-delega* in 1970 and 1975, and then in the 1980s laws which authorised the Government to ensure the appropriate transposition of the large numbers of new directives (law 42 of 1982 and law 183 of 1987)").

78. BGBl. II 753 (July 27, 1957), as translated in Bulmer (1986), 225. On the various categories of supranational normative acts established under the Treaty of Rome, see Chapter 3, nn. 110–112 and accompanying text.

79. Saalfeld (1996), 20–21. According to one report it met six times in five years. Maurer and Wessels (2001b), 437.

established a pattern whereby new Member States would, from the moment of accession, create some kind of scrutiny mechanism, generally including oversight of some kind by a European Affairs Committees (EAC).[80] The fact that Denmark and the United Kingdom took the lead on national parliamentary scrutiny is understandable in part given the timing of their entry. By the early 1970s, the legal consequences of Community membership—in terms of its impact specifically on parliamentary prerogatives and more generally on national sovereignty—were much more evident than in the late 1950s. The Luxembourg Compromise of 1966 had made clear the foundational importance of the national executives in Community decision-making process.[81] Over the course of 1960s and into the early 1970s, the ECJ had also issued an array of decisions on the direct effect of treaty articles,[82] the supremacy of Community law,[83] the implied powers of the Commission,[84] as well as the direct effect of certain decisions.[85] On this basis, in 1974, the ECJ soon would hold in favor of the direct effect of directives in certain circumstances.[86] Thus, timing of entry, as well as the greater awareness of what membership entailed, arguably played a role in prompting greater parliamentary scrutiny for these new Member States.[87]

---

80. Jungar (2007), 8.

81. See generally, Chapter 3.

82. Case 26/62, *Van Gend & Loos v. Nederlandse Administratie der Belastingen*, 1963 E.C.R. 1. See Chapter 4, n. 15 and accompanying text.

83. Case 6/64, *Costa v. ENEL*, 1964 E.C.R. 585. See Chapter 4, n. 41 and accompanying text.

84. Case 22/70, *Commission of the European Communities v. Council of the European Communities*, 1971 E.C.R. 263 (known as *ERTA*).

85. Case 9/70, *Grad v. Finanzamt Traunstein*, 1970 E.C.R. 825.

86. Case 41/74, *Van Duyn v. Home Office*, 1974 E.C.R. 1337. See Chapter 3, nn. 169–172 and accompanying text.

87. Indeed, political scientists have debated whether timing of membership was of such overwhelming importance that it should be excluded from analytical models evaluating cross-national variation in national-parliamentary scrutiny systems for fear that it would overwhelm the effects of all other potential causal variables. See Raunio (2005), 326 (modifying the approach of Bergman (2000) by excluding the timing of membership because "it is quite obvious that parliaments would react to the deepening of integration through more effective scrutiny"). The Irish example, however, should temper any immediate impulse to view timing as the absolutely decisive factor. Despite its simultaneous entry into the Community with Denmark and the UK, parliamentary scrutiny of integration policy in Ireland remained notoriously weak until quite recently (as did that of several subsequent entrants). See generally Conlan (2007). In fact, one summary calls the subsequent entrants of the 1980s—Spain, Portugal, and Greece—together with Belgium, Luxembourg, Ireland, and Italy, "'slow adapting' parliaments" because of the persistence of their relatively weak scrutiny mechanisms. See Maurer and Wessels (2001a), 21.

However, the relative strength of the British and Danish systems, not to mention their very different forms and methods, must also be explained by looking at the political and constitutional contexts of the two countries—in effect, path dependency and institutional history. Consider the British example first: prior to British entry, the government continually assured members of the UK parliament that their sovereign rights would not be "ceded to Brussels but merely delegated."[88] As the 1967 White Paper on membership put it, supranational delegation meant "the acceptance in advance as part of the law of the United Kingdom of provisions to be made in future by instruments issued by the Community institutions."[89] These statements came, however, in the midst of a quite "passionate debate," unrelated to membership in the Community, over how to "restor[e] the influence of the Commons" in governance more generally, in the face of the "widespread agreement that the power of the Executive had grown vis-à-vis Parliament."[90] Inevitably this atmosphere—which developed *before* British entry, contrary to the suggestion of the strong version of the deparliamentarization thesis—undoubtedly influenced the subsequent debate over the European Communities Bill in 1972. Two more specific concerns were commonly expressed: first, "the apparently bureaucratic nature of Community decision-making, with the close interlocking between the Community and the Executives of the Member States;"[91] and second, the general inadequacy of "British Parliamentary control over *all* delegated legislation," with "the power of the Executive consequently increasing."[92]

Thus, from the outset—in contrast with the original six Member States—the parliamentary debate in Britain seemed to focus intuitively on the relationship between European integration and administrative governance as it had evolved on the national level over the postwar decades. The basic

---

Convergence toward a stronger norm would not take place until the 1990s and 2000s, when scrutiny systems throughout the Union were upgraded to address the dramatic extension of supranational authority over the prior decade. Raunio (2005), 337 ("As the European Union has acquired significant new policy powers since the late 1980s, . . . national legislatures have simultaneously invested more resources in holding their governments to account in EU matters.").

88. Denza (1993), 56, citing Membership in the European Community: Report on Renegotiation (1974), 39.

89. Legal and Constitutional Implications of United Kingdom Membership in the European Communities (1967), quoted in Stevens (1976), 269.

90. Ryan and Isaacson (1974), 200.

91. Stevens (1976), 269.

92. Stevens (1976), 269–70 (emphasis added).

connection between the two would also manifest itself in the conceptual vocabulary used to describe European legislation. The 1967 White Paper, for example, referred to European acts as "instruments," a term of art in British public law to refer to delegated legislation (as in "statutory instruments" on the national level).[93] The legislative output of the Community was thus understood in Britain, at least initially, as "secondary legislation, [and] the Treaties forming the Communities' primary legislation"—in effect, something akin to a *loi-cadre*.[94] The European Communities Act itself would reflect this understanding: Section 2(2) specifically provided that, except for measures in sensitive domains like taxation or criminal law, Community directives would be implemented by way of statutory instrument and not by parliamentary legislation.[95]

After the United Kingdom's actual accession, there continued to be a great deal of concern in the British parliament over how to scrutinize delegated legislation in its now supranational form, just as there had been with regard to domestic delegated legislation in the postwar decades.[96] Eventually, parliament referred this deeply contested question to two select committees (the Foster Committee in the Commons, and the Maybray-King Committee in the Lords).[97] These bodies, in turn, defined the dual committee system for parliamentary scrutiny in the UK—one for each house—which has evolved in its details but whose basic contours have remained stable ever since.[98]

---

93. See Chapter 2, n. 95 and accompanying text.

94. Stevens (1976), 279 n. 2. Compare Chapter 3, nn. 62–63 and accompanying text.

95. European Communities Act, 1972 Eliz. 2, c. 68, section 2(2) (subject to the exceptions set out in section 1(1), e.g. "to make any provision imposing or increasing taxation" or "to create any new criminal offence punishable with imprisonment for more than two years").

96. See generally Ryan and Isaacson (1974). Compare, Chapter 2, nn. 95–97 and accompanying text.

97. The Foster Committee issued two reports—Session 1972–73: First Report from the Select Committee on European Secondary Legislation, H.C. 143, Feb. 1973, and Session 1972–73: Second Report from the Select Committee on European Secondary Legislation, H.C. 463-I and H.C. 463-II (Minutes of Evidence), Oct. 1973. The Maybray-King Committee also reported twice—Session 1972–73: First Report by the Select Committee on Procedures for Scrutiny of Proposals for European Instruments, H.L. 67, Mar. 1973, and Session 1972–73: Second Report by the Select Committee on Procedure for Scrutiny of Proposals for European Instruments, H.L. 194, July 1973.

98. The basis of the present regime, with modifications in the late 1980s and late 1990s, remains the "scheme . . . established in accordance with the recommendations of the Foster Committee." Pratt (1998), 222. For additional overviews that also provide a sense of the historical evolution, see Ryan and Isaacson (1974); Stevens (1976); Bates (1991); Denza (1993); Norton (1996b); Carter (2001); Cygan (2001); Clerk of the House (2005); Miller (2005); Mullally and Watts (2006).

Most importantly, like the scrutiny of domestic statutory instruments, these recommendations focused on scrutiny of the documents themselves—primarily, but not exclusively, on Commission legislative proposals.[99]

The British document-based scrutiny system is defined by two core features. The most important and widely copied has been the *scrutiny reserve*.[100] If the scrutiny committee has referred a European document for further consideration (either to a European Standing Committee or the full House), then the scrutiny reserve prohibits the government from taking action on it at the supranational level until national parliamentary scrutiny is complete (other countries often use fixed time limits, but the concept is the same). The reserve was never meant, however, to be applied inflexibly: From its establishment in 1980, a minister could "override" a reserve on a showing of "special reasons"—presumably political considerations at the supranational level would suffice—which the minister in turn must explain to the House in a timely fashion. The scrutiny reserve arguably had greater import in the unanimity environment that prevailed before 1986, posing a genuine complication not just for UK voting but, potentially, for the Community legislative process more generally. And yet it still arguably retains significance after the adoption of QMV, particularly as similar provisions have spread to other Member States.[101] Although government recourse to overrides has garnered criticism recently,[102] this reason-giving obligation has arguably added an important measure of "general discipline" to the scrutiny process.[103]

Reason-giving, in fact, is also at the heart of the second key innovation of the British system—the explanatory memorandum. Early in the development of the British scrutiny system, parliament demanded that, in order to

---

99. Clerk of the House (2005), Appendix 1: Orders of Reference of the European Scrutiny Committee (S.O. No. 143); see also Appendix 2: Standing Order on European Standing Committees (S.O. No. 119). For a discussion of earlier versions of these orders, see Bates (1991), 117.

100. The 1980 version is reproduced in Bates (1991), 119, quoting 991 *HC Debs*, cols. 843–4, 30 Oct. 1980; for the 1990 resolution, see Bates (1991), 121 n. 57, citing 178 *HC Debs*, col. 399; and for the 1998 resolution, see Clerk of the House (2005), app. 3.

101. Carter (2001), 413, quoting interview material of the author: "Ministers do not like being called into the House to give an account of why they have ignored the scrutiny reserve. . . . Civil servants don't like things being held up with a Minister saying 'why can't I agree to this in the Council because my friends want me to' and being told it's because they didn't supply sufficient information to the House of Commons"). On the spread of the scrutiny reserve, see this chapter, nn. 174–177 and accompanying text.

102. Mullally and Watts (2006), 5–6 and 15–17.

103. Carter (2001), 413.

facilitate scrutiny, the government must provide a short memorandum on every European document.[104] These memoranda have evolved into rather elaborate statements describing, among other things: the subject matter of the proposal; where ministerial responsibility lies; its legal basis in the treaties (including the voting procedure—QMV or majority, etc.); its impact on UK law; compliance with the principle of subsidiarity; regulatory impact and/or risk assessment, and so on.[105] The Minister must sign the memorandum, which thus "constitutes the Minister's evidence to Parliament."[106] The memorandum in turn serves as the foundation for all subsequent parliamentary review, whether formally (through referral to Standing Committees, appearance of ministers for questioning, or referral to the full House), or through informal processes.[107]

According to recent numbers, the Commons scrutiny committee considers on average approximately one thousand documents per year, refers approximately forty per year to European Standing Committees for further consideration, and only about three documents per year make it to the full House.[108] This compares favorably to the volume of referrals of purely domestic delegated legislation in the immediate postwar years,[109] and my sense is that it still compares favorably to purely domestic forms of scrutiny. Nevertheless, the system is perhaps only marginally more demanding than the modes of scrutiny that were the subject of heavy criticism in the 1960s in the lead up to British membership.[110] Since the 1970s in fact, British critics—whether on the left in the early 1970s[111] or on the right more recently[112]—have been remarkably consistent in their complaints about the inadequacy of the British document-based system; indeed, they often invoke the simultaneously developed Danish "mandating" system as a clearly

---

104. Bates (1991), 118, citing 874 *HC Debs*, c01.1426.

105. Clerk of the House (2005), 7.

106. Ibid.

107. On the importance of informal control, see Auel (2007b) and (2009).

108. Clerk of the House (2005), 11; see also Pratt (1998), 226, citing the Scrutiny of European Business (1995–96), paras. 28, 39 and 46.

109. Compare, Chapter 2, n. 96 and accompanying text.

110. See this chapter, nn. 90–92 and accompanying text.

111. Ryan and Isaacson (1974), 208 ("as Neil Marten was later to point out, the Danes have devised a satisfactory solution. Peter Shore was to take a similar view in a Fabian pamphlet"), citing Shore (1973).

112. See generally Mullally and Watts (2006).

superior alternative from the standpoint of maintaining parliamentary control.[113]

This admiration for the Danish mandating system ignores, however, that "such an extreme system requires very special political circumstances in order to work."[114] This perhaps explains why, although a large number of new entrants since the 1990s have opted for some form of the mandating system, none has opted for the Danish variant in its strongest form. The most important peculiarity of Danish politics is the regularity of minority (or weak coalition) governments combined with unusually strong party cohesion and discipline.[115] Under its postwar constitution, the Danish parliamentary system is majoritarian.[116] By virtue of its fractured party system, however, this majority principle operates in a somewhat unique, almost inverted sense: Governments survive unless a negative majority can be mobilized against it, whether in the full *Folketing* or its committees.[117] As a consequence of this negative majoritarianism, "there has developed a tradition of seeking broad agreement on major issues even at the expense of meeting some of the non-government parties half way."[118]

The Danish mandating system emerged in the atmosphere of political crisis before and after the 1973 national election.[119] What was then known as

---

113. Fitzmaurice (1979), 201 ("in the House of Commons debate on 29 November 1977, . . . several speakers referred to [the Danish system] in very favourable terms, and the Lord President went so far as to say that the Government would look at it in detail in order to see what, if any, lessons it offered for Britain to learn"). See, more recently, Michael Gove MP, Foreword, in Mullally and Watts (2006), 2 ("Denmark joined the EEC at the same time as Britain, but from the very start Danish MPs ensured that they kept a far tighter grip on what the Danish Government could agree to in Brussels. Indeed, the Danish Government is required to get a 'mandate' from the Europe Committee of the Danish Parliament before it can sign up to any EU proposal.").

114. Fitzmaurice (1979), 202.

115. Damgaard and Jensen (2005); Jensen (1996), 40–41; Fitzmaurice (1979), 205–06.

116. Jensen (1996), 39–40, citing the Constitution of 1953, section 15.

117. Fitzmaurice (1979), 205; see also Laursen (2001), 99. The Danish system compares to the challenge confronting the Brüning government at the end of the Weimar Republic. See Chapter 2, n. 16 and accompanying text.

118. Fitzmaurice (1979), 206.

119. An election in the midst of economic crisis splintered the existing composition of the *Folketing*, doubling the number of parties from five to ten. The new parliament also contained three openly anti-European parties, one from the old parliament, two new ones. (Extraordinarily, the Liberal party formed a minority government with only 22 out of 179 seats, and was able to survive "a surprising fourteen months . . . by concluding five successive pacts on mostly economic, taxation, and government expenditure policy.") Fitzmaurice (1979), 207.

the Market Committee (now as the European Affairs Committee) had been monitoring European affairs since 1961, in conjunction with Denmark's first application for entry.[120] Following Denmark's successful application, the Market Committee took the lead in considering the bill authorizing Denmark's accession in 1972. Similar to the simultaneous discussions on membership in Britain, Danish parliamentarians understood intuitively the relationship between integration, executive power, and, in effect, administrative governance. They viewed the Community's decision-making procedures as fundamentally of an executive character, which needed reconciliation with traditional conceptions of democratic control.[121] Like the German act of accession of 1957 before it, the Danish act of 1972 (in section 6(2)) specified that the government had a duty to inform the Market Committee "of proposals for Council resolutions that will be directly applicable in Denmark or for whose fulfillment the assistance of the *Folketing* is required."[122] In a subsequent series of procedural reports issued by the Market Committee elaborating this obligation, the mandating system emerged.[123]

The system entailed two key commitments on the part of the executive. First, "[t]he Government shall consult the Market Committee of the *Folketing* in questions relating to EC policy of major importance so that the regard for the influence of the *Folketing* as well as the freedom to negotiate are respected." Second, "[p]rior to negotiations in the EC Council of Ministers on decisions of a wider scope, the Government submits an oral mandate for negotiation to the Market Committee. If there is no majority against the

---

120. Danish Folketing (2002), 2.

121. See Fitzmaurice (1979), 209, summarizing the report of the Market Committee: "The report further took notice of the actual power relations among the Community institutions and, in discussing possible ways of exercising democratic control of decision-making, it concluded that control over the Council of Ministers would be essential."

122. Danish Act of Accession, section 6(2), as amended, as translated in "The Legal Basis for the European Affairs Committee in Brief," in Danish Folketing (2002), 2; see also Riis (2007), 189. On the German act of accession, see this chapter, n. 78 and accompanying text.

123. The Market Committee's power under the mandating system was born of a political controversy over, yes, the price of bacon. In February 1973, the minister of agriculture in the minority government of the Social Democrats entered into an interim price agreement for Danish export bacon without prior consent of the *Folketing*. Fitzmaurice (1979), 210; see also Arter (1996), 111. A political crisis ensued, including a motion of no confidence put forward by the opposition Liberals and Conservatives, which was defeated only with the aid of the Radical Liberals and the anti-European Socialist People's Party. The cost for this support was a dramatic upgrading of the authority of the Market Committee, as reflected in a report of March 1973 (reiterated in a report of the following year).

mandate, the Government negotiates on this basis."[124] Thus, negative majoritarianism, which characterizes the Danish political system generally, also extended to the mandating system of the Market Committee (now EAC).[125]

The Danish mandating system has, like the document-based system of the British, evolved in its details over subsequent decades, particularly during the critical period between the SEA in 1986 and the Treaty of Amsterdam of 1997, as part of the general upgrading of national-parliamentary scrutiny systems throughout Europe.[126] But its basic features nevertheless have remained as they were in the 1970s.[127] The government takes the lead in presenting the negotiating mandate.[128] And (at least as compared to mandating systems in other Member States), the Danish EAC sees itself very much as a "bargaining committee," a forum to discuss the contours of the Danish position on key questions of European policy and to pound out compromises among the parties.[129] Thus, outright rejection of the government's proposed mandate rarely occurs, because the government usually changes or modifies "its original mandate for negotiation during the discussions of the Committee."[130] And although its power is formidable, the EAC is not without practical and legal checks. From a practical side, the committee is under a disincentive to impose mandates that are too inflexible or constrained, which run the risk of forcing the Danish minister to abstain or vote against the proposal in the Council, thus marginalizing or diminishing whatever influence Denmark

---

124. "The Legal Basis for the European Affairs Committee in Brief," in Danish Folketing (2002), 2; see also Riis (2007), 189.

125. See this chapter, nn. 116–117 and accompanying text.

126. For a brief summary, see Arter (1996), 111–13; see also Laursen (2001), 103–110; Riis (2007), 192–97.

127. The committee has always been a choice assignment, reserved for leading party figures. Arter (1996), 115 (the committee "has derived considerable authority from [its] 'heavyweight' composition . . . former ministers, party leaders and the like"). The distribution of seats on the committee is determined by party strength in the parliament. It meets every Friday (originally in closed session, now generally in public), regardless of whether the *Folketing* itself is in session, in advance of the Council meeting the following week. Danish Folketing (2002), 4. On the shift to public sessions since 2006, see Riis (2007), 196–97.

128. "How Does the Minister Present the Government's Mandate for Negotiation?" in Danish Folketing (2002), 4; see also Jensen (1996), 43 ("the initiative concerning the formulation of Danish EU policies still rests with the government"); Riis (2007), 192–93.

129. Hegeland and Mattson (1996), 204.

130. Danish Folketing (2002), 5; see also Riis (2007), 192.

might otherwise have had in the negotiations on the issue.[131] And as for legal checks, the government has at least one (admittedly extreme) option: The government can appeal over the head of the parties in the *Folketing* directly to the people by way of referendum. This occurred in 1986 when the Market Committee shockingly rejected the Single European Act, to which the government had previously agreed.[132] Rather than call a general election, the government "surprisingly deployed the referendum as a tactical weapon against the refractory Folketing majority," a gambit that worked.[133]

Certainly the SEA, with its shift to QMV for harmonization directives for the internal market and its other expansions of the Community's regulatory competences, portended significant domestic regulatory impact, not just in Denmark, but throughout the Member States. The SEA is understandably viewed, therefore, as a major turning point in the evolution of national parliamentary scrutiny in the Community.[134] But rumblings for an augmented national parliamentary role in other Member States in fact began to grow over the course of the 1970s. Two interrelated developments in European public law were essential. The first was the *Van Duyn* decision of 1974.[135] In that case, the ECJ held that, in certain circumstances, a directive could have direct effect, regardless of whether it had been properly transposed into national positive law, as the old Article 189 (Article 249 TEC/Article 248 TFEU) seemed to require.[136] The second development dovetailed with the first. Over the course of the 1970s, the ECJ quietly allowed the Community legislative process (Commission and Council) to use market harmonization directives to reach domains not yet within Community jurisdiction—for example, in the area of the free movement of workers, where the Court allowed for harmonization of qualifications for educational grants, even

---

131. See generally Raunio and Hix (2000), 157–58; Benz (2003), 103; Benz (2004), 890–91, 896; Auel (2007b), 492.

132. Hegeland and Mattson (1996), 205.

133. Arter (1996), 112.

134. See, e.g., Norton (1996a), 178; Raunio (2005), 337.

135. Case 411/74, *Van Duyn v. Home Office*, 1974 E.C.R. 1337.

136. As noted in Chapter 3, the conditions that the Court laid down—that the directive was unambiguous in its terms and the time for implementation had passed—simply gave national executives, via the Council, an incentive to impose, through precise directives with clear time limits, a legislative decision on its national parliament. Indeed, subsequent ECJ cases made clear that the scope of this authority extended to the imposition of rules on municipalities and public service providers, regardless of the scope of executive power under national law. See Chapter 3, nn. 170–172 and accompanying text.

though at the time, educational policy was clearly outside Community jurisdiction.[137] Perhaps more importantly, the Court allowed for ever broader use
of the reserve legislative authority under the old Article 235 (Article 308 TEC/
Article 352 TFEU), often for similar purposes.[138]

As the 1970s drew to a close, the combined effect of these developments
did not go unnoticed, particularly in France. In 1978 the French *Conseil d'Etat*,
at a time when it was still resisting the full blown implications of European
legal supremacy, issued a famous decision that effectively rejected the ECJ's
jurisprudence on the direct effect of directives.[139] And nearly simultaneous
with this decision, the National Assembly, in what has been described as a
kind of "sudden awareness" ("*prise de conscience*"), voted down a draft bill to
transpose a directive relating to value-added tax (VAT) harmonization.[140] In
the debate, members of the National Assembly complained about "directives
that are in reality regulations"[141] and called on the government to establish
some mechanism, like those, inter alia, in Denmark and the United Kingdom,
to "consult with their parliaments before deciding [in the Council] on
directives and even regulations."[142]

Although the government was able to enact the bill in question in slightly
altered form only a few days later, the event was startling and unprecedented.
It revealed that even in France—where the parliament was purportedly qui-
escent in the face of the executive's constitutional prerogatives both at home
and in Europe[143]—there existed a limit to the parliament's ability to accept

---

137. See Case 9/74, *Casagrande v. Landeshauptstadt München*, 1974 E.C.R. 773, 777–78. See
Chapter 4, n. 81 and accompanying text.

138. See Chapter 4, nn. 82–86 and accompanying text. As we saw in Chapter 4, the use of
Article 235 as a mechanism for legislative spillover would be among the central
concerns of national high courts in the 1990s. See Chapter 4, nn. 183–186 and
accompanying text.

139. C.E. Ass. 22 déc. 1978, *Min. de l'Intérieur v. Cohn-Bendit, Rec.* 524.

140. Nuttens and Sicard (2000), 62.

141. Statement of Jean Foyer, "Extraits du débat parlementaire du 30 novembre 1978 sur la
transposition de la sixième directive sur la TVA," in Nuttens and Sicard (2000), 63.

142. Statement of Laurent Fabius, in Nuttens and Sicard (2000), 63.

143. This caricature of French legislative-executive relations is common in the literature. See,
e.g., this chapter, n. 72 and accompanying text; see also Szukala and Rozenberg (2001),
223 ("From 1960 up to the 1990s French politics have been extraordinarily non-
parliamentarian"). However, it arguably did not correspond very well to the political
situation in France in the late 1970s, which was fraught and deeply contested, on both
left and right. Although the left coalition of Socialists, Communists and Left-Radicals
led by François Mitterrand failed to force France's first experiment in *cohabitation* with
a victory in the legislative elections of 1978, this did not prevent Mitterrand from taking

supranational "quasi-legislation," which was increasingly seen as "legislation from national ministerial bureaus."[144] By statute adopted the following year,[145] the French government authorized the establishment scrutiny committees in both the National Assembly and the Senate, called *délégations* in view of the French constitutional limitation on the permissible number of actual parliamentary "committees." Henceforth, French parliamentarians would be among the most active in the Community (and later Union) in demanding an increase in the national parliamentary role in European affairs.[146]

It would not be, however, until the decade between the SEA in 1986 and the Treaty of Amsterdam in 1997 that formal (often constitutionally-grounded) rights for national parliamentary scrutiny in many Member States dramatically expanded. In part this was due to the increased volume of supranational legislation under the 1992 internal market program, which also then increased the burden on already established systems of scrutiny.[147] But the SEA also prompted more general anxieties about the place of national parliaments in the European system, as well as the relationship of integration to domestic constitutional traditions and structures. In a recent book, Berthold Rittberger has detailed these concerns, which were interwoven with the shift to QMV in the Council and the expansion of the European Parliament's role in the so-called "cooperation procedure."[148]

Soon after the adoption of the SEA, for example, the scrutiny committee in the British House of Lords (specifically its subcommittee charged with scrutinizing the legal basis in the treaties for Community legislation) critiqued what it saw as the Commission's overly broad interpretation of the new QMV basis in the treaty—the old Article 100a (later Article 95 TEC/Article 114 TFEU)—as well as its reluctance to resort to alternatives

---

the presidency three years later, carrying the parliament in his wake. (Of course, Mitterrand himself would have to endure *cohabitation* with a center-right legislative majority in the mid-1980s.)

144. Foyer (1979), 161, quoted in Nuttens and Sicard (2000), 62.

145. Loi No.79–564 du 6 juillet 1979, *J.O., Lois et Décrets*, July 7, 1979, p. 1643 (rectificatif, *J.O., Lois et Décrets*, July 18, 1979).

146. French parliamentarians, for example, would be instrumental in the creation of Conference of Community and European Affairs Committees of Parliaments of the European Union (COSAC) at the end of the 1980s. COSAC Secretariat (2009), 4–5.

147. The British, for example, reported "an increase from an annual average of 650 Community documents [subject to scrutiny] in the period 1983–5 to an average of 840 between 1986–8." Bates (1991), 110–11, citing Government Evidence to the Procedure Committee, HC (1988–9) 622-II, p. 34.

148. Rittberger (2005), 153–65.

requiring unanimity.[149] But anxieties of this type, at least at this juncture, still had a "low degree of specificity and coherence," as Rittberger puts it, and thus also had little impact on the design of supranational institutions or processes.[150] Rather, as Rittberger continues, some "domestic parliamentarians even viewed this [absence of sustained attention to their role] as part of a strategy on behalf of their governments to further weaken the national parliaments."[151]

To the extent that one began to see greater "specificity and coherence" in the politics of national parliamentary scrutiny, it would express itself almost entirely under national rather than supranational law. In the Netherlands, for example, the adoption of the SEA and the 1992 program finally led the lower house (the *Tweede Kamer*) to definitively establish a Standing Committee on European Affairs. Over the next several years there would be increased pressure from Dutch parliamentarians for better access to information regarding Community developments. This eventually led to the rudiments of a new document-based system, entailing the regular submission of government memoranda (*fiches*) analogous to the explanatory memoranda we encountered in the British case.[152] In the late 1980s, Italy also began to formalize its scrutiny mechanisms, which still remained largely consultative but nevertheless were seen as part of the effort to address its notoriously poor record in transposing European legislation into national law.[153] In the wake of these reforms, both houses of the Italian parliament established standing committees entitled to scrutinize Community documents and express their position to the government.[154]

Feeding into these developments was an intensifying debate over Europe's purported "democratic deficit," a phrase that gained broad currency in the late 1980s as shorthand for a whole range of complaints, including executive

---

149. For an overview, see Denza (1993), 60; Cygan (2001), 108–09.

150. Rittberger (2005), 185–86.

151. Rittberger (2005), 186, citing the statement of Michael Knowles, a pro-Europe Conservative MP in the UK, at Parl. Deb., H.C. (Hansard), 5 December 1985:356.

152. See Tans (2007), 172; for additional background, see van Schendelen (1996), 66. On explanatory memoranda in the United Kingdom, see this chapter, nn. 104–107 and accompanying text. For the German analogue, see Hölscheidt (2001), 136–37.

153. As noted above, this had relied on the periodic adoption of omnibus bills, a highly inefficient means of transposition. See this chapter, n. 77 and accompanying text. For further background on the reforms, see Furlong (1996), 36; Calussi and Grassi (2001), 276.

154. Calussi and Grassi (2001), 276–79.

dominance of the integration process.[155] In addition, the maladroit prediction of then-Commission President Jacques Delors in 1988, that "[t]en years hence, 80% of our economic legislation, and perhaps even our fiscal and social legislation as well, will be of Community origin," added to the sense of concern.[156] France was again at the forefront of these anxieties over the coming years. In the words of one analyst, French parliamentarians became "[o]bsessed" with Delors's statement,[157] ultimately forcing the Socialist government of Michel Rocard to adopt a law in 1990 "to clarify and strengthen the information-provider role of the parliamentary *délégations*."[158] The new legislation made several key changes to the *délégations*, including increasing their size and institutionalizing the practice of ministerial hearings.[159]

But the 1990 statute was really just a prelude to more fundamental reforms in France made two years later in conjunction with the Treaty of Maastricht, contained in the famous Article 88–4.[160] These were designed to entrench the right of parliamentary involvement in European affairs in the national constitution itself.[161] Provisions such as Article 88–4, or Articles 23 and 45 of the German Basic Law, reflected a new direction in the legal contestation over European governance. In constitutionalizing certain rights to information and scrutiny, these provisions reflected the desire for a legal precommitment to an ongoing role for national parliaments, no matter how limited that role might be in some cases.[162] Moreover, by specifically grounding the right of information and scrutiny in the scope of legislative competence under the constitution, reforms like those in France linked the process of integration

---

155. On the emergence of the topic in media, beginning in the late 1980s, see Rittberger (2005), 28.

156. Harryvan and van der Harst (1997), 241, reproducing Debates of the European Parliament, 1988, No. 2, 138.

157. Szukala and Rozenberg (2001), 229.

158. Rizzuto (1996), 50.

159. Ibid., 50–52.

160. See Chapter 4, n. 197 and accompanying text.

161. For detailed analysis, Nuttens and Sicard (2000), 66–91; see also Szukala and Rozenberg (2001), 230–41; Rizzuto (1996), 52–54.

162. See Claes (2007), 35–36. The experience of the 1987–90 *Bundestag*, when no European Affairs Committee was formed, suggests why such a precommitment was necessary. See Saalfeld (1996), 22. After 1993, the EAC became one of four standing committees whose existence was constitutionally prescribed. Hölscheidt (2001), 124. For a comprehensive description of the German system in the 1990s, see Cygan (2001), chaps. 6–7.

directly to a key element of the postwar constitutional settlement.[163] Portugal, and later Finland upon accession in 1995, would take the same approach, using the domestic law-regulation distinction as a means of defining the scope of parliament's rights.[164] In some sense, these approaches can be viewed as another attempt to enforce some minimum degree of respect for the constitutionally defined legislative domain, even if the norms under scrutiny originated at the supranational level.[165]

Formal constitutionalization of information and scrutiny rights was of course not the only path taken in the 1990s, even if the effort to increase national parliamentary access to information and scrutiny had clear implications for both constitutional and political culture in all Member States. Perhaps most prominently, the upheaval in Denmark surrounding the Maastricht Treaty had a profound effect,[166] leading also to a series of reforms aimed at strengthening its mandating system.[167] But even in the still quite pro-European Netherlands, the first half of the 1990s saw, as one commentator put it, a shift away from the "almost unconditional support for supranationalism" toward a new "pragmatism."[168] Throughout the EU in fact, according to a number of different measures—party positions on European institutions, or opinion polls taken of members of national parliaments (MNPs)—there was a discernible demand for greater legitimation of

---

163. See Chapter 2, nn. 80–81 and 90 and accompanying text.

164. See Article 112(8) of the Portuguese Constitution, http://app.parlamento.pt/site_antigo/ingles/cons_leg/Constitution_VII_revisao_definitive.pdf (last visited July 15, 2009); see also Fraga (2001), 362. See Section 96(1) of the Finnish Constitution, reprinted in Nordic EAC (2002), 3.

165. Cf. Acórdão do Tribunal Constitucional, No.184/89, Diário da República, I Série, No. 57, 9 Mar. 1989, cited in Fraga (2001), 362 (prohibiting the executive from transposing a directive by decree-law and instead requiring legislation, where the matter, if domestic, would have fallen within the exclusive competence of the legislature); see also *Meagher v. Minister for Agriculture*, [1994] 1I.R. 347, 365–66 (Denham, J), reprinted in Oppenheimer (1994/2003), 2: 325 (suggesting that the transposition of nondirectly effective provisions of a European directive, or of those not "incidental, supplementary, or consequential" to a directly effective directive, must, under the Irish constitution, be adopted by parliament).

166. See this chapter, nn. 19–21 and accompanying text.

167. These included requiring earlier involvement of the European Affairs Committee in the process of decision making, increasing the transparency of the EAC's operations, improving public access to the documents scrutinized by the committee, and extending its jurisdiction to include the new "second" and "third pillars" of the EU (common foreign and security policy, and justice and home affairs). For succinct overviews, see Arter (1996), 112–13; Krunke (2005), 352–54.

168. van Schendelen (1996), 70–71.

integration through national parliamentary oversight.[169] This coincided with a broader "upswing of Euro-sceptic attitudes," as measured by the Commission's own opinion data over the course of the decade, resulting from "the greater salience of EC/EU policies in the daily life of citizens."[170] On the whole, by the end of the decade a consensus seemed to be emerging among MNPs that favored national parliamentary solutions to the democratic deficit, or at least a "mixed solution" combining both European and national parliamentary oversight (Nordic MNPs most strongly favoring national legitimation).[171] But even in historically more pro-European countries such as the Netherlands, support for increased national parliamentary oversight was clear.[172] Members of the European Parliament (MEPs), by contrast, had a much stronger faith in the capacity of the European Parliament (EP) to provide democratic legitimacy to European governance; nevertheless, they too shared with MNPs the view that more national parliamentary oversight of national executives was needed.[173]

In the competition between models of scrutiny, document-based systems were clearly dominant at the outset of the 1990s, though this too would change, as we will discuss in a moment. Even within document-based systems, procedures varied (and still vary) considerably, whether as to the scope or the timing of scrutiny powers. But they also varied with regard to perhaps the proudest feature of the British model, the scrutiny reserve.[174] The French government instituted a similar reserve in 1994 under

---

169. See Maurer (2001), 54 (party positions); Katz (1999), 28 (opinion data suggesting that "the majority of MNPs appear to favor a mixed solution, in which both the EP and the national parliaments contribute to the overall legitimacy of the EU").

170. Maurer and Wessels (2001b), 432–33, citing European Commission, Eurobarometer 36 (1991) and 47.1 (1997).

171. This survey did not test whether attitudes among MNPs correlated with preferences for a particular model of scrutiny. Certainly it would be plausible to suggest that attitudes of Nordic MNPs favoring national legitimation might also explain their apparent preference for "mandating" systems.

172. Maurer (2001), 54; Katz (1999), 29.

173. Katz (1999), 40.

174. On the scrutiny reserve, see this chapter, nn. 100–103 and accompanying text. For the use of the scrutiny reserve in the various Member States as of 2005, see Overview of the Use of Scrutiny Reserves and Involvement of Sectoral Committees in the Scrutiny Process, http://www.cosac.eu/en/info/scrutiny/scrutiny/overview_/ (last visited July 15, 2009). The admittedly Eurosceptic think tank, Open Europe, reported somewhat different numbers in 2006, adding Germany to the list of countries with a scrutiny reserve. See Mullally and Watts (2006), 29.

pressure from parliament.[175] Moreover, the Protocol on the Role of National Parliaments attached to the Treaty of Amsterdam of 1997 supranationalized a reserve of sorts, by mandating a six-week delay between a new Commission legislative proposal and the date it could be placed on the Council agenda for voting.[176] As for national law, by 2005, a total of five national parliaments or their scrutiny committees explicitly enjoyed some form of scrutiny reserve, although often entailing relatively brief fixed time periods.[177]

Over the course of the 1990s and into the present decade, the Danish-style mandating model gained an increasing number of adherents in other Member States, perhaps out of general dissatisfaction with document-based or consultative systems. In the 1995 and 2004 enlargements, for example, ten out of the thirteen new Member States opted for a mandating system in some form.[178] In part this was the result of a conscious marketing effort on the part of Denmark, joined by Finland and Sweden after 1995, to promote a specifically "Nordic" approach to democratic challenges in the EU.[179] But the success of the mandating model can also be understood in terms of a broader, constructivist "logic of appropriateness" in action.[180] Geographical, historical, and cultural affinities certainly played a role (between, for example, the Baltic and Nordic states). So too did the mandating model's reputation "as the best performing in terms of empowering the national parliaments in relation to the government."[181] But diffusion of the model cannot be fully explained without recourse to changing cultural attitudes regarding what is "more legitimate and consequently more appropriate to emulate," as one analyst put it.[182] Although there were differences in the particulars of the various mandating systems, more interesting were the "symbolic assets" they shared, notably the tighter linkage of European policy with the balance of

---

175. Nuttens and Sicard (2000), 89; Szukala and Rozenberg (2001), 237.

176. Protocol (No. 9) on the Role of National Parliaments in the European Union (1997), 2006 O.J. (C 321) E/227 [hereinafter "Amsterdam PNP (1997)"], section 3.

177. Again, see Overview of the Use of Scrutiny Reserves and Involvement of Sectoral Committees in the Scrutiny Process, http://www.cosac.eu/en/info/scrutiny/scrutiny/overview_/ (last visited July 15, 2009). I exclude from my total those countries that list the reserve as part of a "mandating process."

178. Ibid.; see also Jungar (2007), 14, 16–17.

179. See Jungar (2007), 23, citing Nordic EAC (2002).

180. March and Olsen (2009).

181. Jungar (2007), 26–27.

182. Ibid., 27.

forces within the parliament itself.[183] For many of the newer Member States from Eastern and Central Europe, mandating systems appeared the best way of reconciling integration's functional demands (including a largely executive and technocratic policy process) with their restored national sovereignty and the democratic legitimacy embodied or expressed in the elected legislature.

Another advantage of the mandating system was the stronger sense of ongoing parliamentary control it entailed, although the reality of this factor could be overestimated. There had always been, as we have seen, strong disincentives against adopting overly constraining mandates, which could excessively tie the hands of the national executive in subsequent negotiations at the supranational level.[184] Thus, even in mandating systems, there was an unavoidable separation of power and legitimation, with significant normative discretion conferred on the national executive at the supranational level.

Moreover, on the terrain of legitimation itself, it was not at all clear that mandating systems were necessarily superior to their document-based competitors.[185] The Danish EAC had, until quite recently, historically operated behind closed doors, as a bargaining forum among leading party members.[186] The need for closed sessions suggested the difficulty in optimizing different values—interparty compromise, public accountability, etc.[187] As Katrin Auel has argued, the difficulty in optimizing these conflicting values extends to document-based systems as well.[188] In Germany, for example, parliamentary scrutiny normally "takes place informally within the majority parties, and the direct but informal influence exerted by German MPs at the European level is likewise neither transparent nor subject to public scrutiny."[189] France does a much better job of operating publicly, but its system focuses more on communicating parliamentary positions than on scrutinizing the government's policies themselves. By contrast, "despite its weak institutional position," as Auel sees it, the British scrutiny system "seems to fulfil this

---

183. Ibid.

184. See this chapter, n. 131 and accompanying text.

185. Auel (2007a), 174.

186. See Riis (2007), 197, on the efforts since 2006 to meet in public except in special circumstances.

187. Benz (2004), 896–97.

188. For an overview, see Auel (2007a), 173–74.

189. Ibid., 173.

parliamentary control function best, because it concentrates on forcing the government to explain and defend its negotiating position publicly."[190]

The British success in disgorging explanations takes us back to a central point emphasized in this book—the changing nature of public law in an era of administrative governance. Although no doubt building on earlier traditions (rule of law, *Rechtsstaat, l'état de droit*), public law has shifted away from straightforward validity inquiries toward "the allocation of burdens of reason-giving" in diffuse and fragmented regulatory systems.[191] As in any such transformation, a reconciliation is obviously necessary, balancing functional demands for change with the need to find a way to *experience* the resulting changes as legitimate in a culturally and historically recognizable sense. The evolution in the nature of public law, toward a system of reason-giving rather than outright validity or invalidity, is an extension of a broader effort at reconciliation, pitting the complex socioinstitutional realities of modern administrative governance (now extending to the supranational level) against conceptions of legitimacy still associated primarily with institutions of representative government on the national level.

This is precisely the same challenge that confronted Western European states after 1945, when they sought to surmount the seeming contradiction in administrative governance that Carl Schmitt had claimed was "insurmountable."[192] It is also the same challenge posed by the *Finanzgericht Rheinland-Pfalz* in the context of integration in 1963, when it spoke of an "insuperable obstacle" to constitutionalizing European norm-production in the German system under the current Basic Law.[193] European public law has proven able, through national executive, judicial, and now legislative oversight, to overcome these obstacles while still preserving a sense of plausible representative democracy on the national level.

The strengthening of national parliamentary scrutiny of European policy within national legal systems also reflects the ultimately polycentric distribution of legitimacy resources in Europe's otherwise multilevel system

---

190. Ibid., 174; see also Benz (2004), 897. For a more detailed effort to explain variation in scrutiny methods in various Member States, both formal and informal, see Auel (2009).

191. Somek (2004), 58 ("Der Rechtsstaat verwandelt sich in ein System der Allokation von Begruendungslasten"), quoted in Kumm (2006b), 532 (my translation). See the Introduction, nn. 62–63 and accompanying text.

192. See Chapter 1, n. 111 and accompanying text.

193. See Chapter 4, n. 105 and accompanying text.

of governance.[194] Not surprisingly, such scrutiny has often focused on compliance with subsidiarity,[195] which can be understood as the substantive
expression of both the same polycentricity and struggle for reconciliation.[196]
As we shall see in our next and final section, these institutional and substantive elements—national parliamentary scrutiny on the one hand, and the
principle of subsidiarity on the other—would converge in the explicit incorporation of a role for national parliaments into supranational law over the
coming decade. However, the turn to national parliaments also implicitly
raised a key question. As between the European Parliament and the national
parliaments collectively, which were better positioned to reconnect Europe's
increasingly complex, supranational system of administrative governance
with historically and culturally plausible understandings of democratic legitimacy? It is to that final question we now turn.

🎞 5.3 Toward a Polycentric Constitutional Settlement: National Parliaments and Subsidiarity under Supranational Law in the 2000s

For much of the last three decades, the European Parliament has viewed
itself "as the deepest expression of European democracy and integration."[197]
Given this self-image, it is hardly surprising that the EP sought (often successfully) to expand its prerogatives in European governance, not just legis-
latively, but also in the supervision of the Commission and other forms of
oversight.[198] Berthold Rittberger has analyzed the politics behind this effort
and concluded that the EP's expanding powers reflect an effort by political
elites (not just MEPs, but also members of the Commission and national
politicians) to translate a "model of representative, parliamentary democracy" into workable supranational form in the EU. As Rittberger puts it, this
model has served as "the template which guides political elites' responses to

---

194. See Chapter 1, n. 100 and accompanying text.

195. See, e.g., Nuttens and Sicard (2000), 74 ("The principle of subsidiarity has therefore been
     the principal argument utilized by the assemblies to contest the legitimacy of certain
     proposals formulated by the Commission.") (my translation).

196. See, e.g., this chapter, nn. 18–25 and accompanying text.

197. The quoted phrase comes from recent joint statement of the leaders of the major politi-
     cal groups in the EP. See Daul et al. (2009).

198. See generally Rittberger (2005), chaps. 5–6.

the perceived legitimacy deficit" in European integration—a phenomenon stretching back, in his view, to the 1950s.[199]

Although Rittberger notes the recent turn to national parliaments as an alternative legitimating mechanism, he views this as merely "a shift in emphasis within the representative, parliamentary model of democracy" applied to the supranational level.[200] The discussion that follows questions this final statement. The problem with Rittberger's otherwise compelling analysis is that it suggests, both normatively and descriptively, that national parliaments are merely supplemental to the legitimizing functions of the EP and thus ultimately a part of the same model of "representative, parliamentary democracy" in the context of integration. To the contrary, the historical record suggests that, much less than addressing a legitimacy deficit, as Rittberger emphasizes, the function of national parliamentary scrutiny has been part of the broader effort to *reconnect* European governance to representative democracy on the national level. This, I suggest, implies a very different model of democracy in the EU. It also suggests that the constitutional foundation for European governance is similarly different, being *polycentric* rather than (merely) *multilevel*, as we shall see below.

The notion of a democratic deficit works nicely with an implicit quasi-federal understanding of European governance, rather than one more cognizant of its fundamentally administrative character. In the deficit/federalist view, European governance entails (or should entail) two strongly legitimated sets of institutions—one national, the other supranational—that are (or ought to be) interacting with each other in the European governance process. According to this view, then, the challenge today is one of overcoming a deficit in the legitimacy of supranational institutions that prevents them from achieving the degree of strong legitimation they need to compete with the national level in a truly federal system. The conventional strategy for addressing this deficit, of course, has been to augment the powers of the EP, to replicate a "model of representative, parliamentary democracy," as Rittberger puts it. But scholars have argued for other "deficit"-reducing strategies, including increased participation and transparency in supranational processes, to achieve a sort of novel, nonhierarchical democratic legitimation for the EU. Nevertheless, the purpose of these alternatives is

---

199. Rittberger (2005), 199.

200. Ibid., 200.

still the same: to convince Europeans that the EU is or can be "democratic," perhaps in some new or modified sense, sufficient to legitimize its functions in a quasi-federal, multilevel system of governance.

An administrative reading of European governance and its legitimacy, by contrast, tries to take the distribution of legitimacy resources in the EU as it actually is, rather than how it ought to be according to some implicit quasi-federal teleology. The administrative interpretation recognizes that democratic and constitutional legitimacy is concentrated at the national level even as significant normative power is delegated to the supranational level. Given this distribution of both power and legitimacy, supranational institutions are best understood, in legal-cultural terms, as agents of the Member States, with significant and often autonomous normative power of their own, but without any autonomous capacity for democratic and constitutional legitimation (or at least not yet). The nature of the legitimacy challenge in European governance is thus not one of a deficit at the supranational level. Rather, it is one of augmenting *mediated legitimacy* in terms of the postwar constitutional settlement. This should entail an effort to reconnect European governance with the historically grounded sources of democratic and constitutional legitimacy on the national level—i.e., the *constituted* bodies of representative government (legislative, executive, and judicial). This must be accomplished, however, without endangering the functional effectiveness of the integration project itself—a difficult balance to be sure.

However, the advantage of the administrative interpretation of European governance is not primarily normative but descriptive and analytical, in that it better captures the trajectory of institutional change in European governance over the last several decades. The development of national parliamentary scrutiny, first nationally and then supranationally, is merely the most recent example of the convergence of European governance around the legitimating structures and normative principles of the postwar constitutional settlement. Rather than being simply a shift in emphasis within the representative, parliamentary model of democracy applied to the supranational level (per Rittberger), the increase in the national parliamentary role is a further reflection of the fundamentally administrative character of European integration. Rittberger's model of "representative, parliamentary democracy" does not go far enough in accounting for actual institutional practices in European integration.

These practices reflect a crucial challenge in European law more generally—defining which bodies are the *principals* and which are the *agents* in Europe's complex system of network governance. In terms of socioinstitutional realities (a perspective focusing particularly on the scope of the seemingly autonomous supranational regulatory power), Europe may appear effectively as a system of "agents without principals."[201] This view ignores, however, both the cultural-historical dimension that this study has stressed (with the concentration of legitimacy resources on the national level) as well as the impact of that reality on political action and institutional design over time.[202] What recent history—notably the collapse of the Constitutional Treaty—strongly suggests is that, although Europeans may be willing to accept supranational autonomy *functionally*, they are not yet prepared to do so *constitutionally*. For this reason, one needs an administrative, not constitutional interpretation of integration, one legally and culturally grounded in the idea of delegation from the Member States, with all the national oversight mechanisms that this implies.

To appreciate the delegated/agency character of the EU more fully, consider the evolution of the principle of conferral as expressed in the European treaties over the course of the present decade. In the Convention on the Future of Europe, the federally minded *Praesidium* (and more specifically its chair, Valéry Giscard d'Estaing), initially hoped to include language in the Constitutional Treaty to the effect that EU's competences were "conferred . . . *by the Constitution*."[203] To many members of the Convention, this carried an unacceptable implication that the EU owed its authority to some undefined constituent power apart from the Member States.[204] The Convention thus insisted that the draft be revised to make clear that Union competences were

201. See generally Lindseth (2006); cf. Eberlein and Grande (2005) (characterizing the EU regulatory regime as "beyond delegation"); see also Cohen and Sabel (2004), 164–65; Dehousse (2008), 794–95.

202. See the Introduction, nn. 96–100 and accompanying text.

203. See CONV 369/02, Preliminary Draft Constitutional Treaty, 28 Oct. 2002, Article 8, http://european-convention.eu.int/docs/sessplen/00369.en2.pdf (last visited July 22, 2009); see also CONV 528/03, Draft Articles 1 to 16 of the Constitutional Treaty, 6 Feb. 2003, Article 8(2), http://european-convention.eu.int/docs/Treaty/cv00528.en03.pdf (last visited Oct. 26, 2009) ("the Union shall act within the limits of the competences conferred upon it by the Constitution to attain the objectives the Constitution sets out. Competences not conferred upon the Union by the Constitution remain with the Member States.").

204. CONV 624/03, Summary report on the additional plenary session, Brussels, 5 Mar. 2003, para.1,http://www.europarl.europa.eu/meetdocs_all/committees/conv/20030403/03e_en.pdf (last visited Oct. 26, 2009).

conferred by the Member States themselves.[205] The Treaty of Lisbon would be even more explicit in this respect, following the specific mandate of the European Council in June 2007.[206] Article 5 TEU post-Lisbon would thus read: "the Union shall act only within the limits of the competences conferred upon it by the Member States in the Treaties," adding the modifier "only" to the original language of the Constitutional Treaty.

Consistent with the ultimately delegated/agency character of the EU more generally, European public law has consistently refused to recognize the EP as the ultimate legitimating principal in the system of European governance, akin to a democratic parliament on the national level. Article 10(2) of the TEU post-Lisbon states that "[c]itizens are directly represented at Union level in the European Parliament." But this should be seen, ultimately, as a highly instrumental form of representation, useful in bringing public opinion and perhaps even various interests to bear on the supranational policy process. This is not, however, *constitutional* representation on par with a national parliament, in the sense of the EP being understood as the expression of the democratic will of a political community that sees itself as historically cohesive and capable of self-rule through a legislative body *constituted* for that purpose. "This is why"—borrowing words from Advocate General Miguel Poiares Maduro in a recent opinion—"the European Parliament does not have the same power as national parliaments in the legislative process."[207] In this critical respect, the national parliaments remain the ultimate principals in the European system, while the European Parliament is fundamentally an agent.

This does not mean that the EP cannot have significant regulatory power, as a consequence of delegations from the national level. There are a number

---

205. Norman (2005), 166. See also CONV 574/1/03 Rev. 1, Reactions to Draft Articles 1 to 16 of the Constitutional Treaty—Analysis, http://register.consilium.europa.eu/pdf/en/03/cv00/cv00574-re01.en03.pdf (last visited Oct. 26, 2009). All future drafts and the final version incorporated this change. See CONV 850/03, Draft Treaty Establishing a Constitution for Europe, Article I-9(1), http://european-convention.eu.int/docs/Treaty/cv00850.en03.pdf (last visited July 22, 2009).

206. Brussels European Council, 21/22 June 2007, Presidency Conclusions, Annex I, IGC Mandate [hereinafter "IGC Mandate (2007)"], para. 10 ("it will be specified that the Union shall act *only* within the limits of competences conferred upon it by the Member States in the Treaties.") (emphasis in original), http://www.consilium.europa.eu/ueDocs/cms_Data/docs/pressData/en/ec/94932.pdf (last visited July 22, 2009).

207. Case C-411/06, *Commission v. Parliament and Council*, Opinion of Advocate General Poiares Maduro, 26 Mar. 2009, n. 5, not yet reported, http://eur-lex.europa.eu/LexUriServ/LexUriServ.do?uri=CELEX:62006C0411:EN:HTML#Footref5 (last visited Nov. 3, 2009). This assertion remains true even post-Lisbon.

of functional reasons in support of a strengthened EP role, for example as a means of supervising the Commission or as a forum for forging compromises among disparate cross-national interests. Moreover, there are functional reasons why national parliaments should respect the EP as their designated agent, particularly given the problems of cooperation and coordination that gave rise to delegation in the first place. But on a legal-cultural level, in light of the position of national parliaments as the privileged, if polycentric, repositories of democratic and constitutional legitimacy in the European system, national parliaments are also entitled to some form of oversight, notably on the basis of subsidiarity. Indeed, this right extends to the actions of the EP itself, as well as the actions of all other supranational bodies participating in the supranational legislative process, as agents of the Member States.

The strongest evidence of the culturally distinct (and arguably superior) role of national parliaments can be found, ironically, in the consistent failure of efforts to incorporate the national parliaments directly into the supranational legislative apparatus, through some kind of second chamber at the European level. This may seem paradoxical to some readers, because the very purpose of such proposals was always apparently to *augment* the role of national parliaments in European affairs. The real problem was that such proposals carried with them an unacceptable constitutional quid pro quo— the new centralization of specifically parliamentary legitimacy within the EU, consistent with achieving a strong supranational legitimacy on par with the constituted bodies of the Member States, as in a federal-type system. In 1989, for example, French President François Mitterrand called for the organization of a special conference of parliaments (*Assises*), which would include both MEPs and MNPs, in order to discuss issues of common concern about Europe's future. An initial meeting of this type in fact took place in Rome in 1990. But many national parliamentarians (notably from the UK) "were less enamoured with the experience," in part because the EP had so successfully "harness[ed] the *Assises* to its own agenda."[208] Although the TEU in 1992 would "invite" the convening of future *Assises*,[209] this specific experiment would never repeated.[210]

---

208. Westlake (1996), 171. For more details, see Corbett (1993), 23–26.

209. "Declaration No. 14 on the Conference of Parliaments ('Assises')," reprinted in Krekelberg (2001), 479.

210. COSAC, it should be acknowledged, does now serve as a regular forum for exchange between the European Parliament and the various national parliaments, but its center of gravity is clearly national. For further detail, see Lindseth et al. (2008), 97, 102–05.

Over the course of the 1990s and into the first decade of the 2000s, there were even more ambitious calls for the creation of a genuine second chamber composed of national parliamentarians as a sort of upper house to the European Parliament. In the years immediately following the Maastricht Treaty, for example, both Philippe Séguin (then the President of the French National Assembly) and Sir Leon Brittan (at the time a member of the European Commission) explicitly called for the creation of a second chamber to represent the views of national parliaments in the EU legislative process.[211] The idea, however, never gained traction. The consensus position that emerged over the coming years (reflected in the terms of the protocol on national parliaments attached to the Amsterdam Treaty)[212] favored minimum treaty-based standards regarding information flows to national parliaments, as well as guaranteed time periods for scrutiny on the national level, but not the creation of a second chamber.[213] As the House of Commons Foreign Affairs Select Committee had earlier suggested, the focus going forward would be on "the further development of national parliaments' pre-legislative role,"[214] not the intermixing of national parliaments and the EP in order to augment the latter's weak democratic legitimacy.

A second chamber of sorts, of course, already existed at the EU level in the form of the Council, as many would note.[215] The European treaties would eventually make this explicit as well (specifically in Article 10(2) TEU post-Lisbon), stating the Member States are represented "in the Council by their

---

211. Maurer (2001), 58–59, citing Philippe Séguin in *Le Figaro*, 7 Dec. 1994, and Sir Leon Brittan, specifically Brittan (1994), 227. For more detail on Séguin's position, particularly in relation to his broader efforts to strengthen the French parliament vis-à-vis the national executive, along with his desire to focus on the principle of subsidiarity, see Szukala and Rozenberg (2001), 244.

212. Amsterdam PNP (1997). Section 1 obligated the Commission to forward to national parliaments all consultation documents (that is, green and white papers and communications) used in the process of formulating legislative proposals. Still cognizant of the variation in national scrutiny mechanisms, however, Section 2 once again left it to each Member State government to "ensure that its own national parliaments receive [Commission legislative proposals] as appropriate." But Section 3, in effect, supranationalized a minimum scrutiny reserve with regard to both Commission legislative proposals and third-pillar (justice and home affairs) "common positions," mandating that a "six-week period shall elapse" before either of these could be placed on the Council agenda for decision. See this chapter, n. 176 and accompanying text.

213. Rittberger (2005), 189. On the groundwork for that consensus in the lead up to the IGC, see Maurer (2001), 61–62.

214. Quoted in Westlake (1996), 172.

215. See, e.g., Habermas (2001b), 17.

governments, themselves democratically accountable either to their national Parliaments, or to their citizens." The problem with the Council as a second chamber was that its source of legitimacy is only indirectly parliamentary and much more squarely executive, even if it exercises legislative functions at the supranational level.[216] As such, the Council had to be regarded as unhelpful in augmenting the specifically parliamentary quality of the supranational legislative process. This perhaps explains why, at the outset of the process leading to the drafting of the Constitutional Treaty, proposals for a second chamber composed of purely national parliamentarians again figured prominently in the discussion, ignoring the fate of similar proposals in the negotiations of the Amsterdam protocol on national parliaments.

German Foreign Minister Joschka Fischer, in his famous speech at Humboldt University in May 2000,[217] as well as British Prime Minister Tony Blair, in his speech in Warsaw later that year,[218] both offered ideas in this direction, even as they differed in important particulars. Fischer's was the constitutionally more ambitious proposal, made specifically with an eye to establishing an explicitly federal Europe. Fischer asked for a rethinking of the "division of sovereignty between Europe and the nation-state," which he saw as "the idea underlying the concept of 'subsidiarity,' a subject that is currently being discussed by everyone and understood by virtually no one." In Fischer's view, if a new European federation were to emerge (as he advocated), it would need a truly bicameral legislature on the American model—a "Senate" of national parliamentarians combined with the EP—operating under a full-fledged European constitution worthy of the name. In this way, "there will be no clash between national parliaments and the European Parliament, between the nation-state and Europe"[219]—each would enjoy representation in the new bicameral European legislature, as part of a new, federal-constitutional polity.

Tony Blair, for his part, did not share Fischer's federalist enthusiasm. But in his Warsaw speech he did share the view that the time had "come to

216. Lindseth et al. (2008), 5, 26–36 (including the Council in the category of "executive" oversight mechanism, even though it serves a "legislative" function within the EU). On the general blurring of the lines between executive, legislative, and judicial in administrative governance, see the Introduction 1, nn. 50–51 and accompanying text. In the EU context, see also Cohen and Sabel (2004), 160.

217. Fischer (2000).

218. Blair (2000).

219. See Fischer (2000).

involve representatives of national parliaments . . . by creating a second chamber of the European Parliament." The primary function of this body would not be, in the Prime Minister's estimation, one of legislation (a task he felt should be left to the existing institutional framework). Rather, it would be one of political oversight of the division of competences between the national and supranational levels. He called this a form of "political review by a body of democratically elected politicians,"[220] an implicit dig at the limitations of the existing regime, in which judicial supervision by the ECJ had failed to give effect to subsidiarity in any meaningful sense.[221]

Both speeches no doubt helped to push forward the process that ultimately led to the organization of the Convention on the Future of Europe. But these proposals in fact accomplished little in advancing the cause of a second chamber at the EU level. Well before the Laeken Declaration in December 2001 laid the actual groundwork for the Convention, it was clear that the idea "had little support in other member countries," effectively sounding its "death knell."[222] In the lead up to Laeken as well, the UK House of Lords' Select Committee on European Union issued an extensive report (including submissions from other national parliaments), evocatively entitled *A Second Parliamentary Chamber for Europe: An Unreal Solution to a Real Problem*.[223] "A more significant way forward," the report concluded "would be to strengthen national parliamentary scrutiny of the decisions of national governments in the European context,"[224] while also increasing transparency in the Council.[225] This should be combined, the report stressed, with significant improvements in compliance with subsidiarity by all European institutions, including the EP itself.[226]

The unpopularity of the idea of a second chamber among national parliamentarians, as evidenced by the Select Committee report, in fact suggested a very different understanding of the EU's democratic legitimacy challenges. The report described how "many individual citizens in the EU are fearful that, while 'Europe' is a significant factor in their lives, they cannot

---

220. Blair (2000).

221. See this chapter, nn. 34–38 and accompanying text.

222. Wintour (2001).

223. Select Committee on European Union (2001).

224. Ibid., para. 67.

225. Ibid., paras. 59–63.

226. Ibid., para. 53.

control it."[227] That situation, the report argued, was really one of "'disconnection' rather than 'democratic deficit,'" something that institutional or procedural changes could not solve in the absence of deeper transformations in "'public perceptions'" and "'political culture.'"[228] The report did not elaborate further, but its preference for language of "connection, disconnection and reconnection" is telling, not simply because it seemed "more neatly to summarise what it is that people feel is lacking in Europe at present."[229]

Inscribed into the Select Committee's conceptual vocabulary (as well its conclusions) was a quite different strategy for addressing the difficulties of democratic legitimation in the EU, one that went well beyond the replication of "representative, parliamentary democracy" on the supranational level (per Rittberger)—one that stressed, implicitly, the ultimately administrative character of European governance. In a contribution to these debates in 2002, I also addressed the distinction between the notions of "democratic disconnect" versus "democratic deficit," although at the time I was unaware of the Select Committee's report issued the prior year:

> The notion of a democratic deficit focuses our attention exclusively on the Community level and implies that democratization of supranational norm-production can take place through changes made largely if not entirely within the confines of supranational institutions (e.g., an augmented role of the European Parliament) or within supranational regulatory processes (e.g., greater transparency and participation in the comitology system). The notion of a democratic disconnect, by contrast, focuses our attention on the relationship between supranational institutions and national oversight and control. It does not deny the need for greater transparency and participation in the Community regulatory system, but it suggests that any democratization strategy must, at least in part, include a rethinking of the linkages between supranational norm-production and democratic legitimation derived from the national level.[230]

It is thus no coincidence, I would suggest, that the Select Committee placed significant stress on strengthening national parliamentary scrutiny of

---

227. Ibid., para. 58.

228. Ibid., paras. 56–57, quoting testimony of Lord Norton of Louth.

229. Ibid., para. 56.

230. Lindseth (2002), 151.

European affairs as part of a broader strategy of democratic reconnection. Nor is it a coincidence that the Laeken Declaration would do the same, in the effort to make the EU "more democratic, more transparent and more efficient."[231] This process would culminate, in some sense, in the new Article 12 TEU post-Lisbon, which was placed within Title II ("Provisions on Democratic Principles"). Article 12 outlined the ways in which "National Parliaments contribute actively to the good functioning of the Union," including, among others, oversight of the subsidiarity principle as well as scrutiny of their national executives.

Interestingly, the Laeken Declaration did not exclude the possibility that national parliaments might somehow "be represented in a new institution, alongside the Council and the European Parliament"—indeed, the second chamber idea refused to die easily.[232] But the more likely scenario was always the seemingly more modest "focus on the division of competence between Union and Member States, for example through preliminary checking of compliance with the principle of subsidiarity."[233] In the heady months and days leading to the Convention, when anticipation of a possible constitution for the EU ran high, these sorts of mundane matters were easily discounted or overlooked. (They often still are.) But long after the seemingly more constitutional elements of the Convention's work fell by the wayside,[234] what remained in the Treaty of Lisbon, besides a good deal of technical fine-tuning, was the recognition of national parliaments' key role in the Union, without which its democratic connection to the national level would be much diminished.[235] This role extended beyond ratification, passerelle clauses, and "emergency brakes" in sensitive domains (which, as we saw in Chapter 4, the German Federal Constitutional Court would emphasize

---

231. Presidency Conclusions, European Council Meeting in Laeken, 14 and 15 Dec. 2001, Annex I, Laeken Declaration on the Future of Europe, at 21, http://ec.europa.eu/governance/impact/background/docs/laeken_concl_en.pdf (last visited July 23, 2009).

232. Laeken Declaration on the Future of Europe, at 23. Valéry Giscard d'Estaing, in his capacity as President of the Convention, continued to push for such a body, which he dubbed the "Congress of the Peoples of Europe." It nevertheless failed to garner any support and was eventually dropped. Norman (2005), 122–23.

233. Laeken Declaration on the Future of Europe, at 23.

234. See IGC Mandate (2007), para. 3 (the "*TEU* and the *Treaty on the Functioning of the Union* will not have a constitutional character. The terminology used throughout the Treaties will reflect this change."). See also House of Commons (2007).

235. Again, see Article 12 TEU post-Lisbon, as well as the new protocols on the role of national parliaments and on subsidiarity, discussed in this chapter, at nn. 237–240 and accompanying text.

and strengthen in its own review of the Treaty of Lisbon).[236] Rather, it would now extend to a form of political oversight not merely focused on the activities of national executives but also on the enforcement of the principle of subsidiarity within the European legislative process itself.

The subsidiarity early-warning mechanism contained in the new Subsidiarity Protocol, carried over from the Constitutional Treaty to the Treaty of Lisbon,[237] emerged out of the deliberations of the Convention's working group on subsidiarity. The working group's report recognized that subsidiarity "was a principle of an essentially political nature, implementation of which involved a considerable margin of discretion for the institutions," thus requiring primarily political oversight.[238] Rather than proposing the establishment of a separate institution—a new subsidiarity "watchdog," as the British favored[239]—the working group looked to national parliaments as the logical source of subsidiarity enforcement, complementing their existing functions vis-à-vis their own national executives. The early-warning mechanism was specifically designed to work in conjunction with the new Protocol on the Role of National Parliaments (again carried over to Lisbon).[240] This protocol both broadened the scope of documents that national parliaments were entitled to receive—now including the Commission's annual legislative program—and also guaranteed them a minimum of six weeks (extended to eight by the Treaty of Lisbon) to engage in scrutiny of any draft legislative proposal—again, in effect, a supranationalized scrutiny reserve.[241]

---

236. It is worth noting that, with regard to the general passerelle clause, the Convention's draft contemplated only consultation of the national parliaments. The subsequent IGC changed this to a *nihil obstat* procedure (authorization if no national parliaments raise an objection), in effect a national parliamentary veto of a shift to QMV. Bindi (2008), 293. Even this was not good enough, however, for the German Federal Constitutional Court. See German Lisbon Decision 2009, para. 319, discussed in Chapter 4, n. 229.

237. Protocol (No. 2) on the Application of the Principles of Subsidiarity and Proportionality [hereinafter Lisbon Subsidiarity Protocol], 2008 O.J. (C 115) 206, http://eur-lex.europa.eu/LexUriServ/LexUriServ.do?uri=OJ:C:2008:115:0201:0328:EN:PDF (last visited July 24, 2009).

238. CONV 286/02, Conclusions of Working Group I on the Principle of Subsidiarity, 23 Sept. 2002, para. 5, http://register.consilium.europa.eu/pdf/en/02/cv00/cv00286.en02.pdf (last visited Oct. 26, 2009).

239. See Grice (2002); Menon (2004), 9; Weatherill (2005), 39.

240. Protocol (No. 1) on the Role of National Parliaments in the European Union [hereinafter Lisbon PNP], 2008 O.J. (C 115) 203, http://eur-lex.europa.eu/LexUriServ/LexUriServ.do?uri=OJ:C:2008:115:0201:0328:EN:PDF (last visited July 24, 2009).

241. See this chapter, n. 176 and accompanying text.

In what became known colloquially as the "yellow card" procedure, the Subsidiarity Protocol gave national parliaments six weeks from the submission of a legislative proposal—again, extended to eight weeks by the Treaty of Lisbon—to send a "reasoned opinion" to the Commission objecting to the proposal on subsidiarity grounds. (The protocol limited the right of objection to subsidiarity only, rather than questions of competence, or the expediency of adopting the provision more generally—a potentially significant limitation.)[242] If one-third of all national parliamentary chambers submitted objections—unicameral bodies given two "votes"—the Commission was obligated to reconsider the proposal. If the Commission chose to maintain the proposal, the protocol required a "reasoned opinion" from the Commission itself justifying the decision. This reason-giving obligation came on top of the many other obligations in the protocol, requiring the Commission, before making a proposal at all, to "consult widely" and to issue an initial "detailed statement" justifying the proposal on subsidiarity grounds, including an analysis of its implications for future national implementing legislation, as well as any potential administrative or financial burdens on the Member States.[243] In short, the yellow card procedure was designed to operate within a decisional framework that already generated an extensive administrative-type record, as part of a notice-and-comment type rulemaking process.[244]

The major dispute at the Convention was whether national parliaments should have not merely a right to comment on, but also to reject (on the basis of a two-thirds majority), a draft legislative proposal outright—not merely a yellow but a "red card" procedure. The British member of the *Praesidium,* Gisela Stuart, deeply annoyed many other *conventionnels* by proposing the red card procedure to the full Convention in January 2003. Their anger stemmed from the fact that she had participated in discussions between the working groups on subsidiarity and on national parliaments (the latter she in fact chaired), which had apparently considered and rejected the idea.[245] In the muted words the Convention Secretariat's summary of the

---

242. But see this chapter, nn. 260–272 and accompanying text. For a detailed analysis of the substantive scope of the permissible objections, including possible alternatives, see Weatherill (2005), 40–42.

243. Lisbon Subsidiarity Protocol, arts. 2 and 5.

244. See this chapter, nn. 44–48 and accompanying text.

245. Norman (2005), 167; Menon (2004), 31; Wintour (2003). See also CONV 540/03, Contribution of Ms. Gisela Stuart, "The Early Warning Mechanism—Putting It into

floor debate: "Many Convention members were against this proposal, on the grounds that a 'veto' mechanism would not be acceptable and would infringe the decision-making autonomy of European bodies."[246] The journalist Peter Norman, in his definitive postmortem of the making of the Constitutional Treaty, offered a bit more colorful description, saying the proposal "was trounced, with many conventionnels using unusually forthright language." Lamberto Dini, another leading national parliamentarian, "poured scorn on [the] idea," stating that "'it means giving national parliaments the power of veto over the initiative of the Commission and that we should not do.'"[247]

The debate over the red card proposal was another manifestation of the complex ways in which the legitimacy-control distinction operated as a normative-legal principle in the integration context. The concept of delegation was grounded in its own historically constructed "logic of appropriateness," one that did not necessarily favor direct assertions of control of the type the red card procedure might potentially allow.[248] Manifest in the debate were arguably older understandings of the proper role of a delegating legislature vis-à-vis a more expert agent, the latter functionally entitled to autonomy and discretion in order to carry out its assigned task, without undue parliamentary interference. These understandings have distinct echoes in analogous debates in the interwar period on the national level,[249] as well as in the formative years of European integration.[250]

The debate over the red card procedure, as well as its defeat in the Convention, can also be seen as a further reflection of the need to manage the difficult tension between control and legitimation in the context of integration, which was first raised in the Introduction[251] and encountered more concretely in Chapter 3 in the discussion of the empty chair crisis and the

---

Practice," 6 Feb. 2003, http://register.consilium.eu.int/pdf/en/03/cv00/cv00540en03.pdf (last visited July 24, 2009); Weatherill (2005), 43.

246. CONV 630/03, Summary report on the plenary session of 17 and 18 March 2003, 21 Mar. 2003, http://register.consilium.europa.eu/pdf/en/03/cv00/cv00630.en03.pdf (last visited Oct. 26, 2009); see also Weatherill (2005), 44.

247. Norman (2005), 170, quoting Lamberto Dini.

248. See Chapter 1, nn. 105–106 and accompanying text.

249. See, e.g., Chapter 2, nn. 5, 17–20, and 26–34 and accompanying text.

250. See, e.g., Chapter 3, nn. 20–21 and 64–67 and accompanying text.

251. See the Introduction, nn. 79–81 and accompanying text.

Luxembourg Compromise.[252] What is interesting here, however, is the contrast between executive and legislative prerogatives that this history suggests. In the contestation of the 1960s and 1970s, national executives were able to retain at least *shared* control over the supranational policy process, whereas, in the present decade, national parliaments fell short of even that. This differential outcome might be explained in terms of the functionally and, in some sense, constitutionally superior position of the national executive relative to the national legislature under the postwar constitutional settlement, which was explored in Chapter 2. Beyond adoption of the initial enabling legislation, there were quite limited direct legislative prerogatives vis-à-vis regulatory decision making in the postwar years—although not as limited as they would become in the supranational context for much of its history. Executive prerogatives, by contrast, were clearly greater, ranging from de jure rights of outright hierarchical control to more limited de facto claims for coordination and supervision over an increasingly complex administrative sphere. Combined with the broadly accepted foreign policy character of integration in its earliest decades, this translated into a much greater national executive role at the supranational level.

The compromise "orange card" procedure that eventually emerged in the negotiations of the Treaty of Lisbon might then also be seen as evidence of the sort of adjustments required in parliamentary oversight as the postwar constitutional settlement was translated to the supranational context. The Lisbon Treaty would not permit a national parliamentary veto outright, but it did adopt a rule, perhaps an ultimately unworkable one, in which national parliamentary opposition could trigger an altered voting scheme in the supranational legislative process, thus increasing (slightly) the likelihood that the proposal might be defeated.[253] Even within the national context, however, hierarchical oversight by the national executive alone, even when supplemented (at least in recent years) by transparency and participation rights for outside interests in the administrative domain, has never proven fully adequate to legitimize delegated normative power. The postwar constitutional settlement in effect demanded some additional role for the national

---

252. See Chapter 3, nn. 140–160 and accompanying text; see also nn. 131–132 and accompanying text.

253. Under Article 7(3)(b) of the Lisbon Subsidiarity Protocol, if 55 percent of the members of the Council or a majority of the European Parliament concludes that a proposal challenged by one-third of national parliaments does not comply with the principle of subsidiarity, the draft legislation would fail.

legislature, including in some instances post hoc vetoes, which were often seen as necessary to supplement executive legitimation, even if the veto rights were rarely used.[254] In the integration context, however, the prospect of a general, collective national parliamentary veto was seen as a step too far toward *control*. And yet a strategy of limiting parliamentary oversight to the yellow card did not go far enough to satisfy the normative demands of the postwar constitutional settlement. In this way, the orange card procedure makes a (slight) concession to the greater national parliamentary cultural claims under the postwar constitutional settlement, now adjusted to the functional imperatives of European integration.

The yellow and orange card procedures again raise the question of power versus legitimation in national parliamentary oversight.[255] The British political scientist Simon Hix, in testimony before the House of Common Scrutiny Committee in June 2008, reflected perhaps views typical of his profession by questioning whether these procedures were likely to have significant effect on actual policy outcomes, at least in those parliamentary systems with majority or strong coalition governments.[256] Of course, national procedures may vary, and some national legal systems may choose to give legislative minorities the right to submit subsidiarity objections, precisely because the majority party or coalition will be under the government's effective control. In the slightly different context of maintaining subsidiarity actions before the Court of Justice, for example, the German implementing legislation for Lisbon confers that power on the legislative minority.[257] So too does the new

---

254. See Chapter 2, nn. 92–96 and accompanying text.

255. See this chapter, nn. 65–67 and 185–190 and accompanying text.

256. Oral Evidence, Wednesday 18 June 2008, Professor Simon Hix, in European Scrutiny Committee (2008), EV 10, Q41.

257. See *Gesetz zur Änderung des Grundgesetzes (Artikel 23, 45 und 93)* ("Act Amending the Basic Law (Articles 23, 45 and 93)"), Article 1(1), BGBl. I 1926 (Oct. 8, 2008). The German Federal Constitutional Court specifically upheld this provision as a valid protection of minority rights in a democracy:

> [T]he right to bring a subsidiarity action . . . is to preserve to the parliamentary minority the competence to assert the rights of the German *Bundestag* also where the latter does not wish to exercise its rights, in particular in relation to the Federal Government carried by it. The opposition parliamentary group, and thus the organised parliamentary minority, as the antagonist of the government majority, is intended to be [given] the possibility of recourse before the Court of Justice of the European Union to make possible the actual assertion of the rights reserved to Parliament in the system of European integration.

German Lisbon Decision 2009, para. 403.

Article 88–6(3) of the French Constitution (as revised post-Lisbon).[258] These examples show that there is nothing *in law* that prevents national systems from choosing to grant minorities the right to submit objections to the Commission under either the yellow or orange card procedure.[259]

But even if national parliaments loosened their procedures to allow minority subsidiarity objections to be filed, the high thresholds under both the yellow and orange card procedures could pose significant obstacles to their formal use, thus undermining their likely impact. The same concern applies, of course, to the narrow scope of the procedures, which formally exclude competency or expediency objections.[260] However, the Commission has recently shown great receptivity (and even responsiveness) in its dealing with national parliaments, particularly in the aftermath of the French and Dutch rejections of the Constitutional Treaty. In spring 2006, for example, the Commission announced that, regardless of the seeming demise of the Constitutional Treaty, it would nevertheless begin forwarding all legislative proposals and consultation documents to national parliaments, inviting their comments, which were not specifically limited to subsidiarity, "so as to improve the process of policy formulation."[261] In a speech before a joint meeting of representatives of the European Parliament and national parliaments in Brussels announcing the new policy, Commission President Barroso stated:

[F]or too long national parliaments have been seen as semi-detached players on the European scene. This must change. The involvement of

---

258. See Constitution de la République française, Article 88–6(3) (post-Lisbon): "À la demande de soixante députés ou de soixante sénateurs, le recours est de droit" ("At the request of sixty deputies or sixty senators, the action is as of right").

259. Preliminary research did not reveal any studies specifically on the question of minority rights in national parliaments with regard to the subsidiarity protocol, although it is obviously a pertinent and interesting question to pursue. The COSAC Web site does contain a "Table on Foreseen Models for the Early Warning Mechanism in National Parliaments," http://www.cosac.eu/en/info/earlywarning/overview/ (last visited July 25, 2009). It indicated that, in the EU-25, many parliaments had not yet even adopted formal procedures governing subsidiarity checks, although several had granted their EACs the right to act on behalf of the parliament as a whole. Otherwise, the table contained no category specifically contemplating minority rights in this regard.

260. See this chapter, n. 242 and accompanying text.

261. See Communication from the Commission to the European Council, A Citizens' Agenda: Delivering Results for Europe, Brussels, 10 May 2006, COM (2006) 211 final, at 9, http://eur-lex.europa.eu/LexUriServ/site/en/com/2006/com2006_0211en01.pdf (last visited July 25, 2009).

national parliaments can help make European policies more attuned to diverse circumstances and more effectively implemented. We do not need to wait for an institutional settlement to improve and facilitate the scrutiny by national parliaments of EU legislation.[262]

The Commission initiative to transmit legislative proposals to national parliaments should be seen in the context of the Commission's efforts to respond to the French and Dutch referenda defeats—its so-called "Plan-D for Democracy, Dialogue and Debate."[263] In its announcement of Plan-D in October 2005, the Commission stated: "National Parliaments are the bridge to ensuring effective scrutiny of decisions taken by National Governments on European issues."[264] For its part, the Commission committed to making individual commissioners "accessible and prepared to assist national Parliaments to explain Commission policies and provide an overview of recent EU developments."[265] By April of the following year, according to the Commission's follow-up report to the European Council, "Plan D had added more than 40 Commissioner visits to National Parliaments, covering almost all Member States. Some of these meetings were the first time that national parliaments had received the Commission President or Commissioners in plenary session."[266] A later report covering the year 2008 referred not only to continued visits by members of the Commission (notably by President Barroso and by the Vice President in charge of communications, Margot Wallström) but also to "regular and structured contact with national parliaments" by the Commission's representations in each Member State.[267]

---

262. See Draft Speech, President Barroso at the Joint Parliamentary Meeting on the "Future of Europe," at 3, http://ec.europa.eu/commission_barroso/president/pdf/speech_20060509_en.pdf (last visited July 25, 2009).

263. See The Commission's Contribution to the Period of Reflection and Beyond: Plan-D for Democracy, Dialogue and Debate, Brussels, 13 Oct. 2005, COM (2005) 494 final, http://ec.europa.eu/commission_barroso/wallstrom/pdf/communication_planD_en.pdf (last visited July 25, 2009).

264. COM (2005) 494 final, at 4.

265. Ibid., at 7.

266. Communication from the Commission to the European Council, The Period of Reflection and Plan D, Brussels, 10 Apr. 2006, COM (2006) 212 Provisional Version, at 8, http://www.futureofeurope.europarl.europa.eu/future/webdav/site/event3/users/futureofeurope/public/Background%20documentation/The%20period%20of%20reflection%20and%20Plan%20D.pdf (last visited July 25, 2009).

267. Report from the Commission, Annual Report 2008 on Relations Between the European Commission and National Parliaments, Brussels, 7 July 2009, COM (2009) 343 final, at 7,

Indeed, Vice President Wallström testified before the House of Commons Scrutiny Committee in June 2008, just days after the testimony of Professor Hix discussed above. Wallström made clear that the Commission would take into account national parliamentary observations even if they did not reach the required thresholds under the Subsidiarity Protocol.[268] The logic of her comments, moreover, also suggested that the Commission would be open to comments beyond the limited scope of the subsidiarity protocol, extending to all aspects of the policy process, including questions of competence and expediency.[269] She said that "the attitude [of the Commission] behind giving the national parliaments a voice . . . is the democratic anchoring of the European agenda" more generally.[270]

This recalls the findings of Katrin Auel in the context of parliamentary scrutiny of European affairs under national law, in which she concluded that a "weak institutional position" did not necessarily translate into weak legitimating effects.[271] Indeed, even Professor Hix, despite his general skepticism toward the yellow and orange card procedures, also acknowledged their possible salutary effects in increasing transparency of the EU legislative process, which he hoped would extend beyond the Commission to the Council, "still the most secretive legislature west of Beijing."[272] Thus, the ultimate effectiveness of national parliamentary scrutiny as a legitimating mechanism is likely to be a function not simply of the formal rights under the Subsidiarity Protocol itself. Rather, it also will depend on the informal behavior of supranational institutions, as well as their perceptions of the democratic needs of integration, as Wallström's testimony before the Commons Scrutiny Committee suggested.

In this regard, it is the ECJ that stands as the institution whose behavior is both most difficult to predict and most critical to the legal future of the subsidiarity early-warning mechanism. Article 8 of the Subsidiarity Protocol

---

http://eur-lex.europa.eu/LexUriServ/LexUriServ.do?uri=COM:2009:0343:FIN:EN:PDF (last visited July 25, 2009).

268. Oral Evidence, Monday 23 June 2008, Mrs. Margot Wallström, Vice President, Commissioner for Institutional Relations and Communications Strategy, in European Scrutiny Committee (2008), EV 20–21, Q85–Q86.

269. For data on the number of submissions by national parliaments over the subsequent three years, see Mahony (2009).

270. European Scrutiny Committee (2008), EV 20, Q85.

271. See this chapter, n. 190 and accompanying text.

272. European Scrutiny Committee (2008), EV 10, Q41; see also EV 11, Q44, and EV 13, Q50.

explicitly confers jurisdiction on the Court to exercise ex post judicial review of compliance and further expands standing for subsidiarity challenges to include claims by national parliaments as well as the Committee of the Regions (CoR) (see Article 263 TFEU post-Lisbon). This at least implies a desire on the part of the drafters that the ECJ should involve itself more vigorously on these questions. But as noted at the outset of this chapter, the ECJ's subsidiarity jurisprudence from the late 1990s and early 2000s has been almost embarrassingly limited, particularly with regard to policing the procedural dimension of subsidiarity.[273]

Will this now change? It remains to be seen, although some degree of pessimism is probably in order. It has now become conventional wisdom that the ECJ's limited approach to subsidiarity is evidence of the inherently "political" (and thus borderline nonjusticiable) nature of the subsidiarity principle. In his submission to the subsidiarity working group at the Convention in June 2002, Jean-Claude Piris, Director-General of the Council's Legal Service, called the principle "more for the politician than the judge," a view that clearly had an impact on the working group.[274] Piris noted how the Court had "*never* annulled an act on the grounds of infringement of the principle of subsidiarity" (emphasis in original).[275] He pointed out, by contrast, that the question of competence was "an objective question of a legal nature" and thus amenable to judicial review.[276]

Piris, however, focused exclusively on the *substantive* dimension of the subsidiarity principle, arguably following the example of the Court itself, ignoring the quite objective *procedural* requirements in the governing treaty law.[277] In testimony the week before, Michel Petite, Director-General of the Commission Legal Service,[278] alluded to something that Piris ignored—the

273. See this chapter, nn. 34–38 and accompanying text.

274. WD 04-WG I, 3 July 2002, at 8, Intervention of Mr. Jean Claude Piris, Legal Adviser to the Council of the European Union and Director-General of the Council's Legal Service, at the meeting of the group on 25 June 2002, http://european-convention.eu.int/docs/wd1/1347.pdf (last visited July 26, 2009).

275. WD 04-WG I, at 8.

276. WD 04-WG I, at 5, referring, e.g., to the Court's handling of the tobacco advertising directive in Case C-376/98, *Germany v. Parliament and Council*, 2000 ECR I-8419. See Chapter 4, n. 58 and accompanying text.

277. See this chapter, nn. 25–28, 34–38, and 44–46 and accompanying text.

278. WG I-WD 3, 27 June 2002, Intervention de M. Michel Petite, Directeur Général du Service juridique de la Commission, à la réunion du groupe, le 17 juin 2002, http://european-convention.eu.int/docs/wd1/1336.pdf (last visited July 26, 2009).

embarrassingly large gap between the Court's procedural case law (in which a kind of "implicit" compliance with subsidiarity was acceptable)[279] and the explicit requirements of the then-governing Subsidiarity Protocol under the Treaty of Amsterdam. The Treaty of Lisbon specifically carried over these requirements, mandating that the Commission produce a detailed statement of reasons justifying a proposed legislation on subsidiarity grounds.[280] Petite stated that the Commission, in its actual practice, tried to conform "to the text of the Amsterdam Protocol" rather than follow the more permissive jurisprudence of the ECJ.[281]

Petite's testimony makes clear that, pace Piris, the enforcement of the principle of subsidiarity is not entirely political, and that there is indeed a good deal of objective law to apply. For the new potential claimants in subsidiarity actions before the ECJ—the national parliaments and the CoR—enforcement of this procedural law is likely to loom large in their challenges. As outsiders to the legislative process, their ability to influence the legislative process directly in political and substantive terms will be quite limited. Thus, their incentive will be to pursue political objectives via procedural challenges—a phenomenon not unknown in U.S. administrative law—with the aim of giving effect to the obligations of reasoned decision making in the Subsidiarity Protocol. George Bermann outlined a sensible, balanced approach to the justiciability of subsidiarity in the early 1990s, in terms already partially quoted above but worth repeating: Ex post judicial review of subsidiarity compliance should avoid "profoundly political judgments that [judges are] ill-equipped to make and ultimately not responsible for making."[282] But judicial review should nevertheless "verify whether the institutions themselves examined" all the various questions that the Subsidiarity Protocol in fact demands.[283]

This should not, in principle, be too difficult an inquiry, given the detailed procedural requirements that the Subsidiarity Protocol spells out, as well as the not-inconsiderable rulemaking record that must be assembled.[284] In a more recent article echoing Bermann's earlier argument, Mattias Kumm

---

279. Citing *Biotechnological Inventions*, 2001 E.C.R. I-07079, para. 33; see this chapter, n. 37 and accompanying text.

280. See this chapter, n. 45 and accompanying text.

281. WG I-WD 3, at 5.

282. Bermann (1994), 391; see also this chapter, nn. 27–28 and accompanying text.

283. Bermann (1994), 391.

284. See this chapter, nn. 237–244 and accompanying text.

discussed the Court's role as an "editor" rather than "author" of the subsidiary inquiry: "As an editor of European laws [the Court] does not claim authorial skills or authority. But it does claim that a structured reasoned assessment of the kind the [subsidiarity] framework requires, when supported by a well-developed record supplied by other institutions, allows it to effectively pass judgment on whether or not the arguments provided by the legislator were reasonable or not."[285] This sort of judicial enforcement of reasoned decision-making in the process of making rules is hardly unprecedented. Kumm draws part of his inspiration from the federalism case law of the United States Supreme Court over the last two decades, interpreting the demands of the U.S. constitution against Congress.[286] But the better model for this approach is in fact administrative, not constitutional (as is so much else in European integration).[287] Judicial oversight of reasoned decision making is vastly more developed in the administrative law context in the United States, something touched on at the outset of this chapter: U.S. courts engage in precisely this sort of judicial review when they apply the so-called hard look doctrine to administrative agencies.[288]

And for good reason—the democratic and constitutional legitimacy of an *administrative* agent is at best derivative, thus requiring justification in other terms. Most importantly, the agent must justify its actions in terms of its legislative mandate as well as its purported technocratic expertise, both of which require *reasons* stated simultaneously with the administrative action itself.[289] This reason-giving obligation is deeply bound up with democratic anxieties associated with the fact that it is specifically *delegated* legislative power that is being exercised. The reason-giving obligation not only justifies the actions of the agent but also, in some sense, the judgment of the legislative principal in undertaking the delegation in the first place. Stating good reasons, both in

---

285. Kumm (2006b), 529; see also Bermann (2008), 458.

286. Kumm (2006b), 526 (noting, inter alia, so-called "clear statement rules"); see also Bermann (2008), 458.

287. See Stephenson (2008), which looks to the same federalism jurisprudence as Kumm (particularly with regard to "clear statement rules") but also acknowledges, ibid., 4–5, n. 3, that the approach draws inspiration from the administrative context, more specifically analyzed in Stephenson (2006), as well as in an extended list of cited works in political science on delegation to administrative agencies.

288. See this chapter, nn. 29–30 and accompanying text; see also Stephenson (2006); and Bermann (2008), 458 (suggesting that the "analytic and documentary trail" called for by the Protocols gives the ECJ the opportunity to take a "'harder look' at compliance with the subsidiarity principle").

289. See, e.g., Securities and Exchange Commission v. Chenery Corp. 318 U.S. 80 (1943).

terms of the legislative mandate and purported expertise, demonstrates not only that the delegation to the agent was appropriate, but also that the agent is acting in a manner reasonably within the bounds of its democratic mandate defined by the legislator. Disgorging information reasonably preserves centralized democratic legitimacy in the elected assembly, while also promoting oversight, if not control. In turn, it advances the political-cultural goal of reconciliation between the diffusion of power, on the one hand, and the preservation of democratic and constitutional legitimacy in the representative legislature (that is, on the national level), on the other.[290]

Will the European Court of Justice follow this path? It depends on how it interprets the democratic challenges confronting the Union, either explicitly or implicitly. If it views the challenge in terms of the classic democratic deficit, then it will continue to focus its attention primarily on the supranational level, limiting its subsidiarity analysis. It will try to promote the role of the European Parliament, as it long has, seeing it as the expression of the "fundamental democratic principle that the peoples should take part in the exercise of power through the intermediary of a representative assembly."[291] It will view the problem of the democratic deficit as primarily horizontal, one among European institutions themselves—that is, a problem of "institutional balance"[292]—in which national parliaments play (at best) a marginal and ultimately instrumental role.

But if the Court views the problem as vertical, entailing not a deficit but a democratic disconnect,[293] then the Court may recognize that democratic and constitutional legitimacy remains largely national even as significant normative power has been delegated to the supranational level. In short, if it recognizes the fundamentally *administrative, not constitutional* nature of integration, then it may behave differently. It may then try to enforce the procedural dimension of subsidiarity a bit more aggressively. This would entail promoting heightened transparency and participation rights (an indisputably good thing) but not as some alternative, nonhierarchical means of democratic legitimation for the EU. Rather, it will do so to reduce information costs for *national parliaments,* to reconnect European governance to

---

290. See generally Stack (2007).

291. Case 138/79, *SA Roquettes Frères v. Council,* 1980 E.C.R. 3333, 3360.

292. Cf. Vos (1999b), 88 (discussing how the Court has viewed "institutional balance in a purely horizontal manner (a balance between the 'institutions') and does not include the Member States within it").

293. See this chapter, nn. 228–230 and accompanying text.

its sources of ultimate democratic and constitutional legitimacy on the national level.[294]

Whatever occurs, scholars will no doubt find it difficult to separate political from cultural factors in this process of legal and institutional change. By this, I mean that it will be difficult to determine whether the Court is acting to preserve its own hard-fought institutional advantages (that is, is primarily acting politically) or to further its own conception of legitimate European governance (that is, is primarily acting culturally). Motivated by self-preservation, the Court's response may ultimately turn not on principle but on a strategic political calculation of the likelihood of a negative reaction coming from the national level, particularly in the form of increased activism from national high courts.[295] Motivated by principle, the Court could persist in the its legal-cultural claim that somehow "the genetic code" of the treaties still unambiguously demands a "preference for Europe," whose ultimate *telos* is "'an ever closer union.'"[296] Almost certainly the Court will be motivated by a mix of the two concerns, even as it addresses what it perceives to be the current functional demands of the integration project.

The phrase "ever closer union" is still present in the treaties post-Lisbon; however, much has changed in the last two decades, and more particularly in the last five years. In view of the recent past, it should be hard for the Court to insist on the old teleology of integration with the same confidence it once did. The new motto for the EU proposed in 2000—*In varietate concordia* ("Unity in Diversity")[297]—almost certainly better describes the *telos* of integration today. Sensitive to the demands of diversity even as it strives for unity, the Court might choose to be (at least somewhat) more responsive to the

---

294. For more details on the function of transparency and participation as a means of overcoming the democratic disconnect, see Lindseth (2001), 161–62, and (2002), 158–59. See also the Conclusion, nn. 42–50 and accompanying text.

295. See Kumm (2006b), 504, 530, and 533.

296. Mancini and Keeling (1994), 186. For a recent example of this sort of teleological reasoning in action, see C-105/03, *Pupino*, 2005 ECR I-5285, paras. 41–43 (extending the principle of conforming interpretation to framework decisions adopted under the third pillar). Consider also the analogous teleology that the Court has attempted to define in the context of EU citizenship. See, e.g., Case C-184/99, *Rudy Grzelczyk v. Centre public d'aide sociale d'Ottignies-Louvain-la-Neuve*, 2001 ECR I-6193, para. 31 ("Union citizenship is destined to be the fundamental status of nationals of the Member States.").

297. The Constitutional Treaty infelicitously transformed this motto into "United in Diversity" (see art. I-8) but the Treaty of Lisbon eliminated this provision as part of the effort to purge the more "constitutional" features of the Constitutional Treaty from the TEU and TFEU.

superior legitimacy resources of the Member States and thus enforce the procedural dimension of subsidiarity at least to some extent.

Whatever the ECJ chooses, however, the judges on the Court should not confuse their own institutional autonomy (power) with autonomous democratic and constitutional legitimacy. The Court, too, is ultimately an agent, not a principal. Like all other institutions of the Union, it operates as part of a governance regime whose character is administrative, not constitutional. In this respect, the Court is simply another manifestation of the diffuse and fragmented nature of modern governance more generally, with a legitimacy still derived *normatively* from delegations from the several Member States. In its subsidiarity case law as in other areas, the Court must find a way to come to terms with this polycentric constitutional character of integration even as it oversees the Union's exercise of often extensive, and relatively autonomous, regulatory power penetrating deeply into national legal orders.

Conclusion
The Challenge of Legitimizing Europeanized
Administrative Governance

THIS BOOK ATTEMPTED TO DESCRIBE the democratic and constitutional framework within which supranational governance in the European Union—what we might call *Europeanized administrative governance*—seeks to operate. European governance, this study maintains, should be understood not as sui generis but as a new stage in the diffusion and fragmentation of regulatory power away from the constituted bodies of representative government on the national level, to an administrative sphere that now operates both within and beyond the state. Europeanized administrative governance, because of its very density and complexity, often escapes direct political control. But it has not escaped the demands of mediated legitimacy, whose core features were outlined in Chapter 2. The growth of national parliamentary scrutiny (the focus of Chapter 5), as well as the development of a national jurisprudence of *Kompetenz-Kompetenz* combined with deference (the topic in Chapter 4), are in this sense elements of the same process of historical convergence. They demonstrate the extent to which European public law has increasingly organized itself around the legitimating structures of the postwar constitutional settlement of administrative governance.

Together with national executive oversight (explored in Chapter 3), European public law has come to rely on mechanisms of mediated legitimacy to provide the necessary, although perhaps not sufficient, democratic and constitutional underpinnings of European integration. These mechanisms seek to define, both legally and politically, the broad parameters within which the dense and complex system of Europeanized administrative governance may legitimately produce regulatory norms, consistent with evolving democratic and constitutional principles.

The concluding section of Chapter 3, with its discussion of the emergent committee structure in European integration in the 1960s, gave us a sense of how dense and complex that system would indeed become.[1] Today, there can be little doubt that administrative governance in its Europeanized form has evolved into something even more intricate and complicated than anything contemplated four decades ago. Co-decision, comitology, interinstitutional agreements, European agencies, the open method of coordination, the new approach to technical harmonization (now not-so-new), internal Commission reforms (both structural and procedural), the better regulation initiative, impact analysis, as well as the myriad ways in which national and supranational administrations both formally and informally interact—all constitute elements of Europe's profoundly dense and complex system of regulatory norm-production for a transnational market-polity.[2] The process of generating regulatory norms for the European Union (EU) today operates with a degree of de facto autonomy that is almost certainly greater than even the de jure autonomy envisioned under the treaties.

And that autonomy is even greater still than what is enjoyed by the evolving forms of administrative governance on the national and subnational levels—which brings us to the real challenge of legitimation in the EU. Regulatory power on the supranational level no doubt operates with a significant degree of autonomy, flowing from this density and complexity. But it is an autonomy that remains fundamentally functional, without the capacity for self-legitimation that the institutions of representative government within the constitutional nation-state enjoy. Over time, scholars of European integration have offered any number of labels to describe the elusive nature of this form of European governance. One could see it as an "accumulated executive order,"[3] or perhaps as a multilevel system of "network governance," which "tends to marginalise parliaments as the traditional sites of deliberation and legislative policy-making."[4] Or one might call it "an unprecedented attempt to build a form of continental order without recreating the hierarchical power structure of states."[5] Or one could call it a "confederation" of states, pooling "certain powers for mutual advantage."[6] Indeed, one could even describe it "as an association of sovereign national states

---

1. See Chapter 3, nn. 164–189 and accompanying text.

2. See generally Lindseth et al. (2008); see also Curtin (2009).

3. Curtin and Egeberg (2008).

4. Kaiser (2007), 1.

5. Dehousse (2008), 794.

6. Majone (2005), 41.

(*Staatenverbund*)," as the German Federal Constitutional has done, "in which the peoples of their Member States, i.e., the citizens of the states, remain the subjects of democratic legitim[ation]."[7]

Regardless of the label chosen, one must recognize the profound historical dependence of European governance on the antecedent development of administrative governance as a legitimate form of rule on the national level. It is no coincidence that European integration emerged as a viable political project at precisely the moment in Western history (the 1950s) when the foundations of administrative governance on the national level were also secured, reconciled in some reasonably stable way with the demands of representative government inherited from the past. The development of integration over the last half century should not be understood, as one historian has suggested, as some kind of "technocratic detour" or "technocratic phase,"[8] as if some new period of autonomous democratic and constitutional legitimation of integration were in the offing. The technocratic dimension of integration will almost certainly persist for the foreseeable future; indeed, in the face of the current economic crisis, it is likely to become even more dense and complex, not less.

The challenge is therefore to reconcile *this* functional reality with the political-cultural attachment to the nation-state as the locus of democratic and constitutional legitimacy in Europe. Observers of integration of all inclinations, ranging from the strongly pro-European to the more Eurosceptical, would do well to acknowledge this challenge in order to better understand the nature of the EU's legitimacy going forward. It is administrative, not constitutional.

In making this acknowledgment, however, Europeans should also guard against what might be called the converse error. They should not simply assume, given the largely technocratic and delegated character of Europeanized administrative governance, that it is somehow unproblematically equivalent to its national counterparts in the administrative state in terms of legitimacy.[9] Even as Europeans have attempted to translate the postwar constitutional settlement into workable supranational form (notably in the separation of regulatory power from legitimacy), integration remains a

---

7. German Lisbon Decision (2009), para. 229.

8. Loth (2008), 22, 25.

9. See, e.g., Moravcsik (2005b) (describing the EU as democratically legitimate in this way); see also Moravcsik (2007), 49–50; and Moravcsik (2008). For extended critiques of this thesis from a political science perspective, see Lu (2009); and Bellamy (2006), 736–42.

unique form of administrative governance in one critical respect: the fact that the Member States and their electorates serve as principals *severally* in the system.[10] Although the multiplicity of constitutional principals is hardly unknown in modern administrative states (take, for example, the separation of powers system of the U.S.), the challenge of multiple principals in European governance is of a completely different order of magnitude. In the integration context, there is a vastly larger number of possible "veto players,"[11] which in turn leads to a "joint-decision trap" of significantly greater difficulty than anything experienced on the national level.[12] There are several potential consequences of these factors worth noting.

First, ex ante, the fact of multiple principals in the EU can, in certain domains, lead to exceedingly broad delegations of supranational regulatory power, in order to overcome the problems of cooperation, coordination, and potential defection among the multiple principals—what has been called "principal drift."[13] These delegations are made not just to the Commission and to the Council acting by qualified majority, but also, perhaps most importantly, to the European Court of Justice in its interpretation of the treaties and Community legislation.

Second, once these bodies exercise their relatively autonomous delegated power at the supranational level, then, ex post, the erstwhile principals (the Member States) in some sense become agents themselves, responsible for implementation.[14] In theory, this should only occur within the bounds of the broad policy limits to which Member States themselves originally committed—for example, free movement. Nevertheless, this inversion of roles can have consequences that the Member States may still find deeply disruptive in domestic legal and political orders.

---

10. Lindseth (1999), 637.

11. Tsebelis (2002).

12. Scharpf (1988).

13. Menon and Weatherill (2002), 119. Cf. also Thatcher and Stone Sweet (2002), 6 (discussing "[c]omposite principals" as "a principal comprised of multiple actors whose collective makeup changes periodically through, for example, elections," and which thus "may not possess stable, coherent preferences over time. Instead, they may be competitive with one another over some or many issues, as when member state governments in the EU disagree on matters of policy that fall within the agents' mandate.").

14. Auel (2009), unpaginated, at text accompanying n. 12 ("Once a final decision has been taken at the European level member states become effectively agents of the EU and are in turn accountable for the implementation of European decisions.").

Third, again ex post, if a desire subsequently emerges in one Member State to reverse any of these supranationally devised norms—for example, ones announced by the Court of Justice, interpreting the general provisions of the treaties—the fact of multiple principals (and therefore of even more multiple veto players) means that the sort of political mobilization needed to undertake such a reversal is vastly more challenging than within a purely national administrative polity[15]—not impossible, but challenging.[16]

In these various regards, supranational administrative governance *is* different from its purely national counterparts. From the perspective of a theory of democracy focusing on the circulation of elites,[17] perhaps the biggest problem with integration is the perceived entrenchment of its bureaucratic class in Brussels.[18] From this standpoint, the problem with integration is not so much the normative autonomy of the supranational level but rather the difficulty of exercising strongly legitimated oversight in some coherent way.[19] Under the current rules, "no single parliament [or electorate] can alter the existing system,

---

15. Franchino (2004), 292 ("Tsebelis finds support for his argument in areas, such as adjudication and central banking, that are carried out by actors with considerably more formal autonomy than that of traditional bureaucracies," citing Tsebelis (2002), 222–47).

16. Kassim and Menon (2003), 131.

17. See, e.g., Schumpeter (1976 [1942]), 269–73.

18. The consensus on this point is widespread. See, e.g., the views of a British MP and former member of the *Praesidium* of the Convention on the Future of Europe in Stuart (2009) ("It is virtually impossible to pin down accountability and responsibility in a way which would allow voters to bring about a change in political direction. Once a process has started it just grinds on regardless. The negotiations drag on for years and by the time a decision is made the politicians who started it have long left the stage, immune from the verdict of the ballot box."). Similarly, at the oral argument on the German Lisbon Decision, Udo di Fabio, the *juge-rapporteur* and a leading conservative on the Constitutional Court, apparently pressed counsel on similar themes—the nature of EU democracy, its "government" and its "opposition," and thus its ultimate electoral accountability. Phone conversation, February 23, 2009, with Ingolf Pernice, who appeared as counsel for the German *Bundestag* in the Lisbon hearing before the *Bundesverfassungsgericht* on February 10–11, 2009. As an influential (and generally pro-European) scholar has noted: "The form of European governance is—and will remain for a considerable time—such that there is no 'government' to throw out," much less an opposition to replace it, even though this is normally regarded as a "basic condition of representative democracy." Weiler (1999a), 350. See also Benz et al. (2007), 442 ("the rascals are not elected by the people and can be thrown out only in the most extreme circumstances.").

19. Cf. Krisch (2006), 248 (describing as one of the "central challenge[s] to the use of administrative law concepts for global regulation, namely the fundamental contestation over the question of *to whom* global governance should be accountable," and further arguing that "the strength of this contestation contrasts with the unitary, hierarchical basis on which domestic administrative law rests," which "leads to a peculiarly rugged landscape of accountability mechanisms on the global level") (emphasis in original).

nor indeed even make any formal initiatives to that end."[20] In other words, as a practical matter, given the reality of multiple principals in the European system, the institutional beneficiaries of supranational delegation are entrenched to a degree not found in instances of administrative delegation on the national level, even with regard to independent agencies. The result is that supranational agents appear (at least from a populist, plebiscitary perspective) to enjoy an unusual degree of freedom from the ultimate political sanction in the administrative state—specific legislative deauthorization.

But it should also be stressed that, even in national systems, such a deauthorization (in its most extreme form, a vote of no confidence in the government or minister) "is a blunt and very costly instrument and therefore not likely to be used except in exceptional circumstances."[21] Thus, I tend to agree with Harlow and Rawlings that it is "by no means clear that sanction is an essential element in [administrative] accountability," not merely because it "is very often illusory."[22] Rather, the focus of legitimation in administrative governance today relates much more to "the allocation of burdens of reason-giving" and to "resistance norms" than outright sanction.[23] Even within national administrative states, the focus today is much more on raising the "enactment costs" of delegated rulemaking, primarily through procedural and substantive requirements that can be monitored in less direct ways.[24] In this sense, the difference between administrative institutions nationally and supranationally is, I would suggest, one of degree but not of character.

✥ Beyond Delegation?: Density, Democracy, and Polycentric Constitutionalism in the European Union

By contrast, the difference between European institutions and the strongly legitimated bodies of constitutional democracy on the national level amounts

---

20. Raunio and Hix (2000), 154.

21. Auel (2007b), 502. Indeed, an element of the postwar constitutional settlement was specifically to make it more difficult for the legislature to take these sorts of actions, thus rendering the executive more political secure. See Chapter 2, nn. 86–87 and accompanying text.

22. Harlow and Rawlings (2007), 545.

23. See the Introduction, nn. 63–65 and accompanying text.

24. Cf. Stephenson (2008).

to a vast gulf, one not merely of degree but truly one of character. At this point in history, Europeans have found it extremely difficult, if not impossible, to experience supranational governance as democratic or constitutional in itself, despite the existence of a quite stimulating theoretical literature explaining why they should do so. Instead, Europeans see the EU, even if often inarticulately, as fundamentally administrative, with a legitimacy mediated through the institutions of the various Member States.

Still, given the effective autonomy of European governance, one might well ask: "Is it any longer useful to think of the regulatory system in the [EU] in terms of authority 'delegated' from the national level?"[25] I first raised this question in 2002, in response to a then-emerging literature (now vastly more developed) that depicts the regulatory regime in the EU as "beyond delegation."[26] Admittedly the question, at least as I was posing it then, was rhetorical. My aim was simply to draw attention to the key distinction between delegation as a empirical descriptor (often strained, but still useful), and as a normative-legal principle (which, to my mind, remains absolutely essential in understanding European public law).

The claim that the EU is somehow "beyond delegation" persists, in part because it no doubt captures some of the complexity of European governance below the level of nationally mediated legitimation. But that claim also relies on a surprisingly impoverished understanding of EU complexity, most importantly as to its evolution over time. A fuller appreciation requires attention not merely to functional developments but also to their interaction with political and cultural demands, which is essential to the ultimate process of reconciliation and settlement. Figuring prominently in this dynamic interaction have been historically constructed understandings of delegation—the idea that the historically constituted bodies of the Member State serve as the principals in the integration process, and the EU institutions serve ultimately as their agents. Even if this idea is in tension with functional realities, it has deeply shaped the direction of institutional and legal change in European integration over time. Thus, the claim that today we can adequately come to terms with the complexity of European governance without acknowledging the ongoing role of delegation as a normative-legal principle in integration is, it seems to me, wishful thinking.

---

25. Lindseth (2002), 139.

26. See, e.g., Eberlein and Grande (2005).

Recognizing the legal-cultural role of delegation, moreover, is not merely descriptively helpful but normatively attractive in the effort to reconcile the functional demands of integration with the broadly held desire to preserve some semblance of national democracy and constitutionalism in a historically recognizable sense. In recent years, there has been a decided turn toward administrative law categories in the scholarly literature on European governance, at least descriptively.[27] But there has been little effort to appreciate the full normative and historical implications of integration's fundamentally administrative character. Rather, the literature has remained strangely attached, either explicitly or implicitly, to the idea that European governance somehow could or should be autonomously legitimated in "democratic" and "constitutional" terms, apart from representative government on the national level, to justify the scope of its autonomous regulatory power.

The work of Charles Sabel, the highly innovative theorist of "experimentalist" governance in the EU, both exemplifies this attachment while also suggesting its limitations. Writing with a string of collaborators (Joshua Cohen, Oliver Gerstenberg, William Simon, and Jonathan Zeitlin),[28] Sabel has frankly acknowledged that, to achieve autonomous legitimacy in European governance, nothing less than "a radical re-definition of our democratic and constitutional ideals" would be required.[29] Sabel has summed up the necessary transformation as "directly-deliberative polyarchy," whose functional emergence he believes is already well underway in Europe, offering the possibility of a "radical, participatory democracy with problem-solving capacities useful under current conditions and unavailable to representative systems."[30]

Sabel takes as a given "the failures of representative democracy" and thus seeks the "generalisation of deliberative problem-solving arrangements"[31]— most importantly, the open method of coordination (OMC), complex interactions among networked European and national agencies, peer review, decentralized "learning," and the like—all as elements in an alternative and potentially democratic framework for the EU.[32] The essence of Sabel's project

---

27. This literature is vast. See, e.g., the contributions in Weatherill (2007); Egeberg (2006); Hofmann and Türk (2006); Kassim et al. (2001) and Kassim et al. (2000).

28. See, e.g., Cohen and Sabel (1997), (2004), and (2005); Gerstenberg and Sabel (2002); Sabel and Simon (2006); and Sabel and Zeitlin (2008).

29. Gerstenberg and Sabel (2002), 291.

30. Cohen and Sabel (1997), 313.

31. Ibid., 317.

32. See generally Sabel and Zeitlin (2008).

has been to convince Europeans that their emergent forms of governance can still be understood in democratic terms, even if they deviate radically (and in his mind appropriately) from the institutional forms of representative democracy within the nation-state.[33]

If the reader discerns in Sabel's thinking some traces of the same functionalist spirit that animated scholarly discourse about law and governance in the interwar period, this is no accident. Like the interwar functionalists before him, Sabel is attempting to capture, in theoretical terms, the democratic potential of what he sees as "jurisgenerative social development"—something he readily contrasts with the lagging, formal manifestations of public law and representative democracy that purportedly preoccupy more traditionally minded lawyers and judges.[34] If, however, Sabel's disdain for traditional public lawyers is palpable,[35] he nonetheless acknowledges the need for a kind of legal reconciliation between the old and the new:

Many of the great crises of the development of democracy—the New Deal first and foremost—result from the clash between sub-national advances in governance [or in the European case, supranational advances in governance] and the existing frame of national democracy. The crises are resolved, when they are, by some adjustment of the frame, and the advance that permits a synthesis of the two.[36]

The issue, however, thus becomes: What kind of synthesis is likely to emerge in the case of European governance, both in terms of "democracy" and "constitutionalism," however modified? Will it look more like the system that Sabel anticipates, one that, in his view, cannot be said even to "operate in the state's shadow,"[37] in other words is truly and fully autonomous? Or will it follow the trends outlined here, built on a reconciliation between functional autonomy and normative oversight by national institutions understood as

---

33. See, e.g., Gerstenberg and Sabel (2002); Cohen and Sabel (2004); and Sabel and Simon (2006).

34. Sabel and Simon (2006), 397–403.

35. Sabel and Simon (2006), 403, likening lawyers—"especially administrative lawyers"—to "the unlikely creatures who prosper in the crevices of Antarctic glaciers or the boiling spume of deep-ocean volcanoes that seem utterly inimical to life."

36. Sabel and Simon (2006), 403.

37. Sabel and Zeitlin (2008), 305.

democratically and constitutionally legitimate in a historically and culturally recognizable sense?

Sabel's recent contributions, particularly as to the autonomously democratic potential of "experimentalist" governance, suggest an increasing degree of hesitation in his own thinking, at least as compared to his earlier robust defense of directly-deliberative polyarchy in autonomously democratic terms.[38] "Whether the EU's deliberative decision making," he now writes, "can accredit itself as legitimate by the emergent standards of some alternative deliberative democracy remains a question even for those who strongly suspect that it will turn out to be so."[39] Indeed, he demonstrates a surprising willingness, where needed, to defend European governance in quite orthodox terms, as anchored in democratically legitimate grants of authority from the Member States under the enabling treaties.[40] Moreover, he acknowledges that, by its very density and complexity, European governance seems to "deviat[e] from the norms of representative democracy and principal–agent accountability" and thus "appear[s] to deliver decision making into the hands of a technocratic elite, whose potentially self-interested manipulations are cloaked in the robes of dispassionate deliberation."[41]

Sabel's response to this concern, however, is actually quite typical of contemporary discussions in European governance:[42] He looks to innovations in *administrative* procedure, notably increased participation and transparency rights in rulemaking processes, as a means of checking technocratic overreaching.[43] Although he was once prepared to suggest that such rights could constitute a kind of democratic legitimation "within the review processes themselves,"[44] he no longer seems as willing to do so. Rather, his "claim is not [that] the new architecture of [European governance] is itself intrinsically democratic, but rather that it destabilises entrenched forms of

---

38. See, e.g., Cohen and Sabel (1997), Gerstenberg and Sabel (2002); and Sabel and Zeitlin (2008).

39. Sabel and Zeitlin (2008), 273.

40. Cohen and Sabel (2004), 161.

41. Sabel and Zeitlin (2008), 312–13.

42. See, e.g., Majone (2001a), 265–67; Joerges and Neyer (1997), 283–85; see also Curtin (2009), chaps. 8–10.

43. Sabel and Zeitlin (2008), 313–15; see also Sabel and Simon (2006), 402.

44. Sabel and Simon (2006), 402.

authority—starting with, but not limited to, technocratic authority—in ways that may clear the way for an eventual reconstruction of democracy."[45]

The erosion of the autonomously democratic thrust in Sabel's thinking suggests the great difficulties ahead for those who might seek a new understanding of European governance in novel "democratic" terms apart from representative government on the national level. Without a recognition of the fundamental role still played by national mechanisms of legitimation, European public law would appear to be headed toward its own "political-theoretical cul-de-sac."[46] Mediated legitimacy, Sabel himself seems to imply, remains essential at some point.[47] And yet Sabel's desire to "clear the way for an eventual reconstruction of democracy" still appears strongly biased in favor of a deficit view of the EU's democratic challenges, one that can and should be resolved autonomously, outside the legitimating framework of national representative democracy. Little in Sabel's scholarship over the last decade has suggested a rethinking of the relationship between European governance and national government—little, in other words, that seeks to address what is increasingly, if inarticulately, perceived as a *democratic disconnect* between Europe and the nation-state, not a democratic deficit.[48]

This tension between the deficit and disconnect views of the EU's democratic challenges in fact has a direct bearing on what we might expect from an expansion of administrative-style transparency and participation rights in European governance. Will such rights serve as part of "an eventual reconstruction of democracy" in novel, nonhierarchical, non-"representative" terms, per Sabel? Or do they exist to reinforce *existing* means of democratically legitimate oversight by institutions of representative government that are still largely national, reducing information costs and allowing traditional democratic principals on the national level to oversee their increasingly far-flung administrative agents more effectively? The more persuasive social science on administrative procedure generally, not to mention the historical record regarding the evolution of EU procedures specifically, strongly favors

---

45. Sabel and Zeitlin (2008), 313.

46. See Chapter 2, n. 55 and accompanying text.

47. Cohen and Sabel (2004), 161; see also Sabel and Zeitlin (2008), 274 ("the framework goals, metrics, and procedures themselves are *periodically revised by the actors who initially established them*, augmented by such new participants whose views come to be seen as indispensable to full and fair deliberation") (emphasis added).

48. See Chapter 5, nn. 228–230 and 292–294 and accompanying text.

the second view.[49] As we saw in Chapter 5, an administrative-style procedural code developed in the EU in the late 1990s and early 2000s primarily in response to pressures *from the national level* for more effective oversight and compliance with the principle of subsidiarity.[50]

Sabel's depiction of a novel and autonomous "constitutionalism" to coincide with Europe's novel "democracy" also seems deeply tenuous in light of the historical record. Sabel strongly suggests that the constitutional foundations of European governance must now be decoupled *normatively* from principal-agent thinking—if not entirely, then nearly. In his view, the constitutional legitimacy of regulatory norms cannot (and should not) be grounded in "a pedigree extending from a sovereign people assembled in the electorate through a legislative act as eventually adjusted by administrative

---

49. See, e.g., McCubbins and Schwartz (1987 [1984]). See also Lindseth (2001), 161, n. 69, citing McCubbins and Schwartz (1987 [1984]): "From a principal-agent perspective, transparency and participation rights can be understood as forms of 'fire-alarm oversight,' that is, a way in which legislatures enlist private interests and the courts in the broader project of reducing the inevitable agency costs which flow from delegation." I am not adopting the stronger claim of McCubbins et al. (1987) that administrative procedure somehow "stacks the deck" for favored constituencies, a view that has been questioned conceptually and empirically. See, e.g., Mashaw (1990), Balla (1998); for further overviews, see Rose-Ackerman (2007), xvi-xvii; and Miller (2005), 214–15. Rather, I am relying on the more modest claim that transparency and participation rights in administrative procedure, rather than constituting an alternative, novel, nonhierarchical form of democratic participation, as much or more serve to reinforce oversight by traditional representative institutions.

50. See Chapter 5, nn. 44–48 and accompanying text. Indeed, pressures from the national level arguably account for many of the forms of purported new governance on which Sabel places great weight. For Sabel, the open method of coordination (OMC) is the best example of the "recursive properties of the EU's new experimentalist governance architecture," Sabel and Zeitlin (2008), 289, particularly its "decentralized specification of standards, disciplined by systematic comparison." Cohen and Sabel (2004), 158. In actuality, the prime motivation behind the development of the OMC, studies suggest, was "to prevent a shift of competences from the national to the EU level" on issues of high salience such as employment. See de Ruiter (2008), 898. Moreover, due to its deeply executive-technocratic character, "the OMC is far from meeting the criteria of participatory or deliberative democracy." Benz (2007), 514. As to European agencies, Sabel eyes these as part of a new, networked administrative structure "not built on a 'core of command-and-control,' and [which] cannot be because it does not operate in the state's shadow." Sabel and Zeitlin (2008), 305. But for those who have carefully examined the politics behind the establishment of European agencies, the Commission proposed their creation aware "that additional transfer of power and resources to the European Commission would be unacceptable to the Council of Ministers"—which, in turn, "limited the scope of [the agencies'] authority and demanded that they be controlled by member state appointees." Kelemen (2002), 95. Thus, it is quite plausible to argue, even if Sabel resolutely doubts it, that "what to many governance analysts may appear as a shift *away from* government may turn out to be a path *towards* government." Goetz (2008), 271–72 (emphasis in original).

elaboration."[51] That legitimacy *cannot* be so grounded, he maintains, because of the yawning gap between this pedigree view and the functional realities of diffusion and fragmentation of normative power. And it *should not* be so grounded because any effort to realize such a pedigree linkage would unacceptably interfere with the problem-solving capacities of the new forms of purportedly experimentalist governance, while also deferring the necessary transformations in prevailing notions of legitimacy in a more directly deliberative and polyarchical direction.

My "critically conservative—or conservatively critical"[52] response to this sort of argument is twofold. First, it is not at all clear that administrative governance, as it has evolved particularly over the last quarter of the century, has proven incapable of adapting to the functional requirements of diffuse and fragmented problem-solving. Just as the postwar constitutional settlement surmounted contradictions that Carl Schmitt in the interwar period had claimed were "insurmountable,"[53] so too can European governance achieve a reconciliation of supranational regulatory power and national democratic and constitutional legitimacy, without decoupling itself entirely from the foundations of representative government on the national level. Much of what Sabel claims must now be incorporated into a new constitutionalism is already well reflected in the evolving features of administrative governance—the functional dissolution of boundaries between legislation, execution, and adjudication; the corresponding transformations in the nature of the rule of law; and the emergence of reason-giving as a basic element of dynamic accountability.[54] None of this leads inexorably to the conclusion that we must now abandon the ideal of representative government on the national level as the privileged source of constitutional legitimacy in the European regulatory system.

Nor *should* it, normatively, lead to that conclusion, bringing me directly to my second response to Sabel's argument. It is not merely that a pedigree understanding (that is, one normatively grounded in the idea of delegation) remains essential to the popular capacity of Europeans to experience governance in the EU as democratic and constitutional in a historically recognizable, if evolving, sense. It is also that the alternative posed by Sabel (to paraphrase

---

51. Sabel and Zeitlin (2008), 273; see also Sabel and Simon (2006), 398; Gerstenberg and Sabel (2002), 311.

52. Walker (2006b), 355, commenting on Lindseth (2006).

53. Schmitt (1938 [1936]), 204. See Chapter 2, nn. 47–65 and accompanying text.

54. Sabel and Simon (2006), 409–10; see also ibid., 399 and 400.

Neil Walker in another context) presents disturbing "steering or co-ordination problems. . . . If original authority is found in [diffuse and fragmented 'new governance' mechanisms alone], by whose authority or by what mechanism are these different co-ordinating authorities co-ordinated?"[55] Sabel offers little more than a profound faith in the decentralized forms of experimentalist governance themselves, disciplined by transparency, participation, and reason-giving, to generate sound outcomes in various regulatory domains. "Input legitimacy" is not merely transformed, it is abandoned, with little to replace it but the promise of more "output legitimacy," to put it in the terminology of Fritz Scharpf.[56] This would seem to be a formula for a truly Weberian nightmare—technocratic domination without the possibility of any kind of plebiscitary leadership, strongly legitimated via representative government, capable of breaking through the varied and often questionable claims of expertise, whether within or beyond the state.[57] What would emerge would be, in the words of one political philosopher, a *Sektoralstaat*— that is, "a polity in which different policy spheres are governed by those most closely affected by or interested in them, a development with dire implications for democratic rule, legal authority, and material equality in Europe's future."[58]

As a de facto means of resisting this eventuality, European public law has struggled to retain an understanding of European governance as grounded normatively in *delegation* from the constituted bodies of the Member States severally, as the continuing cultural loci of democratic and constitutional legitimacy in the European system. This is not to deny Sabel's quite accurate insight that, as a descriptive matter, "the very distinction between principal and agent is [often] confounded" in modern governance.[59] But it is to acknowledge that, on the level of political culture, representative government on the national level remains the *privileged* expression of democratic and constitutional legitimacy in the EU, deeply shaping political responses to the challenges of institutional design over time. This, I admit, carries with it its own potential dangers of functional disuniformity in the application of

---

55. Walker (2006b), 355.

56. See generally Scharpf (1999).

57. Cf. Weber (1978 [1922]), 2:1451–59 ("Plebiscitary Leadership and Parliamentary Control," in "Appendix II: Parliament and Government in a Reconstructed Germany (A Contribution to the Political Critique of Officialdom and Party Politics)").

58. McCormick (2007), 177.

59. Sabel and Zeitlin (2008), 304.

European law in the Member States (a topic I take up in the next section). But it does seem to be the best way of "maintaining the connection" between each of the constitutional institutions and "the paradigmatic function which [each such institution] alone is empowered to serve," while also "retaining a grasp on [supranational administrative governance] as a whole that respects our commitments to the control of law."[60]

It is also for this reason that I resist the labels "multilevel constitutional-ism" or "constitutional pluralism" to describe the current legal reality in Europe, despite the sophisticated efforts by eminent scholars to develop these rubrics.[61] My concern is not simply semantic. Rather, these labels suggest a degree of autonomous constitutional legitimacy in the suprana-tional level that is still in serious doubt, both politically and culturally. Europe is not yet a system of multiple or plural forms of strongly legitimated governance levels, some national, others supranational, interacting with each other. In this critical respect, the supranational level is lacking. The events of the last decade, and indeed of the last half century, suggest that the autonomous legitimacy of European governance remains "weak" as com-pared to the nation-state.[62] Although regulatory power may have suprana-tionalized to a considerable extent (in certain domains), democratic and constitutional legitimacy has not. Legitimacy resources, if not control, remain concentrated among the various constitutional centers at the national level and below; they do not yet extend upward to the supranational level, even if significant normative power has upwardly migrated for sound functional reasons.

To the extent that supranational governance enjoys any autonomous legitimacy of its own, that legitimacy remains primarily derivative—in a word, "delegated," or perhaps "mediated"—following the example of the post-war constitutional settlement of administrative governance.[63] It is for this reason that European governance is better described as a system of *polycen-tric constitutionalism*, stressing the failure of constitutional legitimacy to shift to the supranational level in a multilevel or plural sense.

---

60. Strauss (1987), 488; see the Introduction, n. 67 and accompanying text.

61. See, e.g., Pernice (2009); Walker (2002); see also Menon and Weatherill (2008), 410–11.

62. See Lindseth (2001).

63. For reflections on the notion of "weak" constitutionalism in the EU, see Lindseth (2001).

✸ Legitimation and Control Revisited: Toward a European Conflicts Tribunal?

Administrative governance over the last half century has depended, this study has maintained, on the critical distinction between control and legitimation of otherwise (relatively) autonomous forms of regulatory power. Even within national administrative states, some observers suggest hierarchical control still prevails over administrative actors.[64] In my view, however, the breakdown in the capacity for outright control has also made itself felt in modern administrative nation-states as well, particularly over the last several decades.[65] But the phenomenon of Europeanized administrative governance—the diffusion and fragmentation of regulatory power both within and beyond the state—has undoubtedly accentuated, even strained, the legitimacy-control distinction to a considerable extent. And although nationally grounded oversight mechanisms are one response to this problem, they are also an inevitably imperfect one. Here the distinction between control and legitimacy has real bite, particularly in the face of the increasing density and complexity of a Europeanized administrative governance.[66] This in turn feeds anti-EU discourse in national law and politics that we encountered at the very outset of this study.[67] National legitimating mechanisms do *much* to reconcile "Europe" and the nation-state, one might say, but they can never do so *fully.*

For this reason, in the context of integration it is becoming increasingly clear that the Member States cannot relinquish individualized control entirely, at least not at the outer margins where delegation implicates the continued democratic character of the nation-state itself. At these very outer margins, mere legitimation must cede to genuine control—that is, resistance norms must cede to validity norms[68]—in the interest of preserving some semblance of constitutional democracy on the national level. This is the

---

64. See, e.g., Curtin (2007), 524–25 ("In national political systems, administrative actors, even (quasi-) autonomous ones, exist in a relationship of delegation of powers and of control and accountability with the political actors (government and parliament) and ultimately with the citizens.").

65. See, e.g., Chapter 3, nn. 183–186 and accompanying text.

66. Cf. Curtin (2009), 42, quoting Mair (2004), 73, on the "depoliticization of the Europeanization dimension in the national sphere."

67. See the Introduction, nn. 7–11 and accompanying text.

68. See the Introduction, n. 65 and accompanying text.

implicit lesson of the Spanish *Tribunal Constitucional,* for example, in its 2004 ruling on the now-defunct Constitutional Treaty. There the Court held that the "primacy" of European law governs only within the "scopes of application" to which the Member States have democratically committed themselves in the treaties.[69] The "primacy" of European law, the Court reasoned, is itself ultimately dependent upon, and thus constrained by, the "supremacy" of the national constitution, which forms the basis of the state's supranational commitments in the first place. In the same vein but extending beyond the original enactment are the decisions of national high courts encountered in Chapter 4. These decisions made clear that the right to declare a European norm beyond the scope of the power conferred under the treaties—*Kompetenz-Kompetenz*—is necessary to vindicate the democratic character the Member States' original decisions to delegate.

This *Kompetenz-Kompetenz* jurisprudence stands in defiance of those who might argue, along with Charles Sabel, that supranational "agents are [somehow] expected to revise their mandates in the course of implementing them."[70] This claim is no doubt true as to numerous functional policy details but cannot possibly be true as to overarching policy directions, at least not normatively. In its essentials, such a claim amounts to an updated and more sophisticated form of the functional spillover that neofunctionalist theorists

---

69. See DTC 1/2004, at part 4 (ruling on the constitutionality on the Treaty establishing a constitution for Europe), http://www.tribunalconstitucional.es/es/jurisprudencia/restrad/Paginas/DTC122004en.aspx (last visited Nov. 10, 2009).

70. Sabel and Simon (2006), 398. It should perhaps be unsurprising that a context that Sabel has celebrated as a realm of new governance—fundamental rights monitoring across the Member States—may prove precisely the one in which the German courts first enforce *Kompetenz-Kompetenz.* Compare Sabel and Simon (2006), 410 ("in this system the varying national practices of rights enforcement . . . create the benchmarks or precedents against which the others are judged. . . . Member states of the EU are held to constitutional account; but the standards of accountability are set by their peers, on the basis of a comprehensive evaluation of practice") with Herzog and Gerken (2008) (critiquing the analysis of the ECJ in *Mangold* finding that age discrimination is a "general principle of Community law" on the basis of a survey of Member State law); for further detail see Pop (2008). A complaint against *Mangold* is currently pending before the *Bundesverfassungsgericht:* see BverfG, Constitutional Complaint, 2 BvR 2661/06 (against the judgment of the Federal Labour Court, 7 AZR 500/04, 26 Apr. 2006; BAG, 23 Neue Zeitschrift für Arbeitsrecht 1162 (2006)); see also Schorkopf (2009), 1239–40. [The controversy over *Mangold* will no doubt intensify in Germany following the recent decision of the ECJ's Grand Chamber in *Kücükdeveci.* See Case C-555/07, *Seda Kücükdeveci v. Swedex GmbH & Co. KG,* judgment of 19 Jan. 2010, http://eur-lex.europa.eu/LexUriServ/LexUriServ.do?uri=CELEX:62007J0555:EN:HTML (reaffirming *Mangold* both on the basis of "general principles of law" as well as the entry into force of the Charter of Fundamental Rights under the Treaty of Lisbon).]

in the 1950s and 1960s believed would become the driving force behind the integration process over time. These theorists, like Sabel much later, assigned a "leading role to the technocrat" pursuing policies that political actors would ultimately be compelled to follow.[71]

But just as technocratic autonomy did not emerge in quite the way that neofunctionalists expected in the 1950s and 1960s, so too is it unlikely to emerge today, or at least certainly not without a profound cultural struggle, bits of which we witnessed in the last decade. European public law has tolerated and will no doubt continue to tolerate significant discretion for its supranational agents in the interest of integration. But the idea that those agents may then freely "revise their mandates in the course of implementing them," without approval (either implicit or explicit) from the national level,[72] is, for the moment, a normative step too far. To use the evocative words of Giandomenico Majone, such "[i]ntegration by stealth is no longer a viable strategy."[73] In significant part, this is true because of the increasingly "constraining impact of mass publics," whose mobilization over the last decades "has transformed the process of European integration. Whereas elites negotiated with an eye to efficiency and distributional consequences, publics appear to be swayed by identity as well as by economic concerns."[74]

Perhaps this means, as Paul Krugman has claimed, that Europe is condemned to being "structurally weak in a time of crisis."[75] This diagnosis arguably confuses, however, symptom and deeper condition. The activism that Krugman believes Europe needs in order to address economic crisis also demands a degree of autonomous legitimacy that, at this point in their history, European institutions simply do not possess. As the Italian political theorist Stefano Bartolini presciently warned in 2005: "[T]he risk of miscalculating the extent to which true legitimacy surrounds the European institutions and their decisions . . . may lead to the overestimating of the capacity of the EU to overcome major economic and security crises."[76] The mismatch

---

71. See, e.g., Chapter 3, nn. 7–12 and 50–51 and accompanying text.

72. Cf. Stone Sweet (2004), 17–18 (a modern-day neofunctionalist recognizing the role of national executives in ratifying the process of spillover).

73. Majone (2005), 220.

74. Hooghe and Marks (2008), 116, 118. For various observations on the challenges to the European project from the perspective of identity politics, see, e.g., Ladeur (2008); Risse (2001); and Shore (2000).

75. Krugman (2009).

76. See Bartolini (2005), 175.

between regulatory power and governing legitimacy, in other words, almost certainly leads to a downward pressure on the scope of competences that may plausibly be exercised by European institutions alone, without significant national oversight and even control.[77] Functional requirements have been able to take integration "only so far."[78] A specifically *political* mobilization in favor of much greater integration, as well as the concomitant *cultural* adjustments by a European "people" as a whole, must also occur for "Europe" to attain the autonomous legitimacy implied in Krugman's demand for greater activism. Such a mobilization will take the process of European integration out of the realm of administrative governance and place it squarely within that of constitutionalization—but again, this has not yet occurred.

Without making a specifically causal claim (that is, one suggesting that courts are "following popular opinion," so to speak), one can nevertheless see manifestations of this developing identity politics in the realm of national constitutional law, more specifically in national high court jurisprudence over *Kompetenz-Kompetenz*. In the German Lisbon Decision of 2009, for example, the Federal Constitutional Court explicitly made the connection between "*ultra vires* review and identity review" and the need to prevent the application of European rules "that transgress competences or that violate constitutional identity."[79] For observers attached to idea of the European Court of Justice as the final arbiter of legality in the EU (whether for functional or "constitutional" reasons), the prospect of national courts interposing

---

77. No domain proves this point better than that of tax harmonization. See, e.g., Graetz and Warren (2006), 1226–36. But consider also the case of the relatively weak regulatory powers of European "agencies." See Dehousse (2008). Indeed, detailed studies reveal that, historically in the EU, there is in fact a "general bias of delegation in favor of national authorities," and that, under EU legislation, "the Commission is generally more constrained than the member states." Franchino (2004), 286.

78. Hooghe and Marks (2008), 115–16 (asserting that "a functional logic gets us only so far" in understanding the integration phenomenon, in particular in light of "the constraining impact of mass publics—a recent development which . . . has exerted a serious drag on integration."); see also Majone (2009), 234 ("If one clear lesson emerges from the last fifty years, it is that in the age of mass democracy elite-led integration can only go so far."); as well as Majone (2005), 220 ("Integration by stealth is no longer a viable strategy."). [But note also, as the response to the euro crisis in spring 2010 demonstrated, functional demand can still push integration very far indeed, *if* that functional demand is acute and intense enough (such as the fear of contagion of the debt crisis). Nevertheless, it remains to be seen how the resulting "special purpose vehicle" and mammoth bailout fund established in May 2010, or proposals for supranational oversight of national budgets, will fare in the inevitable process of reconciliation that ensues. Cf. the Introduction, nn. 37–38 and accompanying text.]

79. German Lisbon Decision (2009), para. 241.

themselves in this way "is dangerous for the uniformity of EU law, and inimical to the very spirit of integration."[80] But there is good reason to believe, at least based on the language and behavior of the national high courts themselves over the last several decades, that such fears may be overblown.

First of all, the basic deference doctrine that emerged in the 1980s clearly remains in place, even after the recent wave of decisions reiterating *Kompetenz-Kompetenz* (just as it remained after the Maastricht Decision of 1993).[81] Moreover, any successful challenge on the basis of the ultimate supremacy of national constitutional law would probably arise only in extreme circumstances (in fact, no successful challenge of this type has ever been mounted, although that certainly does not preclude one from succeeding in the future).[82] The German Lisbon Decision, for example, speaks only of controlling "obvious transgressions," for which "legal protection cannot be obtained at the Union level,"[83] thus implying an obligation first to exhaust supranational remedies, to use U.S. administrative law terminology.

---

80. Baquero Cruz (2008), 415.

81. See Chapter 4, nn. 202–205 and accompanying text. [Note also the judgment of the *Bundesverfassungsgericht* of May 7, 2010, rejecting an application for a preliminary injunction to block German participation in the emergency loan to Greece. In that judgment, the Court reiterated the basic principle of deference, stating that "[a]mong the constitutional organs, it is above all for the Federal Government to make such assessments [whether a loan to Greece is warranted in the circumstances of the financial crisis], which the *Bundesverfassungsgericht* can only control in a limited fashion (e.g., BVerfGE 97, 350, 376)." BVerfG, Case 2 BvR 987/10 of 7 May 2010, pt. B, para. 2(a), http://www.bundesverfassungsgericht.de/entscheidungen/rs20100507_2bvr098710.html (last visited May 8, 2010) (my translation). Whether the Court will be as indulgent with the "special purpose vehicle" and German contribution to the massive bailout fund remains to be seen, although the same principle of deference would seem to apply there as well. The Court may prove significantly less indulgent toward proposals for supranational oversight of national budgets, at least based on statements contained in the German Lisbon Decision (2009), para. 256 ("[a] transfer of the right of the *Bundestag* to adopt the budget and control its execution by the government which would violate the principle of democracy"). For further detail, see Chapter 4, nn. 232-234 and accompanying text.]

82. As of this writing (December 2009), it is my understanding that there are two complaints currently pending before the German Federal Constitutional Court that may present the opportunity. The first is in *Mangold*: see BverfG, Constitutional Complaint, 2 BvR 2661/06 (against the judgment of the Federal Labour Court, 7 AZR 500/04, 26 Apr. 2006; BAG, 23 Neue Zeitschrift für Arbeitsrecht 1162 (2006)). The second is the *Data Retention Case*; see Schorkopf (2009), 1239–40. [As of May 2010, one could add to this list any complaints made to the Court challenging the constitutionality of German participation in loans to Greece, the general bailout fund in defense of the euro (the "special purpose vehicle"), or the adoption of a proposal requiring EU supervision of national budgets, should the latter occur.]

83. German Lisbon Decision (2009), para. 240.

The Court reiterates later that, "[f]actually at any rate, it is no contradiction to the objective of openness towards European law, ... if *exceptionally*, and *under special and narrow conditions*, the Federal Constitutional Court declares European Union law inapplicable in Germany" (emphasis added).[84] Only at the margins, therefore, has the Court reinterpreted the duty of loyal cooperation, on which the old doctrine of European supremacy had been built, to account for this ultimate national right of control.[85]

This is consistent, both in tone and approach, with the positions previously staked out by other national high courts over many decades. The Italian Constitutional Court in *Frontini* (1973) spoke of "an aberrant interpretation" that brings European law unacceptably into conflict with national constitutional supremacy.[86] And in *Granital* (1984) it spoke of the "unlikely possibility" of such a thing ever occurring.[87] Later, in *Fragd* (1989), the Italian Court stated that any such conflict "whilst being highly unlikely, could still happen."[88] One might dismiss these statements as made before the dramatic expansion of supranational regulatory power in the 1990s and 2000s. But even the Czech decision of 2008, ruling on the constitutionality of the Treaty of Lisbon, stated that "interference by the Constitutional Court should come into consideration as ultima ratio, i.e., in a situation where the scope of discretion was clearly exceeded."[89] And in 2009, in response to the last-ditch petition by Eurosceptical senators opposed to the treaty, the Czech Court added that it would only exercise this power in "exceptional cases."[90] The Polish Constitutional Tribunal earlier spoke of "an irreconcilable inconsistency" that "could not be eliminated by means of applying an interpretation which respects the mutual autonomy of European law and national law."[91] This suggests that the reservation of *Kompetenz-Kompetenz* by even the most Eurosceptical of national high courts is tempered by a still strong impulse

---

84. Ibid., para. 340.

85. Ibid., para. 240.

86. [1974] 2 C.M.L.R. at 389.

87. Oppenheimer (1994/2003), 1:651.

88. Ibid., 1:657.

89. Pl. ÚS 19/08, para. 109, http://angl.concourt.cz/angl_verze/doc/pl-19-08.php (last visited June 11, 2009).

90. Pl. ÚS 29/09, para. 150 ("*případech zcela výjimečných*"), http://www.concourt.cz/clanek/GetFile?id=2150 (last visited Nov. 3, 2009) (trans. Google Translate).

91. K18/04, para. 13, as excerpted in Craig and de Búrca (2008), 372.

toward deference, almost certainly in recognition of evident functional concerns over uniformity.

The more detailed formulation of the Danish Supreme Court in its own Maastricht ruling of 1998 may also be helpful here. The Court stated that it should only uphold a challenge to a constitutionally problematic interpretation of European law "if the extraordinary situation should arise that it can be established with the requisite certainty that an EC act which has been upheld by the European Court of Justice is based on an application of the Treaty which lies beyond the transfer of sovereignty brought about by the Act of Accession."[92] Beyond the reference to "the extraordinary situation," there is again built into this reasoning a requirement of exhaustion of supranational remedies—that is, the condition that the act in question be first "upheld by the European Court of Justice"—as well as the operation of a fairly explicit canon of constitutional avoidance (the standard of "requisite certainty"). This suggests that, although national constitutional courts should serve as a "safety-valve that should always remain open,"[93] they will do so only to a very limited extent, while also giving the supranational level an opportunity to avoid the clash in the first instance. The most important consequence of the reservation of ultimate *Kompetenz-Kompetenz*, this further suggests, is not immediately practical but normative over a longer term. The reservation of authority at the outer margins remains available as an (admittedly deep) background constraint—still perhaps primarily as a *resistance norm*—one that could be activated in the future as a validity norm should an extreme and unlikely need arise.

The danger, of course, is that national high courts could become overly aggressive in this area, thus endangering the functional uniformity of European law in an unacceptable way. But the converse is also a concern: The European Court of Justice (ECJ) might continue to confuse the demands for functional uniformity with constitutional supremacy, deciding on key questions (like Member State liability for violations of European law) in ways insufficiently sensitive to the legitimate constitutional autonomy and ultimate supremacy of the national level.[94] This is not to deny the obvious point

---

92. *Carlsen*, as reprinted in Oppenheimer (1994/2003), 2:191.

93. This is the famous description by Léon Aucoc of the *Conseil d'Etat* under the Second Empire. Quoted, e.g., in Lampué (1954), 380; Auby and Drago (1962), 2:419.

94. See, e.g., Case C-224/01, *Gerhard Köbler v. Republik Österreich*, 2003 E.C.R. I-10239, paras. 52–53 (holding that a Member State may incur liability on the basis of the judicial decision of a national court of last instance even as the Court adjusted the normal

that a national high court's misinterpretation of EU law, without a reference to the ECJ, can constitute a breach of a Member State's obligations under the treaties.[95] Rather it is simply to point out that, where that purported violation of EU flows from principled belief that the EU has exceeded the scope of its delegated competence, then national law should, in that narrow circumstance, prevail.

The challenge then is to manage and balance, both substantively and procedurally, the legitimate concerns of both legal orders (the EU in legal uniformity and compliance, the Member States in preserving ultimate democratic and constitutional legitimacy). Substantively, European law needs to acknowledge *explicitly* the inherent right of national high courts to *Kompetenz-Kompetenz*, which, if properly exercised, should never be understood as a breach of the duty of loyal cooperation under European law.[96] Procedurally, the sensible approach may also require the establishment of an additional tribunal, composed of judges from both national high courts and the ECJ, with limited jurisdiction to review rulings of the Court of Justice on questions of competence, subject to the substantive and procedural conditions precedent of the sort suggested by the Danish Supreme Court in 1998.

Over the last two decades, there have been numerous proposals for some kind of "competence court" along these lines.[97] Defenders of the existing system, however, have generally regarded such proposals as not merely conservative in orientation but ultimately destined to undermine the very structures of integration by subjecting the ECJ to review by a body whose defining

---

"sufficiently serious breach" requirement somewhat, stating rather that the national high court must "manifestly infringe the applicable law"); see also Case C-173/03, *Traghetti del Mediterraneo SpA v. Italy*, 2006 E.C.R. I-5177, para. 44 (reaffirming *Köbler*). For an overview, see Craig and de Búrca (2008), 332–37.

95. See, e.g, Case C-154/08, *Commission v. Spain*, judgment 12 Nov. 2009, not yet reported in E.C.R., (in French), http://curia.europa.eu/jurisp/cgi-bin/form.pl?lang=EN&Submit=Submit&numaff=C-154/08 (last visited Nov. 16, 2009).

96. Cf. German Lisbon Decision (2009), para. 240 ("The exercise of this competence of review, which is rooted in constitutional law, follows the principle of the Basic Law's openness towards European Law (*Europarechtsfreundlichkeit*), and it therefore also does not contradict the principle of loyal cooperation (Article 4(3) TEU Lisbon)"). Cf. also the Opinion of Advocate General Kokutt delivered on 4 Sept. 2008, in Case C-185/07, *Allianz*, para. 57 (referring to "the general principle that every court is entitled to examine its own jurisdiction (doctrine of Kompetenz-Kompetenz)"), not yet reported in ECR, http://eur-lex.europa.eu/LexUriServ/LexUriServ.do?uri=CELEX:62007C0185:EN:NOT (last visited Nov. 5, 2009).

97. For an overview, including discussion of my proposal in Lindseth (1999), see Mayer (2001), 601–05.

spirit would be Euroscepticism.[98] What I mean to suggest here, however, is that such an institution, if properly designed, could actually be integration-reinforcing.

Since the 1980s, the national high courts have been working to define the deference they owe to the European Court of Justice as the "lawful judge" of integration.[99] Their effective response has been "a great deal"—subject to the ultimate constitutional limitation of *Kompetenz-Kompetenz*. Emerging out of this jurisprudence has been the understanding of the national-supranational judicial relationship as, in effect, a kind of *dualité de juridiction*, different from its French counterpart in many particulars (no doubt), but nevertheless inspired by a similar principle.[100] The historical struggle at the heart of French state-building over several centuries (the pursuit of national integration in the face of social and territorial divisions) ultimately demanded an autonomous judge to rule on disputes over the legality of state power—the *Conseil d'Etat* and inferior administrative tribunals. Similarly, in the ongoing struggle of the EC/EU to pursue European integration (as against Europe's own centrifugal forces, both social and territorial), integration too has been given an autonomous judge—the European Court of Justice and inferior European tribunals.

In pursuit of their respective goals of integration, both national and supranational, the French administrative judge and the European "administrative" judge each enjoy the right to decide *souverainement* on matters within their jurisdiction. But the comparison to the French *dualité de juridiction* offers an additional helpful analogue: Under the monarchical and imperial regimes that governed France up to 1870, the *Conseil d'Etat* had the power to determine the scope of administrative jurisdiction relative to the ordinary courts—in effect, *Kompetenz-Kompetenz*—subject only to the technical requirement that the head of state retained ultimate authority (*la justice retenue*). In the reform of the *Conseil d'Etat* in 1872 following the collapse of the Second Empire, however, the *Conseil d'Etat* gained the right to decide

---

98. These concerns might not be wholly baseless, as evidenced by the recent campaign of criticism directed at the ECJ by the former German President Roman Herzog, in which calls for a new competence tribunal figured prominently. See, e.g., Herzog and Gerken (2008). Additional articles can be found on the Web site of the Centrum für Europäische Politik (CEP), a conservative German think tank associated with the Friedrich-August-von-Hayek-Stiftung, http://www.cep.eu/en/home/ (last visited Oct. 4, 2009).

99. See Chapter 4, n. 130 and accompanying text.

100. See Chapter 4, nn. 135–144 and accompanying text.

souverainement, without reference to the head of state (*la justice déléguée*),[101] but only by relinquishing *Kompetenz-Kompetenz.* Henceforth, questions of jurisdiction became the responsibility of a separate body—the *Tribunal des conflits*—composed of judges both from the ordinary and administrative systems.[102]

This reform, I suggest, points to a basic principle of administrative justice: Jurisdictions of an administrative character should not enjoy the right to define the scope of their own authority.[103] The same principle should apply to "administrative" justice in its now supranational guise, which emphatically includes the ECJ, not merely as to the legality of supranational norms, but also as to Member State compliance with obligations under supranational law. It is in that latter regard that the authority of the national and the supranational are brought most clearly into legal tension. The competing claims of the ECJ and the national high courts should not be understood as pluralist dialogue of equals, a "conflict between right and right in which there is no praetor."[104] Precisely because of the superior legitimacy resources of the national level, the national high courts have retained the inherent constitutional right to *Kompetenz-Kompetenz*—albeit always subject to the countervailing functional concerns over uniformity, which then translates into a broad obligation of deference.

Given, however, the risks of heightened conflict between the national and the supranational going forward, it may now be time for a new *praetor* to adjudicate these conflicts—what we could call a *European Conflicts Tribunal* (ECT). The ECT would be composed of judges from the ECJ and national high courts, to rule on competence disputes between the national and the supranational levels.[105] The effect of establishing such a tribunal, I would suggest, would be twofold. First, like the establishment of the French *Tribunal des conflits* before it, it would serve as a kind of historical quid pro quo for the ECJ's right to exercise a kind of *justice déléguée,* deciding *souverainement* on matters relating to European integration to which the national judge must generally defer. Second, it would temper the effects of the national high courts' inherent reservation of *Kompetenz-Kompetenz,* lessening its potential

---

101. Chevallier (1970), 200–01.

102. Burdeau (1995), 202.

103. See generally Lindseth (2005a).

104. Beck (2005).

105. For details, see Lindseth (1999), 731–34.

adverse functional impact on European legal uniformity. In my view, the rulings of the ECT would become one of the supranational remedies that a litigant must exhaust before it could ask a national high court to exercise its inherent jurisdiction of *Kompetenz-Kompetenz* under the national constitution.[106] In other words, a national high court cannot be deprived of its right to *Kompetenz-Kompetenz,* but the exercise of that right should still be subject to procedural and substantive conditions precedent, that is, review by a European Conflicts Tribunal under a new body of "supranational conflicts of laws."[107]

The *telos* of such an institution and its legal doctrine would be integration-stabilizing, not Eurosceptical. Its purpose would be to strike a balance between deference to the European courts as the "lawful judge" of integration, on the one hand, and the ultimate responsibility of national high courts to preserve democratic and constitutional legitimacy in a historically recognizable sense, on the other. In this way, the ECT would seek to build directly on the postwar constitutional settlement of administrative governance, as well as on the complex translation of that settlement into supranational terms over the last half century. It would hopefully promote deliberation and reason-giving as an aspect of a European version of the rule of law, requiring that the litigant and national courts "state in *legal* terms [their] objection to [supranational] competence, thus favoring the development of legal principles—including subsidiarity—to define the relative boundary between national and [supranational] authority."[108]

Admittedly, after a decade of institutional distractions, some have thought it is time for European leaders to take "a solemn pledge to avoid tinkering with European institutions."[109] It remains to be seen, however, whether the Treaty of Lisbon constitutes a durable institutional settlement for Europe or

---

106. When I first advanced the idea of an ECT in 1999, I also argued for a political dimension to the proposed procedure—review by the European Council, as well as the ultimate right of opt-out by the Member State should that review not go its way—as, in effect, a modest revival of *la justice retenue* in the integration context. I continue to regard that dimension as desirable (particularly in reinforcing national executive political responsibility for normative outcomes at the supranational level), although I think it unlikely that national executives would ever seek that ultimate responsibility. I would thus no longer regard political review by the European Council and the right of national opt-out as "[t]he most important dimensions" of the ECT procedure. Lindseth (1999), 733.

107. Cf. Joerges (2007) (calling for a deliberative "supranational conflict of laws" in place of the old notion of EU law "supremacy").

108. Lindseth (1999), 732.

109. Presseurop (2009), translating de Volkskrant (2009).

whether the pressure for institutional change will persist—functionally, politically, or culturally. If more change proves necessarily, serious consideration should then be given to the establishment of a new European Conflicts Tribunal. Such a body would in fact be a modest addition to the EU's institutional apparatus, one that would build on integration's administrative character as well as on its deeper grounding in the evolution of administrative governance. The ECT would also constitute, if established, the final step in the convergence of European public law around the legitimating structures of the postwar constitutional settlement of administrative governance.

ℳ Sovereignty, the Nation-State, and Integration History

In a recent perceptive critique, one of Europe's most thoughtful legal scholars described "the maze of *idées reçues* of state-based constitutional dogmatics" that were seemingly on display in the *Kompetenz-Kompetenz* decisions of the last two decades.[110] He claimed these rulings defended "a static and unrealistic image of the nation-state [that] goes against a process that is well under way." He summarized that process through several interrelated assertions—

> that the nation-state, the historical form that most sovereign political communities have taken for a while in Europe, has radically changed; that public power is now almost invariably shared between two or more coordinated levels of government; that sovereignty has become relative and pooled; that it no longer defines the political community.[111]

There is obvious truth in many of these assertions, at least on a functional level. There can be no doubt that the nation-state "has radically changed," and that "public power is almost invariably shared." But it is not at all clear that sovereignty "no longer defines the political community," at least in the political culture of Member State populations outside Europeanized elites. Like so many other descriptions of the national-supranational relationship in the scholarly literature, this one fails to distinguish the functional, political, and cultural dimensions of institutional and legal change. Rather, it

---

110. Baquero Cruz (2008), 408.

111. Ibid.

equates functional change with change itself and ignores its interaction with the cultural and political dimensions, which has given rise to the precisely dynamic of resistance and reconciliation that has been the object of this study.

James Sheehan, one of America's most eminent historians of Europe, has presented a somewhat contrasting view on the current state of national sovereignty. In his presidential address to the American Historical Association in 2005, Sheehan discussed what he called "the problem of sovereignty in European history."[112] He noted the deeply contested nature of state claims to sovereignty over time. Moreover, he stressed how the realm of law, particularly that of constitutional law, had served as a critical terrain for this contestation. But when he turned to the recent era of European integration, Sheehan observed that constitutional theorizing in the EU remained, at this point at least, "so poorly articulated" in significant part because "we continue to view European politics in terms of the state's rise (or fall)."[113] He continued:

> To understand contemporary Europe, we must set aside the teleological narrative of state making [(or unmaking)] and see the Union as the latest, and in many ways the most remarkable, chapter in Europeans' continuing efforts to imagine and organize political space, define and limit political power, calibrate and contest political boundaries. In these efforts, sovereignty remains, but with new meaning.[114]

Throughout the present study, I have explored ways in which European public law has provided a terrain for coming to terms, over time, with administrative power in its new supranational guise. European public law (encompassing both the national and supranational levels) has done so, I suggest, by translating the basic legitimating mechanisms of the postwar constitutional settlement—executive, legislative, and judicial—into workable supranational form. It has further done so by retaining, but also refining, delegation as a normative legal principle. It has been through the legitimating mechanisms and normative commitments of the postwar constitutional settlement that European public law has, in effect, sought to preserve some semblance of the state's "sovereignty," albeit "with new meaning" in light of integration's

---

112. Sheehan (2006).

113. Ibid., 14, citing Weiler (1999a), 8.

114. Ibid., 15.

pressing demands. It is on the level of institutional practice, and not in writings of integration's many stimulating legal theorists, that we can discern, *in law,* how Europeans have struggled over the last half century "to imagine and organize political space, define and limit political power, calibrate and contest political boundaries," to borrow Sheehan's formulation.[115]

Focusing on the legitimating structures and normative principles of administrative governance allows us to avoid the temptation, so strong in the legal-theoretical literature on integration, to assume that supranational regulatory power must somehow demand a new form of "non-statal constitutionalism" or "constitutionalism beyond the state" in order to be properly understood and legitimized. The grip that such concepts have had in the literature (at least until the rejection of the Constitutional Treaty in the French and Dutch referenda in 2005) is perhaps one of the main reasons why "the constitutional theory of contemporary Europe" has remained "so poorly articulated" for so long.[116]

From the perspective of administrative governance, a misplaced assumption animates much of this theorizing—that forms of relatively autonomous regulatory power *require* an equally autonomous capacity for democratic and constitutional legitimation, without mediation by national executives, legislatures, or judiciaries, as in the administrative state. The postwar constitutional settlement of administrative governance suggests that regulatory power and democratic and constitutional legitimacy can in fact be separated, at least to a very significant extent. The concepts of *delegation* and *mediated legitimacy* have provided the normative-legal framework—the "logic of appropriateness"—to justify this state of affairs. And although some may find a delegation-based system of mediated legitimation contrary to what the EU *should be* (an autonomously democratic and constitutional entity in itself), the ensemble of mechanisms explored in this study in fact serve an essential and normatively attractive purpose. Each mechanism has sought to address, albeit from different angles, the seeming contradiction at the heart of European integration: On the one hand, significant normative power has migrated to the supranational level; on the other hand,

---

115. Jan-Werner Müller's description of Rudolf Smend's theory of "social integration" as articulated in the interwar and postwar decades in West Germany would apply equally well to the European context: "Integration was not so much a matter of theoretical reflection, as of empirical observation. The process of integration had to be understood, rather than philosophically constructed." Müller (2003), 69.

116. Sheehan (2006), 14; see also Avbelj (2008b), 24 (describing the "wrong track" of European constitutionalism).

there has been little or no corresponding shift in specifically democratic and constitutional legitimacy out of national bodies—executive, legislative, and judicial—despite the creation of roughly corresponding institutions at the supranational level for precisely this purpose.

Although some commentators may lament the "suboptimal" policy outcomes that flow from the diffuse and fragmented character of governance in the EU,[117] the presence of national legitimating mechanisms has arguably allowed Europeans, over time, to experience the process of integration as something approaching their own, or at least not wholly foreign, despite their struggle with the perceived distance between "Brussels" and their daily lives. This is no small achievement. National oversight is a means of ensuring that the rules and norms produced supranationally do not violate core legal commitments that are understood, historically, to *constitute* one's own legal order in some fundamental way, while nevertheless allowing integration to proceed. Much less than rendering European integration suboptimal, the persistence of national legitimation in European public law may well have been responsible for integration's longer-term durability and success. In this way, integration is developing a "praxis of self-determination that makes sense" in light of both its functional and political-cultural realities, one which may in turn lead to "a deeper theory of sovereignty."[118]

Stressing nationally grounded legitimating mechanisms is not to deny that the system also relies (heavily) on controls operating at the supranational level. These include not just decisions of the supranational judiciary (acting as a kind of supranational *juridiction administrative*) but also mechanisms of hierarchical oversight within the European Commission itself (through "better lawmaking" and antifraud requirements, for example), or through scrutiny by the European Parliament as well as increased transparency and participation rights for outsiders in supranational policy processes. Over time, some of these more supranationally oriented controls, through the European Parliament perhaps, or perhaps through a genuinely democratic supranational executive, may gain an independent capacity to legitimize the regulatory output of European institutions in an autonomously democratic and constitutional sense. As a historian, I will leave it to more

---

117. See Ludlow (2006a), 276 (describing "the phenomenon of 'structural capture' in the decision-making process of the European Union"), citing Baquero Cruz (2005), 209, 211. For a very different take on the "suboptimal performance of the EU," see Majone (2009), 10.

118. Haltern (2007), 51, although I doubt Ulrich Haltern would be altogether satisfied with the institutional settlement described here. See ibid., 52–53.

forward-thinking legal and political theorists to reflect on how and when this might occur.

If supranational institutions do eventually attain some autonomous capacity for self-legitimation, then Europe will have reached a point contemplated by Ernest Renan in 1882 in his classic lecture, "What Is a Nation?" Although Renan spoke there of "nations," his meaning clearly extended to nation-*states,* which he viewed as "not something eternal. They had their beginnings and they will end. A European confederation will very probably replace them." But, as Renan continued, in terms undoubtedly true for his era, "such is not the law of the century in which we are living."[119]

The surprising lesson of the present study may be that Renan's caveat of 1882 retains more than a residual measure of validity in our own era. Despite all that has come to pass in the intervening century and a quarter, a constitutionally autonomous European polity has not (yet) eclipsed the nation-state, at least not in law, and almost certainly not in culture or political practice. What has emerged is not a return to some neomedieval system of "mixed government," as some observers would have it, "characterized by the presence in the legislature of the territorial rulers and of the 'estates' representing the main social and political interests in the polity."[120] Looking to the distant past distorts the fundamentally *modern* nature of Europeanized administrative governance, with its foundations in constitutional self-government as it evolved on the national level over the last two centuries.[121] As a consequence of this history, the democratic nation-state "remains the key contemporary frame of reference for meaningful discussion of constitutionalism" in the EU.[122] As a matter of legitimacy, if not of actual regulatory power, supranational administrative governance remains anchored "in the Member States' constitutional orders."[123]

It has been through the adaptation of the legitimating mechanisms and normative principles of the postwar constitutional settlement of administrative governance that Europe has arguably found its way, pragmatically, to an institutional formula that conforms to Europe's new slogan, "Unity in Diversity." Unity is achieved by way of shared institutions whose character is

---

119. Renan (1996 [1882]), 53.

120. Majone (2005), 46; Majone (2002), 320; see also Wind (2003).

121. See Bartolini (2005); cf. also Rubenfeld (2001).

122. Walker (2006c), 53–54.

123. Joerges (2002), 27.

fundamentally *administrative,* creating nevertheless a deeply *political* system exercising some measure of delegated normative power on the supranational level, operating on behalf of a set of polycentric constitutional principals on the national level. Diversity is preserved, however, precisely because ultimate legitimation (if not control) remains in the polycentric *constituted* bodies of self-government—executive, legislative, and judicial—of the Member States. In this way, European public law has found a way to maintain the connection to the strong expressions of democratic self-rule on the national level in what is otherwise, functionally, a multilevel and even polyarchical system of governance.

Such is the law of the age in which *we* are living—different from Renan's, no doubt, but surprisingly less so than one might suppose after reading the many fascinating, but still ultimately doubtful reflections on the possible forms of democracy or constitutionalism beyond the state that have proliferated in Europe over the last two decades. Nationally grounded legitimating mechanisms in European public law remind us that constitutional democracy still emanates *from the state* in crucial respects. How long that will last, I cannot say. But at this point in European history, these mechanisms are probably best viewed in terms that Ernest Renan would have well understood. They remind us that national institutions are still looked upon, in terms of political culture, as a "guarantee of liberty" in a collective, constitutional sense, something that "would be lost if [Europe] had only one law and only one master."[124]

---

124. Renan (1996 [1882]), 53.

References

Adenauer, Konrad. 1966. *Memoirs 1945–53.* Chicago: Henry Regnery.

———. 1967. *Erinnerungen. 1955–1959.* Stuttgart: Deutsche Verlags-Anstalt.

Alter, Karen J. 1996. The European Court's political power. *West European Politics* 19 (3):458–87.

———. 2001. *Establishing the supremacy of European law: The making of an international rule of law in Europe.* Oxford, UK and New York: Oxford Univ. Press.

Alter, Karen J., and Sophie Meunier-Aitsahalia. 1994. Judicial politics in the European Community: European integration and the pathbreaking *Cassis de Dijon* Decision. *Comparative Political Studies* 26 (4):535–61.

Alter, Karen J., and David Steinberg. 2007. The theory and reality of the European Coal and Steel Community. In *The state of the European Union.* Vol. 8, *Making history: European integration and institutional change at fifty,* ed. Sophie Meunier and Kathleen R. McNamara. Oxford, UK: Oxford Univ. Press.

Amphoux, Jean. 1962. *Le chancelier fédéral dans le régime constitutionnel de la République fédérale d'Allemagne.* Paris: L.G.D.J.

Anderson, Svein S., and Tom Burns. 1996. The European Union and the erosion of parliamentary democracy: A study of post-parliamentary democracy. In *The European Union: How democratic is it?,* ed. Svein S. Anderson and Kjell A. Eliason. London: Sage.

Aron, Raymond. 1956. Esquisse historique d'une grande querelle idéologique. In *La Querelle de la C.E.D.: Essais d'analyse sociologique. Cahiers de la Fondation Nationale des Sciences Politiques, no. 80,* ed. Raymond Aron and Daniel Lerner. Paris: Armand Colin.

Arter, David. 1996. The Folketing and Denmark's "European Policy": The case of an "Authorising Assembly." In *National parliaments and the European Union,* ed. Philip Norton. London and Portland, OR: Frank Cass.

Auby, Jean-Marie, and Roland Drago. 1962. *Traité de contentieux administratif,* vol. 2. Paris: LGDJ.

Auel, Katrin. 2006. The Europeanisation of the German Bundestag: Institutional change and informal adaptation. *German Politics* 15 (3):249–68.

———. 2007a. Adapting to Europe: Strategic Europeanization of national parliaments. In *Democratic governance and European integration: Linking societal and state processes of democracy,* ed. Ronald Holzhacker and Eric Albæk. Cheltenham, UK and Northampton, MA: Edward Elgar.

———. 2007b. Democratic accountability and national parliaments: Redefining the impact of parliamentary scrutiny in EU affairs. *European Law Journal* 13 (4):487–504.

———. 2009. "Servants of the people" or "masters of the government"? Explaining parliamentary behaviour in EU affairs. In *European Union Studies Association, 11th Biennial International Conference,* http://www.unc.edu/euce/eusa2009/papers/auel_02D.pdf (accessed June 17, 2009).

Auel, Katrin, and Arthur Benz. 2005. The politics of adaptation: The Europeanisation of national parliamentary systems. *Journal of Legislative Studies* 11 (3):372–93.

———. 2007. Expanding national parliamentary control: Does it enhance democracy? In *Debating the democratic legitimacy of the European Union,* ed. Beate Kohler-Koch and Berthold Rittberger. Lanham, MD: Rowman and Littlefield.

Auel, Katrin, and Berthold Rittberger. 2006. Fluctuant nec merguntur: the European Parliament, national parliaments, and European integration. In *European Union: Power and policy-making,* ed. Jeremy Richardson. 3rd ed. London: Routledge.

Avbelj, Matej. 2008a. Questioning EU constitutionalisms. *German Law Journal* 9 (1):1–26.

———. 2008b. The pitfalls of (comparative) constitutionalism for European integration. Eric Stein Working Paper 1/2008, http://ssrn.com/abstract=1334216 (accessed July 19, 2009).

Babelparis. 2008. Henri Guaino est-il eurosceptique?, http://paris.cafebabel.com/fr/post/2008/03/15/Henri-Guaino-est-il-eurosceptique (accessed June 8, 2009).

Bache, Ian, and Matthew Flinders, eds. 2004. *Multi-level governance.* Oxford, UK: Oxford Univ. Press.

Badel, Laurence, Stanislas Jeannesson, and N. Piers Ludlow, eds. 2005. *Les Administrations nationales et la construction européenne: Une approche historique (1919–1975).* Brussels: P.I.E.-Peter Lang.

Balakrishnan, Gopal. 2000. *The enemy: An intellectual portrait of Carl Schmitt.* London and New York: Verso.

Balla, Steven. 1998. Administrative procedures and the political control of the bureaucracy. *American Political Science Review* 92:663–73.

Baquero Cruz, Julio. 2002. *Between competition and free movement: The economic constitutional law of the European Community.* Oxford, UK and Portland, OR: Hart.

———. 2005. Beyond competition: Services of general interest and European Community law. In *EU Law and the Welfare State: In Search of Solidarity,* ed. Gráinne De Búrca. Oxford, UK: Oxford Univ. Press.

———. 2006. The Luxembourg Compromise from a legal perspective: Constitutional convention, legal history, or political myth? In *Visions, votes, and vetoes: The empty chair crisis and the Luxembourg Compromise forty years on,* ed. Jean-Marie Palayret, Helen Wallace, and Pascaline Winand. Brussels: P.I.E.-Peter Lang.

———. 2008. The legacy of the *Maastricht-Urteil* and the pluralist movement. *European Law Journal* 14 (4):389–422.

Bartolini, Stefano. 2005. *Restructuring Europe: Centre formation, system building, and political structuring between the nation state and the European Union.* Oxford, UK: Oxford Univ. Press.

Bates, David. 2006. Political theology and the Nazi state: Carl Schmitt's concept of the institution. *Modern Intellectual History* 3 (3):415–42.

Bates, T. St J. N. 1991. European Community legislation before the House of Commons. *Statute Law Review* 12 (1):109–134.

Beck, Gunnar. 2005. The problem of Kompetenz-Kompetenz: A conflict between right and right in which there is no praetor. *European Law Review* 30 (1):42–67.

Becker, Carl L. 1943 [1940]. The Cornell tradition: Freedom and responsibility. In *Cornell University: Founders and the founding*. Ithaca, NY: Cornell Univ. Press.

Bellamy, Richard. 2006. Still in deficit: Rights, regulation, and democracy in the EU. *European Law Journal* 12 (6):725–42.

Benz, Arthur. 2003. Compounded representation in EU multi-level governance. In *Linking EU and national governance*, ed. Beate Kohler-Koch. Oxford, UK and New York: Oxford Univ. Press.

———. 2004. Path-dependent institutions and strategic veto players: National parliaments and the European Union. *West European Politics* 27 (5):875–900.

———. 2007. Accountable multilevel governance by the open method of coordination? *European Law Journal* 13 (4):505–22.

Benz, Arthur, Carol Harlow, and Yannis Papadopoulos. 2007. Introduction. Special issue: Accountability in EU Multilevel Governance, *European Law Journal* 13 (4):441–46.

Berghahn, Volker R. 1986. *The Americanization of West German industry, 1945–1973*. Leamington Spa, NY: Berg.

Bergman, Torbjörn. 2000. The European Union as the next step of delegation and accountability. *European Journal of Political Research* 37 (3):415–29.

Bergman, Torbjörn, and Erik Damgaard, eds. 2000. *Delegation and accountability in European integration: The Nordic parliamentary democracies and the European Union*. London and Portland, OR: Frank Cass.

Bergström, Carl-Fredrik, Henry Farrell, and Adrienne Héritier. 2007. Legislate or delegate? Bargaining over implementation and legislative authority in the EU. *West European Politics* 30 (2):338–66.

Bergström, Carl Fredrik. 2005. *Comitology: Delegation of powers in the European Union and the committee system*. Oxford, UK and New York: Oxford Univ. Press.

Bermann, George A. 1994. Taking subsidiarity seriously: Federalism in the European Community and the United States. *Columbia Law Review* 94 (2):331–456.

———. 2008. National parliaments and subsidiarity: An outsider's view. *European Constitutional Law Review* 4:453–59.

Bermann, George A., Roger J. Goebel, William J. Davey, and Eleanor M. Fox, eds. 1998. *1998 supplement to cases and materials on European Community law (including European Union materials)*. Eagan, MN: West.

Bernard, Nick. 2004. *Multilevel governance in the European Union*. New York: Aspen.

Bertram, Christoph. 1967. Decision-making in the E.E.C.: The management committee procedure. *Common Market Law Review* 5:246–64.

Besselink, Leonard F. M. 2006. National parliaments in the EU's composite constitution. In *National and regional parliaments in the European constitutional order*, ed. Philipp Kiiver. Groningen: Europa Law.

Bevan, Aneurin. 1953. Memorandum. In *Report of the Select Committee on Delegated Legislation, together with the proceeding of the committee, the minutes of evidence, and appendices*. London: H. M. Stationery Office.

Bignami, Francesca. 2005. Creating European rights: National values and supranational interests. *Columbia Journal of European Law* 11:241–353.

Bindi, Federiga. 2008. Italy and the Treaty Establishing a European Constitution: The
decline of a middle-size power? In *The rise and fall of the EU's constitutional treaty*,
ed. Finn Laursen. Leiden, Netherlands and Boston: Martinus Nijhoff.

Blair, Tony. 2000. Speech to Polish Stock Exchange (June 10, 2000), http://www.
number10.gov.uk/Page3384 (accessed July 21, 2009).

Blümel, Barbara, and Christine Neuhold. 2001. The Parliament of Austria: A large
potential with little implications. In *National parliaments on their ways to Europe:
Losers or latecomers*, ed. Andreas Maurer and Wolfgang Wessels. Baden-Baden,
Germany: Nomos.

Borgwardt, Elizabeth. 2005a. *A New Deal for the world: America's vision for human
rights*. Cambridge, MA: Belknap Press.

———. 2005b. Re-examining Nuremberg as a New Deal institution: Politics, culture,
and the limits of law in generating human rights norms. *Berkeley Journal of
International Law* 23:401–62.

Börzel, Tanja A., and Carina Sprungk. 2007. Undermining democratic governance in
the member states? The Europeanization of national decision-making. In
*Democratic governance and European integration: Linking societal and state pro-
cesses of democracy*, ed. Ronald Holzhacker and Eric Albæk. Cheltenham, UK and
Northampton, MA: Edward Elgar.

Bossuat, Gérard. 1995. The French administrative elite and the unification of Western
Europe, 1947–58. In *Building postwar Europe: National decision-makers and
European institutions 1948–63*, ed. Anne Deighton. New York: St. Martin's Press.

Bovens, Mark. 2007. Analysing and assessing accountability: A conceptual framework. Special issue: Accountability in EU Multilevel Governance, *European Law
Journal* 13 (4):447–68.

Braibant, Guy. 1993. Du simple au complexe, quarante ans de droit administratif
(1953–1993). *Etudes et Documents du Conseil d'Etat* 45:409–20.

Bright, Charles, and Michael Geyer. 2002. Where in the world is America?: The history
of the United States in the global age. In *Rethinking America in a global age*,
ed. Thomas Bender. Berkeley: University of California Press.

Brittan, Leon. 1994. *Europe: The Europe we need*. London: Hamish Hamilton.

Brittan, Samuel. 1975. The economic contradictions of democracy. *British Journal of
Political Science* 5 (2):129–59.

Bullen, Roger. 1988. The British government and the Schuman Plan May 1950–March
1951. In *Die Anfänge des Schuman-Plans, 1950/51*, ed. Klaus Schwabe. Baden-
Baden, Germany: Nomos.

———. 1989. Britain and "Europe" 1950–1957. In *Il rilancio dell'Europa e i trattati di
Roma*, ed. Enrico Serra. Brussels: Bruylant.

Bulmer, Simon. 1986. *The domestic structure of European Community policy-making in
West Germany*. New York: Garland.

Burchell, Graham, Colin Gordon, and Peter Miller, eds. 1991. *The Foucault effect:
Studies in governmentality*. Chicago: University of Chicago Press.

Burdeau, François. 1995. *Histoire du droit administratif.* Paris: Presses Universitaires de France.

Burley, Anne-Marie, and Walter Mattli. 1993. Europe before the court: A political-theory of legal integration. *International Organization* 47 (1):41–76.

Calabresi, Steven G., and Christopher S. Yoo. 2008. *The unitary executive: Presidential power from Washington to Bush.* New Haven, CT: Yale Univ. Press.

Calussi, Federiga Bindi, and Stefano B. Grassi. 2001. The parliament of Italy: From benevolent observer to active player. In *National parliaments on their ways to Europe: Losers or latecomers,* ed. Andreas Maurer and Wolfgang Wessels. Baden-Baden, Germany: Nomos.

Camera dei Deputati. 1990. *Costituzione della Repubblica italiana: Deutsch, English, Español, Français, Italiano.* Roma: Segreteria generale.

Carr, Cecil T. 1955. Legislative control of administrative rules and regulations: II. Parliamentary supervision in Britain. *New York University Law Review* 30:1045–56.

Carré de Malberg, Raymond. 1984 [1931]. *La loi, expression de la volonté générale: Etude sur le concept de la loi dans la Constitution de 1875.* Paris: Economica.

Cartabia, Marta. 1998. The Italian Constitutional Court and the relationship between the Italian legal system and the European Union. In *The European Court and National Courts—Doctrine and jurisprudence: Legal change in its social context,* ed. Anne-Marie Slaughter, Alec Stone Sweet, and J. H. H. Weiler. Oxford, UK: Hart.

Carter, Caitriona A. 2001. The parliament of the United Kingdom: From supportive scrutiny to unleashed control? In *National parliaments on their ways to Europe: Losers or latecomers,* ed. Andreas Maurer and Wolfgang Wessels. Baden-Baden, Germany: Nomos.

Cassese, Antonio. 1982. *Parliamentary foreign affairs committees, the national setting: Essays.* Vol. 1, *Control of foreign policy in Western democracies.* Padova: Cedam.

Cassese, Sabino, and Giacinto della Cananea. 1992. The Commission of the European Economic Community: The administrative ramifications of its political development (1957–1967). In *Die Anfänge der Verwaltung der Europäischen Gemeinschaft,* ed. Erk Volkmar Heyden. Baden-Baden, Germany: Nomos.

Cederman, Lars-Erik. 2001. Nationalism and bounded integration: What it would take to construct a European demos. *European Journal of International Relations* 7 (2):139–74.

Chapus, René. 1953. La loi d'habilitation du 11 juillet 1953 et la question des décrets-lois. *Revue du Droit public et de la Science politique en France et a l'Étranger:* 954–1006.

Charlemagne. 2009a. Cameron on the EU: A scary picture he paints. *The Economist,* http://www.economist.com/blogs/charlemagne/2009/05/cameron_on_the_eu_unaccountabl.cfm (accessed June 6, 2009).

———. 2009b. Just for the record. *The Economist,* http://www.economist.com/blogs/charlemagne/2009/06/just_for_the_record.cfm (accessed July 21, 2009).

Chevallier, Jacques. 1970. *L'Elaboration historique du principe de séparation de la juridiction administrative et de l'administration active.* Paris: L.G.D.J.

Chiti, Edoardo. 2000. The emergence of a Community administration: The case of European agencies. *Common Market Law Review* 37:309–43.

Cini, Michelle. 2007. *From integration to integrity: Administrative ethics and reform in the European Commission.* Manchester, UK: Manchester Univ. Press.

Claes, Monica. 2005. Constitutionalising Europe at its source: Europe provisions in national constitutions: Evolution and typology. *Yearbook of European Law 2003* 24:81–125.

———. 2006. *The national courts' mandate in the European constitution.* Oxford, UK: Hart.

———. 2007. The Europeanisation of national constitutions in the constitutionalisation of Europe: Some observations against the background of the constitutional experience of the EU-15. *Croatian Yearbook of European Law and Policy* 3 (3):1–38.

Claes, Monica, and Bruno de Witte. 1998. Report on the Netherlands. In *The European court and national courts—Doctrine and jurisprudence: Legal change in its social context,* ed. Anne-Marie Slaughter, Alec Stone Sweet, and Joseph Weiler. Oxford, UK: Hart.

Clemens, Elisabeth S. 2003. Rereading Skowronek: A precocious theory of institutional change. *Social Science History* 27 (3):443–53.

Clerk of the House. 2005. The European scrutiny system in the House of Commons: A short guide for members of parliament by the staff of the European Scrutiny Committee, www.parliament.uk/documents/upload/TheEuroScrutinySystemintheHoC.pdf (accessed June 17, 2009).

Cohen, Antonin, and Mikael Rask Madsen. 2007. Cold War law: Legal entrepreneurs and the emergence of a European legal field (1945–1965). In *European ways of law: Toward a European sociology of law,* ed. Volkmar Gessner and David Nelken. Oxford, UK and Portland, OR: Hart.

Cohen, Joshua, and Charles F. Sabel. 1997. Directly-deliberative polyarchy. *European Law Journal* 3 (4):313–42.

———. 2004. Sovereignty and solidarity: EU and U.S. In *Public governance in the age of globalization,* ed. Karl-Heinz Ladeur. Aldershot, UK and Burlington, VT: Ashgate.

———. 2005. Global democracy? *International Law and Politics* 37:763–97.

Cohn-Bendit, Daniel, and Henri Guaino. 1999. *La France, est-elle soluble dans l'Europe?* Paris: Albin Michel.

Comité national chargé de la publication des travaux préparatoires des institutions de la Ve République, ed. 1987. *Documents pour servir à l'histoire de l'élaboration de la constitution du 4 octobre 1958.* 3 vols. Paris: La Documentation Française.

Committee on Administrative Tribunals and Enquiries. 1957. Report. London: H. M. Stationery Office. Cmnd. 218.

Committee on Ministers' Powers. 1932. Report. London: Stationery Office. Cmd. 4060.

Conlan, Patricia. 2007. Ireland: Enhanced parliamentary scrutiny of European affairs: But is it effective? In *National parliaments within the enlarged European Union: From "Victims" of integration to competitive actors?,* ed. John O'Brennan and Tapio Raunio. London and New York: Routledge.

Cooper, Ian. 2006. The watchdogs of subsidiarity: National parliaments and the logic of arguing in the EU. *Journal of Common Market Studies* 44 (2):281–304.

Coppolaro, Lucia. 2006. The empty chair crisis and the Kennedy round of GATT negotiations (1962–67). In *Visions, votes, and vetoes: The empty chair crisis and the*

Luxembourg Compromise forty years on, ed. Jean-Marie Palayret, Helen Wallace, and Pascaline Winand. Brussels: P.I.E.-Peter Lang.

Corbel, Pierre. 1969. *Le parlement français et la planification.* Paris: Éditions Cujas.

Corbett, Richard. 1993. *The Treaty of Maastricht from conception to ratification: A comprehensive reference guide.* Harlow, Essex, UK: Longman Current Affairs.

COSAC Secretariat. 2009. History of COSAC, http://www.cosac.eu/en/cosac/ (accessed July 16, 2009).

Court of Justice of the European Communities. 2009. The Treaty of Lisbon and the Court of Justice of the European Union, press release 104/09, Luxembourg, November 30, 2009. http://europa.eu/rapid/pressReleasesAction.do?reference=C JE/09/104&format=HTML&aged=0&language=EN&guiLanguage=en.

Craig, Paul. 2003. EU law and national constitutions: The U.K. In *F.I.D.E. XX Congress London 30 October–2 November 2002, Vol. II Reports and conclusions.* London: British Institute of International and Comparative Law.

Craig, Paul, and Gráinne de Búrca, eds. 2008. *EU law: Text, cases, and materials.* 4th ed. Oxford, UK: Oxford Univ. Press.

Craig, Paul, and Adam Tomkins, eds. 2006. *The executive and public law: Power and accountability in comparative perspective.* Oxford, UK and New York: Oxford Univ. Press.

Cristi, F.R. 1984. Hayek and Schmitt on the rule of law. *Canadian Journal of Political Science* 17 (3):521–35.

Currie, David P. 1993. Separation of powers in the Federal Republic of Germany. *The American Journal of Comparative Law* 41 (2):201–60.

Curtin, Deirdre. 1997. *Postnational democracy: The European Union in search of a political philosophy.* The Hague and London: Kluwer Law International.

———. 2007. Holding (quasi-)autonomous EU administrative actors to public account. *European Law Journal* 13 (4):523–41.

———. 2009. *Executive power of the European Union: Law, practices, and the living constitution.* Oxford, UK and New York: Oxford Univ. Press.

Curtin, Deirdre, and Morten Egeberg. 2008. Tradition and innovation: Europe's accumulated executive order. Special issue: Towards a New Executive Order in Europe?, *West European Politics* 31 (4):639–61.

Cygan, Adam Jan. 2001. *National parliaments and an integrated Europe: An Anglo-German perspective.* The Hague, London, and New York: Kluwer Law International.

Dahl, Robert. 1999. Can international organizations be democratic? A skeptic's view. In *Democracy's edges,* ed. Ian Shapiro and Casiano Hacker-Cordón. London and New York: Cambridge Univ. Press.

Damgaard, Erik, and Henrik Jensen. 2005. Europeanisation of executive-legislative relations: Nordic perspectives. *Journal of Legislative Studies* 11 (3):394–411.

Danish Folketing. 2002. *The European Affairs Committee of the Folketing: Parliamentary control of government policy in the EU.* Copenhagen: EU Information Centre of the Folketing.

Danish National Compromise. 1992. EU Information Centre of the Folketing, http://www.euo.dk/upload/application/pdf/97ca9e4c/EU%20kompromis.pdf (accessed June 15, 2009).

Darnstädt, Thomas. 2009. The future of European democracy. *Spiegel Online International*, July 17, 2009, http://www.spiegel.de/international/europe/ 0,1518,636706,00. html (accessed July 19, 2009).

Daul, Joseph, Martin Schulz, and Guy Verhofstadt. 2009. Joint statement to the press by Joseph Daul, on behalf of the EPP group, Martin Schulz, on behalf of the S&D group, and Guy Verhofstadt, on behalf of the ALDE group, July 14, 2009, http://www.eppgroup.eu/Press/showpr.asp?PRControlDocTypeID=1&PRControl ID=8674&PRContentID=15026&PRContentLG=en (accessed September 21, 2009).

de Búrca, Gráinne. 1995. The quest for legitimacy in the European Union. *Modern Law Review* 59 (3):349–76.

———. 2008a. Developing democracy beyond the state. *Columbia Journal of Transnational Law* 46:221–78.

———. 2008b. Reflections on the EU's path from the Constitutional Treaty to the Lisbon Treaty. Fordham Law Legal Studies Research Paper 1124586, http://papers. ssrn.com/sol3/papers.cfm?abstract_id=1124586#PaperDownload (accessed June 2, 2008).

de Gaulle, Charles. 1965. Conférence de presse de Charles de Gaulle (9 septembre 1965). European Navigator: La première bibliothèque numérique sur l'histoire de l'Europe, http://www.ena.lu/conference_presse_charles_gaulle_septembre_1965-010002252.html (accessed March 27, 2009).

de Ruiter, Rik. 2008. Developing multilevel surveillance in the EU. *West European Politics* 31 (5):896–914.

de Schoutheete, Philippe. 2006. The European Council. In *The institutions of the European Union*, ed. John Peterson and Michael Shackleton. Oxford, UK: Oxford Univ. Press.

de Schoutheete, Philippe, and Helen Wallace. 2002. The European Council. Groupement d'Etudes at de Recherches Notre Europe, Research and European Issues 19, http://www.notre-europe.eu/uploads/tx_publication/Etud19-en.pdf (accessed June 13, 2007).

de Volkskrant. 2009. Eindelijk een verdrag. *de Volkskrant*, November 4, 2009, http:// extra.volkskrant.nl/opinie/artikel/show/id/4474/Eindelijk_een_verdrag (accessed November 8, 2009).

de Witte, Bruno. 1991. Community law and national constitutional values. *Legal Issues in European Integration* 18(2):1–22.

———. 1995. L'encadrement communautaire des services publics: le chevauchement des notions d'Etat et d'entreprise. In *Les mutations du droit de l'administration en Europe: pluralisme et convergences*, ed. Gérard Marcou. Paris: L'Harmattan.

———. 1998. Sovereignty and European integration: The weight of legal tradition. In *The European court and national courts—Doctrine and jurisprudence: Legal change in its social context*, ed. Anne-Marie Slaughter, Alec Stone Sweet, and Joseph Weiler. Oxford, UK: Hart.

———. 2002. The closest thing to a constitutional conversation in Europe: The semi-permanent treaty revision process. In *Convergence and divergence in European public law*, ed. Paul Beaumont, Carole Lyons, and Neil Walker. Oxford, UK and Portland, OR: Hart.

———. 2003. Do not mention the word: Sovereignty in two Europhile countries: Belgium and the Netherlands. In *Sovereignty in transition,* ed. Neil Walker. Oxford, UK and Portland, OR: Hart.

Dehousse, Renaud. 2008. Delegation of powers in the European Union: The need for a multi-principals model. *West European Politics* 31 (4):789–805.

Dell, Edmund. 1995. *The Schuman plan and British abdication of leadership in Europe.* Oxford, UK: Oxford Univ. Press.

Denza, Eileen. 1993. Parliamentary scrutiny of community legislation. *Statute Law Review* 14 (1):56–63.

DiMaggio, Paul J., and Walter W. Powell. 1991. The iron cage revisited: Institutional isomorphism and collective rationality in organizational fields. In *The new institutionalism in organizational analysis,* ed. Walter W. Powell and Paul J. DiMaggio. Chicago: University of Chicago Press.

Dowding, Keith. 2000. Institutionalist research on the European Union: A critical review. *European Union Politics* 1 (1):125–144.

Dubin, Martin David. 1983. Transgovernmental processes in the League of Nations. *International Organization* 37 (3):469–93.

Duchêne, François. 1994. *Jean Monnet: The first statesman of interdependence.* New York: Norton.

Duhamel, Olivier. 1980. *La gauche et la Ve République.* Paris: Presses Universitaires de France.

Eberlein, Burkhard, and Edgard Grande. 2005. Beyond delegation: Transnational regulatory regimes and the EU regulatory state. *Journal of European Public Policy* 12 (1):89–112.

Edinburgh Agreement. 1992. Decision of the heads of state and government, meeting within the European Council, concerning certain problems raised by Denmark on the Treaty on European Union, http://www.euo.dk/emner_en/forbehold/edinburgh/ (accessed June 15, 2009).

Edinburgh European Council. 1992. *Bulletin of the European Communities* 12-1992: 7–40.

Egeberg, Morten. 2008. European government(s): Executive politics in transition? *West European Politics* 31 (1-2):235–57.

———, ed. 2006. *Multilevel Union administration: The transformation of executive politics in Europe.* Houndmills, UK and New York: Palgrave Macmillan.

Eley, Geoff. 1995. The social construction of democracy in Germany, 1871–1933. In *The social construction of democracy, 1870–1990,* ed. George Reid Andrews and Herrick Chapman. New York: New York Univ. Press.

European Commission. 1985. Completing the internal market. White Paper, Commission to the European Council (Milan, June 28–29, 1985). COM (85) 310 final, http://aei.pitt.edu/1113/01/internal_market_wp_COM_85_310.pdf (accessed July 10, 2008).

———. 2001. European governance. White Paper (July 21, 2001). COM(2001) 428 final, http://eur-lex.europa.eu/LexUriServ/site/en/com/2001/com2001_0428en01.pdf (accessed June 6, 2007).

European Institute of Public Administration. 1991. *Subsidiarity: The challenge of change, proceedings of the Jacques Delors colloquium.* Maastricht: EIPA.

European Scrutiny Committee. 2008. Subsidiarity, national parliaments and the Lisbon Treaty. *Thirty-third Report of Session 2007-08, House of Commons,* http://www.publications.parliament.uk/pa/cm200708/cmselect/cmeuleg/563/563.pdf (accessed July 25, 2009).

Everson, Michelle. 1995. Independent agencies: Hierarchy beaters? *European Law Journal.* 1 (2):180–204.

———. 1999. The constitutionalization of European administrative law: Legal oversight of a stateless internal market. In *EU committees: Social regulation, law and politics,* ed. Christian Joerges and Ellen Vos. Oxford, UK: Hart.

Feld, Werner. 1964. *The court of the European Communities: New dimensions in international adjudication.* The Hague: Martinus Nijhoff.

Fennelly, Nial. 1997. Legal interpretation at the European Court of Justice. *Fordham International Law Journal* 20:656–79.

Fischer, Joschka. 2000. From confederacy to federation: Thoughts on the finality of European integration. Speech at the Humboldt University in Berlin (May 12, 2000), http://www.futurum.gov.pl/futurum.nsf/0/1289AFAAE84E5075C1256DA2003D1 306 and http://www.jeanmonnetprogram.org/papers/00/joschka_fischer_en.rtf (accessed July 20, 2009).

———. 2009. Ein nationaler Riegel. *Die Zeit* (July 9, 2009), http://www.zeit.de/2009/29/ Lissabon (accessed July 17, 2009).

Fitzmaurice, John. 1979. The Danish system of parliamentary control over European Community policy. In *The European parliament and the national parliaments,* ed. Valentine Herman and Rinus van Schendelen. Farnborough, UK: Saxon House.

Foundation for Foreign Affairs. 1947. A constitution for the Fourth Republic. Foundation Pamphlet 2. Trans. French Press and Information Service. Washington, DC: Foundation for Foreign Affairs.

Foyer, Jean. 1979. Le contrôle des parlements nationaux sur la fonction normative des institutions communautaires. *Revue du Marché Commun* (226):161–68.

Fraga, Ana. 2001. The parliament of Portugal: Loyal scrutiny and informal influence. In *National parliaments on their ways to Europe: Losers or latecomers?,* ed. Andreas Maurer and Wolfgang Wessels. Baden-Baden, Germany: Nomos.

Franchino, Fabio. 2001. Delegation and constraints in the national execution of the EC policies: A longitudinal and qualitative analysis. *West European Politics* 24 (4): 169–92.

———. 2002. Efficiency or credibility? Testing the two logics of delegation to the European Commission. *Journal of European Public Policy* 9 (5):677–94.

———. 2004. Delegating powers in the European Community. *British Journal of Political Science* 34:269–93.

———. 2005. A formal model of delegation in the European Union. *Journal of Theoretical Politics* 17 (2):217–47.

———. 2007. *The powers of the Union: Delegation in the EU.* Cambridge, UK and New York: Cambridge Univ. Press.

Fransen, Frederic J. 2001. *The supranational politics of Jean Monnet: Ideas and origins of the European Community.* Westport, CT: Greenwood Press.

Frears, J. R. 1975. The French parliament and the European Community. *Journal of Common Market Studies* 14 (2):140–56.

Furlong, Paul. 1996. The Italian parliament and European integration—Responsibilities, failures, and success. In *National parliaments and the European Union,* ed. Philip Norton. London: Frank Cass.

Ganshof van der Meersch, Walter Jean. 1968. Réflexions sur le droit international et la revision de la constitution. *Journal des tribunaux* 83 (4626):485–96.

———. 1969. Le juge belge à l'heure du droit international et du droit communautaire. *Journal des tribunaux* 84 (4671):537–51.

Gaudemet, Yves, Bernard Stirn, Thierry Dal Farra, and Frédéric Rolin, eds. 1997. *Les grands avis du Conseil d'Etat.* Paris: Dalloz.

Gaudet, Michel. 1963. Incidences des Communautés européennes sur le droit interne des états membres. *Annales de la Faculté de droit de Liège:5–26.*

German Lisbon Decision. 2009. BVerfG, 2 BvE 2/08, June 30, 2009 [provisional translation in English], http://www.bundesverfassungsgericht.de/entscheidungen/es20090630_2bve000208en.html (accessed July 3, 2009).

Gerstenberg, Oliver, and Charles F. Sabel. 2002. Directly-deliberative polyarchy: An institutional ideal for Europe? In *Good governance in Europe's integrated market,* ed. Christian Joerges and Renaud Dehousse. Oxford, UK: Oxford Univ. Press.

Gillingham, John. 1991. *Coal, steel, and the rebirth of Europe, 1945–1955: The Germans and French from Ruhr conflict to economic community.* Cambridge, UK: Cambridge Univ. Press.

———. 2003. *European integration, 1950–2003: Superstate or new market economy?* Cambridge, UK and New York: Cambridge Univ. Press.

Global Administrative Law Bibliography. 2005. *Law and Contemporary Problems* 68:357–77.

Goetz, Klaus H. 2008. Governance as a path to government. *West European Politics* 31 (1–2):258–79.

Golub, Jonathan. 2006. Did the Luxembourg Compromise have any consequences? In *Visions, votes, and vetoes: The empty chair crisis and the Luxembourg Compromise forty years on,* ed. Jean-Marie Palayret, Helen Wallace, and Pascaline Winand. Brussels: P.I.E.-Peter Lang.

Goodnow, Frank J. 1900. *Politics and administration: A study in government.* New York and London: Macmillan.

Graetz, Michael J., and Alvin C. Warren. 2006. Income tax discrimination and the political and economic integration of Europe. *Yale Law Journal* 115:1186–1255.

Grice, Andrew. 2002. Hain warns of "creeping federalism" in EU. *Independent on Sunday,* July 22, 2002. http://www.independent.co.uk/news/uk/politics/hain-warns-of-creeping-federalism-in-eu-649083.html (accessed July 26, 2009).

Griffith, J.A.G. 1955. The Crichel Down affair. *Modern Law Review* 18:557–570.

Griffiths, Martin. 1999. *Fifty key thinkers in international relations.* London and New York: Routledge.

Grimm, Dieter. 1997. The European court and national courts: The German constitutional perspective after the Maastricht Decision. *Columbia Journal of European Law* 3 (2):229–42.

————. 2005. The constitution in the process of denationalization. *Constellations* 12 (4):447–63.

Guaino, Henri. 2009. Guaino: "L'Europe est devenue un projet bureaucratique." *La Provence*, June 2, 2009. http://www.laprovence.com/articles/2009/06/02/831249-France.php (accessed June 2, 2009).

Gusy, Christoph. 1994. La dissolution de la constitution de Weimar. In *Weimar, ou de la démocratie en Allemagne*, ed. Gilbert Krebs and Gérard Schneilin. Paris: Publications de l'Institut d'Allemand.

Haas, Ernst B. 1963. Technocracy, pluralism, and the new Europe. In *A new Europe?*, ed. Stephen R. Graubard. Boston: Houghton Mifflin.

————. 1964. *Beyond the nation-state: Functionalism and international organization.* Stanford, CA: Stanford Univ. Press.

————. 1971. The study of regional integration: Reflections on the joy and anguish of pretheorizing. In *Regional integration: Theory and research*, ed. Leon N. Lindberg and Stuart A. Scheingold. Cambridge, MA: Harvard Univ. Press.

————. 2004 [1958]. *The uniting of Europe: Political, social, and economic forces, 1950–1957.* Notre Dame, IN: University of Notre Dame Press. (Orig. pub. Stanford Univ. Press 1958.)

Habermas, Jürgen. 1976 [1973]. *Legitimation crisis.* London: Heinemann.

————. 1992. Citizenship and national identity: Some reflections on the future of Europe. *Praxis International* 12 (1):1–19.

————. 2000 [1998]. *The inclusion of the other: Studies in political theory.* ed. Ciaran P. Cronin and Pablo De Greiff. Cambridge, MA: MIT Press.

————. 2001a. *The postnational constellation: Political essays.* Trans. Max Pensky. Cambridge, MA: MIT Press.

————. 2001b. Why Europe needs a constitution. *New Left Review* 11 (September-October 2001):5–26.

————. 2008. Krise der Europäischen Union: Ein Lob den Iren. *Süddeutsche Zeitung* (June 16, 2008), http://www.sueddeutsche.de/ausland/artikel/310/180753/ (accessed November 26, 2008).

Halberstam, Daniel. 2005. The bride of Messina: Constitutionalism and democracy in Europe. *European Law Review* 30 (6):775–801.

Halberstam, Daniel, and Christoph Möllers. 2009. The German constitutional court says "*Ja zu Deutschland!*." *German Law Journal* 10 (8):1241–57.

Hall, Peter A. 1986. *Governing the economy: The politics of state intervention in Britain and France, Europe and the international order.* New York: Oxford Univ. Press.

Hall, Peter A., and Rosemary C. R. Taylor. 1996. Political science and the three new institutionalisms. *Political Studies* 44 (4):936–57.

Hallstein, Walter. 1972. *Europe in the making.* Trans. Charles Roetter. New York: Norton.

Haltern, Ulrich. 2007. A comment on Von Bogdandy. In *Debating the democratic legitimacy of the European Union*, ed. Beate Kohler-Koch and Berthold Rittberger. Lanham, MD: Rowman and Littlefield.

Hansen, Lene. 2002. Sustaining sovereignty: The Danish approach to Europe. In *European integration and national identity: The challenge of the Nordic states*, ed. Lene Hansen and Ole Wæver. London: Routledge.

Harlow, Carol. 2002. *Accountability in the European Union.* Oxford, UK and New York: Oxford Univ. Press.

Harlow, Carol, and Richard Rawlings. 2007. Promoting accountability in multilevel governance: A network approach. Special issue: Accountability in EU Multilevel Governance, *European Law Journal* 13 (4):542–62.

Harryvan, Anjo G., and Albert E. Kersten. 1989. The Netherlands, Benelux and the relance Européenne 1954–1955. In *Il relancio dell'Europa e i trattati di Roma,* ed. Enrico Serra. Brussels: Bruylant.

Harryvan, Anjo G., and Jan van der Harst. 1997. *Documents on European Union.* New York: St. Martin's Press.

———. 2001. For once a united front: The Netherlands and the "empty chair" crisis of the mid-1960s. In *Crises and compromises: The European project 1963–1969,* ed. Wilfried Loth. Baden-Baden, Germany and Brussels: Nomos and Bruylant.

Hauriou, Maurice. 1925. La théorie de l'institution et de la fondation. *Cahiers de la Nouvelle Journée* 4:2–45.

Hayes-Renshaw, Fiona, and Helen Wallace. 2006. Changing the course of European integration—or not? In *Visions, votes, and vetoes: The empty chair crisis and the Luxembourg Compromise forty years on,* ed. Jean-Marie Palayret, Helen Wallace, and Pascaline Winand. Brussels: P.I.E.-Peter Lang.

Hegeland, Hans, and Ingvar Mattson. 1996. To have a voice in the matter: A comparative study of the Swedish and Danish European committees. *Journal of Legislative Studies* 2 (3):198–215.

Héritier, Adrienne, and Catherine Moury. 2009. Contested delegation: The European Parliament and comitology. In *European Union Studies Association, 11th Biennial International Conference,* http://www.unc.edu/euce/eusa2009/papers/heritier_10 A.pdf (accessed July 30, 2009).

Herzog, Roman, and Lüder Gerken. 2008. Stop the European Court of Justice. *EU Observer,* 10 September 2008, http://euobserver.com/9/26714 (accessed October 2, 2009).

Hewart of Bury, Lord. 1929. *The new despotism.* London: Ernest Benn.

Hirst, Paul. 2000. Democracy and governance. In *Debating governance,* ed. Jon Pierre. Oxford, UK and New York: Oxford Univ. Press.

Hofmann, Herwig H. C., and Alexander H. Türk. 2006. *EU administrative governance.* Cheltenham, UK and Northampton, MA: Edward Elgar.

———. 2007. The development of integrated administration in the EU and its consequences. *European Law Journal* 13 (2):253–71.

Hölscheidt, Sven. 2001. The German Bundestag: From benevolent weakness towards supportive scrutiny. In *National parliaments on their ways to Europe: Losers or latecomers?,* ed. Andreas Maurer and Wolfgang Wessels. Baden-Baden, Germany: Nomos.

Holton, Robert J. 1998. *Globalization and the nation-state.* Houndmills, UK and New York: Macmillan and St. Martin's.

Honig, Bonnie. 1993. *Political theory and the displacement of politics.* Ithaca, NY: Cornell Univ. Press.

Hooghe, Liesbet, and Gary Marks. 2001. *Multi-level governance and European integration.* Lanham, MD: Rowman and Littlefield.

————. 2008. European Union? *West European Politics* 31 (1–2):108–29.

Hopt, Klaus. 1966. Report on recent decisions. *Common Market Law Review* 4:93–101.

House of Commons, Library. 2007. EU reform: A new treaty or an old constitution? Research Paper 07/64, 24 July 2007, http://www.parliament.uk/commons/lib/research/rp2007/rp07-064.pdf (accessed July 24, 2009).

Huber, John D., and Charles R. Shipan. 2002. *Deliberate discretion: The institutional foundations of bureaucratic autonomy.* Cambridge, UK and New York: Cambridge Univ. Press.

Immergut, Ellen M., and Karen M. Anderson. 2008. Historical institutionalism and West European politics. *West European Politics.* 31 (1–2):345–69.

Ipsen, Hans Peter. 1972. *Europäisches Gemeinschaftsrecht.* Tübingen: Mohr.

————. 1993. Zur Exekutivrechtsetzung in der Europäischen Gemeinschaft. In *Wege und Verfahren des Verfassungslebens,* ed. Peter Badura and Rupert Scholz. München: Beck Verlag.

Jachtenfuchs, Markus. 2002. *Die Konstruktion Europas: Verfassungsideen und institutionelle Entwicklung.* Baden-Baden, Germany: Nomos.

Jachtenfuchs, Markus, Thomas Diez, and Sabine Jung. 1998. Which Europe?: Conflicting models of a legitimate European political order. *European Journal of International Relations* 4 (4):409–45.

Jensen, Jørgen Alboek. 1996. Prior parliamentary consent to Danish EU policies. In *National parliaments as cornerstones of European integration,* ed. Eivind Smith. London and Boston: Kluwer Law International.

Joerges, Christian. 2002. The law's problems with the governance of the European market. In *Good governance in Europe's integrated market,* ed. Christian Joerges and Renaud Dehousse. Oxford, UK: Oxford Univ. Press.

————. 2003. Europe a Großraum? Shifting legal conceptualisations of the integration project. In *Darker legacies of law in Europe: The shadow of national socialism and fascism over Europe and its legal traditions,* ed. Christian Joerges and Navraj Singh Ghaleigh. Oxford, UK and Portland, OR: Hart.

————. 2006. "Deliberative political processes" revisited: What have we learnt about the legitimacy of supranational decision-making. *Journal of Common Market Studies* 44 (4):779–802.

————. 2007. Reconceptualizing the supremacy of European law: A plea for a supranational conflict of laws. In *Debating the democratic legitimacy of the European Union,* ed. Beate Kohler-Koch and Berthold Rittberger. Lanham, MD: Rowman and Littlefield.

————. 2009. *Sozialstaatlichkeit* in Europe? A conflict-of-laws approach to the law of the EU and the proceduralisation of constitutionalisation. Special issue: The Law of the Network Society—A Tribute to Karl-Heinz Ladeur, *German Law Journal* 10 (4):335–60.

Joerges, Christian, and Jürgen Neyer. 1997. From intergovernmental bargaining to deliberative political processes: The constitutionalisation of comitology. *European Law Journal* 3 (3):273–99.

Jones, Eric Lionel. 1987. *The European miracle: Environments, economies, and geopolitics in the history of Europe and Asia.* 2nd ed. New York: Cambridge Univ. Press.

Jungar, Ann-Catherine. 2007. The rules of attraction: Policy transfer and the design of parliamentary EU scrutiny mechanisms in new EU member states. *European Union Studies Association, 10th Biennial International Conference,* http://aei.pitt.edu/7928/01/jungar-a-11h.pdf (accessed July 16, 2009) (cited with permission).

Kaiser, Wolfram. 2006. From state to society? The historiography of European integration. In *Palgrave advances in European Union studies,* ed. Michelle Cini and Angela K. Bourne. Houndmills, UK and New York: Palgrave Macmillan.

——. 2007. *Christian democracy and the origins of European Union, new studies in European history.* Cambridge, UK and New York: Cambridge Univ. Press.

——. 2008. History meets politics: Overcoming interdisciplinary volapük in research on the EU. *Journal of European Public Policy* 15 (2):300–13.

——. 2009. Transnational networks in European governance: The informal politics of integration. In *The history of the European Union: Origins of a trans- and supranational policy 1950–72,* ed. Wolfram Kaiser, Brigitte Leucht and Morten Rasmussen. New York and London: Routledge.

Kassim, Hussein. 2004. The Kinnock reforms in perspective: Why reforming the commission is an heroic, but thankless, task. *Public Policy and Administration* 19 (3): 25–41.

Kassim, Hussein, and Anand Menon. 2003. The principal-agent approach and the study of the European Union: Promise unfulfilled? *Journal of European Public Policy* 10 (1):121–39.

Kassim, Hussein, Anand Menon, B. Guy Peters, and Vincent Wright. 2001. *The national co-ordination of EU policy: The European level.* Oxford, UK and New York: Oxford Univ. Press.

Kassim, Hussein, B. Guy Peters, and Vincent Wright. 2000. *The national co-ordination of EU policy: The domestic level.* Oxford, UK and New York: Oxford Univ. Press.

Katz, Richard S. 1999. Representation, the locus of democratic legitimation, and the role of national parliaments in the European Union. In *The European parliament, the national parliaments, and European integration,* ed. Richard S. Katz and Bernhard Wessels. Oxford, UK and New York: Oxford Univ. Press.

Katznelson, Ira, and Barry R. Weingast. 2005. Intersections between historical and rational choice institutionalism. In *Preferences and situations: Points of intersection between historical and rational choice institutionalism,* ed. Ira Katznelson and Barry R. Weingast. New York: Russell Sage Foundation.

Kelemen, R. Daniel. 2002. The politics of "Eurocratic" structure and the new European agencies. *West European Politics* 25 (4):93–118.

——. 2005. The politics of Eurocracy: Building a new European state? In *The state of the European Union.* Vol. 7, *With us or against us? European trends from an American perspective,* ed. Nicolas Jabko and Craig Parsons. Oxford, UK: Oxford Univ. Press.

——. 2006. Suing for Europe: Adversarial legalism and European governance. *Comparative Political Studies* 39 (1):101–127.

——. 2009. The strength of weak states: Adversarial legalism in the US and the EU. In *European Union Studies Association, 11th Biennial International Conference,* http://www.unc.edu/euce/eusa2009/papers/kelemen_10B.pdf (accessed June 5, 2009).

Kennedy, Duncan. 2006. Three globalizations of law and legal thought: 1850–1968. In *The new law and economic development: A critical appraisal*, ed. David M. Trubek and Alvaro Santos. Cambridge and New York: Cambridge Univ. Press.

Kershaw, Ian. 2008 [1993]. "Working towards the Führer": Reflections on the nature of the Hitler dictatorship. In *Hitler, the Germans, and the final solution*. New Haven; London: Yale Univ. Press (Orig. pub. *Contemporary European History* 2(2): 103–18, 1993).

Kiiver, Philipp, ed. 2006. *National and regional parliaments in the European constitutional order*. Groningen: Europa Law.

King, Anthony. 1975. Overload: Problems of governing in the 1970s. *Political Studies* XXIII (2-3):284–96.

Kingsbury, Benedict, Nico Krisch, and Richard B. Stewart. 2005. The emergence of global administrative law. *Law and Contemporary Problems.* 68:15–61.

Kischel, Uwe. 1994. Delegation of legislative power to agencies: A comparative analysis of United States and German law. *Administrative Law Review* 46:213–56.

Klaus, Václav. 2009. Statement of President Václav Klaus on the Ratification of the Lisbon Treaty (October 9, 2009), http://www.hrad.cz/en/president-of-the-cr/current-president-of-the-cr-vaclav-klaus/selected-speeches-and-interviews/96.shtml (accessed October 19, 2009).

Knudsen, Ann-Christina L. 2001. Creating the common agricultural policy. Story of cereals prices. In *Crises and compromises: The European project 1963–1969*, ed. Wilfried Loth. Baden-Baden, Germany and Brussels: Nomos; Bruylant.

Knudsen, Ann-Christina L., and Morten Rasmussen. 2008. A European political system in the making 1958–1970: The relevance of emerging committee structures. *Journal of European Integration History.* 14 (1):51–67.

Kohler-Koch, Beate, and Berthold Rittberger. 2007. Charting crowded territory: Debating the democratic legitimacy of the European Union. In *Debating the democratic legitimacy of the European Union*, ed. Beate Kohler-Koch and Berthold Rittberger. Lanham, MD: Rowman and Littlefield.

Konstadinides, Theodore. 2009. *Division of powers in European Union law: The delimitation of internal competence between the EU and the member states*. Alphen aan den Rijn: Kluwer Law International.

Krekelberg, Astrid. 2001. The reticent acknowledgement of national parliaments in European treaties: A documentation. In *National parliaments on their ways to Europe: Losers or latecomers*, ed. Andreas Maurer and Wolfgang Wessels. Baden-Baden, Germany: Nomos.

Krisch, Nico. 2006. The pluralism of global administrative law. *European Journal of International Law.* 17 (1):247–78.

Krugman, Paul. 2009. A continent adrift. *New York Times*, March 16, 2009, http://www.nytimes.com/2009/03/16/opinion/16krugman.html (accessed March 19, 2009).

Krunke, Helle. 2005. Peoples' vengeances—from Maastricht to Edinburgh: The Danish solution. *European Constitutional Law Review* 1:339–56.

Kuisel, Richard F. 1981. *Capitalism and the state in modern France: Renovation and economic management in the twentieth century*. Cambridge, UK and New York: Cambridge Univ. Press.

Kumm, Mattias. 2006a. Beyond golf clubs and the judicialization of politics: Why Europe has a constitution properly so called. *American Journal of Comparative Law* 54 (Suppl.): 505–30.

———. 2006b. Constitutionalising subsidiarity in integrated markets: The case of tobacco regulation in the European Union. *European Law Journal* 12 (4): 503–33.

———. 2006c. The jurisprudence of constitutional conflict: Constitutional supremacy before and after the constitutional conflict. *European Law Journal* 11:262–307.

Küsters, Hanns Jürgen. 1988. Die Verhandlungen über das institutionelle System zur Gründung der Europäischen Gemeinschaft für Kohle und Stahl. In *Die Anfänge des Schuman-Plans 1950/51*, ed. Klaus Schwabe. Baden-Baden, Germany: Nomos.

La Pergola, Antonio, and Patrick Del Duca. 1985. Community law and the Italian constitution. *American Journal of International Law* 79:598–621.

Ladeur, Karl-Heinz. 2008. "We, the European people . . ."—Relâche? *European Law Journal* 14 (2):147–67.

Lagrange, Maurice. 1979 [1976]. La Court de Justice des Communautés Européennes du Plan Schuman à l'Union Européenne. In *Mélanges Fernand Dehousse*, ed. Pierre-Henri Teitgen. Paris and Brussels: Fernand Nathan and Editions Labor.

Lampué, Pierre. 1954. Le développement historique du recours pour excès de pouvoir depuis ses origines jusqu'au début du XXe siècle. *Revue Internationale des Sciences Administratives* (2):359–92.

Landis, James. 1938. *The administrative process*. New Haven, CT and London: Yale Univ. Press and Oxford Univ. Press.

Laursen, Finn. 2001. The Danish Folketing and its European affairs committee: Strong players in the national cycle. In *National parliaments on their ways to Europe: Losers or latecomers*, ed. Andreas Maurer and Wolfgang Wessels. Baden-Baden, Germany: Nomos.

Lecourt, Robert. 1931. Nature juridique de l'action en réintégrande: Etude de la jurisprudence française. PhD thesis, Université de Caen.

———. 1963. L'unification du droit européen est aussi un moyen de construire l'Europe. *France-Forum*:27–31.

———. 1964. Le rôle du droit dans l'unification européenne. *Bulletin de l'Association des Juristes Européens* 17-18:5–23.

———. 1976. *L'Europe des juges*. Brussels: Emile Bruylant.

———. 1991. Quel eut été le droit des communautés dans les arrêts de 1963 et 1964? In *Mélanges en hommage à Jean Boulouis: L'Europe et le droit*. Paris: Dalloz.

Lee, Sabine. 1995. German decision-making elites and European integration: German "Europolitik" during the years of the EEC and free trade area negotiations. In *Building postwar Europe: National decision-makers and European institutions 1948–63*, ed. Anne Deighton. New York: St. Martin's Press.

Legal and constitutional implications of United Kingdom membership in the European communities. 1967. Cmnd. 3301.

Lenaerts, Koen. 1990. Constitutionalism and the many faces of federalism. *American Journal of Comparative Law* 38:205–63.

———. 1992. Some thoughts about the interaction between judges and politicians. *University of Chicago Legal Forum*:93–134.

Lieshout, Robert H., Mathieu L. L. Segers, and Anne L. van der Vleuten. 2004. De Gaulle, Moravcsik, and The Choice for Europe: Soft sources, weak evidence. *Journal of Cold War Studies* 6 (4):89–139.

Lindberg, Leon N. 1963. *The political dynamics of European economic integration.* Stanford, CA: Stanford Univ. Press.

Lindseth, Peter L. 1999. Democratic legitimacy and the administrative character of supranationalism: The example of the European community. *Columbia Law Review* 99 (3):628–738.

———. 2001. "Weak" constitutionalism? Reflections on comitology and transnational governance in the European Union. *Oxford Journal of Legal Studies* 21 (1):145–63.

———. 2002. Delegation is dead, long live delegation: Managing the democratic disconnect in the European market-polity. In *Good governance in Europe's integrated market,* ed. Christian Joerges and Renaud Dehousse. Oxford, UK: Oxford Univ. Press.

———. 2003a. The contradictions of supranationalism: Administrative governance and constitutionalization in European integration since the 1950s. *Loyola of Los Angeles Law Review* 37:363–406.

———. 2003b. The "Maastricht Decision" ten years later: Parliamentary democracy, separation of powers, and the Schmittian interpretation reconsidered. Robert Schuman Centre for Advanced Studies/EUI Working Papers, RSC 2003/18, http:// cadmus.eui.eu/dspace/bitstream/1814/1893/1/03_18.pdf (accessed February 9, 2009).

———. 2004. The paradox of parliamentary supremacy: Delegation, democracy, and dictatorship in Germany and France, 1920s–1950s. *Yale Law Journal.* 113 (7):1341–1415.

———. 2005a. "Always embedded" administration?: The historical evolution of administrative justice as an aspect of modern governance. In *The economy as a polity: The political constitution of contemporary capitalism,* ed. Christian Joerges, Bo Stråth, and Peter Wagner. London: UCL Press.

———. 2005b. Reconciling with the past: John Willis and the question of judicial review in inter-war and post-war England. *University of Toronto Law Journal* 55:657–689.

———. 2006. Agents without principals?: Delegation in an age of diffuse and fragmented governance. In *Reframing self-regulation in European private law,* ed. Fabrizio Cafaggi. Alphen aan den Rijn, Netherlands: Kluwer Law International.

Lindseth, Peter L., Alfred C. Aman, and Alan Charles Raul. 2008. *Administrative law of the European Union: Oversight,* ed. George A. Bermann, Charles H. Koch, and James T. O'Reilly. Chicago, IL: ABA.

Locke, John. 1980 [1690]. *Second treatise of government,* ed. C. B. McPherson. Indianapolis, IN and Cambridge, UK: Hackett.

Lodge, Martin. 2008. Regulation, the regulatory state and European politics. *West European Politics* 31 (1–2):280–301.

Long, Marceau, Prosper Weil, Guy Braibant, Pierre Delvolvé, and Bruno Genevois. 1993. *Les grands arrêts de la jurisprudence administrative.* 10 ed. Paris: Dalloz.

Loth, Wilfried. 2008. Explaining European integration: The contribution from histori- ans. *Journal of European Integration History* 14 (1):9–26.

Loughlin, Martin. 2005. The functionalist style in public law. *University of Toronto Law Journal* 55:361–404.

Lu, Chien-Yi. 2009. EU as the fourth branch of member state governments? In *European Union Studies Association, 11th Biennial International Conference,* http://www.unc.edu/euce/eusa2009/papers/lu_11H.pdf (accessed June 5, 2009).

Lübbe, Hermann. 1962. Zur politschen Theorie der Technokratie. *Der Staat* 1:19–30.

Luchaire, François. 1992. L'Union Européenne et la constitution. *Revue de Droit Public* (3):589–616.

Lüdemann, Jörn. 2004. Die verfassungskonforme Auslegung von Gesetzen. *Juristische Schulung*:44.

Ludlow, N. Piers. 1999. Challenging French leadership in Europe: Germany, Italy, the Netherlands and the outbreak of the empty chair crisis of 1965–1966. *Contemporary European History* 8 (2):231–48.

———. 2001. The eclipse of the extremes: Demythologising the Luxembourg compro- mise. In *Crises and compromises: The European project 1963–1969,* ed. Wilfried Loth. Baden-Baden, Germany and Brussels: Nomos; Bruylant.

———. 2005. Mieux que six ambassadeurs: L'émergence du COREPER durant les pre- mières années de la CEE. In *Les Administrations nationales et la construction euro- péenne: Une approche historique (1919–1975),* ed. Laurence Badel, Stanislas Jeannesson, and N. Piers Ludlow. Brussels: P.I.E.-Peter Lang.

———. 2006a. *The European Community and the crises of the 1960s: Negotiating the Gaullist challenge.* London and New York: Routledge.

———. 2006b. De-commissioning the empty chair crisis: The Community institutions and the crisis of 1965–66. In *Visions, votes, and vetoes: The empty chair crisis and the Luxembourg Compromise forty years on,* ed. Jean-Marie Palayret, Helen Wallace, and Pascaline Winand. Brussels: P.I.E.-Peter Lang.

———. 2009. The European Commission and the rise of COREPER: A controlled experiment. In *The history of the European Union: Origins of a trans- and suprana- tional policy 1950–72,* ed. Wolfram Kaiser, Brigitte Leucht, and Morten Rasmussen. New York and London: Routledge.

Lynch, Frances. 1988. The role of Jean Monnet in setting up the European Coal and Steel community. In *Die Anfänge des Schuman-Plans, 1950/51,* ed. Klaus Schwabe. Baden-Baden, Germany: Nomos.

MacCormick, Neil. 1999. *Questioning sovereignty: Law, state, and nation in the European commonwealth.* Oxford, UK and New York: Oxford Univ. Press.

Magnette, Paul. 2003. *Contrôler 'Europe: Pouvoirs et responsabilité dans l'Union euro- péenne.* Brussels: Editions de l'Université de Bruxelles.

Mahony, Honor. 2009. Portuguese MPs most active in monitoring EU law. *EU Observer,* September 14, 2009. http://euobserver.com/18/28657 (accessed September 16, 2009).

Maier, Charles S. 1975. *Recasting bourgeois Europe: Stabilization in France, Germany, and Italy in the decade after World War I.* Princeton, NJ: Princeton Univ. Press.

———. 1987. The two postwar eras and the conditions for stability in twentieth-century Western Europe. In *In search of stability: Explorations in historical political economy*. Cambridge, UK: Cambridge Univ. Press.

Mair, Peter. 2004. The Europeanization dimension. *Journal of European Public Policy* 11 (2):337–48.

Majone, Giandomenico. 1994a. The European community: An "independent fourth Branch of government?." In *Verfassungen Für Ein Ziviles Europa*, ed. Gert Brüggemeier. Baden-Baden, Germany: Nomos.

———. 1994b. The rise of the regulatory state in Europe. *West European Politics* 17 (3):77–101.

———. 1996. *Regulating Europe*. London and New York: Routledge.

———. 1998. Europe's "democratic deficit": The question of standards. *European Law Journal* 4 (1):5–28.

———. 2001a. Regulatory legitimacy in the United States and the European Union. In *The federal vision: Legitimacy and levels of governance in the United States and the European Union*, ed. Kalypso Nicolaidis and Robert Howse. Oxford, UK and New York: Oxford Univ. Press.

———. 2001b. Two logics of delegation: Agency and fiduciary relations in EU governance. *European Union Politics* 2:103–22.

———. 2002. Delegation of regulatory powers in a mixed polity. *European Law Journal* 8 (3):319–39.

———. 2005. *Dilemmas of European integration: The ambiguities and pitfalls of integration by stealth*. Oxford, UK and New York: Oxford Univ. Press.

———. 2009. *Europe as the would-be world power: The EU at fifty*. Cambridge, UK and New York: Cambridge Univ. Press.

Maleville, Georges. 1954. Les décrets pris en application des articles 6 et 7 de la loi du 17 août 1948 tendant au redressement économique et financier. *Etudes et Documents du Conseil d'Etat* 8:56–96.

Mancini, G. Federico, and David T. Keeling. 1994. Democracy and the European Court of Justice. *Modern Law Review* 57:175–90.

Mann, Clarence J. 1972. *The function of judicial decision in European economic integration*. The Hague: Nijhoff.

Mannori, Luca, and Bernardo Sordi. Forthcoming. Science of administration and administrative law. In *A treatise of legal philosophy and general jurisprudence*. Vol. 9, *A history of the philosophy of law in the civil law world, 1600–1900*, ed. Hasso Hofmann, Paolo Grossi, and Damiano Canale. New York: Springer.

March, James G., and Johan P. Olsen. 1989. *Rediscovering institutions: The organizational basis of politics*. New York: Free Press.

———. 1998. The institutional dynamics of international political orders. *International Organization* 52 (4):943–69.

———. 2009. The logic of appropriateness. Centre for European Studies, University of Oslo, ARENA Working Papers, WP 04/09, http://www.arena.uio.no/publications/wp04_9.pdf (accessed July 3, 2009).

Marcou, Gérard. 1995. Introduction. In *Les mutations du droit de l'administration en Europe: Pluralisme et convergences*, ed. Gérard Marcou. Paris: L'Harmattan.

Marjolin, Robert. 1989. *Architect of European unity: Memoirs 1911–1986*. London: Weidenfeld and Nicholson.

Mashaw, Jerry L. 1990. Explaining administrative process: Normative, positive, and critical stories of legal development. *Journal of Law, Economics, and Organization* 6:267–98.

———. 2005. Norms, practices, and the paradox of deference: A preliminary inquiry into agency statutory interpretation. *Administrative Law Review* 57:501–42.

———. 2007. Agency-centered or court-centered administrative law: A dialogue with Richard Pierce on agency statutory interpretation. *Administrative Law Review* 59:889–904.

———. 2008. Administration and "the Democracy": Administrative law from Jackson to Lincoln, 1829–1861. *Yale Law Journal* 117:1568–1693.

———. 2009. Center and periphery in antebellum federal administration: The multiple faces of popular control. *University of Pennsylvania Journal of Constitutional Law* (forthcoming), http://papers.ssrn.com/sol3/papers.cfm?abstract_id=1432016 (accessed July 10, 2009).

Mason, Henry L. 1955. *The European Coal and Steel community: Experiment in supranationalism*. The Hague: Nijhoff.

Maurer, Andreas. 2001. National parliaments in the European architecture: From latecomers' adaptation towards permanent institutional change? In *National parliaments on their ways to Europe: Losers or latecomers?*, ed. Andreas Maurer and Wolfgang Wessels. Baden-Baden, Germany: Nomos.

Maurer, Andreas, and Wolfgang Wessels. 2001a. Major findings. In *National parliaments on their ways to Europe: Losers or latecomers*, ed. Andreas Maurer and Wolfgang Wessels. Baden-Baden, Germany: Nomos.

———. 2001b. National parliaments after Amsterdam: From slow adaptors to national players? In *National parliaments on their ways to Europe: Losers or latecomers*, ed. Andreas Maurer and Wolfgang Wessels. Baden-Baden, Germany: Nomos.

———, eds. 2001c. *National parliaments on their ways to Europe: Losers or latecomers*. Baden-Baden, Germany: Nomos.

Mayer, Franz C. 2001. Die drei Dimensionen der europäischen Kompetenzdebatte. *Zeitschrift für ausländisches öffentliches Recht und Völkerrecht* 61 (2/3):577–640.

Mayntz, Reynate. 1980. Executive leadership in Germany: Dispersion of power or "Kanzlerdemokratie"? In *Presidents and prime ministers*, ed. Richard Rose and Ezra N. Suleiman. Washington, DC: AEI.

Mazower, Mark. 2000 [1998]. *Dark continent: Europe's twentieth century*. New York: Vintage.

———. 2008. *Hitler's empire: How the Nazis ruled Europe*. New York: Penguin Press.

McCormick, John P. 2007. *Weber, Habermas, and transformations of the European state: Constitutional, social, and supranational democracy*. Cambridge, UK and New York: Cambridge Univ. Press.

McCubbins, Mathew D., Roger G. Noll, and Barry R. Weingast. 1987. Administrative procedures as instruments of political control. *Journal of Law, Economics, and Organization* 3:243–77.

McCubbins, Mathew D., and Thomas Schwartz. 1987 [1984]. Congressional oversight overlooked: Police patrols versus fire alarms. In *Congress: Structure and policy*, ed.

Mathew D. McCubbins and Terry O. Sullivan. Cambridge, UK and New York: Cambridge Univ. Press. (Orig. pub. *American Journal of Political Science* 1984, 28:16–79).

Meier, Gert. 1994. Der Streit um die Umsatzausgleichsteuer aus integrationspolitischer Sicht. *Recht der Internationalen Wirtschaft* 40 (2):149–51.

Membership in the European Community: Report on renegotiation. 1974. Cmnd. 6003.

Menon, Anand. 2004. Leading from behind: Britain and the European Constitutional Treaty. *Notre Europe: Research and European issues No. 31,* http://www.notre-europe.eu/uploads/tx_publication/Etud31-en-2_01.pdf (accessed July 24, 2008).

Menon, Anand, and Stephen Weatherill. 2002. Legitimacy, accountability, and delegation in the European Union. In *Accountability and legitimacy in the European Union,* ed. Anthony Arnull and Daniel Wincott. Oxford, UK: Oxford Univ. Press.

———. 2008. Transnational legitimacy in a globalising world: How the European Union rescues its states. *West European Politics* 31 (3):397–416.

Merkel, Angela, and Nicholas Sarkozy. 2009. Pour une Europe qui protège. *Le Journal du Dimanche,* May 31, 2009. http://www.lejdd.fr/cmc/elections-europeennes-2009/200922/pour-une-europe-qui-protege_213259.html (accessed June 2, 2009).

Merle, Marcel. 1962. Inventaire des apolitismes en France. In *La dépolitisation: Mythe ou réalité? In Cahiers de la Fondation Nationale des Sciences Politiques, No. 120,* ed. Georges Vedel. Paris: A. Colin.

Merlini, Stefano. 1995. Il governo constituzionale. In *Storia dello Stato Italiano dall'Unità a oggi,* ed. Raffalele Romanelli. Roma: Progetti Donzelli.

Meunier, Sophie, and Kathleen R. McNamara. 2007. Making history: European integration and institutional change at fifty. In *The state of the European Union.* Vol. 8, *Making history: European integration and institutional change at fifty,* ed. Sophie Meunier and Kathleen R. McNamara. Oxford, UK and New York: Oxford Univ. Press.

Miller, Gary J. 2005. The political evolution of principal-agent models. *Annual Review of Political Science* 8:203–25.

Miller, Vaughne. 2005. The UK Parliament and European business. House of Commons Library Research Paper 05/85, www.parliament.uk/commons/lib/research/rp2005/rp05-085.pdf (accessed June 17, 2009).

Milward, Alan S. 1984. *The reconstruction of Western Europe, 1945–51.* Berkeley and Los Angeles: University of California Press.

———. 1992. *The European rescue of the nation-state.* Berkeley: University of California Press.

———. 1993. *The frontier of national sovereignty: History and theory, 1945–1992.* London and New York: Routledge.

———. 1995. Allegiance: The past and the future. *Journal of European Integration History* 1 (1):7–19.

———. 2000 [1992]. *The European rescue of the nation-state.* 2nd ed. London: Routledge. (1st ed. 1992).

———. 2002. *The rise and fall of a national strategy, 1945–1963.* Vol. 1, *The UK and the European community.* London and Portland, OR: Whitehall History/Frank Cass.

———. 2005. *Politics and economics in the history of the European Union, the Graz Schumpeter lectures.* London and New York: Routledge.

Milward, Alan S., and Vibeke Sørensen. 1993. Interdependence or integration? A national choice. In *The frontier of national sovereignty: History and theory, 1945-1992*, ed. Alan S. Milward, Frances M. B. Lynch, Ruggero Ranieri, Federico Romero, and Vibeke Sørensen. London and New York: Routledge.

Ministre des affaires étrangères. 1951. La Communauté Européenne du charbon et de l'acier, Rapport de la délégation française sur le Traité et la Convention signés à Paris le 18 Avril 1951.

Mitrany, David. 1933. *The progress of international government, William Dodge lectures, Yale University, 1932.* New Haven, CT: Yale Univ. Press.

——. 1946 [1943]. *A working peace system: An argument for the functional development of international organization.* 4th ed. London: National Peace Council.

Moe, Terry. 1987. Interests, institutions and positive theory: The politics of the NLRB. *Studies in American Political Development* 2:236-299.

——. 1989. The politics of bureaucratic structure. In *Can the government govern?*, ed. John E. Chubb and Paul E. Peterson. Washington, DC: Brookings Institution.

Monnet, Jean. 1978. *Memoirs.* Trans. Richard Mayne. Garden City, NY: Doubleday.

Moravcsik, Andrew. 1994. Why the European Community strengthens the state: Domestic politics and international cooperation. Center for European Studies Working Paper 52, http://www.princeton.edu/äamoravcs/library/strengthen.pdf (accessed November 5, 2008).

——. 1998. *The choice for Europe: Social purpose and state power from Messina to Maastricht.* Ithaca, NY: Cornell Univ. Press.

——. 2000a. De Gaulle between grain and grandeur: The political economy of French EC policy, 1958-1970 (pt. 1). *Journal of Cold War Studies* 2 (2):3-43.

——. 2000b. De Gaulle between grain and grandeur: The political economy of French EC policy, 1958-1970 (pt. 2). *Journal of Cold War Studies* 2 (3):117-42.

——. 2000c. The origins of human rights regimes: Democratic delegation in postwar Europe. *International Organization* 54 (2):217-52.

——. 2002. In defence of the democratic deficit: Reassessing legitimacy in the European Union. *Journal of Common Market Studies* 40 (4):603-24.

——. 2004. Is there a "democratic deficit" in world politics? A framework for analysis. *Government and Opposition* 39 (2):336-363.

——. 2005a. Europe without illusions: A category error. *Prospect Magazine* 112:1-5.

——. 2005b. The European constitutional compromise and the neofunctionalist legacy. *Journal of European Public Policy* 12 (2):349-86.

——. 2007. The European constitutional settlement. In *The state of the European Union.* Vol. 8, *Making history: European integration and institutional change at fifty*, ed. Sophie Meunier and Kathleen R. McNamara. Oxford, UK and New York: Oxford Univ. Press.

——. 2008. The myth of Europe's democratic deficit. *Intereconomics: Journal of European Public Policy* (November-December 2008): 331-40.

Mößle, Wilhelm. 1990. *Inhalt, Zweck und Ausmaß: Zur Verfassungsgeschichte der Verordnungsermächtigung.* Berlin: Duncker and Humboldt.

Mullally, Lorraine, and Barry Watts. 2006. *Getting a grip: Reforming EU scrutiny at Westminster,* ed. Neil O'Brien. London: Open Europe. http://www.openeurope.org.uk/scrutiny.pdf (accessed June 17, 2009).

Müller, Jan-Werner. 2003. *A dangerous mind: Carl Schmitt in post-war European thought.* New Haven, CT: Yale Univ. Press.

———. 2009. The triumph of what (if anything)? Rethinking political ideologies and political institutions in twentieth-century Europe. *Journal of Political Ideologies* 14 (2):211–26.

Nordic EAC. 2002. The EU and democracy in the Nordic region: European affairs committees in Finland, Sweden, and Denmark (pamphlet). http://www.eu-oplysningen.dk/upload/application/pdf/6f93001d/nordiske_engelsk_03.pdf (accessed July 12, 2009).

Norman, Peter. 2005. *The accidental constitution: The making of Europe's constitutional treaty.* 2nd ed. Brussels: EuroComment.

North, Douglass Cecil. 1990. *Institutions, institutional change, and economic performance: The political economy of institutions and decisions.* Cambridge, UK and New York: Cambridge Univ. Press.

Norton, Philip. 1996a. Conclusion: Addressing the democratic deficit. In *National parliaments and the European Union,* ed. Philip Norton. London: Frank Cass.

———. 1996b. The United Kingdom: Political conflict, parliamentary scrutiny. In *National parliaments and the European Union,* ed. Philip Norton. London and Portland, Or.: Frank Cass.

———, ed. 1996c. *National parliaments and the European Union.* London: Frank Cass.

Nosemonkey. 2009. The dishonesty of the EU debate. In *Nosemonkey's EUtopia: In search of European identity,* http://www.jcm.org.uk/blog/?p=2282 (accessed July 21, 2009).

Novak, William J. 2008. The myth of the "weak" American state. *American Historical Review* 113:752–72.

Nuttens, Jean-Dominique, and François Sicard. 2000. *Assemblées parlementaires et organisations européennes.* Paris: La Documentation française.

O'Brennan, John, and Tapio Raunio. 2007a. Introduction: Deparliamentarization and European integration. In *National parliaments within the enlarged European Union: From "victims" of integration to competitive actors?,* ed. John O'Brennan and Tapio Raunio. London and New York: Routledge.

———, eds. 2007b. *National parliaments within the enlarged European Union: From "victims" of integration to competitive actors?* London and New York: Routledge.

Offe, Claus. 1972. *Strukturprobleme des kapitalischen Staates.* Frankfurt am Main: Suhrkamp.

Olsen, Johan P. 2002. The many faces of Europeanization. *Journal of Common Market Studies* 40 (5):921–52.

Oppelland, Torsten. 2001. "Entangling alliances with none"—Neither De Gaulle nor Hallstein: The European politics of Gerhard Schröder in the 1965/66 crisis. In *Crises and compromises: The European project 1963–1969,* ed. Wilfried Loth. Baden-Baden, Germany and Brussels: Nomos and Bruylant.

Oppenheimer, Andrew, ed. 1994/2003. *The relationship between European Community law and national law: The cases.* 2 vols. Cambridge, UK and New York: Cambridge Univ. Press.

Padgett, Stephen. 1994. Introduction: Chancellors and the chancellorship. In *Adenauer to Kohl: The development of the German chancellorship,* ed. Stephen Padgett. London and Washington, DC: Hurst and Company and Georgetown Univ. Press.

Palayret, Jean-Marie. 2006. De Gaulle challenges the Community: France, the empty chair crisis and the Luxembourg Compromise. In *Visions, votes, and vetoes: The empty chair crisis and the Luxembourg Compromise forty years on,* ed. Jean-Marie Palayret, Hellen Wallace, and Pascaline Winand. Brussels: P.I.E.-Peter Lang.

Palayret, Jean-Marie, Hellen Wallace, and Pascaline Winand, eds. 2006. *Visions, votes, and vetoes: The empty chair crisis and the Luxembourg Compromise forty years on.* Brussels: P.I.E.-Peter Lang.

Parsons, Craig. 2002. Showing ideas as causes: The origins of the European Union. *International Organization* 56 (1):47–84.

———. 2003. *A certain idea of Europe.* Ithaca, NY: Cornell Univ. Press.

Patch, William L. 1998. *Heinrich Brüning and the dissolution of the Weimar republic.* Cambridge, UK: Cambridge Univ. Press.

Pech, Laurent. 2009. The rule of law as a constitutional principle of the European Union. In *European Union Studies Association, 11th Biennial International Conference,* http://www.unc.edu/euce/eusa2009/papers/pech_01D.pdf (accessed June 5, 2009).

Pedersen, Susan. 2007. Review essay: Back to the League of Nations. *American Historical Review* 112 (4):1091–117.

Peers, Steve. 2009. The Beneš decrees and the EU charter of fundamental rights. *Statewatch.org,* October 12, 2009, http://www.statewatch.org/news/2009/oct/lisbon-benes-decree.pdf (accessed October 19, 2009).

Pernice, Ingolf. 2009. The Treaty of Lisbon: Multilevel constitutionalism in action. *Columbia Journal of European Law* 15 (3):349–407.

Pescatore, Pierre. 1981. Les travaux du "groupe juridique" dans les négociations des Traités de Rome. *Studia Diplomatica* 34 (1–4):159–78.

Phelan, Diarmuid Rossa. 1997. *Revolt or revolution: The constitutional boundaries of the European Community.* Dublin: Round Hall Sweet and Maxwell.

Phelan, William. 2002. Does the European Union strengthen the state? Democracy, executive power, and international cooperation. Harvard University, Center for European Studies Working Paper 95, http://www.ces.fas.harvard.edu/publications/docs/pdfs/Phelan95.pdf (accessed November 5, 2008).

Philip, André. 1951. *The Schuman Plan: Nucleus of a European Community.* Brussels: European Movement.

Pierson, Paul. 2004. *Politics in time: History, institutions, and social analysis.* Princeton, NJ: Princeton Univ. Press.

Pine, Melissa. 2008. European integration: A meeting ground for history and political science? A historian responds to Andrew Moravcsik. *Journal of European Integration History* 14 (1):87–104.

Pinto, Roger. 1948. La loi du 17 août 1948 tendant au redressement économique et financier. *Revue du Droit Public et de la Science Politique* 64 (4):517–48.

Pittaro, Paolo. 1980. Sospensione delle Garanzie Fondamentali e Diritti dell'Uomo. *Annali della Facoltà di Scienze Politiche* 2:469–508.

Poetzsch, Fritz. 1921. Verfassungsmässigkeit der vereinfachten Gesetzgebung. *Archiv des öffentlichen Rechts* 40 (2):156–72.

———. 1922. Bericht. In *Verhandlungen des 32. Deutschen Juristentages.* Berlin and Leipzig: Jansen.

———. 1925. Vom Staatsleben unter der Weimarer Verfassung (vom 1. Januar 1920 bis 31. Dezember 1924). *Jahrbuch des öffentlichen Rechts der Gegenwart* 13: 1–248.

Poiares Maduro, Miguel. 1998. *We the court: The European Court of Justice and the European economic constitution.* Oxford, UK: Hart.

———. 2003. Europe and the constitution: What if this is as good as it gets? In *European constitutionalism beyond the state*, ed. J. H. H. Weiler and Marlene Wind. Cambridge, UK and New York: Cambridge Univ. Press.

Polanyi, Michael. 1951. *The logic of liberty: Reflections and rejoinders.* London: Routledge and Kegan Paul.

Pollack, Mark A. 2003. *The engines of European integration: Delegation, agency, and agenda setting in the EU.* Oxford, UK and New York: Oxford Univ. Press.

———. 2005. Theorizing the European Union: International organization, domestic polity, or experiment in new governance? *Annual Review of Political Science* 8:357–98.

———. 2006a. Delegation and discretion in the European Union. In *Delegation and agency in international organizations*, ed. Darren G. Hawkins, David A. Lake, Daniel L. Nielson, and Michael J. Tierney. Cambridge, UK and New York: Cambridge Univ. Press.

———. 2006b. Rational choice and EU politics. In *Handbook of European Union politics*, ed. Knud Erik Jørgensen, Mark A. Pollack, and Ben Rosamond. London and Thousand Oaks, CA: Sage.

Pop, Valentina. 2008. Former German president bashes EU court. *EU Observer*, September 10, 2008. http://euobserver.com/9/26712/?rk=1 (accessed October 3, 2009).

Pratt, Timothy. 1998. The role of national parliaments in the making of European law. *The Cambridge Yearbook of European Legal Studies* 1:217–31.

Presseurop. 2009. Lisbon Treaty: Signed at last, time to move on. *Presseurop.eu,* November 4, 2009. http://www.presseurop.eu/en/content/article/131031-signed-last-time-move (accessed November 8, 2009).

Prieur, Raymond. 1962. *La Communauté européenne du charbon et de l'acier: Activité et évolution.* Paris: Montchrestien.

Radaelli, Claudio. 2000. Policy transfer in the European Union: Isomorphism as a source of legitimacy. *Governance* 13 (1):25–43.

Rasmussen, Morten. 2008. Costa v. ENEL to the Treaties of Rome— A brief history of a legal revolution. In *The future of European law: Revisiting the classics in the 50th anniversary of the Rome Treaty*, ed. Miguel Poiares Maduro and Loïc Azoulai. Oxford, UK: Hart.

———. 2009. Supranational governance in the making: Towards a European political system. In *The history of the European Union: Origins of a trans- and supranational policy 1950–72*, ed. Wolfram Kaiser, Brigitte Leucht, and Morten Rasmussen. New York and London: Routledge.

Raunio, Tapio. 2005. Holding governments accountable in European affairs: Explaining cross-national variation. *Journal of Legislative Studies* 11 (3):319–42.

Raunio, Tapio, and Simon Hix. 2000. Backbenchers learn to fight back: European integration and parliamentary government. *West European Politics* 23 (4):142–68.

Renan, Ernest. 1996 [1882]. What is a nation? In *Becoming national: A reader,* ed. Geoff Eley and Ronald Grigor Suny. Oxford, UK and New York: Oxford Univ. Press.

Reuter, Paul. 1953. *La Communauté européenne du charbon et de l'acier.* Paris: Librairie générale de droit et de jurisprudence.

———. 1979 [1977]. Aux origines du Plan Schuman. In *Mélanges Fernand Dehousse,* ed. Pierre-Henri Teitgen. Paris and Brussels: Fernand Nathan and Editions Labor.

Riis, Peter. 2007. National parliamentary control of EU decision-making in Denmark. In *National parliaments in European democracy: A bottom-up approach to European constitutionalism,* ed. Olaf Tans, Carla Zoethout, and Jit Peters. Groningen: Europa Law.

Rioux, Jean-Pierre. 1987. *The Fourth Republic 1944–1958.* Cambridge, UK: Cambridge Univ. Press.

Risse, Thomas. 2001. A European identity? Europeanization and the evolution of nation-state identities. In *Transforming Europe: Europeanization and domestic change,* ed. Maria G. Cowles, James Caporaso, and Thomas Risse. Ithaca, NY: Cornell Univ. Press.

Rittberger, Berthold. 2005. *Building Europe's Parliament: Democratic Representation Beyond the Nation-State.* Oxford, UK and New York: Oxford Univ. Press.

Rizzuto, Franco. 1996. The French parliament and the EU: Loosening the constitutional straitjacket. In *National parliaments and the European Union,* ed. Philip Norton. London: Frank Cass.

Rodgers, Daniel T. 1998. *Atlantic crossings: Social politics in a progressive age.* Cambridge, MA: Belknap Press/Harvard Univ. Press.

Rokkan, Stein. 1999. *State formation, nation-building, and mass politics in Europe: The theory of Stein Rokkan,* ed. Peter Flora, Stein Kuhnle, and Derek Urwin. Oxford, UK and New York: Oxford Univ. Press.

Rosanvallon, Pierre. 1990. *L'Etat en France de 1789 à nos jours.* Paris: Seuil.

Rose-Ackerman, Susan. 2007. Introduction. In *Economic approaches to administrative law,* ed. Susan Rose-Ackerman. Cheltenham, UK and Northampton, MA: Edward Elgar.

Roussel, Eric. 1996. *Jean Monnet.* Paris: Fayard.

Rubenfeld, Jed. 2001. *Freedom and time: A theory of constitutional self-government.* New Haven and London: Yale Univ. Press.

Rubin, Edward L. 1989. Law and legislation in the administrative state. *Columbia Law Review* 89:369–426.

Rutgers, Mark R. 2000. Public administration and the separation of powers in a cross-Atlantic perspective. *Administrative Theory & Praxis* 22 (2):287–308.

Ryan, Michael, and Paul Isaacson. 1974. Parliament and the European Communities. *Parliamentary Affairs* 28:199–215.

Saalfeld, Thomas. 1996. The German houses of parliament and European legislation. In *National parliaments and the European Union,* ed. Philip Norton. London: Frank Cass.

Sabel, Charles F., and William H. Simon. 2006. Epilogue: Accountability without sovereignty. In *Law and new governance in the EU and the US,* ed. Gráinne de Búrca and Joanne Scott. Oxford, UK and Portland, OR: Hart.

Sabel, Charles F., and Jonathan Zeitlin. 2008. Learning from difference: The new architecture of experimentalist governance in the EU. *European Law Journal* 14 (3):271–327.

Saurer, Johannes. 2009. The accountability of supranational administration: The case of European Union agencies. *American University International Law Review* 24 (3): 429–88.

Scharpf, Fritz Wilhelm. 1988. The joint-decision trap. Lessons from German federalism and European integration. *Public Administration* 66 (2):239–78.

———. 1999. *Governing in Europe: Effective and democratic?* Oxford, UK and New York: Oxford Univ. Press.

Schechtman, Joseph B. 1963. *Postwar population transfers in Europe 1945–1955.* Philadelphia: University of Pennsylvania Press.

Scheuermann, William E. 1997. The unholy alliance of Carl Schmitt and Friedrich A. Hayek. *Constellations* 4 (2):172–88.

Scheuner, Ulrich. 1967. Die Anwendung des Art. 48 der Weimarer Reichsverfassung unter den Päsidentschaften von Ebert und Hindenburg. In *Staat, Wirtschaft Und Politik in Der Weimar Republik: Festschrift Für Heinrich Brüning,* ed. Ferdinand A. Hermens and Theodor Schieder. Berlin: Duncker and Humblot.

Schmidt, Vivien A. 2006. *Democracy in Europe: The EU and national polities.* Oxford, UK and New York: Oxford Univ. Press.

Schmitt, Carl. 1936. Vergleichender Überblick über die neueste Entwicklung des Problems der gesetzgeberischen Ermächtigungen (legislative Delegationen). *Zeitschrift für ausländisches öffentliches Recht und Völkerrecht* 6:252–68.

———. 1938 [1936]. Une étude de droit constitutionnel comparé: L'évolution récente du problème des délégations legislatives. In *Introduction à l'étude du droit compare: Recueil d'études en l'honneur d'Edouard Lambert.* Paris: Sirey.

———. 1985 [1926]. *The crisis of parliamentary democracy.* Trans. Ellen Kennedy. Cambridge, MA: MIT Press.

———. 1990 [1944]. The plight of European jurisprudence [Die Lage der europäischen Rechtswissenschaft (1943/44)]. *Telos* 83:35–70.

———. 2008 [1928]. *Constitutional theory.* Trans. Jeffrey Seitzer. Durham, NC: Duke Univ. Press.

Schneider, Gerald, and Mark Aspinwall, eds. 2001. *The rules of integration: The institutionalist approach to the study of Europe.* Manchester, UK: Manchester Univ. Press.

Schönberger, Christoph. 2009. *Lisbon* in Karlsruhe: *Maastricht's* epigones at sea. *German Law Journal* 10 (8):1201–18.

Schönwald, Matthias. 2001. Walter Hallstein and the "empty chair" crisis 1965/66. In *Crises and compromises: The European project 1963–1969,* ed. Wilfried Loth. Baden-Baden, Germany and Brussels: Nomos; Bruylant.

Schorkopf, Frank. 2009. The European Union as an association of sovereign states: Karlsruhe's ruling on the Treaty of Lisbon. *German Law Journal* 10 (8): 1219–40.

Schuman Declaration. 1950. http://europa.eu.int/abc/symbols/9-may/decl_en.htm (accessed February 21, 2009).

Schuman, Robert. 1953a. Preface. In *La Communauté européenne du charbon et de l'acier*, ed. Paul Reuter. Paris: Librairie générale de droit et de jurisprudence.

———. 1953b. French foreign policy towards Germany since the war. Stevens Memorial Lecture 4, Royal Institute of International Affairs.

Schumpeter, Joseph A. 1976 [1942]. *Capitalism, socialism, and democracy*. New York: Harper.

Schütze, Robert. 2009. *From dual to cooperative federalism: The changing structure of European law*. Oxford, UK and New York: Oxford Univ. Press.

Scott, Colin. 2002. The governance of the European Union: The potential for multi-level control. *European Law Journal* 8 (1):59–79.

Scott, Joanne, and David M. Trubek. 2002. Mind the gap: Law and new approaches to governance in the European Union. *European Law Journal.* 8 (1):1–18.

Scrutiny of European Business. 1995–96. Twenty-seventh report HC 51-xxvii.

Seidel, Martin. 1995. Basic aspects of a European constitution. *Assenwirtschaft* 50 (1):221–36.

Select Committee on European Union. 2001. A second parliamentary chamber for Europe: An unreal solution to a real problem. *Seventh Report, Session 2001-2002, House of Lords,* http://www.publications.parliament.uk/pa/ld200102/ldselect/ldeucom/48/4801.htm (accessed July 22, 2009).

Sheehan, James J. 2006. Presidential address: The problem of sovereignty in European history. *American Historical Review* 111 (1):1–15.

———. 2009. *Where have all the soldiers gone?: The transformation of modern Europe*. 1st ed. Boston: Mariner Books.

Shore, Cris. 2000. *Building Europe: The cultural politics of European integration*. London and New York: Routledge.

Shore, Peter. 1973. *Europe: The way back*. London: Fabian Society.

Slaughter, Anne-Marie. 2004. *A new world order*. Princeton: Princeton Univ. Press.

Smith, Brendan P. G. 2002. Constitution building in the European Union: The process of treaty reforms. The Hague and New York: Kluwer Law International.

Somek, Alexander. 2003. On delegation. *Oxford Journal of Legal Studies* 23:703–09.

———. 2004. Dogmatischer Pragmatismus. Die Normativitätskrise der Europäischen Union. In *Demokratie und sozialer Rechtsstaat in Europa. Festschrift für Theo Öhlinger,* ed. Stefan Hammer, Alexander Somek, Manfred Stelzer, and Barbara Weichselbaum. Vienna: WUV-Universitätsverlag.

———. 2009. Administration without sovereignty. University of Iowa Legal Studies Research Paper 09-04, http://ssrn.com/abstract=1333282 (accessed July 20, 2009).

Southern, David. 1994. The chancellor and the constitution. In *Adenauer to Kohl: The development of the German chancellorship,* ed. Stephen Padgett. London: Hurst.

Spaak Report, Comité intergouvernemental créé par la Conférence de Messine. 1956. Rapport des Chefs de Délégation aux Ministres des Affaires Etrangères. Brussels.

Spierenburg, Dirk, and Raymond Poidevin. 1993. *Histoire de la Haute Autorité de la Communauté Européenne du Charbon et de l'Acier: Une expérience supranationale*. Brussels: Bruylant.

Stack, Kevin M. 2007. The constitutional foundations of *Chenery. Yale Law Journal* 116 (5):952–1021.

Stein, Eric. 1981. Lawyers, judges, and the making of a transnational constitution. *American Journal of International Law* 75:1–27.

Stephenson, Matthew C. 2006. A costly signaling theory of "hard look" judicial review. *Administrative Law Review* 58:753–813.

———. 2008. The price of public action: Constitutional doctrine and the judicial manipulation of legislative enactment costs. *Yale Law Journal* 118 (1):2–62.

Stevens, Anne. 1976. Problems of parliamentary control of European community policy. *Millenium Journal of International Studies* 5 (3):269–81.

Stolleis, Michael. 2001. *Public law in Germany, 1800–1914.* New York: Berghahn Books.

Stone Sweet, Alec. 2000. *Governing with judges: Constitutional politics in Europe.* Oxford, UK: Oxford Univ. Press.

———. 2004. *The judicial construction of Europe.* Oxford, UK: Oxford Univ. Press.

Stone Sweet, Alec, and James A. Caporaso. 1998a. La Cour de Justice et l'intégration européenne. *Revue française de science politique.* 48 (2):195–244.

———. 1998b. From free trade to supranational polity: The European court and integration. In *European integration and supranational governance,* ed. Wayne Sandholtz and Alec Stone Sweet. Oxford, UK: Oxford Univ. Press.

Stone Sweet, Alec, and Wayne Sandholtz. 1998. Integration, supranational governance, and the institutionalization of the European polity. In *European integration and supranational governance,* ed. Wayne Sandholtz and Alec Stone Sweet. Oxford, UK: Oxford Univ. Press.

Strauss, Peter L. 1987. Formal and functional approaches to separation-of-powers questions—a foolish inconsistency? *Cornell Law Review* 72:488–526.

———. 1989. Considering political alternatives to "hard look" review. *Duke Law Journal* 1989 (3):538–50.

———. 2007. Forward: Overseer, or "the decider"? The president in administrative law. *George Washington Law Review* 75:696–760.

Strumia, Francesca. 2009. Supranational citizenship and the challenge of diversity: Immigrants, citizens and member states in the EU. SJD dissertation, Harvard Law School.

Stuart, Gisela. 2009. Time for a change. Speech by Gisela Stuart MP to St. Antony's College, University of Oxford (March 5, 2009), http://www.giselastuartmp.co.uk/time-for-a-change/ (accessed July 20, 2009).

Sunstein, Cass R. 2000. Nondelegation canons. *University of Chicago Law Review* 67:315–43.

Szukala, Andrea, and Olivier Rozenberg. 2001. The French parliament and the EU: Progressive assertion and strategic investment. In *National parliaments on their ways to Europe: Losers or latecomers,* ed. Andreas Maurer and Wolfgang Wessels. Baden-Baden, Germany: Nomos.

Tallberg, Jonas. 2006. *Leadership and negotiation in the European Union.* Cambridge: Cambridge Univ. Press.

Tans, Olaf. 2007. The Dutch parliament and the EU: A constitutional analysis. In *National parliaments in European democracy: A bottom-up approach to European constitutionalism*, ed. Olaf Tans, Carla Zoethout, and Jit Peters. Groningen: Europa Law.

Tans, Olaf, Carla Zoethout, and Jit Peters, eds. 2007. *National parliaments in European democracy: A bottom-up approach to European constitutionalism.* Groningen: Europa Law.

Teasdale, Anthony L. 1993. The life and death of the Luxembourg Compromise. *Journal of Common Market Studies* 31 (4):567–79.

Thatcher, Mark. 2005. The third force? Independent regulatory agencies and elected politicians in Europe. *Governance* 18 (3):347–73.

Thatcher, Mark, and Alec Stone Sweet. 2002. Theory and practice of delegation in non-majoritarian institutions. *West European Politics* 25 (1):1–22.

———, eds. 2003. *The politics of delegation.* London and Portland, OR: Frank Cass.

Thompson, E. P. 1994. History and anthropology, lecture given at the Indian History Congress (Dec. 30, 1976). In *Making history: Writings on history and culture.* New York: Norton.

Tilly, Charles. 2002. *Stories, identities, and political change.* Lanham, MD: Rowman and Littlefield.

———. 2003. *Contention and democracy in Europe, 1650–2000.* New York: Cambridge Univ. Press.

Tocqueville, Alexis de. 1889 [1835]. *Democracy in America.* Trans. Henry Reeve, ed. Bruce Frohnen. Vol. 1. London: Longmans. (Reprint Regnery 2002.)

Treaties Establishing the European Communities. 1987. Office of Official Publications of the European Communities.

Treaty Establishing the European Coal and Steel Community. 1951. London: Fanfare Press.

Trenz, Hans-Jörg. 2005. *Europa in den Medien. Die europäische Integration im Spiegel nationaler Öffentlichkeit.* Frankfurt, Germany and New York: Campus.

Triepel, Heinrich. 1922. Bericht. In *Verhandlungen des 32. Deutschen Juristentages.* Berlin and Leipzig: Jansen.

Tsebelis, George. 2002. *Veto players: How political institutions work.* Princeton, NJ: Princeton Univ. Press.

Türk, Henning. 2006. "To face De Gaulle as a community": The role of the Federal Republic of Germany during the empty chair crisis. In *Visions, votes, and vetoes: The empty chair crisis and the Luxembourg compromise forty years on,* ed. Jean-Marie Palayret, Helen Wallace, and Pascaline Winand. Brussels: P.I.E.-Peter Lang.

Usher, John A. 1988. The gradual widening of European Community policy on the basis of article 100 and 235 of the EEC Treaty. In *Structure and dimensions of European Community policy,* ed. Jürgen Schwarze and Henry G. Schermers. Baden-Baden, Germany: Nomos.

Vaïsse, Maurice. 2001. La politique européenne de la France en 1965: Pourquoi "la chaise vide"? In *Crises and compromises: The European project 1963–1969,* ed. Wilfried Loth. Baden-Baden, Germany and Brussels: Nomos and Bruylant.

van der Harst, Jan. 2008. Introduction—History and theory. *Journal of European Integration History* 14 (1):5–8.

van Houtte, Albert. 1955. La Communauté Européenne du Charbon et l'Acier, conference faite à l'Université de Naples (December 15, 1955).

van Schendelen, M.P.C.M. 1996. The Netherlands: From founding father to mounding baby. In *National parliaments and the European Union*, ed. Philip Norton. London: Frank Cass.

Vauchez, Antoine. 2008. "Integration-through-law": Contribution to a socio-history of EU political commonsense. Robert Schuman Centre for Advanced Studies, EUI Working Papers, RSCAS 2008/10, http://cadmus.iue.it/dspace/handle/1814/8307 (accessed April 17, 2009).

Verhey, Luc, Hansko Broeksteeg, and Ilse van den Driessche, eds. 2008. *Political accountability in Europe: Which way forward? A traditional concept of parliamentary democracy in an EU context.* Groningen: Europa Law.

Vignes, Daniel. 1956. *La Communauté européenne du charbon et de l'acier: un exemple d'administration économique internationale.* Liège: G. Thone.

Volcansek, Mary L. 2000. *Constitutional politics in Italy: The constitutional court.* Houndmills, UK: Macmillan.

von Bogdandy, Armin. 2008. General principles of international public authority: Sketching a research field. *German Law Journal* 9 (11):1909–38.

Vos, Ellen. 1999a. EU committees: The evolution of unforeseen institutional actors in European product regulation. In *EU committees: Social regulation, law and politics*, ed. Christian Joerges and Ellen Vos. Oxford, UK and Portland, OR: Hart.

———. 1999b. *Institutional frameworks of community health and safety legislation: Committees, agencies, and private bodies.* Oxford, UK and Portland, OR: Hart.

Walker, Neil. 2002. The idea of constitutional pluralism. *Modern Law Review* 65 (2): 317–59.

———. 2003b. From Großraum to condominium: A comment. In *Darker legacies of law in Europe: The shadow of national socialism and fascism over Europe and its legal traditions*, ed. Christian Joerges and Navraj Singh Ghaleigh. Oxford, UK and Portland, OR: Hart.

———. 2004. After the constitutional moment. In *A constitution for the European Union: First comments on the 2003-draft of the European convention*, ed. Ingolf Pernice and Miguel Poiares Maduro. Baden-Baden, Germany: Nomos.

———. 2005. Legal theory and the European Union: A 25th anniversary essay. *Oxford Journal of Legal Studies* 25 (4):581–601.

———. 2006a. A constitutional reckoning. *Constellations* 13 (2):140–50.

———. 2006b. Epilogue: On regulating the regulation of regulation. In *Reframing self-regulation in European private law*, ed. Fabrizio Cafaggi. Alphen aan den Rijn, Netherlands: Kluwer Law International.

———. 2006c. European constitutionalism in the state constitutional tradition. *Current Legal Problems* 59:51–89.

———. 2006d. The migration of constitutional ideas and the migration of the constitutional idea: The case of the EU. In *The migration of constitutional ideas*, ed. Soujit Choudhry. Cambridge, UK: Cambridge Univ. Press.

Warlouzet, Laurent. 2008. Relancer la CEE avant la Chaise vide: Néo-functionnalistes vs. fédéralistes au sein de la Commission européenne (1964–1965). *Journal of European Integration History.* 14 (1):69–86.

Weatherill, Stephen. 1995. *Law and integration in the European Union.* Oxford, UK: Oxford Univ. Press.

———. 2005. Competence creep and competence control. *Yearbook of European Law 2004* 23:1–55.

———. 2007. *Better regulation.* Oxford, UK and Portland, OR: Hart.

Weber, Max. 1978 [1922]. *Economy and society: An outline of interpretive sociology.* 2 vols. Trans. Ephraim Fischoff, et al. and ed. Guenther Roth and Claus Wittich. Berkeley: University of California Press.

Weiler, J. H. H. 1991. The transformation of Europe. *Yale Law Journal* 100:2403–83.

———. 1995. Does Europe need a constitution? Demos, telos, and the German Maastricht Decision. *European Law Journal* 1 (3):219–58.

———. 1999a. *The constitution of Europe: "Do the new clothes have an emperor" and other essays on European integration.* Cambridge, UK and New York: Cambridge Univ. Press.

———. 1999b. The constitution of the common market place: Text and context in the evolution of the free movement of goods. In *The evolution of EU law,* ed. Paul Craig and Gráinne de Búrca. Oxford, UK: Oxford Univ. Press.

Weiler, J. H. H., Ulrich R. Haltern, and Franz C. Mayer. 1995. European democracy and its critique. *West European Politics* 18 (3):4–39.

Weiler, J. H. H., and Joel P. Trachtman. 1996–1997. European constitutionalism and its discontents. *Northwestern Journal of International Law and Business* 17:354–97.

Weiler, J. H. H., and Marlene Wind. 2003. Introduction: European constitutionalism beyond the state. In *European constitutionalism beyond the state,* ed. J. H. H. Weiler and Marlene Wind. Cambridge, UK and New York: Cambridge Univ. Press.

Wessels, Wolfgang. 1995. Walter Hallsteins integrationstheoretischer Beitrag—überholt oder verkannt? In *Walter Hallstein: Der vergessene Europäer,* ed. Wilfried Loth, William Wallace, and Wolfgang Wessels. Bonn: Europa Union Verlag.

Westlake, Martin. 1996. The view from "Brussels." In *National parliaments and the European Union,* ed. Philip Norton. London: Frank Cass.

White, Jonathan P. J. 2003. Theory guiding practice: The neofunctionalists and the Hallstein EEC commission. *Journal of European Integration History.* 9 (1):111–31.

Willis, John. 1933. *The parliamentary powers of English government departments.* Cambridge, MA: Harvard Univ. Press.

———. 1935. Three approaches to administrative law: The judicial, the conceptual, and the functional. *University of Toronto Law Journal* 1:53–81.

Wincott, Daniel. 1998. Does the European Union pervert democracy? Questions of democracy in new constitutionalist thought on the future of Europe. *European Law Journal* 4 (4):411–28.

Wind, Marlene. 2003. The European Union as a polycentric polity: Returning to a neo-medieval Europe? In *European constitutionalism beyond the state,* ed. J. H. H. Weiler and Marlene Wind. Cambridge, UK and New York: Cambridge Univ. Press.

Wintour, Patrick. 2001. Blair's idea for second EU chamber rejected. *The Guardian,* November 6, 2001. http://www.guardian.co.uk/politics/2001/nov/06/uk.eu (accessed July 22, 2009).

———. 2003. Red card scheme to curb EU power. *The Guardian,* January 30, 2003. http://www.guardian.co.uk/politics/2003/jan/30/uk.eu (accessed July 24, 2009).

Wolff, Bernhard. 1952. Die Ermächtigung zum Erlaß von Rechtsverordnungen nach dem Grundgesetz. *Archiv des öffentlichen Rechts* 78:194–227.

Wouters, Jan. 2000. National constitutions and the European Union. *Legal Issues of Economic Integration* 27 (1):25–91.

Young, Ernest A. 2000. Constitutional avoidance, resistance norms, and the preservation of judicial review. *Texas Law Review* 78:1549–1614.

Table of Cases

317

〽 Italy

Ireland

Netherlands

Poland

Spain

United Kingdom

United States

Index

A

Accountability, 6, 19, 22, 22*n*64, 25, 48,
48*n*74, 52–53, 202, 255*n*18, 255*n*19,
263, 266*n*64, 267*n*70, 285
  democratic, 47*n*65, 284
  electoral, 255*n*18
  parliamentary, 171, 202
  political and legal, 48
  principal-agent, 260
  public, 223
  reason-giving and, 22, 25
  sanction and, 23*n*68, 256
Act of accession
  Danish, 135, 213, 213*n*122, 272
  German, 169, 171, 206, 213, 213*n*122,
Adenauer, Konrad, 82–84, 106*n*71, 118,
119*n*125
Administrative-executive distinction, 2,
15–16, 37, 37*n*25, 39, 39*n*34, 42, 50,
84–85
Administrative governance, 2–3, 15–16,
20–22, 33–44, 47, 253, 256
  and autonomy, 3, 14, 21, 29, 85, 98
  and constitutional government, 49
  and the control-legitimation
    distinction, 14–23, 25, 266. *See also*
    individual entry
  and the executive. *See* Administrative-
    executive distinction
  Europeanized, 1, 3–4, 49–51, 91, 132,
    251–56, 266, 281
  evolution of, 51, 263
  and the evolution of public law. *See*
    Public law (evolution of)
  historiographical theory of, 37–44
  and the "leaky" modern state, 16, 18, 41

legitimation of, 2, 14, 21, 23, 74-90,
104, 279
and mediated legitimacy, 23, 88-90,
180–81, 279
and the New Deal, 97, 161
and oversight. *See individual entry*
the postwar constitutional settlement
of, 3, 13, 17, 44, 51, 58–59, 74-88,
251, 279
and representative government, 1, 18,
38, 40, 49, 72, 89–90, 251–53
and separation of regulatory power
from legitimacy/legitimation, 27,
59, 155, 279. *See also* Legitimacy
"Administrative, not constitutional," 1, 3,
19, 41, 49, 53, 228, 246–47, 249, 253
Administrative procedure, 262. *See also*
Subsidiarity
consultation with stake-holders,
199–200
exhaustion of remedies, 270, 272, 276
impact assessment, 199–200
judicial review, 196, 198, 245–46, 270,
272, 276. *See also* Hard look
doctrine
participation and transparency, 226,
260, 262*n*49
reason-giving (*also* reasoned decision
making *and* justification), 22, 25,
196, 197*n*36, 199–200, 210–11, 224,
237, 245–47, 256, 263–64, 276
recours pour excès de pouvoir (action for
breach of authority),
141*n*28, 198
"Agents without principals," 52, 228
Aquinas, Thomas, 71

Ingram Content Group UK Ltd.
Milton Keynes UK
UKHW020301220423
420618UK00003B/67